IN THE TRENCHES

Volume 3

IN THE TRENCHES

Selected Speeches and Writings
of an American Jewish Activist
Volume 3: 2002-2003

DAVID A. HARRIS
Executive Director,
The American Jewish Committee

KTAV Publishing House, Inc.

Library of Congress Cataloging-in-Publication Data

Harris, David A.
 In the trenches : selected speeches and writing of an American Jewish
activist / David A. Harris.
  v. cm.
 Contents: v. 1. 1979-1999
 ISBN 0-88125-693-5
 1. Jews--Politics and government--1948- 2. Jews--Soviet Union--Emigration
and immigration. 3. Arab-Israeli conflict. 4. Jews--Europe--Social
conditions--20th century. 5. Antisemitism. 6. American Jewish Committee--
Officials and employees--Biography. 7. Holocaust, Jewish (1939-1945)--
Influence. I. Title.
DS140.H36 2001
305.892'4'009045--dc21   00-058958

 Contents: v. 2. 2000-2001
 ISBN 0-88125-779-6
 Contents: v. 3. 2002-2003
 ISBN 0-88125-842-3

Distributed by
KTAV Publishing House, Inc.
930 Newark Avenue
Jersey City, NJ 07306
www.ktav.com

To the blessed memory of the Righteous among the Nations,
who set an example of courage and humanity
that will shine brightly for eternity.

CONTENTS

2. SPEECHES & TESTIMONY

3. MEDIA ACTIVITY

4. TRANSLATIONS

5. AJC INSTITUTIONAL

FOREWORD

As president of the American Jewish Committee for the past three years, I have traveled around the world and to many Jewish communities across the United States. I have witnessed enormous global change. I have observed firsthand the extent to which David Harris is recognized as a thoughtful, perceptive, and influential spokesman for the Jewish community.

David consistently demonstrates a keen ability to identify issues, to address emerging problems, and to speak truth to world leaders in a way that befriends the listener and advances the Jewish agenda. He saw the challenge to our open democratic society posed by terrorist groups and by Islamic extremism long before September 11 brought it agonizingly home to all Americans. He recognized the reemergence of anti-Semitism in Europe—sometimes disguised as opposition to Israel, sometimes manifest in acts of violence—long before it became the subject of banner headlines. He reached out to American Jews and helped shake them from complacency.

This volume is a record of David's thinking, encompassing his letters, speeches, and writings over the years 2002–03. The collection reveals both his exceptional vision and his eloquent passion.

The American Jewish Committee has been blessed to have David Harris as its spokesperson and its helmsman during this period of rough waters. I have been privileged to have had him as a companion, mentor, friend, and partner in leading this agency's efforts to secure a brighter future for the Jewish people and for humanity.

Harold Tanner
President, American Jewish Committee
Spring 2004

IN THE TRENCHES

TRENCHES

Volume 3

INTRODUCTION

I remember vividly how, in some high-school classes, the forty-five minute periods never seemed to end. Time simply stood still. The monotonous teachers not only brought to a screeching halt our curiosity, such as it was, but the wall clock as well.

In midlife, it all appears quite different. Somewhere along the way, sight unseen, someone shifted the clock to a fast-forward mode. As a result, the days and years now simply race by.

It seems like only yesterday, even if it was actually two years ago, that I sat down to write the Introduction to Volume II of *In the Trenches*. The ensuing twenty-four months have been eventful, to say the least.

Indeed, September 11 and its aftermath defined an entirely new historic era. If, we were told, history had for all practical purposes come to an end in the 1990s with the global ascendancy of liberal democracy, spearheaded by the United States, then history restarted with a vengeance after the attack on America.

The ever-growing threat of international terrorism—the stratagem of choice used by radical Islamic groups and their state sponsors—coupled with their ominous quest for weapons of mass destruction, has created a clear and present danger for the United States, the West generally, and, of course, moderate Muslim nations.

For the Jewish people, this has been a particularly challenging time. First, the vast majority of Jews live precisely in those countries facing the gravest terrorist danger. Second, the terrorists have made abundantly clear that Jews and their institutions figure prominently on the menu of possible targets. Third, Israel is at the epicenter, both ideologically and geographically, of this global war waged by terrorists and the fanatical belief systems that fuel them. Fourth, the search for Arab-Israeli peace, never simple to begin with, has been rendered still more complicated by recent developments. And fifth, anti-Semitism, both in

3

familiar forms and new guises, has resurfaced with a fervor that many observers, including some Jews, thought well-nigh impossible just a few years ago.

Accordingly, it should come as no surprise to readers of this third volume of *In the Trenches* that the topics covered here largely, though not exclusively, coincide with these five challenges. I should also note that there's one new section in this book—selected translations.

Let me explain. Since I've followed events in Europe with particular attention in recent years, there were a number of items that originally appeared in either French or Italian which I felt ought to be shared with an English-speaking audience. I'm especially pleased to have been the first to translate into English some important articles of the hard-hitting Italian journalist Oriana Fallaci, and the equally outspoken Spanish author and politician Pilar Rahola, who originally came to my attention in an interview she gave to the French-language web site *proche-orient.info*.

Believe me, I derive no special pleasure from constantly writing about the challenges we face. I am by nature both an optimist and an idealist, albeit with some scars to show for both. But the nature of my work prevents me from yielding to the temptation of subordinating facts to fantasies. The stakes are too high and the dangers too real.

At the same time, I refuse to succumb to a fatalistic despair either, no matter how bleak a situation may look at any given moment. I've seen enough remarkable breakthroughs in my own lifetime—from Israel's valiant struggle for sheer survival against all the odds to the signing of peace treaties with Egypt and Jordan; from the successful Soviet Jewish emigration struggle to the end of the Cold War and the break-up of the USSR; from the ouster of the Taliban regime in Afghanistan to the capture of Saddam Hussein; from the desegregation of the University of Mississippi and its academic kindred spirits to the relegation of South African apartheid to the dustbin of history—to believe unshakably in the ultimate triumph of, yes, good over evil.

I've been blessed by many things, among them the privilege of spending the past two decades of my professional life at the American Jewish Committee. This has given me the chance to deal with both sides of the coin—the opportunities and the minefields—in the company of a steady, surefooted, and savvy institution.

There are those who have difficulty sorting out one organization from another in a Jewish community that, shall we say, doesn't suffer from a lack of agencies. I admire the work of many of these agencies, which are engaged in truly indispensable efforts on behalf of the Jewish people. But for me the American Jewish Committee remains a unique institution, as I discuss at length elsewhere in this book (see "Letter from a Bar Mitzvah Employee").

If I could start from scratch and create a vehicle for the Jewish community to interact with the larger world in which we live, it would look remarkably like the American Jewish Committee.

These days, there are those who labor under the mistaken notion that he (or she) who shouts the loudest wins. AJC's approach is deliberately different. The goal isn't to receive any sound-and-fury awards. Rather, formulaic though it may sound, it's to try and make a difference, and if that means submerging institutional or individual egos to get results, so be it.

In an era increasingly defined by a desire for instant gratification, AJC understands that the societal issues with which we are grappling—combating anti-Semitism and other forms of bigotry, helping Israel achieve peace and security, promoting interethnic and interfaith harmony, strengthening human rights, and advancing democratic values—don't conveniently lend themselves to quick or easy solutions. Rather, they require heavy doses of preparation, perseverance, and, at the end of the day, patience.

In today's world of instant experts, AJC recognizes that there simply is no substitute for adequate research, analysis, and discussion, as well as informed debate, all of which require a knowledgeable professional staff and an engaged lay leadership.

And at a time when we are too often surrounded by self-assured and uncompromising notions of "right" and "wrong," "hawk" and "dove," or "liberal" and "conservative," AJC stubbornly refuses to be pigeon-holed, believing that complex policy issues in democratic societies like the United States and Israel don't always lend themselves to a purist's approach, but instead demand carefully nuanced thinking.

I grew up in a relatively assimilated environment (see "Letter from a Jewish Late Bloomer"). Thoughts of one day becoming a Jewish civil servant were far from my mind. In any case, I could hardly have imagined an organization that spoke to me in quite the way the American Jewish Committee does—blending American democratic principles and Jewish ethical values, balancing public advocacy and private diplomacy, rejecting ideological labels, and, above all, getting important, even historic, things done.

Moreover, as I've written on previous occasions, AJC is that all-too-rare oasis of civility, where notions of collegiality, integrity, and mutual respect aren't just promotional lines for outside consumption, but essential ingredients of our institutional ethos.

Given such a description of the American Jewish Committee, it should come as little surprise that I've been able to benefit from the help of a number of exceptional people with this book project.

During the period covered in this volume, Harold Tanner has served with distinction as AJC's president. He has always encouraged me to write on current issues, and whenever I share a draft text with him, I unfailingly receive insightful feedback. I cannot say enough good things about this remarkably caring and committed mentor and friend.

Roselyn Bell and Larry Grossman, our gifted in-house editors, microscopically scrutinize just about every piece I write and always make helpful suggestions, both conceptual and stylistic. I am grateful for their efforts now, as in the past.

Cyma Horowitz and Michele Anish of AJC's wonderful Blaustein Library are treasures, both for our organization and the outside world. No request of mine has ever proved too difficult for these information sleuths *sans pareil.*

Rebecca Neuwirth, AJC's director of special projects, works closely with me on all aspects of my work, which makes me a very lucky person. I value her keen mind and sharp eye, and I can always rely on her honest, unsparing critique of everything I write.

Ken Bandler, AJC's director of communications, helped place a number of the pieces in this volume in various media outlets, for which I am most appreciative.

Sam Kliger, a former Jewish activist from Moscow, joined the AJC staff in the spring of 2003 as our principal link with the Russian-speaking world. He hit the ground running. He has overseen the translation into Russian of many of the pieces that appear in this volume and their placement in a variety of Russian-language publications.

Jason Isaacson, the director of AJC's Office of Government and International Affairs and an unusually skilled writer with a journalist's background, offered valuable comments on a number of the articles in this book.

Richard Foltin, AJC's legislative director, had the idea for the testimony submitted to the House of Representatives on Arab school curricula that appears in this volume. He wrote the first draft.

I have been able to count on Linda Krieg's well-honed skills as a graphic artist to design the covers for all three volumes in this series.

Regrettably, Alina Warda-Viera, my cherished administrative assistant, became seriously ill midway through this two-year span. Helen Allen, with grace and dedication, stepped in to help out until Alina is well enough to return. Both Alina and Helen have played an important part in the preparation of this book.

I'd like to express a special word of gratitude to Adam Janvey, AJC's senior fellow this year. Mature beyond his years, Adam took on the daunting task of collecting all the material for this book, coordinating the various responsibilities with colleagues, and offering important ideas along the way. With individuals like Adam coming up in the ranks, the Jewish organizational world is sure to be well-served in the years to come.

The staff at KTAV Publishing House, and in particular Bernie Scharfstein, has made this project sheer pleasure for Roselyn Bell, our liaison to KTAV, and me. Bernie and his colleagues have been our publishing partners for all three volumes of *In the Trenches,* and they are tops at what they do.

Finally, I cannot ever sufficiently thank my wife, Jou Jou, and our three children, Danny, Mishy, and Josh, for their love, support, understanding, and, not least, good humor. They infuse everything I do with additional layers of meaning and satisfaction.

And my mother, Nelly Harris (see "Letter from an Octogenarian"), gave me the two most precious gifts any parent can give a child—roots and wings. I could not have asked for more.

New York, January 2004

I. LETTERS

Letter from the Road
January 30, 2002

The road I'm talking about is Roaring Brook Road. It's normally a quiet country thoroughfare in northern Westchester County, except on school mornings, when it becomes a frustratingly long line of cars, minivans, and SUVs snaking down a steep hill and headed eastward for the local high school on the other side of the Saw Mill Parkway.

By the time the vehicles make it across the parkway on the quick green light, they are joined by others that have exited the highway from both the north and south on their way to the same destination. They inch up the hill, with the sprawling, verdant campus of Reader's Digest on the left, while another caravan of vehicles approaches the school from the west, both lines alternating to make the turn into the school and drop off students or, in the case of young licensed drivers, search for a parking space.

I've never made a proper count of the ratio of cars to light trucks (SUVs, etc.), but with each passing year it seems to be getting closer to parity.

The scene repeats itself day in and day out: literally hundreds of cars headed for a school with barely one thousand students.

Anyone who wants to understand America's energy challenge should watch this morning ritual.

The bright yellow school buses arrive practically empty. The few students who ride them are ninth-graders. No older student would be caught dead in the "loser cruiser," as local kids call the school bus. So, as many as 750–800 students who avoid the buses at all costs must arrange for other transportation. In some cases, it's parents who drive; in others, especially for juniors and seniors, it's quite likely to be kids in their own cars. That's another feature of life here—the expectation

9

that shortly after passing the driver's test, there'll be an additional car in the garage.

Doubtless, the same story repeats itself in suburban and rural communities across the country. With only limited public transportation, scarce sidewalks, few bike lanes, and "uncool" school buses, it's all about cars.

When one concerned parent approached a local school official and suggested a student-led energy conservation initiative as a response to the events of September 11, the official essentially responded that he wouldn't touch the idea with a ten-foot pole. Not only would it go nowhere, he said, but it could easily provoke a backlash. Cars, you see, are a sacrosanct subject in places like this. Perhaps, said the persistent parent, but shouldn't the students be challenged to do something tangible to help our nation while our servicemen and servicewomen are defending us abroad? The official wouldn't budge.

The problem extends far beyond the high school. For example, parents sometimes wait for the school buses carrying their elementary school children in cars with engines running to ensure enough warmth in winter, cool air in summer, or uninterrupted news or entertainment on the radio. And then there are the sports travel teams, a subject on which I can claim some expertise. With two of our sons having participated for years in competitive hockey programs that took us all over the tristate area on weekends, the idea of a team bus or even carpooling was never taken seriously. Instead, as a rule, each of the fifteen or twenty players would travel separately with a parent as much as a couple of hundred miles every week for games, most often in a large vehicle, the preferred mode of transportation for hockey parents, at least in this part of the world.

Meanwhile, our recent yearlong experience in Europe revealed some significant differences.

Cars are most assuredly an important feature of the Continental landscape—just try navigating the streets of Rome at rush hour or the French highways heading to the Riviera at the beginning of August—but there are at least two major distinctions.

First, Europe has invested very heavily in energy-efficient railroads, and, with few exceptions, the networks are comprehensive, efficient, and fast. Moreover, they are integrated into the larger transportation system, so that a passenger arriving at, say, Geneva or Frankfurt airport can board a train and either go into the city center or head directly for his final destination, for example, Lausanne or Bonn. In stark contrast, passengers arriving at JFK or La Guardia have no train options whatsoever, and even when the long-in-coming train connection is finally completed at JFK, it will be a far cry from the European model. Add to this the impressive urban and suburban public transportation systems in many European metropolitan areas and you have a highly competitive rival for the car.

Second, SUVs are still a relative rarity on European streets. What discourages many prospective buyers from purchasing large vehicles, apart from any possible environmental considerations, is the simple fact that gasoline is heavily taxed and thus two to three times as expensive as in the United States.

When Americans visit Europe, they are often struck by the small size of many cars, not to mention the surprisingly large number of motorcycles and motor scooters. When we first took our children to Italy in the early 1980s, they fell in love with the adorable Cinquecento, the legendary Fiat 500, and wanted to take one home, as a play toy, that is. But together with the Morris Mini and the Volkswagen Beetle, the Fiat 500, now in its remodeled form, has been a popular family car on the streets and highways of Europe. Today there's the Smart car as well, a two-seater that can more or less fit in a standard closet and appears to be selling well, its principal features being high fuel mileage and easy parking.

Vehicle use is not the only way that Europe differs from the U.S. When it comes to electricity, per capita use in Europe is surely lower than in the United States.

Each time I travel to Germany, I am struck by the limited use of lighting in offices, even for senior government officials. The same was true for the modern apartment building in Geneva in which our family lived for a year. The lobby and corridor lighting was a fraction of what it would have been in an equivalent New York building. Anyone who has visited an apartment building in Paris will surely remember dark public spaces that are illuminated by pushing a time-controlled button that barely allows you to get between the entrance and an apartment. And when it comes to heating British homes in winter, I don't remember removing my sweater very much during three-and-a-half years living in London and Oxford. (Britain's per capita energy consumption is 46 percent of the U.S. figure.)

I fully recognize that energy conservation is not an especially popular subject in the United States. As Maureen Dowd wrote in the *New York Times* on May 20, 2001:

> We want big. We want fast. We want far. We want now. We want 345 horsepower in a V-8 engine and fifteen miles per gallon on the highway. We drive behemoths. We drive them alone. This country was not built on H.O.V. lanes. We don't have limits. We have liberties.... We don't care for cardigans. Give us our sixty-nine degrees, winter and summer. Let there be light—no timers, no freaky-shaped long-life bulbs.

The mention of cardigans presumably was a reference to an American president who took seriously the issue of energy conservation—Jimmy Carter—and the ridicule he endured when he announced that he was turning down the wintertime thermostat at the White House and wearing a sweater to compensate. Rather than follow his laudable example, many pooh-poohed the gesture, suggesting that this was hardly a sure-fire formula to enhance a politician's popularity.

But President Carter was reacting to the traumatic events of the 1970s—first, the Arab oil embargo of 1973, followed by the jacking up of oil prices by the OPEC cartel. He understood that America's Achilles' heel was our dependence on foreign, especially Middle East, oil, and we needed to wean ourselves off this dangerous addiction, or risk the possibility of further political and economic blackmail.

He wasn't alone in understanding the danger. One month before Carter took office, the American Jewish Committee adopted a far-reaching Statement on Energy:

> The American Jewish Committee believes that the development of a comprehensive U.S. energy program is essential to the economic and social well-being of our country, to our national security, and to the con-

tinuance of our broad role in world affairs.... The American public seems to have forgotten the 1973 crisis and the quadrupling of oil prices that followed. Indeed, our dependence on foreign oil, particularly Arab oil, has increased over the past three years. In 1973, we imported only 28 percent of the oil we consumed; today [in 1976] we import close to 43 percent, and the trend is upward.

AJC offered a targeted six-point plan to achieve a substantial reduction in U.S. dependence on imported energy supplies that included "reducing wasteful energy consumption, increasing domestic supplies, and developing alternative sources of energy and the means to cope with supply cutoffs."

The statement served us well as we responded to specific energy policy issues in the ensuing years. In fact, during the 1970s and 1980s, there was real progress. New fuel economy standards (Corporate Average Fuel Economy Standards, or CAFE) were adopted that averaged 27.5 miles per gallon for cars and 20.1 m.p.g. for trucks. A Strategic Petroleum Reserve was created to help the nation in case oil supplies were again disrupted or prices manipulated. Research into alternative sources of energy, including geothermal, solar, wind, and shale, was undertaken. And more stringent energy standards for appliances and construction materials were introduced.

But all this encouraging momentum came to a screeching halt about a decade ago. Fuel economy standards were allowed by Congress and the administration to loosen. The fleet fuel economy standards have now dropped to the lowest in the last fifteen years. More generally, energy consciousness pretty much disappeared, except among a very few.

Instead, complacency settled in. Sure, there were those who continued to alert us to the danger of dependence on Middle East oil, but their warnings went largely unheeded. America was seemingly awash in cheap and plentiful oil, and we thought we could confidently ignore the prophets of doom and promising new energy-saving technologies.

(According to a 2001 National Academy of Sciences study [*Economist,* December 15, 2001], "[W]ith technologies that are readily available, reductions in fuel use of up to 20 percent for cars and light trucks could be achieved comfortably.")

As a consequence, we've actually experienced backsliding. Since SUVs are classified as light trucks, not cars, they are governed by the lower mileage standards. In 1975, light trucks accounted for only 19 percent of all automotive sales, while today that figure is 50 percent.

A recent article in the *Toronto Star* (January 4, 2002) revealed some rather startling facts:

> [I]f SUVs were required to have the same average fuel economy as cars, the gasoline saved in the U.S. would represent more oil than could be pumped from the Alaskan wildlife refuge over the thirty years it would take to deplete its oil stocks.... To look at the wastefulness of SUVs in another way, consider this: the amount of extra gas they use on average in one year, compared with cars, equals the amount of energy you'd waste if you left your refrigerator door open for six years.

With America constituting less than five percent of the world's population, "today one out of every seven barrels of oil produced in the world is consumed on American highways" (*New York Times*, January 2, 2002). As domestic sources of oil dry up, we today import 52 percent of our crude oil, of which, according to the Department of Energy, 29 percent comes from the Persian Gulf, principally Saudi Arabia, Kuwait, and Iraq (yes, Iraq).

The one piece of good news is that we have managed to diversify our sources of imported oil to include other, more stable suppliers as well. Europe and Japan, on the other hand, remain far more dependent on Middle East oil. The advanced European nations, for example, import 57 percent of their oil needs from North Africa and the Persian Gulf; in the case of Japan, the figure is over 75 percent.

After the horrific events of September 11, we have another window of opportunity to talk about energy questions. There is far greater understanding today that the principal Middle East suppliers of oil are not necessarily our friends. They most certainly do not share our basic values of democracy, the rule of law, emancipation of women, and religious tolerance. In some cases, they've been playing a double game—alleging friendship with the West while financially propping up anti-Western regimes in the region and inculcating anti-Western hatred in their own youth. And for years they've been turning a blind eye to groups within their borders that often masqueraded as "charitable organizations," while funneling oil money to terrorist networks that target Americans and other Westerners.

As *New York Times* columnist Tom Friedman recently wrote:

> I don't want to be dependent on Mideast oil anymore. Countries in that region haven't had a good century in 700 years—and they're not going to soon. Oil is their curse, as well as ours. It's corrupted their rulers, enabled them to keep their women backward and out of the work force, and prevented them from developing innovative economies that make things instead of just taking things from the ground. They have a lot of homework to do before they will be stable allies.

If these regimes are inherently unstable, then their oil supplies can be disrupted, making it all the more important for America not to be caught off guard.

No one should be under any illusion about the complexity of developing a national energy policy. There are no simple, neat formulas, no silver bullets. Virtually all major energy decisions entail difficult trade-offs involving political, economic, diplomatic, environmental, and consumer considerations. Elected officials, foreign governments, energy companies, power companies, car and truck manufacturers, environmental groups, and others all have a profound stake in the outcome of any debate on energy questions, and will fight tooth and nail to defend their respective interests.

AJC today is once again deepening its involvement in these issues, just as it did in the 1970s. Presciently, AJC reestablished an Energy Task Force last spring to build on the foundations of the old policy with the addition of some new issues and emphases. Its work has only become more important since September 11. It has drafted a proposed statement that will be debated by the Board of Governors at its February meeting in Dana Point, California.

At the end of the day, perhaps, the true test of success will be measured mornings on Roaring Brook Road and its environs. While I'd be reluctant to predict any positive short-term change in driving habits to and from school, car purchasing patterns, or, for that matter, energy consumption at home, I had one pleasant surprise this morning.

At our suburban train station, I discovered that there are now ten choice parking spots for electric cars, each fitted with a recharging unit. Now that's an interesting and unexpected development.

Letter from a School Parent[*]
February 4, 2002

As a parent of two Horace Greeley High School graduates and one child currently enrolled in the school, I would like to bring to the attention of the Board of Education a matter of serious concern.

On Friday, February 1, an assembly entitled "Living as an American and as a Member of the Islamic Faith, Before and After September 11" was convened for the entire Greeley student body.

The notice indicated that the "assembly program will consist of a panel, members of the Niazi family, our Chappaqua neighbors, who will share their culture and beliefs with us. Following their remarks, we will provide time for some questions and answers from the audience. After that, we will break into Forum groups for continuing discussion and reflection."

I do not question the good intentions of the Greeley administration in planning such a program, or the equally good intentions of the Niazi family in their willingness to appear before the school community and talk about their religion and values.

What I do question, however, is whether this was the appropriate way to present an enormously complex subject to an impressionable audience, and especially at a particularly sensitive moment in American and world history. Incidentally, this very concern was expressed in a phone conversation with a senior school administrator on January 31, but clearly to no avail.

* This letter was sent to every member of the School Board of Chappaqua, New York. Subsequently, the Board notified the high school administration that it had not followed proper procedure.

Rather than assemble a panel reflecting a range of thinking on the many and varied currents in Islam, the school instead chose to invite members of one family who, in their remarks, reinforced each other's idealized and uncritical views of their religion. They, of course, have every right to their beliefs and those beliefs deserve respect, but this cannot be the beginning and end of a discussion on Islam, any more than the mirror images of this family's views in other great religious traditions could suffice to represent those religions in their entirety.

As an editorial in the *Financial Times* (December 27, 2001) said:

> Just like Christianity, Islam is open to a wide range of interpretations. There has long been a heated debate over whether a justification for suicide attacks can be found in the Koran. There is no consensus on the Koranic teachings regarding women's rights.... The blurred separation between church and state makes interpreting Islam all the more difficult.

In preparation for the assembly, the students were given two brief and, if I may say, rather selective articles to read from among the multitude written since September 11. One was a sympathetic assessment of Islam and the other an examination of five typologies of anti-Americanism in the world today, including in the Middle East.

The students also had available to them an article written by Zareen Niazi, a Greeley student and one of the four family members who spoke at the assembly. This article appeared in the Greeley *Tribune* on November 15, 2001.

Ms. Niazi is entitled to her views. Nevertheless, her opinion piece was replete with historical inaccuracies (e.g., comparing the treatment of Japanese Americans during World War II, as shameful as it was, to Hitler's policy of extermination of European Jewry), glaring omissions (e.g., referring to those who killed thousands on September 11 as merely "a small group of confused human beings" or speaking of "whoever did this atrocious deed," as if it were unknown who committed these horrific acts, and in the name of what), and hyperbole (e.g., describing "Muslim men beaten and burned to death" in America, or asking "How can Americans claim to want to bring justice overseas when they are the cause of injustice in their own home?").

These statements should have alerted school officials to the need for adequate planning, preparation, and a balancing viewpoint for any assembly on such a "hot" topic.

Greeley assemblies with outside speakers are far from a daily occurrence. Thus, there is almost inevitably a certain authority conferred on those outsiders invited to address the entire school body. They become the filter through which the students are introduced to a particular issue.

There were no other voices at the assembly—neither outside guests nor administrators and teachers—to present what the *Financial Times* referred to as the "wide range of interpretations," whether about the various meanings of jihad, the different schools of Islamic thought, the status of women in Muslim society, the record of treatment of non-Muslims in Muslim-dominated countries, the tense relationship of Islam to modernity and democracy, or the very real struggle between moderate Muslims who seek accommodation with the West and extremist Muslims, like the Taliban, Al-Qaeda, Hezbollah, Islamic Jihad, Osama bin Laden, and others who seek to wage war against us.

Further, it was abundantly clear in the question-and-answer period that the students were either ill-equipped or simply hesitant to broach these entirely legitimate—and controversial—issues.

Moreover, there was one particularly disturbing moment in the assembly.

Mr. Niazi asked the students to repeat the Arabic words "*Allahu Akbar*" ("God is great"). He was disappointed with the response after the first attempt, so he called on the students to repeat them more emphatically a second time.

He may have simply been trying to introduce a central phrase of the religion to the students, but that was nonetheless unfortunate. It is precisely these words that are widely known to be the very last words uttered by radical Islamic suicide bombers. Thousands of Americans and other victims of terrorism have perished as a direct result of the abuse of these very words. Again, there was no intervention on the part of the school to put things in perspective for the students.

I understand that the smaller Forum groups were designed to address issues in greater depth, but they could not possibly deal with the full impact of what took place in the gym in front of the entire student body.

Finally, lest there be any misunderstanding, this letter should not in any way be construed as casting aspersions on the Muslim religion or seeking to deny the children of Chappaqua the opportunity to learn more about Islamic tradition and faith (or, for that matter, the tradition and faith of any other religion, consistent with Constitutional safeguards).

Rather, it is, as I said at the outset, an expression of deep concern that this important and complex topic was not handled by school officials with the skill and nuance that we have come to expect from Horace Greeley. As a result, in my view a potentially important educational opportunity was lost.

Letter from a Professional Worrier
March 12, 2002

You know the classic Jewish telegram—"Start worrying. Letter follows." Please consider this a telegram and letter rolled into one.

When summarizing my job description, I often refer to myself as a professional worrier. My line of work is also somewhat akin to political oncology, in that my colleagues and I deal all too often with the societal consequences of such gruesome pathologies as war, terrorism, intolerance, and bigotry.

The Italians have a wonderfully apt term—*deformazione professionale*—which in English means "professional bias," even if it doesn't sound quite as good in translation.

So, in the interests of truth in advertising, I put my cards on the table. I am a professional worrier, whose views may well be colored by the dark issues I deal with daily and whose judgment, therefore, could well be clouded by a professional bias.

That said, as an American Jew, I am deeply concerned today, perhaps more so than at any time in a communal career that began in 1975.

Mind you, there have been many other tough moments for the

Jewish world along the way: the adoption of the infamous "Zionism is racism" resolution by the UN General Assembly in 1975; the dramatic slowdown in the rate of Soviet Jewish emigration after the high point in 1979; the indescribable plight of Soviet Jewish prisoners of conscience and refuseniks; the enormous hurdles in rescuing Ethiopian Jews; the repeated acts of terror against Israel and Israeli targets abroad; the first Palestinian intifada, which began in 1987; the thirty-nine Scud missiles that Iraq launched against Israel in the Gulf War; the bombing of the Argentine Jewish community's central building in 1994; the assassination of Prime Minister Yitzhak Rabin by a fellow Israeli in 1995; the arrest of thirteen Iranian Jews on trumped-up charges; and the incessant preoccupation of the United Nations with Israel's every alleged misdeed.

At the same time, the period from 1975 onward had a bright side, so much so that it may well be viewed as a golden age in modern Jewish history.

After all, at the end of the day, not only did the Soviet gates open wide and 1.5 million Jews walk through to new lives in the West, but the Soviet Union imploded and its empire collapsed, which, among many other consequences, had a dramatically positive impact on both Jewish life and Israel's strategic picture.

Although several thousand Ethiopian Jews tragically died en route to neighboring countries in the hope of eventually reaching Israel, many more successfully made the full journey and established a significant presence in the land that had been at the center of their prayers and dreams.

It took sixteen years, but the UN General Assembly finally voided the "Zionism is racism" canard, only the second time the UN reversed a resolution it had previously adopted.

Israel grew, especially with the influx of one million Soviet Jews, and prospered, as it reached historic peace agreements with Egypt and, later, Jordan, signed what many thought to be the promising Oslo Accords with the Palestinians, and established links with a number of North African and Persian Gulf countries.

And American Jews reached new heights of access and influence, as we mobilized in one campaign after another to assist Israel and Jewish communities in need, all the while witnessing a sharp decline in the remaining barriers to full Jewish participation in the entire spectrum of American life. The culmination, of course, came with the nomination of Senator Joe Lieberman to the Democratic ticket in 2000. One surely didn't have to be a Democrat to appreciate this remarkable moment in the nearly 350-year history of Jews on America's soil.

I am an inveterate long-term optimist. The trajectory of history since the end of the Second World War, while most certainly not linear, has essentially been in a positive direction for the things that matter the most—the leadership of the United States as a bastion and defender of freedom, the well-being of Israel and the Jewish people, the health of democracy worldwide, and respect for human rights and promotion of mutual understanding.

But who among us can be optimistic in the short term? The sky is darkening and claps of thunder can be heard with increasing frequency.

First, the hourly news from Israel is beyond devastating. And bad as it is, many fear it will get worse before it gets better. There simply is no obvious way out, much as we may yearn for an atmosphere conducive to serious peace talks. No one has convincing answers for how to bring the daily carnage of Israelis by Palestinian groups—ranging from Hamas and Islamic Jihad to Yasir Arafat's own forces—to an end. The Pentagon has an acronym it uses for moments like this—AOS ("all options stink").

If Israel chooses to withdraw unilaterally from certain areas, such as Gaza, it could send the unintended signal of a weakening resolve, and thus embolden the Palestinians to intensify their terrorist campaign.

If Israel goes the other way and seeks to reoccupy the West Bank and Gaza, Israel could come under unrelenting international pressure and face enormous military—and moral—challenges.

In essence, Israel is at war, but forced to fight with one hand tied behind its back. As a democracy, there are certain things Israel cannot or will not do. Ironically, the Palestinians, for all their condemnation of Israeli military actions, still understand this better than anyone.

Consider how other countries in the region have dealt with real or perceived threats.

When Arafat yet again backed the wrong horse during the Gulf War, Saddam Hussein, Kuwait summarily expelled all 300,000 Palestinians overnight, fearing that their continued presence in the country represented a potential fifth column.

When Yemen also sided with Saddam Hussein, Saudi Arabia ousted 600,000 Yemenis from the country.

When the Muslim Brotherhood began posing a threat to the Syrian president Hafez Assad, he sent an unmistakable message by leveling Hama, a center of their activity, killing as many as 15,000 residents.

When Egyptian President Hosni Mubarak faced the danger of growing Islamic radicalism in his own country, he imprisoned, under the radar, thousands of suspects, throwing due process to the wind. How many of these suspects have been killed by Egyptian authorities? And how many continue to languish in prison?

And it's not worth wasting time talking about how Saddam Hussein has chosen to deal with insurgent Kurds and Shiites, or the methods employed by the Algerians or the Sudanese in protracted and grisly civil wars.

No, Israel is totally different, and thank goodness for that, but the fact is that Israel's adversaries see its democracy as a strategic advantage for them. After all, they reason, if four Israeli mothers could lead a successful campaign to withdraw Israeli forces from southern Lebanon, just think what 300 army reservists who refuse to serve in the territories might bring about.

How long can Israel continue to cope with massive daily casualties across the length and breadth of this tiny nation? Or with the massive economic impact of recession and a drying up of tourism revenue that coincides with mounting military costs? Or with the growing international political pressure from nations whose motto might as well be, "My mind's made up; don't confuse me with the facts"? Or from those in the international media who obsessively examine every Israeli action and, often ignoring balance, context, or objectivity, portray Israel in the worst possible light?

Speaking of the media, it's fascinating to see what goes on. I fully appreciate the challenges any major media outlet has in presenting a story as complex and multifaceted as the Middle East, and I also recognize that, as a friend of Israel, I may not always be the most objective observer. But sometimes I can't believe what I read in print or hear on the news.

When the *New York Times* last week announced in banner headlines on page one, above the fold, that Syria had accepted the so-called Saudi peace initiative, only to report in the story's third paragraph that the acceptance was conditioned on, among other things, "the right of return for Palestinian refugees"—which, of course, is a formula for Israel's destruction as a Jewish state—what are we to think? And it was the same paper, the week before, I might add, which delicately described the Syrians as exercising "effective authority" over Lebanon, when, in reality, Syria is an occupier, pure and simple.

Meanwhile, an MSNBC interviewer was asking former Prime Minister Ehud Barak when Israel would "return" the territories to the Palestinians, suggesting that Israel had seized land that once belonged to the Palestinians, rather than to Egypt and Jordan, which were the territories' governing authorities at the start of the Six-Day War.

My favorite came from a CNN reporter who interviewed—or rather lobbed softballs to—Hanan Ashrawi shortly after the September 11 terror attacks, including this whopper: "Ms. Ashrawi, it is very possible that more American lives have been lost in this terrorist attack—in this tragedy—than even the countless Arab [i.e., Palestinian] lives in the last five years...." Remember that at the time the death toll from September 11 was variously estimated at 5–15 thousand.

Israel's national will is being tested as never before in this wave of terror that Arafat initially launched in the fall of 2000. While I am confident that Israelis will once again withstand this test and, at the same time, continue to protect their democratic institutions, they are paying an extraordinarily high price, more than those of us living outside Israel's borders can imagine.

Second, anti-Semitism is on the rise again.

As Andrew Sullivan trenchantly wrote in the *Sunday Times* of London on December 23:

I'm not talking merely about editorials that seem to deny the right of Jews to emigrate to Israel; or leaders that come close to blaming Israel itself for the mass murder of its own citizens by Hamas terrorists. It is simply routine at this point to see "balanced" news reports from the BBC and the broadsheet British press that morally equate the actions of Israeli self-defense with the deliberate murder of civilian Jews by Palestinian terrorists. While Britain and America are allowed to fight a war against terrorism, Israel is urged to practice self-restraint every time another terrorist massacres another group of civilians in a restaurant or disco. Supporting Israel as a matter of right versus wrong is almost unheard of in polite society.

In normal times, this is lamentable but not disastrous. The Jews know something about survival. They can and will defend themselves. But in abnormal times, when anti-Semitism is spreading across the globe like a brushfire, it is deeply dangerous. Not since the 1930s has such blithe hatred of Jews gained this much acceptability in world opinion. Across the Arab world, in particular, the past decade or so has seen a shift from mere passive resentment of Jews to a paranoid anti-Semitism. That European elites want to ignore it, or—worse—pander to it, suggests we have learnt nothing from history.

The taboo on expressions of anti-Semitism that descended on much of the civilized world after the Shoah is eroding. Durban should have been a wake-up call. A UN conference convened to explore strategies for combating racism instead became a venue for promoting raw, unvarnished anti-Semitism, especially at the parallel nongovernmental forum. Everything was up for grabs; nothing was sacrosanct. The Holocaust, Zionism, and anti-Semitism—you name it and it was in dispute. Jewish delegates were harassed and intimidated, and required police protection.

Meanwhile, Arabic-language editions of the notorious *Protocols of the Elders of Zion* were readily available, and booklets with vile anti-Semitic caricatures were distributed by groups accredited by the conference. Three days after the conference ended, terrorists struck at the World Trade Center and Pentagon, and Durban disappeared from public consciousness. But we ignore the lessons of Durban at our collective peril.

In the Muslim world, with a few notable exceptions, anti-Semitism is quite widespread and deeply ingrained, as a forthcoming AJC-commissioned study will show in graphic detail. Yet where is it condemned in the international community?

When was the last time anyone remembers a discussion on the topic under UN auspices? Okay, I'm dreaming, but how about a major global campaign to shine the spotlight of exposure on the teaching of incitement in the Muslim world? After all, anti-Semitism is usually coupled with hatred of all "infidels," emphatically including Christians.

Isn't the fabric of religious tolerance for all faiths threatened in a country like the United States when, as the *Washington Post* reported on February 25, eleventh-graders at the elite Islamic Saudi Academy in Northern Virginia "file into their Islamic studies class, where the textbooks tell them the Day of Judgment can't come until Jesus Christ returns to Earth, breaks the cross and converts everyone to Islam, and until Muslims start attacking Jews"? In Saudi-funded schools around the world the teaching isn't much different.

For many diplomats and editorial writers, the subject is simply too radioactive, and they don't want to risk antagonizing the Muslim world. Better, the thinking goes, to live in denial as long as possible or simply to resort as needed to ritualistic and platitudinous language about all religions having their extremist factions that distort the true meaning of faith.

For each of the past three years, the fifty-three-member UN Commission on Human Rights approved a resolution under the innocent-sounding title of "defamation of religion" that cited only Islam, among the world's many religions, as the victim of defamation. Believe it or not, as I learned during a recent trip to Geneva, the Commission may be presented with a companion resolution at this year's session. This one would cite the hardships that Muslim minorities around the world—and no other religious minorities—have faced, ignoring the plight of Christians in Sudan, Bahais in Iran, etc.

Anti-Semitism has also been rearing its ugly head in Western Europe. Its sources are threefold: growing Muslim communities, extreme right-wing movements, and the fashionable "salon" anti-Semitism of some elites.

Reminiscent of the 1970s, much of the anti-Semitism is thinly masked as anti-Israelism, but in truth, it doesn't criticize specific Israeli policies but questions Israel's very right to exist.

One illustration was a long op-ed piece last fall in the respected Italian national daily *La Stampa*. The author called on Israel and its friends to engage in a collective mea culpa for the "original sin" of Israel's creation and the damage it inflicted on the Palestinian population. The piece caused a stir in Italy, with a number of prominent left-of-center personalities supporting the author, and others taking her to task.

France, a country to which I am deeply attached, is an especially telling case in point. While French Jews publicly debate among themselves the extent of anti-Semitism, what is indisputable is that there have been several hundred documented cases of anti-Semitism since October 2000, a frightening rise from previous years.

What is also beyond question is that poorer and more religious French Jews, who often live cheek by jowl with North African Muslims in the suburbs surrounding France's principal cities, are most vulnerable.

When the historic Jewish cemetery in Carpentras, in Provence, was desecrated in 1990, more than 200,000 people, including then-President Francois Mitterand and leaders of all the major political parties, marched in Paris in protest, after 10,000 gathered in Carpentras a day earlier for a solidarity service. A decade later, by contrast, France has become eerily quiet when Jews are targeted.

President Jacques Chirac recently announced that France was not an anti-Semitic country, as if this would instantaneously end all discussion, and Foreign Minister Hubert Vedrine cited negative images of Israel seen by French Muslim youths on Arab television as seeming justification for their violent behavior.

In fact, when an American Jewish Committee delegation met with the French foreign minister in New York in November 2001 and raised the subject of anti-Semitic incidents, he immediately dismissed it as a problem and added that resolution of the Arab-Israeli conflict would end the danger for French Jewry.

Can this be a satisfactory answer, especially coming from a country that has only recently emerged from a fifty-year period of denial of responsibility for the crimes of Vichy? Of what long-term value is facing history if its essential lessons are ignored or lost? Can anything serve to justify or excuse anti-Semitic behavior, regardless of what French Muslim youth believe to be happening in the Middle East, or what they think French policy is toward the region?

Might it be that, rather than exercising principled leadership in the face of French Jewish anxieties, the political leaders have deliberately chosen to "play down"—in the words of Roger Cukierman, the president of CRIF, the French Jewish umbrella organization—these concerns for domestic and external reasons? Could this be a harbinger of things to come in other countries with growing Muslim populations and strong ties to the Arab world?

France is now in the midst of a hotly contested presidential election. The outcome is likely to be close. French Jews number 600,000 and are prominent in every facet of the nation's life. But there are four to six million Muslims in France, mostly from North Africa, and, while some are there illegally, many are not, and will vote on Election Day. Indeed, last summer several French newspapers reported on an internal Socialist Party memorandum recommending that the party take strong pro-Palestinian positions to attract more French Arab voters.

Similarly, neither major French political party wants to upset ties with Arab countries. There is simply too much at stake for the French economy, which relies heavily on exports to North Africa and the Middle East and the jobs they create at home, not to speak of France's enduring diplomatic ambitions.

Remember that after a decisive downturn in Franco-Israeli relations in 1967, France sought to deny Israel ownership of five gunboats built under contract in Cherbourg, and Israel had to smuggle them out of the French harbor to Israel in 1969.

While Chirac was prime minister in the 1970s, France sold the Osirak nuclear reactor to Iraq. It was subsequently dubbed "Ochirac," and eventually—and fortunately—destroyed by the Israeli air force in 1981.

There's no doubt that Paris went soft on Iranian and Palestinian terrorism in an effort to ingratiate itself with Iran and the Arab world. In the same spirit, Paris refused to provide air space to American fighter jets taking off from Britain and targeting Libya in 1986, after Washington linked Colonel Muammar Qaddhafi with the bombing of a West Berlin discotheque in which an American soldier was killed and dozens were injured. As a result, the jets had to travel around France, more than doubling the length of the trip.

More recently, when the French ambassador to the Court of St. James referred to Israel as "that shitty little country" at a private dinner, what happened? Given the chance to retract his words, the ambassador instead only grumbled that an off-the-record conversation had been reported to the press. Meanwhile, it appears, the French government has taken no disciplinary action against the envoy.

Imagine that instead of Israel the ambassador had spoken of, say, Saudi Arabia. My guess is that he'd have been recalled to the Quai d'Orsay within minutes and never heard from again.

And while on the subject of the recrudescence of anti-Semitism, what can one say about the brutal slaying of Daniel Pearl and his reported last words, "I am a Jew, my mother is a Jew"? As Leon Wieseltier wrote in the *New Republic Online* (February 25): "I cannot recall in recent memory a more unreconstructed example of what we prefer to think of as 'medieval' anti-Semitism."

Yet many in the press, writing about Pearl's murder, inexplicably chose to minimize or completely ignore his last words and their meaning. I was in Europe at the time and noticed this in the papers there. Jonathan Mark, who writes a column entitled Media Watch for New York's *Jewish Week*, reported on some striking findings of his own (March 8):

> The *New York Times* story on Pearl's videotaped death (Feb. 23) buried his Jewish last words in the eighteenth paragraph, and then mentioned it just one other time amid numerous other reports and columns on the case. Pearl's own *Wall Street Journal*, in a 2,016-word story (Feb. 21), didn't mention "Jew" at all.... Post-mortem editorials in the *New York Times*, *Washington Post*, *Baltimore Sun* ... and dozens of other papers didn't mention the word Jew.

On the other hand, Mark points out that in *Pravda*, of all places, Pearl's identity as a Jew was not only noted, but "this very fact is quite enough for the militants."

This brings me to my third and final point. What worries me almost as much as the tragic situation confronting Israel and the reemergence of anti-Semitism in some noteworthy places is the reaction—or lack thereof—of some American Jews. The meaning of these developments hasn't fully penetrated.

Maybe it's a vacuum in communal leadership. Maybe the message hasn't been effectively conveyed by agencies and synagogues beyond their immediate constituencies. Maybe it's plain and simple uncertainty about what to do at such a moment. Maybe it's the disconnection between the privileged life we as American Jews lead in this blessed land and what's going on beyond our borders. Maybe it's an emotional detachment from Israel. Maybe it's discomfort with media images of Israeli military action. Maybe it's disagreement with the current Israeli government. Maybe it's a lack of personal identification with Jews in other countries.

There are lots of possible maybes.

The bottom line is that some people seem largely untouched or unaffected by what's going on, or, from my perspective, fail to see the larger issues at stake.

Somehow, Jewish leaders have to make the case for more awareness and activism, more organizational involvement, more political advocacy, and more contact with Jews abroad and especially in Israel.

If I needed reinforcement for my view, the point was driven home to me the other day by an Israeli diplomat stationed in the States. I called to check in and exchange views, as I periodically do.

He began a long discourse on American Jewry. In this hour of need, when Israel's very existence was being challenged as never before, he was dismayed to discover that American Jewish friends were rather few and far between. Normally mild-mannered and rather upbeat, he was as depressed as I've ever heard him. His bitterest complaint was directed at local Jewish leadership in his region of the country. They went on with their lives as before, he asserted, focusing on local Jewish needs and broader civic concerns, seemingly indifferent to Israel's struggle for survival. Israel was simply one among a number of agenda items, nothing more.

In the meantime, he said, Israel's adversaries in the United States, smelling blood, were organizing as never before, seeking coalition partners among racial, religious, labor, and human rights groups, finding support on local college campuses, inundating the media with letters, corresponding with elected officials, and organizing demonstrations.

The bottom line, for him, was that now more than ever Israelis need to believe they are not alone in their bitter struggle. Yet increasingly they feel abandoned by fellow Jews who seem unfazed by events far off in the Middle East. Bad as that is psychologically, it could have long-term political consequences as well.

Do something, he pleaded.

In 1863, Nikolai Chernyshevsky, a prominent Russian writer and political activist, wrote a classic novel entitled *Shto Dyelat?* or *What Is to Be Done?* The title is apt for us today, if not the contents.

I don't think there's any mystery about the kinds of things that need to be done. We need to educate ourselves and those around us, raise public consciousness, approach potential coalition partners, talk with elected officials, attend rallies, reach out to Israeli and Diaspora communities, participate in missions to Israel, and strengthen advocacy organizations like the American Jewish Committee. Most of all, we need to move from a business-as-usual attitude to a heightened state of activism.

Institutions and individuals are ultimately defined by how they act at moments they do not control. Those moments come, linger, and depart. But in those brief periods, we are challenged to show who we really are and what we truly stand for.

Years from now, what will be said of our response to the crisis at hand? Will we—Jews in the most successful Diaspora community in the history of our people—be able to assert that we did everything within our power to meet the challenges before us?

One of the victims of September 11, a recent graduate of Columbia University, lived by a simple philosophy passed on to him by his Greek grandmother: "Yesterday is history, tomorrow is a mystery, and today is a gift from God."

May we use that gift wisely.

Letter from a DOT-CONNer
April 1, 2002

No, it's not a typo. I'm not talking about the DOT-COMMers, but the DOT-CONNers. I'm referring to "Dot-Connecters," that is, people who are capable of connecting the dots.

As I watch the nightmarish events unfold day after day from Jerusalem to Tel Aviv, from Haifa to Netanya, I cry out in anguish.

Israel is under attack from vicious enemies who celebrate the culture of death and find joy not only in the path to so-called martyrdom but in killing innocent men, women, and children along the way. Everything and everyone is fair game: the sacred space of a Passover Seder or a bar mitzvah celebration; the targeting of the elderly and children; a restaurant that attracts both Arabs and Jews. The object is to slay as many people as possible.

There are allegedly heavenly rewards awaiting these Palestinian kamikazes. And there are earthly rewards as well, at least for their families. Iraq's Saddam Hussein gleefully dispatches checks to the surviving relatives.

Under the circumstances, it would be nice to believe that the world is able to connect the dots and get what's going on, but, with only a few notable exceptions, that would be asking too much, it seems.

Thank goodness for the United States.

President George W. Bush, I believe, has connected the dots and gets what's going on. Rather than choose the path of least resistance (which in this case would be craven appeasement of the Arab world), he has had the courage on several occasions to say what needs to be said.

He understands the fundamental point that Israel is a democratic nation fighting against an enemy that is linked to the global terror network and can no longer be trusted to do anything it promises. Using the essential guidepost, "Tell me who your friends are and I'll tell you who you are," he has concluded that Yasir Arafat's incontrovertible links with Iran, Hamas, Islamic Jihad, Hezbollah, and perhaps Al-Qaeda as well, reveal all too clearly on which side of the fence Arafat sits.

President Bush grasps the bottom-line point that there can be no moral equivalence between a nation trying by all means necessary to defend itself against suicide bombers bent on killing civilians and those who recruit, train, brainwash, and dispatch those killers.

And there are a handful of other world leaders who also see the situation for what it is, though only a few have had the guts to speak out publicly.

At the same time, I wouldn't hold my breath waiting for the United Nations to convene an emergency session to explicitly condemn the killing of Israelis. That's never happened, nor is it likely to start tomorrow. The UN is a political body, and the deck is overwhelmingly stacked against Israel.

Nor would I expect, however much I might still hope, that the European Union would at long last issue a clear-cut, unambiguous statement criticizing Chairman Arafat for his encouragement of terrorism, his violation of one cease-fire after another, and his abject failure to lead the Palestinian people down the promising path of peace offered to them by President Bill Clinton and Prime Minister Ehud Barak. After all, when was the last time that anyone can remember the EU doing any better than the carefully crafted utterances that regularly issue forth from Brussels, almost always tilted toward the Palestinians, regardless of events on the ground?

No, the member nations of the EU—usually with two notable exceptions, Britain and Germany—seem so blinded by their antipathy for Ariel Sharon, so reluctant to admit that their confidence in Arafat over the years might have been misplaced, so hesitant to incur the wrath of the Arab world and local Muslim populations, and so tied to a policy of evenhandedness, come what may, that they refuse to connect the dots.

Actually, the EU may be suffering from a form of cognitive dissonance, which is a psychological affliction reflecting the inability or

unwillingness to reconcile conflicting or contradictory beliefs and attitudes.

After all, the EU knows down deep that Israel is a fellow democracy—the only one in the Middle East; that it tried in vain to achieve
peace with the Palestinians on remarkably forthcoming terms, only to
be met with the claim that there has never been a historical link
between the Jewish people and Jerusalem and the demand for 3-4 million Palestinians to be given the so-called right of return to Israel; and
that it now faces the deadly scourge of terrorism encouraged, if not
directed, from the top. As the old proverb goes, "The fish stinks from
the head."

Yet the EU is unwilling to draw the obvious conclusions, instead
lamely demanding still more proof of a PA-Iranian link, calling repeatedly for Israeli restraint notwithstanding the nature of the provocation,
holding back on declaring Hezbollah a terrorist organization, and offering Arafat, as "the only game in town," just one more chance to prove his
bona fides ... and just one more chance ... and just one more chance.

The only known cure for cognitive dissonance is a reality check, but
that requires a willingness to admit that previously held beliefs may
have been either mistaken or overtaken by events.

Nor can I expect all that much from the media. To be sure, there are
certainly those with a firm grasp of the complexities of the Israeli-
Palestinian conflict and an ironclad commitment to fair, balanced
reporting, but too often what gets aired or published is a whole lot less.

In some cases, there are reporters who've been assigned to the beat
only yesterday because editors seek broader coverage of an ascending
news story, but these reporters simply don't have a clue about what's
going on, and it shows in their naive questions and uninformed comments.

In some cases, there are reporters who've succumbed to the roman-
ticized notion that the basic narrative line is oppressor vs. oppressed,
and, come hell or high water, that's the departure point for the stories
they file.

In some cases, reporters work for government-controlled media outlets, such as Agence France-Presse (AFP), and understand that there's
a certain line they're expected to follow.

And in some cases, there are reporters who follow the unwritten rules of the game: If you want access to Palestinian leaders, you have to play along, or else you will be left talking to yourself, or worse, face intimidation. After all, unlike Israelis who migrate to microphones like bees to honey, Palestinian spokesmen are deliberately few in number and can play hard to get, which allows them to control their message much more effectively than Israelis.

Much as American friends of Israel on occasion find fault with reporting here, and rightly so, the situation in Europe continues to be much more problematic. Sympathetic editorial writers and columnists are all but impossible to find, the traditional separation of news and opinion is frequently blurred, and the ingratiating, sometimes sycophantic reporting of the Palestinian side of the conflict is simply impossible to ignore.

Perhaps most disturbing of all is the appropriation of Holocaust imagery.

While *La Repubblica* (March 16), one of Italy's two leading dailies, referred to the American camp for Al-Qaeda detainees in Guantanamo as a "concentration camp," *El Periódico*, a prominent Spanish daily, carried a profoundly offensive cartoon on March 15. The first panel, entitled "Warsaw 1940," showed Nazi troops pointing their guns at Jewish children. The second panel, entitled "Ramallah 2002" and intended as a mirror image, showed Israeli troops pointing their guns at Palestinian children, with one Israeli soldier saying: "Our case is different. We are the chosen people."

Meanwhile, *El Pais*, Spain's most influential daily, has carried two long op-eds in the last two months by an unaffiliated American Jew who compared Israel's actions in the West Bank to those of Yugoslavia under Slobodan Milosevic and who, in previous writings, suggested that Israel was behaving like the Nazis from 1933 to 1945. The first piece was entitled "Letter from an American Jew." I submitted a reply suggesting that there were other American Jews who felt rather differently, but was told by the paper's editors that, as they don't believe in "polemics," there was no room to publish it.

Incidentally, the first of the two pieces written by this harsh critic of Israel was also carried in *Der Spiegel*, Germany's most prominent weekly news magazine. At least, the magazine published a protesting letter, even if the four other published letters were supportive of the author's line.

While this is not the time to go into what's happening in Germany these days, it's a subject to which I'll return in future letters. Suffice it to say that there seems to be a gradual but perceptible change taking place in Germany about Israel and the nature of the special German-Israeli relationship, certainly among younger people, but not only, and this does not augur well.

The one group that could be expected to understand and identify with Israel's plight is fellow American Jews. That would seem a no-brainer. After all, aren't we Israel's international lifeline? Aren't we the ones who to this day rue the fact that we could do so little during the Shoah to rescue fellow Jews and say "Never again" ad nauseam? Aren't we the ones who in our fundraising campaigns speak of "one people?"

Needless to say, there are any number of American Jews who have expressed their support for Israel in tangible ways in recent months. These Jews understand that this is no time for silence. To the contrary, this is a moment to set aside business as usual. The moment will not wait for them. The time to act, they understand, is now.

They have traveled to Israel despite the obvious danger, kept in touch with Israeli relatives and friends by phone or e-mail, contacted elected officials about Israel, written letters to the editor, called in to talk-radio shows, protested when the media has dealt unfairly with Israel, arranged pro-Israel programs and rallies, donated funds to pro-Israel organizations, bought Israeli products, discussed Israel with their non-Jewish neighbors and colleagues, and given their children a crash course in what's going on and how to stand up for Israel in schools and colleges.

But, truth be told, there are too many others who have not.

Among them are many who care deeply about Israel, instinctively support the democratically elected government of the day, and worry profoundly about the threat to Israel. The problem is that they haven't been sufficiently mobilized yet. Other than following the news and anguishing over it, they're not sure what else to do or where to turn. It is time to reach these individuals and offer them concrete ways to demonstrate their support for Israel. It can be done, but it will require the sustained efforts of national and local leadership.

Regrettably, there are others who couldn't care less. They live in a self-contained, self-satisfied world. Israel is simply not a part of their lives, and they do not connect what's going on there—or even the virulent expressions of anti-Semitism in the Arab world or, for that matter, the anti-Semitic incidents in such European countries as France and Belgium—with their own lives in the United States. Some in this group are identified Jews who find fulfillment of their identity needs within the framework of the American Jewish community and seek nothing more; others are detached or even alienated from the community for one reason or another.

According to American Jewish Committee surveys, approximately 20–25 percent of American Jewry feel no identification with Israel.

And then there is an important third group. It's hard to quantify numbers. These are people who care about Israel but have qualms about what's going on. They feel that they cannot in good conscience support the current Israeli government policy, they are pained by the plight of the Palestinians and the image of Israel as the aggressor nation, and they believe that peace talks must replace military actions.

Of course, within this group there are those whose views range across a spectrum. Some express their opinions publicly, while others choose not to; some propose what many would consider extreme measures, while others are far more moderate in their views.

I wouldn't suggest spending much time trying to convince Adam Shapiro, the Jewish-born Palestinian activist, to come home from Ramallah, or the "more than 600 [Jewish] contributors" who sponsored the quarter-page ad in the *New York Times* on March 17 calling for the suspension of U.S. military aid to Israel and a reduction in economic aid, and declaring that "Israel's security policies harm all the peoples of the Middle East," to consider the dangerous consequences of their misguided initiative.

On the other hand, I would devote far more attention to those American Jews who are open to discussion, seek answers to difficult questions, and want to do the right thing for Israel.

All in all, I believe, American Jews could benefit from a wake-up call.

What we witnessed on September 11 was a declaration of war against the United States and Western values. It was also an attack on Jews.

In the aftermath of September 11, the widespread efforts in the Arab and larger Muslim worlds to peddle elaborate conspiracy theories about the alleged role of Israel, the Mossad, and Jews generally—in order to divert world attention from those who were truly responsible for the terrorist attacks—cannot simply be dismissed.

The brutal kidnapping and murder of Daniel Pearl, the *Wall Street Journal* reporter, in Pakistan, and his chilling last words about being a Jew, must not be forgotten.

The widespread anti-Semitism in the Arab and Muslim media is real. When a medical professor at King Faisal University writes a column in a leading Saudi paper (*Al-Riyadh*, March 10) that asserts the Jewish need for Christian and Muslim blood to fulfill ritual obligations for Purim and Passover, we ignore at our peril the meaning of this age-old blood libel accusation.

And incidentally, the current Syrian defense minister has written a widely disseminated book also pinning the blood libel canard on Jews. It's safe to say that the book hasn't hurt his standing in the Syrian government.

The growing number of anti-Semitic incidents in Europe needs to be taken very seriously. When synagogues in Marseilles, Strasbourg, Lyon, Brussels, and other cities are attacked, when Orthodox Jews in France are hesitant to wear a *kippah* in public, and when Jewish schools are the focus of intense security, does this not touch us? Have we learned so little from history, especially about the slippery slope of anti-Semitism? Do we not feel a sense of kinship and interdependence with fellow Jews in other lands? Didn't the events of September 11 once and for all puncture the myth of America's distance from the events emanating from the Middle East?

Finally, we should be under no illusions. Israel is fighting for its very existence. If those who perpetrate terrorist acts in Israel believe they can succeed in bringing the country to its knees, it will only invite more and more such bombings. Remember that Hamas, which claimed responsibility for the recent attack on the restaurant in Haifa, referred to the port city as "occupied" land.

Israel cannot be expected to negotiate under the threat of terror. It's a formula for disaster, and not just for Israel. If the terrorists succeed in Israel, they will apply the lessons to other parts of the world as well; make no mistake about it.

The political solution that we all must continue to pray for, however remote it may appear for the foreseeable future, can only come about once the Palestinians realize that the terror campaign is entirely counterproductive; in point of fact, it is only serving to unify Israelis in a way that we haven't seen for decades. Ariel Sharon, once considered the darling of the right wing, today reflects the center of the Israeli political spectrum.

A couple of weeks ago, a number of European newspapers reported the results of a *Ma'ariv* poll showing that 60 percent of Israelis were unhappy with Sharon's policies. The papers implied that the Israeli public was moving to the left, but in reality the same poll showed that those dissatisfied Israelis felt Sharon was not tough enough and saw Benjamin Netanyahu in a more favorable light.

It was only a few years ago that many thought they saw the light at the end of the tunnel. Some Israeli leaders spoke about a new era dawning in the Middle East and a golden age for Jews worldwide. Some American Jews openly questioned the continued need for Jewish defense organizations and began to devote more of their time and resources outside the Jewish community. Now, it seems, we've been given yet another jarring reminder that history takes unexpected turns and that we have, as Robert Frost wrote, "miles to go before we sleep."

The more we Jews go down that road together, united by common purpose and resolve, the more likely we are to succeed. And a first step might be for all of us to connect the dots.

Letter from Dublin
· June 11, 2002

Speaking of change.

I first caught a glimpse of Ireland in 1960, when the transatlantic ocean liner SS *America*, on which my mother and I were traveling, docked in the charming harbor of Cobh en route to Le Havre, France, but it wasn't until 1971 that I actually spent any time in the country.

I crossed the Irish Sea by ferry from England and spent ten days hitchhiking around Ireland with little more than a backpack. As an aside, had I been more inventive, I would have brought along a refrigerator as well, as the British writer Tony Hawks did years later, parlaying a bet in a bar into a memorable month-long hitchhiking trek around Ireland and a best-selling book based on the unusual experience.

The Ireland I remember was verdant and friendly—perhaps the friendliest country in Europe—but strikingly poor. The cities and towns, with the exception of some Dublin districts, weren't anything to write home about. In effect, they resembled the prevailing weather—gray and despondent. And everyone I met, it seemed, had family members abroad and were themselves thinking about leaving. The only diversity in the country at the time was the tiny Protestant population and the even more miniscule Jewish community.

That was thirty years ago. Back in Dublin for the first time a week ago, together with Jason Isaacson, AJC's director of government and international affairs, I was overwhelmed by the changes.

Ireland has become a prosperous country. In the past decade, largely fueled by the high-tech boom (and surviving the high-tech bust), Ireland has rapidly risen in the European Union rankings from near-bottom to near-top in per capita income. Unemployment is so low that the country has welcomed foreign workers. Indeed, the number of Asians, Africans, East Europeans, and other residents is striking. Some women, I was told, come only in order to give birth, knowing that their children will then enjoy Irish citizenship automatically and they can follow suit. Dublin alone has three mosques, including the imposing Islamic Cultural Center, built with funds from the United Arab

Emirates. And perhaps for the first time in their history, the Irish are no longer emigrating; in fact, many Irish abroad are returning home to take advantage of the good times.

What hasn't changed for the better, though, is the consumption of alcohol. During my stay, the Irish press reported on the findings of a new EU study. From 1990 to 2000, alcohol use dropped in ten of the fifteen EU countries and increased by no more than 5 percent in four other countries (Germany, Greece, Portugal, and the United Kingdom), but in Ireland jumped by a whopping 41 percent.

To illustrate, the Irish consumed 12.3 liters of pure alcohol per capita in 2000, 2.5 liters more than in France and Germany and four liters more than in the U.K. And when it comes to beer, the average Irishman drinks 153 liters per year, compared to 125 liters in Germany. As a result, one in five hospital patients has been seriously abusing alcohol, and one in four admissions to hospital emergency rooms is alcohol related.

In one of Dublin's curious anomalies, where else would you find a one-time hospital for recovering alcoholics located just across the street from the sprawling Guinness brewery?

Ireland never had a large Jewish population, but at its peak in the late 1940s the community numbered 5–6 thousand. Since then, the total has steadily declined to around 1,200 today, mostly in Dublin, with a few score in Cork, according to Mark Sofer, Israel's departing ambassador in Dublin. In his daughter's class at the Jewish school in Dublin, only seven of the thirty children are actually Jewish.

The dramatic drop is explained by two principal factors—emigration to Europe and North America and aliyah. It is said that today there are more Irish Jews in Israel than Ireland, and undoubtedly the most famous Irish contribution to Israel has been the Herzog family, symbolized by Chaim Herzog, Israel's former president, who was born in Belfast and grew up in Dublin.

Despite its small size, Irish Jewry has played an important role in the life of Ireland. Until national elections last month, there had always been at least one Jew—and at times as many as three (of 166 members)—in the Dáil Éireann, the Irish parliament.

Both Dublin and Cork have had Jewish mayors. It was one of those mayors who prompted the legendary story of the two Jews standing on New York's Fifth Avenue watching the start of the annual St. Patrick's Day Parade in 1956. As Robert Briscoe, the lord mayor of Dublin, kicked off the parade, one Jew turned to the other and said: "Isn't that amazing? Did you know that the lord mayor of Dublin is Jewish?" The other replied: "No kidding. Only in America!"

But perhaps the most famous Irish Jew of all was Leopold Bloom, the central character in James Joyce's classic 1922 novel, *Ulysses*, arguably the most lauded and least read book in the English language. As a tour guide noted, this is a book that every Irishman begins reading, but few are able to finish, without considerable help at least, as it requires vast knowledge of theology, history, mythology, languages, and much more to fully grasp. Once asked about the demands his writing made on the reader, Joyce replied: "The demand I make of my reader is that he should devote his whole life to reading my works."

Joyce, acclaimed as Ireland's greatest writer in a country with a remarkable literary tradition that includes the likes of Samuel Beckett, William Butler Yeats, Oscar Wilde, and Seamus Heaney, went abroad in 1902, at the age of twenty, never to live in the land of his birth again. He expressed his reasons through the words of Stephen Daedalus, the hero in the essentially autobiographical *Portrait of the Artist as a Young Man*:

> I will not serve that in which I no longer believe, whether it call itself my home, my fatherland, or my church: and I will try to express myself in some mode of life or art as freely as I can, using for my defence the only arms I allow myself to use—silence, exile, and cunning.

Indeed, in this one sentence, Joyce has touched on perhaps the principal themes that have defined the Irish soul—family, nationalism, and church—although, in his case, he rebelled against all three.

At least two of these themes—nationalism and the church—may also have affected Ireland's approach to Israel.

Ireland was the last European country to permit a resident Israeli ambassador. Hard as it is to believe, it was not until 1995 that the first

Israeli ambassador arrived in Dublin. Until then, Ireland was served by the Israeli embassy in London.

There is some dispute over the reasons for this long delay. Officially, the Irish contended that budgetary and security factors prevented the opening of embassies in Dublin and Tel Aviv. But some observers argue that Ireland did not want to jeopardize its trade relations with Egypt, Iraq, and Libya, to which it exported meat, and that it did not want to get ahead of the Vatican, which only established formal ties between the Holy See and Israel in 1994.

Whatever the real explanation, Ireland and Israel have experienced substantial growth in their bilateral relationship in the ensuing seven years. This is especially noticeable in the volume of trade. Ireland now ranks as Israel's sixth leading trading partner in Europe. Surprisingly, Ireland's trade with Israel exceeds the combined total of its trade with the Arab world. As Ireland moved from an economy based primarily on meat and agricultural products to one based on information technology, it found a compatible partner in Israel, which was undergoing precisely the same kind of change.

Interestingly, Dublin is home to only two Arab embassies—Egypt and Morocco—and the latter has been downgraded in recent years. The Palestinian Authority has a resident "delegate general" in Dublin, and there are rumors the Libyans will soon open an embassy in the Irish capital.

There have been a few Algerians and Egyptians arrested for links to terrorist groups and reports of some fundraising efforts for these groups, but in comparison with Britain, France, Germany, and other European countries, there appears to be relatively little Islamic extremist activity, at least to date.

What is particularly worrisome, however, is the longstanding link between the Irish Republican Army and Palestinian terrorist groups. Indeed, in the recent military operation in Jenin, Israeli troops found a cache of pipe bombs identical to known IRA prototypes.

Ireland offers an interesting case study in attitudes toward Israel. Unlike France or Italy, Ireland is not dependent on energy imports from the Middle East, nor does it have major export markets in the region. Geographically, it's quite far removed from the Middle East and North Africa. And its Muslim population remains relatively small, perhaps 18–20 thousand in a population of four million.

If Ireland is considered quite pro-Palestinian, then it can't be explained by political or economic expediency, as it can for some other European countries.

Rather, it appears to derive principally from seeing the Israeli-Palestinian conflict through the lens of Irish history and the experience of Northern Ireland.

For nearly 700 years Ireland was occupied and dominated by the British. It was not until 1921 that Ireland, minus the six counties of the north, gained independence from Britain following the War of Independence, but it remained a British dominion. And it was only in 1949 that the Republic of Ireland came into being, after which it withdrew from the British Commonwealth.

To most Irish, the word "occupation" is simply anathema. Israel is seen as the occupying power; thus the natural sympathy is extended to the Palestinians. The Israelis are cast in the role of the unloved British.

In the same vein, there is less sympathy for the Israeli argument that negotiation with an avowed enemy is, for all practical purposes, impossible, as the Irish insist that, at the end of the day, there is no alternative but to negotiate with your enemy.

There are other elements that go into the shaping of Irish attitudes, few of which are in Israel's favor.

Despite the close family ties between Ireland and the United States, there is a discernible strain of anti-Americanism in Irish society. Israel and the U.S. are seen as close allies, only reinforcing the prevailing Irish view regarding Israel.

Within the European Union, Ireland is generally quite close to France, Israel's most outspoken critic, and distant from the United Kingdom, together with Germany, Israel's most ardent supporter.

In fact, as our visit coincided with the opening of the World Cup soccer tournament, it was noteworthy that Irish fans had two consuming passions: (1) energetically rooting for their team to hold their own against a stronger Cameroon squad in the opening match (the game ended in a 1-1 tie, leading one journalist to comment elegantly that "their [the Irish squad's] self-respect and ours was snatched from the jaws of ignominy") and (2) equally energetically cheering on Sweden in its first match against the despised English.

On the international scene, Ireland is a strong supporter of the United Nations and an outspoken defender of human rights. Remember that the controversial United Nations High Commissioner for Human Rights, Mary Robinson, is the former president of Ireland. To state the painfully obvious, neither the UN nor Mrs. Robinson can be counted among Israel's friends today.

With a built-in aversion to military options other than UN peace-keeping operations, Ireland has never been a member of NATO, remained neutral during the Second World War, and devotes no more than one percent of its current GDP to defense spending (compared to Israel's 11.6 percent). In this light, Israel is seen as "excessively aggressive."

And there are those observers who believe that into the mix must also be added a certain residual religiously based anti-Semitism, a resentment that the Jews rule over Jerusalem and many of the Christian holy places. After all, despite growing secularism, Ireland remains a deeply Catholic country, whose roots can be traced to the fifth century C.E. when St. Patrick converted the Irish to Christianity. While I am not in a position to comment on the degree to which anti-Semitism remains a factor in Irish attitudes toward Israel, if at all, it was noted by enough knowledgeable people—Jews and Catholics alike—to warrant mentioning.

Ireland today is among the EU nations less sympathetic to Israel, but not nearly as outspoken as, say, France or Sweden. And while Bertie Ahern, the Taoiseach—the widely used Irish name referring to the prime minister—spontaneously offered public words of sympathy for the "stress endured" by the two Palestinian terrorists accepted by Ireland (of the total of thirteen) to end the standoff at the Church of the Nativity, the statements coming recently from the Foreign Ministry have shown at least some degree of balance.

Within Ireland, it must be said, there are also strong voices of support for Israel. Israel is blessed with an energetic and articulate ambassador who, I am told, may be the most interviewed foreign envoy in the country. Despite its small size, the Jewish community has several outspoken and effective advocates for Israel. And in the press there are a few gems. Best known is Conor Cruise O'Brien, the historian, diplomat, politician, and writer. Author of the highly acclaimed *The Siege: The Saga of Israel and Zionism* (1985), O'Brien is a regular columnist in the press and a consistently staunch defender of Israel (and America, too). Eoghan Harris and Kevin Myers, two other regular columnists, are equally pro-Israel. And the *Sunday Independent*, Ireland's most widely circulated newspaper, takes a pro-Israel line as well, though it is among the very few media outlets to do so.

Moreover, I visited a bookshop and picked up a book entitled *An Accidental Diplomat: My Years in the Irish Foreign Service, 1987-1995* by Eamon Delaney. To my pleasant surprise, I discovered that at least one recent diplomat, apart from the legendary O'Brien, who served as Ireland's ambassador to the UN from 1956 to 1960, sees things in the Middle East the way some of the rest of us do. Delaney writes:

> One time, I was chatting to the Liechtenstein delegate when a Kuwaiti delegate turned around and glared at me; we were "talking" during the Palestine debate.... This was just Kuwait "getting back to normal." After the Gulf War, when the Kuwaitis had got their country back, and exiled or killed thousands of Palestinians in the process, they wanted to show that they were back "being concerned" about Palestine again, just like the rest of the Arab world.
>
> In fact, the Palestine debate takes up to three days [at the UN General Assembly], "debate" being a rather glorious name for a series of almost identical statements attacking Israel which, ironically, they do not recognize as actually being in the chamber.... The issue of Palestine takes up to 20 percent of the GA's time, while the situation of the Kurds, for example, gets none. No wonder Ed Koch, mayor of New York, wanted the UN moved out of the city, especially when it passed the infamous "Zionism is Racism" resolution.

It will take more American Jewish Committee visits to learn just how unusual this point of view is.

As a young man, Eamon de Valera, certainly the best-known Irish statesman of the twentieth century, who served as prime minister three times and as president once, visited France. On his return to Ireland, he famously announced: "All I can say is that sex in Ireland is as yet in its infancy."

The American Jewish Committee visit to Dublin, we were told, was the first ever by an American Jewish group, as was our hour-long meeting with Ireland's respected foreign minister, Brian Cowen. As such, it represented the infancy of our program there. But there is so much to discuss regarding the Middle East, international terrorism, and the transatlantic relationship, not to mention the obvious natural affinity between the Irish and the Jews, which I couldn't help noticing during this visit. Thus, without doubt we shall return to the captivating Emerald Isle.

Letter from the Campus Front
June 24, 2002

A number of colleges and universities have become the front line in the Israeli-Palestinian struggle in the United States. Pro-Israel college students are in the thick of that struggle and need our understanding, support, and help.

Nowhere else in this country have the battle lines been drawn as sharply or has the atmosphere turned more poisonous. Nowhere else do pro-Israel activists experience such intense forms of hostility, and even intimidation and harassment.

Among the recent incidents:

At the University of California at Berkeley, the *Los Angeles Times* reported (April 11, 2002):

> A spate of anti-Semitic vandalism has stung Jewish students, leading some to question their safety at the school.... The glass door at Berkeley Hillel, the center of Jewish life on campus, was smashed with a cinder block March 27, as Jews marked the first night of the holy days of Passover.... A group of students was pelted with eggs 18 months ago as they emerged from services celebrating the Jewish New Year.

Moreover, two Orthodox Jewish students were assaulted this spring one block from the Berkeley campus. And an anti-Israel rally—deliberately scheduled to coincide with Holocaust Remembrance Day, April 9—featured signs equating Israel with the Third Reich and the apartheid regime of South Africa. Seventy-eight demonstrators from the rally were arrested for occupying a university building.

At San Francisco State University (SFSU), an American Jewish Committee eyewitness described a chilling scene in which nearly 1,000 people, also gathered on April 9, cheered those who likened the Star of David to the swastika, lauded suicide bombers, and called for a one-state solution that would liquidate Israel. "Occupied Palestine is all of Palestine," said a speaker. Also heard were such statements as: "The Germans should hook you all up"; "You should go back to Germany"; and "It's the rise of the Jewish Cracker."

But wait, there's more. On May 7, Hillel students organized a "Peace in the Middle East" rally. Dr. Laurie Zoloth, the director of Jewish studies at SFSU, described the scene:

> As soon as the community supporters left, the fifty students who remained praying in a minyan for the traditional afternoon prayers, or chatting, or cleaning up after the rally, or talking—were surrounded by a large, angry crowd of Palestinians and their supporters. But they were not calling for peace. They surrounded the praying students, and the elderly women who are our elder college participants, who survived the Shoah, who helped shape the Bay Area peace movement, only to watch as a threatening crowd shoved the Hillel students against the wall of the plaza....
>
> As the counterdemonstrators poured into the plaza, screaming at the Jews to "Get out or we will kill you" and "Hitler did not finish the job," I turned to the police and to every administrator I could find and asked them to remove the counterdemonstrators from the Plaza.... The police told me that they had been told not to arrest anyone, and that if they did, "it would start a riot." I told them it already was a riot.

A few days later, Robert A. Corrigan, the university's president, sent an open letter in which he said that in his fourteen years at SFSU, "I have never been as deeply distressed and angered by something that happened on this campus as I am by the events of last week." He spoke of "a small but terribly destructive number of pro-Palestinian demon-strators, many of whom were not SFSU students, who abandoned themselves to intimidating behavior and statements too hate-filled to repeat." He went on to say that "if we identify violations of public law, we will refer cases to the district attorney."

At New York University last October, Nadeen Al-jijakli, the presi-dent of Arab Students United, sent an e-mail to the members of the group that included an article by former Ku Klux Klan Grand Dragon David Duke excoriating the Jews for every sin under the sun, includ-ing responsibility for September 11.

Asked about the piece by a reporter for the *Washington Square News* (October 8, 2001), Al-jijakli responded: "I read the article by David Duke and I'm not going to deny that I agree with some of its content.... I feel like the article is valid. I don't feel like whether the article is anti-Semitic is something I need to explain."

On April 9, Ms. Al-jijakli received the university's prestigious President's Service Award.

At Hunter College, a Hillel official reported, an attempt by students to organize an affiliate of AIPAC was prevented when pro-Palestinian activists blocked entry to the meeting room.

At the University of Colorado this spring, "There was a wave of highly abusive graffiti daubed around the campus, bearing the same message: 'Zionazis'" (*Ha'aretz*, June 18, 2002).

And at Columbia University, according to the campus newspaper (April 18, 2002), a pro-Palestinian rally on April 17 included the par-ticipation of several faculty members. Joseph Massad, a professor of Middle Eastern languages and cultures, decried Israel as "a Jewish supremacist and racist state" and stated that "every racist state should be threatened." Not to be outdone, Nicholas de Genova, a professor of Latino studies, declared: "The heritage of the Holocaust belongs to the Palestinian people. The State of Israel has no claim to the heritage of the Holocaust."

To be sure, there are thousands of American colleges and universi-ties, and the situation varies from place to place.

No two campuses are identical. Some are harmonious or just plain quiet, even indifferent to events in the Middle East. (A recent survey of college students nationwide, reported on MSNBC last week, revealed a strikingly high level of ignorance about current affairs generally. Fewer than 20 percent of the students, for example, could properly identify either Condoleezza Rice or Donald Rumsfeld.)

On a handful of campuses, observant Jewish and Muslim students share dining facilities and, in doing so, seek to break down barriers. On some campuses, the principle of a "hate-free zone" prevails, and violations are dealt with severely. But there are quite a few schools that have become hotbeds of pro-Palestinian, anti-Israel activity, and these bear close scrutiny.

What is indisputable is that pro-Palestinian activists have targeted the campuses and see them as particularly ripe for building support. Is there one central body organizing the effort? Hard to tell, but doubtful. Are funds coming from overseas or their proxies here? Again, difficult to say, but it wouldn't come as a complete surprise if they were.

I've spent a good chunk of time over the last two years trying to understand the campus situation. Having led a graduate seminar at a large university during the past two academic years, I interacted with dozens of students. Serving, until recently, as a trustee of a New England liberal arts college offered me another perspective. Traveling to a number of diverse campuses as a guest of pro-Israel students, I have met with many students and talked with them late into the night about their concerns. I've also benefited from the presence at the American Jewish Committee of thoughtful interns who attend a broad range of undergraduate and graduate schools. And as the father of two college-age sons, I have also seen the situation through their experiences.

Who are the pro-Palestinian activists?

First and foremost, they are drawn from the growing number of Arab and Muslim students to be found on American campuses, whether foreign students on student visas, or immigrants, or the children of immigrants.

Usually, they are not alone. Their claims that Israel is a "colonialist, racist, occupying" power find a receptive ear among the sometimes overlapping anti-globalization crowd, other minority communities, human rights activists, the far—and, sometimes, not so far—left, and the America-can-do-no-right believers. These individuals are drawn from the ranks of students and, in the case of large, urban campuses, sometimes from part-time, older students, and non-students as well.

More surprising, on a number of campuses, some Jewish, even Israeli, students have openly identified themselves with pro-Palestinian groups.

As the *New York Times* reported (April 8, 2002):

> The groups have attracted support from non-Muslim and non-Arab students. At Berkeley, Mr. Shingavi said, less than one-fifth of the core seventy members of his organization [Students for Justice in Palestine] are Arab or Muslim. They have also drawn support from Jewish students.
>
> "I always had this view that Jews wouldn't do anything bad," said Laura Pearl, a Jewish student who is a member of the Palestine Committee at the University of Michigan. "Once I started to question that assumption, I saw how many things there were that Israel had done that were really bad."

One pro-Israel activist at a leading law school indicated that a majority of the Jewish students in her year took the Palestinian side in the current conflict with Israel.

For me, the pièce de résistance was an evening spent this winter with students at a prestigious college near New York. The meeting was organized by the pro-Israel group on campus, but was open to all. Three students affiliated with a campus group known as FIST—Fight Israeli State Terrorism—showed up and participated in the discussion. It turned out that one of them, in fact the most assertive, was a Jew.

After several hours of responding to questions from the students, I turned to this particular student from FIST.

"Before I go, do you mind if I ask you just one question?" I inquired.

"Sure," he replied.

"You've talked a lot this evening about Israeli confiscation of Palestinian lands, settlements, IDF brutality, denial of health care, and other allegations. Let's assume for a moment, though, that the Palestinians and Israelis could reach a peace agreement. If so, would you accept Israel's right to exist as a sovereign Jewish state in the Middle East?"

He did not answer. Instead, he met my question with silence and averted his eyes.

I don't know the number of pro-Israel activists on each campus, but surely they constitute a minority of the total number of Jewish students in each instance. In effect, the Jewish students are divided into three groups—the pro-Israel activists, the anti-Israel activists, and the silent majority (except, perhaps, in that law school cited above, where the silent majority appears to be a minority).

The pro-Israel campus community has stepped up its efforts over the past year and merits tremendous admiration. These courageous and principled students are being helped by various Jewish groups, most notably Hillel and AIPAC. Other Jewish organizations and foundations are also paying increasing attention to the campus, providing, among other things, speakers and information. The American Jewish Committee, for example, has prepared several basic fact sheets on the Arab-Israeli conflict that have been widely circulated on campuses.

All these initiatives are laudable and necessary. However, as more and more actors involve themselves in trying to address the campus situation, there will be a need for greater coordination, not always the Jewish community's strongest suit.

Remember the story about the rowing team at Yeshiva University?

University officials decided they wanted to upgrade the school's public image. They conducted a study and learned that many of the major American universities, including the members of the Ivy League, had rowing teams, so they decided to start a team of their own.

In the first race, though, the Yeshiva crew barely got going when the Harvard crew was already crossing the finishing line. Embarrassed university officials ordered their new coach to observe the training techniques of the Harvard crew before the next regatta. The coach did as he was told and then reported back: "We've got it all wrong. In the Harvard crew, eight men row and one guy shouts orders. In our crew, eight guys shout orders and only one man rows!"

The key challenge is how to reach the silent majority of Jewish students. Ranging in age from, say, eighteen to twenty-two or twenty-three, they were born long after the seminal events that shaped the identity of many adult Jews—1948, 1967, and 1973.

To the extent they know anything about the Middle East—and most have never been to the region—they see the conflict largely as presented through the media, namely in strictly political or human rights terms, but not as a larger existential struggle of the Jewish people.

Few, it appears, have been exposed to Zionism or are sufficiently knowledgeable to debate the intricacies of the Middle East conflict. Sadly, as I've learned, in some of their families Israel did not loom large, if at all, so there's an underlying question about why Israel should even matter.

And the debate is especially tough these days because Israel is seen as an "illiberal" cause, even if the Jewish state is the only democracy in the region and the only society in the Middle East that protects free expression—not to mention feminism, gay rights, and multiculturalism—which is an essential part of the liberal agenda here at home.

Many of our Jewish children are raised in homes where they are encouraged to be open to all ideas, to consider the many sides of an argument, and to be sensitive to the feelings of others.

Thus, they can find it very difficult to know how to defend Israel against the unending barrage of accusations and condemnations. When one of the chants of the anti-Vietnam period, "Hey, hey, LBJ, how many kids did you kill today?" gets morphed into "How many kids did Israel kill today?" some Jewish kids simply do not want—or know how—to respond, so they don't. Instead, they take a pass.

They aren't necessarily eager to find themselves in a position where they are forced to defend a "right-wing" government in Israel, or the actions of an "occupying" army, or the litany of Israel's alleged human rights violations, or to be associated with Evangelical Christians or campus conservatives who are often the main, if not the only, allies of pro-Israel Jewish activists today.

Faced with Arab students who come from the region, they are simply no match in a debate. What is the well-intentioned but largely uninformed Jewish student supposed to say if a Palestinian student claims that his own family has experienced Israeli "brutality?" Call him a liar? Justify the IDF action?

Yet, this silent majority, for whatever reason, also doesn't choose to join the anti-Israel Jewish activists. Rather, it remains on the sidelines.

Incidentally, it's not just the silent majority who can be off duty. One of the students I met this year, who was pursuing a master's degree in politics, had spent several years working for AIPAC. Although both knowledgeable and committed to Israel, she told me matter-of-factly that she was taking a breather during her two-year program. The level of debate was so intense and bitter, she said, that she feared it would spoil her experience and, so, with some reluctance, she simply opted out.

As more Jewish institutions line up to help out on the campuses, it will be important to do some analysis about intended audiences and objectives.

In political campaigns with which I am familiar, a candidate segments voters more or less into five blocs—enthusiastic supporters, mild supporters, uninformed or undecided, mild opponents, and zealous opponents.

The object of the exercise, of course, is to get elected by cobbling together a majority of voters on Election Day, but to do so requires sophisticated knowledge of what makes each of the groups tick, especially the first three—the continuum from the most ardent supporters to the middle group. There's no point in wasting time on trying to change the minds of your most determined adversaries, though there could possibly be utility in trying to soften the hostility of the fourth group.

In some respects, it's the same on the campuses. There are multiple constituencies, and therefore multiple strategies are required. One outside speaker may be needed to reach the "silent Jewish majority" or motivate the "mild Jewish supporters" to get active, while another might be more effective with the committed activists.

Some speakers will be far more effective than others for campus-

wide events that seek to attract large numbers of uninformed or undecided students. Some speakers, by dint of their reputation and credibility, will have far more drawing power to attract not only students but
also faculty. One kind of pamphlet—or CD, poster, or campus newspaper ad—may work better than another, depending on the individual
campus and the specific audience being targeted.

A moment ago, I mentioned faculty. This is a subject unto itself, but
terribly important to the discussion.

At some colleges, pro-Israel students have faculty advisers or men-
tors; at others, they don't.

As a monthly visitor to a graduate program, I unexpectedly found
myself in the role of mentor, largely because the Jewish students had
no full-time faculty member to whom to turn, yet it was clear that they
desperately needed someone with whom to talk.

For some students, it was to get additional information and talking
points, as well as advice on outside speakers; for others, it was to
explore their relationship to their Jewish identity against the backdrop
of rapidly unfolding events in the Middle East that were seeping into
the life of the school. All too typical of the latter group was one student
who posed the following question to me: "Other than remembering the
Holocaust, what is it about being Jewish that I should know?"

In some cases, faculty members who specialize in the Middle East
in particular, including a few Jews, openly side with the pro-
Palestinian cause, and much less frequently with a pro-Israel position.
This is not necessarily limited to campus rallies. At times, it pene-
trates the classroom. But for those who have read Martin Kramer's
important book, *Ivory Towers on Sand: The Failure of Middle Eastern
Studies in America*, this will come as no surprise. In assessing the
state of Middle Eastern studies on American campuses, Dr. Kramer,
the editor of *Middle East Quarterly* and a distinguished scholar, concluded that:

> Middle Eastern studies used to resemble a quaint guild, emphasizing
> proficiency. Now they more closely resemble a popular front, demand-
> ing conformity.

Or take the example of a course announcement in the English Department at Berkeley for Fall 2002, entitled "The Politics and Poetics of Palestinian Resistance." The official course description reads as follows:

> The brutal Israeli military occupation of Palestine, an occupation that has been ongoing since 1948, has systematically displaced, killed, and maimed millions of Palestinian people.... This class takes as its starting point the right of Palestinians to fight for their own self-determination.

It earlier included an additional line—"Conservatives need not apply"—but that was dropped under pressure.

And the reading list, predictably, includes at least one book by an obviously Jewish author—in this case, the infamous Norman Finkelstein, who stands alongside MIT professor Noam Chomsky in the pantheon of self-hating Jewish academics—presumably to provide "cover" against any possible accusation of anti-Semitism.

Or take the case of a Columbia University professor far removed from Middle Eastern studies who sent an e-mail to his students encouraging them to miss his class so they could attend the April 17 rally against Israel.

Incidentally, by way of stark contrast, my son just took a semester-long course on the Arab-Israeli conflict with Martin Kramer at Brandeis University. Although Dr. Kramer has strong political views that he doesn't hide off campus, my son and his classmates insist that there wasn't even a hint of the professor's own leanings on the conflict during four months of teaching. He presented all sides in a dispassionate academic fashion, exposed the students to conflicting viewpoints, and left it entirely to the students to reach their own political conclusions. In other words, he did precisely what we want to believe still happens as a matter of course in the college classroom.

In the summer of 2001, pro-Palestinian groups prepared themselves for a stepped-up effort in the fall. As the *New York Times* reported (August 25, 2001):

Arab-American groups plan a campaign this fall, modeled on the anti-apartheid movement of the 1980s, to urge universities to divest themselves of holdings in companies doing business with Israel.

These plans, of course, were disrupted by the events of September 11 and their aftermath, but only temporarily. Strikingly, within a few months Arab and Muslim groups once again sought to flex their muscles, aided by an atmosphere on many campuses that bent over backwards to demonstrate respect and tolerance for those from Arab countries or who espouse the Muslim faith. Thus, this spring we saw the first signs of the delayed campaign to turn Israel into the new pariah state, which follows the playbook from the popular campus campaign to oppose apartheid.

Archbishop Desmond Tutu, the South African Nobel Peace Prize recipient in 1984, confirmed the objective—and the analogy—in a recent op-ed in the *International Herald Tribune* (June 14, 2002):

> If apartheid ended, so can the occupation, but the moral force and international pressure will have to be just as determined. The current divestment effort is the first, though certainly not the only, necessary move in that direction.

At Princeton University, the *Bergen Record* reported (June 10, 2002):

> A petition demanding that Princeton, which has about $8 billion in investments, divest from Israeli-connected companies gained the support of more than 300 students and forty-two faculty members, including the history department chairman. Some of the companies identified by the group include General Electric, Lucent Technologies, McDonald's Corp., Merck & Co., and Lehman Bros.
>
> The divestment petition prompted at least one hundred students to sign an opposing petition, delivered the same day, urging the university to retain its Israeli-connected stock. In addition, forty-three professors signed a letter to the *Daily Princetonian* condemning their colleagues for endorsing the divestment campaign.

Meanwhile at Berkeley, the campus newspaper, on June 4, carried a story that a divestment campaign was starting with support from some faculty and students. One professor associated with the campaign was quoted as saying that "the petition seeks to change public opinion and, in this way, to influence the course of political debate."

Other universities have witnessed similar developments, most notably Harvard and MIT, but strong countermovements have emerged, not only among faculty and students but also among alumni. As the Harvard law professor Alan Dershowitz warned:

> Any effort to divest from Israel would fail because it would destroy any university that attempted it. Faculty would leave, students would refuse to attend, and the contributors would refuse to contribute.

Barring unforeseen circumstances, come September, when colleges start the academic year, we can expect more rallies and demonstrations, more petition drives for divestment, and more harassment of pro-Israel groups on campus.

Friends of Israel need to be prepared on every level. Fortunately, when it comes to America's colleges and universities, we are not without considerable resources of our own. There are many outstanding college presidents and numerous well-disposed trustees, donors, active alumni, and professors who are becoming increasingly alert to the dangers not only for Jews, but also for such fundamental college values as mutual respect and tolerance, of this campus blitz. And, not least, there is a significant group of caring and committed students.

With them stand Jewish organizations, including the American Jewish Committee, ready to harness their experience, expertise, and relationships to ensure that our nation's cherished colleges and universities are never used—or, should I say, misused—as a battering ram to damage Israel or intimidate its supporters.

Letter from an Anguished Soul
August 5, 2002

The bad news just keeps coming. One terror attack after another. More and more fatalities. No place in Israel today is safe. No Israeli can feel immune from the danger.

Tragically, the response to each calamity takes on a rather eerie predictability.

Israelis are killed, and the mourners, together with an entire nation, weep, while the government vows to crush the terrorists, and the people stoically resolve to carry on their "normal" lives. Of course, this government, just like its predecessors, is unable to find a foolproof method to stop the terrorists. Who could? And what constitutes a normal life these days in a totally abnormal situation?

Israeli spokesmen are too many in number, perhaps the price to be paid for a democratic society where everyone is eager to speak, and foreign journalists, who are in Israel by the hundreds, are in need of filing a story and always looking for an angle.

Some Israeli spokesmen are on message, others not; some come across well on television, others do not; some speak fluent English, others do not; some talk the language of war, others of peace. In other words, to borrow a favorite Israeli expression, it's a bit of a *balagan*, chaos, and efforts to control the messenger and the message have been only partially successful.

In the wake of President George Bush's landmark June 24 speech, glib Palestinian spokesmen—Yasir Arafat's minions—now appear before Western reporters to ritualistically denounce the terror attacks against Israelis, but then never fail to add that, in the final analysis, these attacks are all Ariel Sharon's fault and certainly not the Palestinians'. Following a carefully controlled script, they then quickly slip in the Palestinian buzzwords that inevitably surface whether the interview lasts five seconds or fifty—Israeli "occupation," "humiliation," "economic strangulation."

Not only are the Palestinians better at controlling the message and the messenger—unless it's Arafat speaking—but they have another advantage. They are practiced liars.

They can look unblinkingly at the television cameras and declare that hundreds of Jenin residents were massacred by Israeli troops, or that Israeli doctors have injected HIV in Palestinian children, or that the Israeli army is using depleted uranium shells, or whatever other outrageous fabrication comes to mind. These spokesmen know all too well that such accusations will be reported dutifully—and often uncritically—by an often gullible media that's "only doing its job," and that there are a certain number of nations, human rights groups, and individuals who are only too ready to believe the latest charge against Israel and repeat it ad nauseam. History has taught us something about the "big lie" theory, hasn't it?

Meanwhile, back in Gaza or Nablus, the deaths of Israelis, whatever their age, ideology, or denomination, are cause for feverish celebration among the many who take to the streets. Compare this to the anguished discussion within Israel when Palestinian civilians, especially children, become unintended casualties of military action to combat terror.

The United States, to its everlasting credit, can be counted on to quickly and unambiguously denounce the terror, express its understanding of Israel's situation, and defend Israel's right to strike back.

The Europeans, by contrast, stumble all over themselves, trying, but never terribly convincingly, to show sympathy for the Israeli victims, but unable to hide their profound antipathy for the Sharon-led government and their general dislike of military responses to what they believe to be political problems.

In fact, to this day the European Union cannot even bring itself to agree on designating Hezbollah, a group openly dedicated to Israel's destruction, as a terrorist organization, largely due to French objections that there are other, more "benign" aspects to the group, such as its "social welfare" agenda and participation in the Lebanese "political" process. (By contrast, Hezbollah, together with Hamas and Islamic Jihad, have been on the U.S. terrorism list for many years.)

The media, with few exceptions, feeds us the "moral equivalence," "cycle of violence," and "an eye for an eye" lines, essentially two sides in an atavistic struggle to the end, with no clear distinction between democrats and dictators. The *New York Times* is still not prepared to label Hamas, which is hell-bent on Israel's complete destruction according to its own charter, a terrorist group, instead antiseptically referring to its members as "militants." And, as we know, the *Times* is far from the worst offender. That title would clearly go to one of several European candidates.

Countries like Egypt and Jordan, which, in private, express undisguised contempt for Arafat, are fearful of saying anything remotely similar in public.

The United Nations, needless to say, is a hostage of the numbers game, and the numbers are heavily stacked against Israel. That helps explain why the Geneva-based Commission on Human Rights, for example, was able to devote 30-40 percent of its time at this year's six-week session to bashing Israel. It passed no fewer than eight anti-Israel resolutions, when no other problematic regional situation was the object of more than one resolution, if that.

When was the last time anyone remembers the UN meeting in special session because of a Palestinian terror attack against Israel? Don't count on it anytime soon, either.

American Jews react in various ways. There are those—the clear majority, according to a national survey just released by AJC—who identify ever more closely with Israel and recoil in horror at these repeated terrorist attacks.

Then there is a significant minority that remains essentially indifferent to the attacks, devoting, at best, passing attention, but then moving on, since Israel is far from their lives.

And finally, there is a much smaller minority, but a vocal one at that, people who have essentially determined that Israel has only itself to blame for its current situation, and are ready to sign on to any ad or join any protest to heap scorn on Sharon et al, while self-righteously wrapping themselves in the mantle of the Jewish ethical tradition.

Thus, on the day after the horrific tragedy at Hebrew University, one Jewish letter-writer to the *Times* could contemptuously blame it all on Sharon, while others publicly call on the American government to pressure Israel by withholding foreign aid.

I confess that sometimes I just don't get it.

A spokesman for Hamas publicly declares that the group's objective is to rid Israel of its Jewish population. He couldn't be more clear, nor could the Hamas charter. The same goes for Islamic Jihad, Hezbollah, and other terror groups. Israel is in a war for its survival against an enemy that celebrates death, especially Jewish death. What exactly is Israel supposed to do in response? If there's a playbook for this crisis, I'm not aware of it.

Israel has just about tried it all.

The dovish Shimon Peres replaced the slain Yitzhak Rabin as prime minister, eager to continue the work of building peace, and was almost immediately faced with one deadly terrorist bombing after another in the spring of 1996. As a result, he lost the election to his rival, Benjamin Netanyahu, who promised the nation security.

Under Prime Minister Ehud Barak of the Labor Party, and with the full support of President Clinton, Israel made a breathtakingly tantalizing offer to the Palestinians for peace and statehood on 97 percent of the disputed land less than two years ago, only to see it turned down flat. Now the Palestinians, once again seeking to rewrite history, flail about, asserting variously that the offer was never actually made in writing, or was less than meets the eye, or would have created Bantustans, but the people actually in the know—President Clinton, Prime Minister Barak, Ambassador Dennis Ross, and Foreign Minister Shlomo Ben-Ami—all reject these contentions out of hand.

Israel has tried unilateral ceasefires, restraint in the face of severe provocation, offers to ease economic conditions, and even expressions of regret when IDF mistakes occur, but that hasn't done much good either.

Let's acknowledge certain inescapable truths.

The Palestinian leadership has not prepared its people for peace with Israel or even acceptance of Israel's right to exist as a Jewish state, whatever its final boundaries. To the contrary, the years since the 1993 Oslo Accords have been devoted to quite the opposite—the teaching of hatred and incitement, and the creation of a military/terrorist infrastructure.

Remember that this is the very same Palestinian leadership that introduced the world to a whole new era of international terrorism in the 1970s, that was expelled from Jordan, that caused a domestic civil war in Lebanon, that violated more ceasefires in Jordan and Lebanon alone than Barry Bonds hit home runs last season, that has been utterly corrupt in the use of aid money, that supported Saddam Hussein in the Gulf War, that colluded with Iran to purchase sophisticated weapons, and that, during the Cold War, embraced just about every communist dictator from the Soviet Union's Leonid Brezhnev to Cuba's Fidel Castro.

Despite all the attempts at spin and recasting, Arafat has not changed his spots. It's tough to admit, perhaps, but he managed to pull the wool over the eyes of just about everyone, including the Nobel Peace Prize Committee.

To state the painfully obvious, there are no easy or off-the-shelf answers for Israel in the face of this situation. As I've written on previous occasions, both the left and the right have flawed approaches.

The left has a blind spot. It refuses to see things as they are. Instead, it substitutes wishful thinking for reality. Since it cannot bring itself to admit that its analysis was so off base, it chooses, instead, to persist in its dangerous thinking.

The right lives under its own illusion. The Palestinians cannot be crushed militarily. Or, let me put it differently: They can be, but Israel is not prepared to do what would be required, because there are built-in restraints on Israeli behavior, both as a democracy and as a Jewish state. And don't think the Palestinians, for all their accusations against Israel, don't know it. They know it very well.

To be sure, the Palestinians can be made to pay a heavy price for their support of terror, but, as we've seen, it didn't take long after the Israeli-launched Operation Defensive Shield for the Palestinian terror infrastructure to regroup and launch more attacks.

I don't pretend to have the answers. Indeed, for years I have contended, whatever the government of the day in Jerusalem, that it is for Israel to decide how to respond most appropriately to the challenges both of war and peace.

Those of us on the outside—however close to the situation, however well-intentioned—need to exercise restraint and intellectual modesty. It would be sheer chutzpah to believe that we want peace for

Israel more than Israel wants peace for itself, or that we have solutions to Israel's military challenges that Israel, which has managed to defend itself against all the odds since 1948, has not yet come up with. And do we still need reminders that, at the end of the day, it is Israel and its citizens—and not we in the Diaspora—who will bear the most direct consequences of decisions made?

Our job, I believe, is to help Israel achieve the time and space it needs to make its own decisions on these existential questions. That does not necessarily mean that Israel is incapable of making mistakes, or that its highly pressurized society doesn't come up with some pretty bad policy from time to time. Of course it does.

Israel is an imperfect society, but then so is every other democracy. But those other nations are not faced with the same immediate threats as Israel is today. Yes, the United States and India, in particular, currently understand the menace of terrorism, but surely few citizens in either country ever stop to wonder whether their national existence is imperiled.

Israel is fighting tooth and nail to defend its citizens, who have been declared fair game by a whole host of terrorist groups fueled by hatred and a sense that they have found the Israeli Achilles' heel through suicide bombings and remote-controlled explosions.

Israel desperately needs our support, now more than ever. We have our work cut out for us here in the United States, but we've also been given an extraordinary opportunity.

How will history judge us at this defining moment?

Do we have any excuse for passivity or indifference?

Are there those who will be able to claim, down the road, that they were unaware of what was actually going on?

Are some so focused on the trees—grievances about this or that Israeli policy or tactic—that they fail to see the forest, namely, the attempt to destroy all of Israel, to kill as many Jews as possible, and to propagate a vicious anti-Semitism unknown since the days of Hitler and Stalin?

Do some hold Israel to such an unrealistically high standard of behavior that Israel will never be able to meet it, if it is to survive and win this ugly war?

It's long overdue for everyone in the American Jewish community to wake up and, as they say, smell the coffee.

We need to stand up and be counted. Now. Not at some distant time down the road, but now. Events aren't going to wait for us. There is much to be done by us, and if we're not going to do it, who will?

What do we need to do?

More than anything, we need to find ongoing ways to express our collective solidarity with Israel and its people.

We need to engage fellow Jews who don't yet grasp the importance of the moment or may not have a full appreciation for the history that led to this point.

We need to make certain that all of our political leaders know exactly where we stand, and that we support candidates for elected office of both major political parties who share our views and are prepared to act on them.

We need to reach out to our non-Jewish friends, colleagues, and neighbors more than ever and help them understand what Israel is up against and why America must continue to stand foursquare with our democratic ally.

We need to make the point to the world that if Israel succumbs to the scourge of suicide bombing, then every democratic nation becomes vulnerable to the very same threat.

We need to go out of our way to buy Israeli products and otherwise support the battered Israeli economy.

We need to continue traveling to Israel, in spite of the dangers or, yes, maybe because of the dangers. We cannot allow Israelis to feel alone and abandoned. Their struggle is our struggle. They must not be asked to shoulder it by themselves.

We need to be vigilant with the media, on university campuses, and in civic groups, where anti-Israel activists are seeking to make inroads.

We need to stress that Israel's yearning for peace is unquenchable and has been demonstrated again and again, but that peace with the Palestinians requires a willing and credible partner.

We need to ask our rabbis, who are soon to preside over High Holy Day services, when vast numbers of American Jews will be attending services, to use the occasion to mobilize the community.

And we need to support those Jewish organizations that are on the front lines in this battle. As individuals, our influence is usually quite limited, but as members of influential groups we leverage our power.

The Israeli people time and again have shown the world what they are made of. It's now time for us American Jews, asked to play a supporting role, to do the same. Given our track record of support for Israel over the past fifty-four years, I have no doubt that we can and will rise to the challenge.

Letter from the Home Front
August 12, 2002

Israel's well-being, security, and quest for peace depend, first and foremost, on the will and resolve of the Israeli people. Time and again, their determination has left us in awe. We should never underestimate it or, heaven forbid, succumb to despair.

But in the final analysis, Israel is simply too small to survive over the long haul without powerful friends, principal among them the United States.

While other major countries, notably Germany, Britain, Australia, Canada, Turkey, India, China, Russia, and Japan, all play an important part in Israel's political, economic, or strategic life, none begins to approach the American role or is likely to in the foreseeable future.

No other country provides such generous and essential economic and military assistance year after year.

No other country has the capacity to furnish state-of-the-art weapons to help ensure Israel's qualitative, if not quantitative, edge over its adversaries.

No other country rivals American technological know-how in the intelligence field or has closer cooperation with Israel in intelligence-sharing.

No other country would have, indeed could have, taken on Saddam Hussein in 1991 or would even consider it again today.

No other country has both the capacity and will to face the menace of Islamic extremism—from groups planning terrorist attacks to states seeking weapons of mass destruction.

No other country is able to mobilize its diplomatic machinery in the Arab world as persuasively to urge moderation and the path toward peace.

No other country could offer any credible guarantees to help ensure Israel's security should Jerusalem cede land in exchange for the promise of peace.

I could go on at length. Suffice it to say that Israel's yearning for peace and security depends to an unprecedented degree on the United States.

If the Arab world senses the prospect of any reversal in the airtight U.S.-Israel relationship, the incentive for coming to terms with Israel diminishes. It is only the recognition that all the Arab efforts over the years to drive a wedge between Washington and Jerusalem have failed that may one day lead to peace in the Middle East, with the U.S. playing an active role in monitoring compliance with any peace agreement and wielding both the carrot and stick to ensure that the Arab world does not renege on its agreement.

Parenthetically, those in the American Jewish community who publicly call for American pressure on Israel may not fully appreciate this essential point. The Arab world might conclude that its long-desired aim of separating American Jewry from Israel—and thereby presumably giving the American government a freer hand to move away from Israel and closer to the Arabs—becomes more realistic, thus providing less, not more, incentive to reach a peace agreement with Israel.

Let's not kid ourselves. The U.S.-relationship is not on automatic pilot. There is no amendment to the Constitution that guarantees American support for Israel. No, what undergirds the American role in Israel's life more than anything else is American Jewish activism. To be sure, there are other essential factors.

It helps greatly that Israel, like the U.S., is a democracy, a reliable ally, and the cradle of Judeo-Christian civilization. It also helps that a clear majority of the American people identifies with Israel's story line—the dramatic return to the birthplace of the Jewish people, the need for a Jewish state after the devastation wrought by the Shoah, and the successful struggle to build and defend a viable democratic country against all the odds.

But I have long believed that if the American Jewish factor were removed from the equation, or even reduced, it might not be long before American foreign policy, driven by a more detached assessment of the narrow national interest (i.e., energy needs, Arab versus Israeli population numbers, etc.) would begin to more closely resemble the evenhanded approach of the Europeans, and that would be an unmitigated disaster for Israel.

We American Jews have an extraordinary opportunity and responsibility. The opportunity is to help sustain and develop the state that has been at the center of Jewish prayer and yearning since time immemorial. In fact, if I describe this as an opportunity, I misstate the case. It's more accurately a privilege that has been given us.

And yes, it's a responsibility. In effect, it's the flip side of the famous Pogo line—"We have met the advocates and they are us."

Blessed to live in this extraordinary country, we have the chance to impact on the foreign policy of the single most powerful nation in the world and to do so in a way that harmonizes our American and Jewish selves. After all, to believe in democracy, the rule of law, and respect for human dignity is to be both pro-American and pro-Israeli. We needn't apologize for our support for Israel; to the contrary, we should celebrate it as embodying our highest values.

There will be those who raise questions about specific Israeli policies and ask whether they are compatible with those values. The answer, of course, is that Israel does not always live up to its own aspirations.

As Jews, steeped in a proud moral and ethical tradition, we are at times uneasy when the messy realities of statecraft clash with the prophetic values we embrace, but we dare not forget that Israel is obligated to operate in a region where no neighbor even pretends to abide by Israel's core value system.

So, if the United States is critical to Israel's existence, and if American Jewry is key to the American position, what are the dangers lurking ahead as we look at the chessboard?

Broadly speaking, there are two—one internal, the other external.

The internal danger could emerge if the American Jewish commitment to Israel wanes. The fear is that the passage of time works to weaken the ties between Israel and American Jewry. The societies grow farther apart, the links between the two great centers of world Jewry become more tenuous, and the shared history begins to sound more like a slogan than reality.

According to this reasoning, fewer young people feel closely connected to Israel than their parents or grandparents. As the rate of intermarriage grows, poll after poll reveals that in such families the ties to Israel are likely to be thinner. And in light of the fact that Jewish numbers in the U.S. overall have been static for decades and are only likely to decrease, if slowly, in the years ahead, the Jewish percentage of the American population will continue to drop, with all of its attendant political and other consequences.

That's why the current emphasis on educating our young people, taking advantage of the new communications technologies, preparing them for the inevitable discussions and debates at schools and colleges, and offering links to Israel becomes more important than ever. And finding ways to reach those in their thirties and forties—the "missing generation," as someone dubbed this group—is absolutely vital, especially as the next generation of communal leadership will come from this age cohort.

While these internal trends are at work, there is an external factor that must not be overlooked.

In recent years, there has been a sharp increase in Arab and Muslim American political activity in the United States. With their numbers growing—more about that in a minute—and their self-confidence developing, they have surged on to the political battlefield. They know they have an uphill struggle. They recognize the formidable strength of the pro-Israeli advocacy movement in this country, but they believe it is assailable.

First, they believe that their communities must now be taken into account by politicians running for office in such key states as New Jersey, Michigan, California, and Illinois, where Arab and Muslim immigrants have settled.

Second, they contend that the American public is less certain of its support for Israel since the so-called Al-Aqsa intifada began nearly two years ago.

Third, they see an opportunity to create new coalitions, especially with minority communities such as African Americans and Latinos by portraying the Palestinians as the "oppressed Third Worlders" and Israelis as the "neo-colonialist oppressors."

Fourth, they perceive a splintering in the American Jewish community, including those who care little about Israel and others prepared to be openly critical of Israel.

And fifth, their organizations have been encouraged by the ease with which they have gained entrée into the White House, State Department, and other centers of power, even when these organizations represent extremist viewpoints.

For years, I've been struck by the obvious manipulation of Muslim numbers in the United States. How else to explain jumps in estimates from two to four to six to eight million Muslims within a matter of a few years? It's much harder to do the same for Arab numbers, since those figures are available through the decennial census and annual immigration data, but federal law prohibits any questions about religion, so it's pretty much left to the religious groups themselves and academic researchers to come up with estimates. (The 2000 census indicated just over one million Arabs in the United States, many of them Christians, e.g., Lebanese Maronites, Egyptian Copts, Iraqi Chaldeans, etc.)

While the Jewish community painstakingly plans the complex methodology of the National Jewish Population Survey, some Muslim spokesmen have found a much easier—and less time-consuming—approach. They simply toss out numbers with abandon, and the media, with only a handful of exceptions, has dutifully and uncritically reported these numbers as facts.

Last fall, the American Jewish Committee approached Dr. Tom Smith of the University of Chicago to study the numbers. We knew that some would question our motives, but we felt we had no choice. It was abundantly clear that Muslim leaders, appearing ever more frequently in the media after September 11, were using the opportunity to exaggerate their community's size for obvious reasons, and no one was challenging them. We went to the blue-ribbon specialist. Dr. Smith is the head of the General Social Survey and is considered the best in his field. After months of study, he presented us with his findings. Based on all the quantitative data he could find, Dr. Smith came up with a best-guess estimate of 1.8 million Muslims, allowing for at most another million uncounted Muslims.

Unbeknownst either to Dr. Smith or us, the City University of New York was conducting its own study of religious affiliation in the United States, and their figures became available at more or less the same time as Dr. Smith's. Lo and behold, their bottom-line figure for Muslims in this country was 1.8 million.

Predictably, Muslim spokesmen attacked Dr. Smith's study by impugning our motives, and then sought to cast doubt on the CUNY study by noting that the two researchers were both Jewish and therefore, by definition, must have had ulterior motives. These spokesmen realized, not without reason, that if they simply kept repeating their numbers the media would soon forget the two studies and play along. The alternative would be to invite squabbles with Muslim organizations that would not hesitate to level racism charges at the drop of a hat, something the media would obviously prefer to avoid.

The latest numbers I've heard come from the director of the American Muslim Council. In the span of one week, I saw him on two of the cable news network shows touting the fact that there are today "seven million Muslim citizens" in the United States. That's a new one. Overnight they've all become citizens, no less.

If these Muslim organizations can persuade American opinion molders and policy makers that they are truly such a formidable force in American life, the political consequences will be considerable.

The Muslim population in the U.S. is variegated, but the organizations that claim to represent the community are not. Moderate groups have valiantly sought to emerge, but they have been kept at bay by the more extreme groups, who, strange as it may seem, have actually been helped by the government and media.

The Islamic Supreme Council of America is a good case in point. A genuinely moderate organization that openly rejects Islamic fundamentalist politics, it can barely get its foot in the door inside the Beltway or have the chance to comment in the media, while spokesmen for such radical groups as the Council on American-Islamic Relations (CAIR), the American Muslim Council (AMC), and the Islamic Society of North America (ISNA) are openly courted.

I confess that it's one of the biggest mysteries to me. The Clinton administration—both the White House and State Department—began the practice and the Bush administration has followed suit. In both cases, there seems to have been a political calculation high up in the White House that it is important to have an open-door policy to Muslim groups, that for better or worse the more radical groups are the ones with the most prominence and longevity, and that the Muslim community has come of age as a voting bloc and therefore electoral considerations become paramount.

Or take the recent case of the FBI. Who should know better than the FBI exactly what's what among these groups, yet, to our dismay, Director Robert Mueller agreed to speak before the annual convention of the American Muslim Council in June despite being presented with evidence from many sources, including the American Jewish Committee, that the group was a leading apologist for Islamic extremism.

In fact, the AMC cosponsored the "National Rally for Free Jerusalem and Al-Aqsa" on October 28, 2000, where one of the speakers, an AMC board member, declared: "We are all supporters of Hamas. I wish they added that I am also a supporter of Hezbollah." Both Hamas and Hezbollah have been on the U.S. terrorism list for years.

More recently, the AMC honored the Holy Land Foundation for its "strong global vision." The Texas-based organization had its assets frozen by President Bush after 9/11 for collecting funds "used to support the Hamas terror organization." The AMC responded to the president's action by condemning it as "particularly disturbing, unjust, and counterproductive."

Yet, despite this knowledge, the FBI director went ahead, contending that the AMC was now a mainstream group. With great respect for the FBI and the enormous responsibility it is shouldering, I cannot for the life of me figure out why it decided in this case to turn a blind eye to reality.

Or, for that matter, take the case of the shooting incident, in June, at the El Al ticket counter at Los Angeles International Airport. Can there be any serious doubt that this was an act of terrorism, which is defined in the Federal Register as "the unlawful use of force and violence against persons or property to intimidate or coerce a government, the civilian population, or any segment thereof, in furtherance of political or social objectives"? But then again it took the FBI six years to reclassify the 1994 murder of Ari Halberstam, the sixteen-year-old student killed by an Arab gunman on the Brooklyn Bridge, as an act of terrorism. Until then, the crime, believe it or not, was listed as an act of "road rage."

What difference does the classification make? Not only is this about truth and accuracy, but it also determines the extent of the resources devoted to an investigation.

It's important to be clear about a related matter. No major American Jewish organization has more energetically pursued Muslim-Jewish dialogue in this country than the American Jewish Committee. But, truth be told, we have constantly run into difficulties.

Beginning in 1992, we were among the first to highlight the plight of Bosnian Muslims and thought it might also serve as a good bridge to links with Muslim groups in this country who involved themselves in the same issue, but we quickly learned that we were wrong; these groups had a radical political agenda when it came to the Middle East and international terrorism.

We sponsored the first national conferences on Muslim-Jewish relations, held at the University of Denver, two years running, but we couldn't continue when our Muslim partners were revealed to have a sharply different view than we of the killing of Israeli civilians by bus bombers.

At the urging of the State Department in the wake of the optimism generated by the 1993 Oslo Accords, we met with several delegations of Muslim clerics from the Middle East and elsewhere in the Islamic world, who were brought to the U.S. as guests of our government to learn about American concepts of religious freedom and pluralism.

Some of these meetings were extremely difficult. There were individuals among the visitors who clearly did not want to be in the room, others whose only impressions of Jews had been formed by reading anti-Semitic books published in the Middle East, and still others who would not have their pictures taken with us in the group shots.

What was abundantly clear was that many of these Muslim clergymen had essentially no information about Jews and Judaism from Jewish—or even dispassionate third-party—sources. Thus was born the idea for AJC to commission two volumes—one on Islam for Jews, the other on Judaism for Muslims. The goal was to bring Muslims and Jews closer together through greater understanding of the two religious traditions. It was a wonderful concept, and it generated a lot of excitement in many quarters, including the State Department.

Plans were developed to try to partner synagogues and mosques around the country to use the books as the basis for discussion and familiarization, and to invite the two authors—both distinguished scholars, one Jewish, the other Muslim—to travel together to moderate Muslim countries (and to Israel) to promote interfaith conversation.

But, as one of my favorite expressions goes, "No good deed goes unpunished."

The books had just been published in the spring of 2000 and we issued our first press release. It didn't take long for a Jordanian extremist cleric to issue a fatwa, endorsing the killing of the Muslim scholar, Khalid Duran, for the "crime" of collaborating with the Jews and defaming Islam. Incidentally, the cleric hadn't even read the book because it had not yet been distributed.

In any case, it's fair to say that he wouldn't have liked the book, as it was written by a moderate Muslim who rejected the Islamists and their politicization of the faith. And a representative of the Council on American-Islamic Relations, which defends radical Islam in this country, also immediately pounced on the Duran book and maligned our motives, although he was forced to admit to the press that he hadn't seen the book, either.

As a result of the fatwa, Khalid Duran and his family were forced to go into hiding here in the United States. Inexplicably, the story received only brief coverage in the media and then quickly faded.

Despite these experiences—or maybe because of them—we are all the more determined to identify potential partners in the American Muslim community with whom we can talk. We know they are there. And the same goes for overseas, where we sometimes find it easier to establish links with responsible Muslim leaders, with whom we may not always agree but with whom we have a common interest in building bridges and preventing civilizational clashes.

In sum, we need to be alert to the elements of the external challenge.

First, there is a physical threat to Jews. There have been enough terrorist incidents in the past decade, enough thwarted attempts, and enough warnings, especially in recent months, to put us all on notice that Jews and Jewish institutions are possible targets of the Islamic terrorist network. We have no choice but to take security issues far more seriously than we have until now, just as European Jewish communities have had to do since the outbreak of terrorist attacks—often jointly conducted by Arab and extreme left-wing European terrorist groups—began there in the 1970s.

Second, there is a political threat. There is ample evidence that Muslim organizations in the United States, claiming exaggerated numbers, are determined to assert themselves in the political arena and no longer believe, as they once did, in the "invincibility of the Jewish lobby," to quote one of their spokesmen. This is a long-term process, and it has already begun.

Take this year's gubernatorial race in Michigan. David Bonior, who is leaving the U.S. Congress, where he rose to be number two in the Democratic Party, chose to run in the Democratic primary. (The primary was held on August 6 and he lost.) Here's what he said to one predominately Muslim audience:

I think the political growth, the political sophistication, and the political understanding have increased tremendously within the [American Muslim] community. But there are still many, many steps to go. One step, of course, is electing a governor of a large state. When that happens, several other things will happen. That person will make sure that your sons and your daughters and the adults in the community are placed on the boards, the commissions, the judgeships, the staff positions, and the cabinet positions of the government. That in itself creates an infrastructure for the community to progress even further.

This is not the only example. The current congressional primary fight in Georgia between the incumbent, Cynthia McKinney, who has received substantial support from Arab and Muslim sources, and her challenger, Denise Majette, who is being helped by the pro-Israel community, is another good case in point, with the added dimension that both candidates are African Americans, and black-Jewish and black-Muslim relations have become factors as well. A rather similar story was played out in Alabama earlier this year.

And third, there is the challenge of encouraging the emergence of genuinely moderate voices in the American Muslim community. They most certainly do exist, but many are cowed into silence, bullied by the extremists. As I said earlier, to date they have gotten precious little help from the government and media, who have largely ignored (or, worse, marginalized) them. The Council on American-Islamic Relations and the American Muslim Council are benignly seen as counterparts of the American Jewish Committee or the National Urban League, though they are anything but.

One thing that can be said about the American Jewish agenda— never a dull moment.

Letter from One Jew to Another
October 29, 2002*

I sometimes fantasize that I'm a hotel switchboard operator, making wake-up calls to all those Jews who remain fast asleep, or in a daze, or buried under the blankets. I visualize the struggle—I keep phoning; they keep ignoring the call. Eventually, I win the first round, as they

* A shorter version of this letter was published in the *Forward* on November 21, 2002.

pick up the receiver, if only to stop the irritating ring. But do I win the second round, when I try to get their attention and convince them to come out of their airtight bubble and see what's going on?

To be fair, the decade of the 1990s was so comforting that it lulled many Jews into a deep sleep.

Despite some very difficult moments, for America, Israel, and world Jewry, it was a particularly uplifting period.

It was a decade of remarkable economic growth and prosperity.

America's international prestige was ascendant, not only because of the dissolution of the Soviet empire, but also due to the successful U.S.-led military campaign to oust Iraq from Kuwait.

The frontiers of democracy were extended in Central and Eastern Europe, Latin America, Asia, and Africa. The Middle East, however, remained largely impervious to the growing democratic revolution.

The implosion of the Soviet Union removed the Iron Curtain. It deprived Egypt and Syria, among other Third World nations, of the chance to continue playing one superpower against another. It denied home and haven to Middle Eastern terrorist groups that had used the Warsaw Pact countries for training and support. And it brought new life to Jewish communities that had been systematically repressed under Communist rule.

During the decade of the '90s, Israel witnessed some rather extraordinary developments.

The Gulf War removed Iraq, a nation bent on Israel's destruction, from the strategic calculus, at least temporarily. It created a new environment making possible the 1991 Madrid Conference and the first glimmerings of the possibilities of regional peace. Bolstered by the arrival of one million Jews from the Former Soviet Union, Israel's mood turned buoyant. Zionism received a significant lift, and Israeli science, engineering, medicine, and the arts benefited immensely. In fact, during the '90s the high-tech boom catapulted Israel into the top tier of nations advancing the frontiers of scientific knowledge.

Two years after Madrid came the Oslo Accords. While some were openly skeptical, many more hoped that this was the breakthrough that would finally bring to an end the Arab conflict with Israel.

In the wake of Oslo, there was more heady news.

In 1994, Israel and Jordan signed a treaty, codifying a de facto peace that had long been among the region's poorest kept secrets.

A series of annual Middle East and North African economic summits took place, bringing Arab, Israeli, and other business leaders together to help make peace a reality through enlightened mutual self-interest.

Several Arab countries, including Oman, Qatar, Morocco, and Tunisia, established formal subambassadorial links with Israel, while Mauritania went the extra mile and announced full diplomatic ties with Israel. Meanwhile, a number of other Arab leaders were meeting with their Israeli political, military, and intelligence counterparts just below the radar.

India, China, Japan, South Korea, the newly democratic countries of Central and Eastern Europe, and countless other nations were rapidly upgrading their relations with Israel. It reached the point where, like a busy New York bakery on a Sunday morning, they had to take a number and wait on line for visits to an Israel that loomed large in the public imagination, but that was too small to handle all the interest and attention at once.

During the annual American Jewish Committee diplomatic marathon coinciding with the opening of the UN General Assembly, foreign ministers regularly pleaded for our intercession with Jerusalem to act on sometimes longstanding requests to pay official calls on Israeli leaders.

Meanwhile, American Jews were also doing quite nicely.

There were even Jewish leaders who went so far as to suggest that anti-Semitism had been largely relegated to remote stretches of Idaho and Montana, and that any other discussion of anti-Semitism was nothing more than a fund-raising ploy by Jewish organizations rapidly losing their raison d'être.

At the same time, some Israeli leaders were telling American Jews that their help was no longer needed, and that it was time instead to attend to the internal life of American Jewry, lest it succumb to the temptation of assimilation and disappear.

American Jewish political, economic, social, and cultural influence reached new heights.

Jews could be found near the top of most key sectors of American life, since there were no longer discriminatory impediments in their path. This culminated with the nomination of Joe Lieberman to the Democratic presidential ticket in 2000.

It didn't matter whether one was a Republican or a Democrat to appreciate such a milestone. Here was a Jew—a proud, observant Jew, no less, with a wife whose name was not plain vanilla but Hadassah— who had been added to a ticket to give it life when polls in the summer of 2000 showed that Al Gore was running behind the Republican team.

As an aside, I cannot help but think of the generational difference in reaction to the Lieberman nomination.

Had my grandparents been alive, though they were classic, Roosevelt-era Democrats, my bet is they would have voted for Bush and Cheney. Why? Because, according to their thinking, if things turned sour under Gore and Lieberman, no doubt the Jews would be blamed.

For me, the news came like a bolt from the blue. I couldn't stop saying, "Isn't this incredible? I never thought I'd live to see the moment. American Jewry has truly arrived."

And for my children, their response was essentially, "What's the big deal? Jews are in lots of high places, so why not on a presidential ticket?"

Again, putting aside partisan issues, the sheer number of Jews appointed to senior posts in the Clinton administration, including two Jews to fill the two Supreme Court vacancies, was additional proof that we had fully arrived. And the fact that the religion of both appointees aroused nary a murmur only underscored the welcome new reality.

Politicians seeking elected office energetically sought out the Jewish community during the decade, again boosting our sense of confidence and place in America. We knew we could rely on many friends in Congress to be responsive to our principal concerns, especially regarding the Middle East.

In an odd way, even the much-touted 52 percent intermarriage figure—the disputed finding of the 1990 National Jewish Population Study—reinforced the point, for some, that American Jews had made it in America and could finally put down their Jewish guard and relax. After all, according to this line of reasoning, not only was anti-Semitism at an all-time low, but non-Jews in large numbers viewed us as desirable marriage partners.

Underscoring this point, an informal survey of our numerous inter-married neighbors in Westchester County showed they no longer even felt a need to take surnames into account. Thus, a Mr. Shapiro could marry a Ms. Smith and give the children the name Shapiro without any intention of raising the kids as Jews, yet unconcerned that carrying such an obviously Jewish name might create difficulties in today's America, or beyond.

The decade also witnessed considerable attention paid to the Holocaust and its legacy. The Holocaust Memorial Museum in Washington opened and, to everyone's surprise, it became an instant hit, with more than 80 percent of the visitors turning out to be non-Jews. Holocaust curricula were adopted in a number of countries and in several American states. And, more or less willingly, numerous countries and institutions, including but not limited to Europe, began a process of self-examination about their acts of omission and commis-sion during the Holocaust. This included, of course, the issue of resti-tution to the victims.

Far from being forgotten, then, it seemed that the Holocaust was now indelibly etched on the world's conscience as the ultimate exam-ple of man's capacity for evil.

In sum, it was a rather extraordinary decade in Jewish history. We came as close as we ever have to the long-sought goal of the normal-ization of the Jewish people—a people with a state that had become a full member of the community of nations, a people with a voice that was heard in the corridors of power and decision-making, and a people that, with only a few exceptions, enjoyed equal rights and opportuni-ties as fellow citizens elsewhere.

To borrow from the title of Francis Fukuyama's much discussed book, it seemed like the "end of history" as we had known it, and the start of something new and ever so promising. It felt so good, so com-forting, so long in coming.

And then we got mugged in 2000.

It wasn't that everything that happened in the '90s vanished—far from it. It's just that we were reminded that life as a Jew is a bit more complicated, and that progress is not necessarily as linear as we lulled ourselves into believing during that golden decade.

Some Jews got the message pretty quickly; others preferred to live in denial, despite the mounting evidence over the past two years that something had gone terribly wrong.

Whether dove or hawk, any serious supporter of Israel had to be stunned by the rapidity of Israel's changed international standing after September 2000.

Despite a left-of-center government in power racing against its own self-imposed deadline to achieve a historic peace with the Palestinians, Israel found itself the target of a calculated campaign of Palestinian-instigated terror. Seeking to defend itself, as any government would under similar circumstances, it learned once again that the rules of international relations apply differently to Israel.

Suddenly, the Barak government received little credit for its far-reaching peace initiative, but much condemnation for its efforts to stem the violence.

The UN Commission on Human Rights even went so far as to condemn Israel for "war crimes," a charge rarely invoked by the world body.

And the media, with a few notable exceptions, came down hard on Israel, almost with a vengeance, giving rise to the impression that it had been lying in wait for just such a moment to return to the more familiar story line of "occupier" and "occupied," "overdog" (sic) and "underdog."

The performance of the media was almost surreal to witness, as if the preceding period of frenetic Israeli peacemaking, with U.S. assistance, had never happened; as if there had never been a far-reaching plan for a two-state solution put on the negotiating table by Israel; and as if Israel's credibility as a democratic nation—struggling against a corrupt, violent, dictatorial adversary—counted for little in the court of world opinion.

It went on like this for five months while Ehud Barak was prime minister, though that's conveniently forgotten by those who seek to put all the blame at Ariel Sharon's doorstep, as if he alone, by dint of his "warrior" reputation, is somehow responsible for the current conflict.

But wait a minute—Israel cannot make peace with the Palestinians in a vacuum.

With whom exactly is Israel to negotiate an accord? What is Israel to do in the absence of a credible peace partner and faced by an unending wave of terror? Is it simply to turn the other cheek in order to assuage the humanistic instincts of some well-intentioned but utterly clueless sideline observers, while getting pummeled and burying its growing number of dead? Is there to be one set of constraining rules for Israel's defense and quite another set of rules for every other sovereign nation?

Are we to ignore Arafat's direct complicity in terror up to this very day, and will him, through some chic séance perhaps, to be the peacemaker that we might wish him to be? Are we to live in la-la land and pretend that Israel is not fighting for its life against those nations and terror groups that refuse to recognize a Jewish birthright to any part of the land, and seek, however long it takes, to remove the "modern-day crusaders" from "Arab soil"?

Are we to rationalize the unending and deadly attacks on Israeli civilian targets, as if the Palestinians had no other means to achieve their political aims, assuming they are serious about a peaceful compromise with Israel?

Are we to look the other way while Palestinians cheered in the streets on 9/11, or lionize the latest "martyrs" who kill newborn children and elderly women with abandon in the streets of Israel?

Are we to succumb to a moral equivalence between Israeli and Palestinian behavior over the last two years, as if there were no fundamental difference between those plotting acts of terror and those seeking to prevent acts of terror?

Are we to dismiss as meaningless the threats of the Iranian leader Ayatollah Khamenei who said, in a typical comment, on January 15, 2001, "The foundation of the Islamic regime is opposition to Israel and the perpetual subject of Iran is the elimination of Israel from the region"?

Or the fact that Iran's closest ally in the region is Syria, Israel's neighbor, and that Iran's proxy in Lebanon is Hezbollah, which is amassing short-range missiles provided by Iran at an alarming rate, and placing them just north of Israel's border? Or that Iran provides funding to other anti-Israel terror groups operating in the region, including Hamas and Islamic Jihad?

To be sure, Israel is fully capable of making policy and operational errors, but then again, there's no neat, clean, and surgical response to such a situation, as other countries fighting wars against terror, including the U.S., Russia, India, and Turkey, have discovered.

Are we to overlook the meaning of endless UN assemblies, commissions, committees, subcommittees, emergency sessions, special rapporteurs, and staff reports that long ago threw objectivity and fairness to the wind and simply reflect a world body hopelessly stacked against Israel and held hostage to the whim of the Arab bloc? A world body where Israel has never, in the fifty-three years of its membership, sat on the Security Council, while Syria presided as Security Council president in June? A world body where Libya—yes, Libya—will assume the chairmanship of the UN Commission on Human Rights in January, while Israel has no chance even to participate as a member of the commission? A world body that devotes an inordinate amount of time to microscopically examining Israel, while blithely ignoring politically inconvenient but truly egregious violations of human rights elsewhere in the world?

And are we simply to dismiss the fact, as if it had no larger significance, that only twice in the fifty-three-year history of the Fourth Geneva Convention were the High Contracting Parties (i.e., signatories) convened to discuss a specific country or regional situation, and both times it involved—guess who?—Israel and Israel alone? Incidentally, the first time was while Ehud Barak of the Labor Party was Israel's prime minister. Absolutely nothing else in the past half century of war, genocide, occupation, invasion, and expulsion has galvanized the signatories. Nothing, that is, but Israel.

And are we to ignore the fact that Israel and Israel alone is excluded from full membership in the International Red Cross—a movement that professes neutrality—regardless of what government is in power in Jerusalem, while all the Arab countries, of course, enjoy full membership?

Isn't it time to wake up and recognize that Israel is in danger and needs our help, that there is a worldwide campaign being waged to isolate, condemn, and weaken Israel? If we Jews aren't going to respond to the call, who will?

This is not about right-wing or left-wing politics. In fact, this transcends partisanship. Rather, it is about standing together as Jews who care about Israel, and doing whatever we can to help the first and only Jewish state in the past 1,900 years get through yet another profoundly trying period. This is about fighting the cockiness of some who feel that they alone know what's best for Israel, and others who suffer from a psychological detachment from Israel, as if it were unconnected to the fate of American and world Jewry.

And are we to bury our heads in the sand while anti-Semitism once again rears its head?

Have some forgotten—or chosen to ignore—the anti-Semitic hate fest that erupted at Durban under the aegis of the UN in September 2001?

Or the breadth and depth of anti-Semitism in the Arab and Islamic world that has been revealed particularly in the post-9/11 period, including the revival of the notorious blood libel charge, the airing on Egyptian television of a forty-one-part serialization based on the infamous *Protocols of the Elders of Zion* during Ramadan this year, and the teaching of hatred of Jews—all Jews—in the Saudi-funded *madrassas* from the Persian Gulf to Pakistan?

Or the wave of documented anti-Semitic incidents—hundreds, if not more—that have taken place in Western Europe since the fall of 2000, largely the work of youth who are part of rapidly increasing Muslim communities throughout the continent? And how many other planned anti-Semitic attacks were foiled, as when the German authorities last April arrested twelve Arab men suspected of plotting attacks on Jewish and Israeli targets throughout Germany?

Or, equally disturbing, the hesitant, often equivocal response by governments, human rights institutions, intellectuals, and the media to this wave of hatred and violence?

Needless to say, the UN was largely silent about all this, or at best muttered concern in the context of "Islamophobia" and every other purported social ill.

But shouldn't we have expected more from the governments of Europe, which, after all, had only just gone through an examination of their own records during the Holocaust?

Instead of rushing to put out the fires, they hemmed and hawed, as if acknowledging a problem of anti-Semitism might stain their self-image as open, tolerant countries. Or was it fear of further arousing restive Muslim minorities that had already proved resistant to traditional patterns of integration? Or was it kowtowing to the Muslim vote, as in France, where a closely contested presidential election was looming and the Muslim vote could tip the scales one way or the other?

Striking, isn't it, that since the French presidential and parliamentary elections this spring there are markedly fewer reports of anti-Semitic incidents in France, which means that the government knows how to deal with the problem when it sets its mind to it. So why did it take eighteen months? Why did French Jews have to live in fear, wondering whether they should wear a *kippah* in public or if their children were safe in a Jewish school? Was this the price they were compelled to pay for French domestic politics? It's hard to escape such a conclusion.

And it wasn't just the UN and governments that diddled. Where were the European human rights and anti-racist groups that are so quick to speak out, hold press conferences, organize demonstrations, and issue reports when Palestinians are seen as the victims of human rights abuses, but not Jews, much less Israelis?

To be sure, there were a few outspoken voices of conscience: a human rights group here and there, some Catholic and Protestant church leaders, several politicians—most notably German Foreign Minister Joschka Fischer and Interior Minister Otto Schilly—and a handful of intellectuals, including a powerful statement from a distinguished Polish group.

By and large, the institutions we counted on to speak out against any reemergence of anti-Semitism were largely silent or tongue-tied. Perhaps they were fearful of antagonizing the Islamic world, or they retained a certain residual ambivalence about Jews and their place in the world, or they were unwilling to recognize anti-Semitism only sometimes thinly camouflaged as anti-Israelism, or perhaps they subliminally sought payback for the guilt heaped on Europe about the failure to protect Jews against Hitler's Final Solution.

The self-justifying mantra I heard a hundred times across Western Europe was that this was really all about Israel and not about Jews, as if the burning of a synagogue in Marseilles or shouts of "Death to the Jews" in Brussels could ever conceivably be justified.

And then things moved closer to home.

Near-riots against Jewish students from San Francisco to Montreal, requiring police intervention; the imam of New York's leading mosque—seen by some Jews as a dialogue partner—who suddenly disappears and resurfaces in Cairo to repeat the vilest anti-Semitic canards; the New Jersey poet laureate who asserts that Israel was linked to 9/11, and a school principal in the state who makes a point of bringing his pupils to hear this "public intellectual"; two killed at the El Al counter at LAX on July 4; government warnings to synagogues, Jewish schools, and organizations like the American Jewish Committee of possible terror attacks; arrests of terror cells from Charlotte to Buffalo to Portland; and the closure of terrorist-linked Muslim institutions from Virginia to Illinois to Texas that propagated hatred of America, Israel, and Jews.

While many Jews are alert to the dangers and are determined to do what they can to support Israel, fight anti-Semitism, and aid our government in the worldwide struggle against radical Islamic terrorism, there are others—and I see them every day—who, tragically, still don't get it, or, perhaps, don't want to get it. They cannot accept the new realities, or feel they can somehow remain insulated by keeping their distance, or, in classic fashion, they wonder how the instigator might be pacified.

Personally, despite profound concern about all the challenges we face, I remain stubbornly optimistic about the future. I have no doubt that we, the Jewish people, will get through this unsettling period. But surely it will help to stand together and in large numbers, even as we look to our friends to stand with us, and we have no better friend, thankfully, than the United States.

I am optimistic because the entire sweep of Jewish history is a metaphor for the triumph of hope over despair.

I am optimistic because I have come to believe that Jewish history defies logical analysis and linear projections. By those standards alone, we would have been goners long ago, yet we, the custodians of an extraordinary civilizational heritage, are as strong today as we have ever been.

I am optimistic because I do believe that, while the struggle is never cost-free, good will vanquish evil.

I am optimistic because the Jewish people have succeeded against all the odds, whether in establishing the democratic State of Israel and fending off the standing armies of five Arab countries; rebuilding Jewish life in Europe after the devastation wrought by the Holocaust; mounting one of history's most successful human rights campaigns on behalf of the Jews of the Soviet Union; maintaining Jewish life in Ethiopia for two thousand years with no outside contact; or witnessing an American Jewish community that has grown in influence and stature, after its failure to save European Jewry in World War II revealed its impotence.

I am optimistic because the people of Israel refuse to bend or break in the face of Palestinian terror; to the contrary, Israeli will and resolve have only grown stronger despite the horrors inflicted by suicide bombers and the campaign to isolate the state internationally. And throughout, the yearning for peace—including, I have no doubt, the willingness to compromise in the name of peace when a truly credible Palestinian partner finally emerges—remains undiminished.

I am optimistic because I have spent enough time in Europe to see that, no matter how outnumbered or overwhelmed by attempts to demonize Israel, the Jewish communities—often alone, it must be said—stand tall and proud, refusing to cower or run for cover.

I am optimistic because I believe that the panoply of American

Jewish organizations will do whatever is required to ensure the right responses to the challenges before us.

And in that same spirit of optimism, I continue to hope that those who haven't yet answered the wake-up call will do so, and heed the message. Isn't it time for all of us to stand up and be counted?

Letter from a Jewish Late Bloomer
December 3, 2002

There's much talk these days about the delayed American Jewish population survey. I'm as interested in the data as the next person, but I suspect I don't need a mega-study to understand the basic story line of American Jewry today. In essence, it's the familiar words from the opening of *A Tale of Two Cities*, "It was the best of times, it was the worst of times.... It was the spring of hope, it was the winter of despair."

Or, to put it in contemporary Israeli terms: Moshe meets Rafi on the street. "Moshe, my friend, how are you?" "In a word, good," replies Moshe. "In two words, not good."

All I need to do is look around me. Encouraging news abounds, but then again so does the opposite.

In the past decade, since the 1990 National Jewish Population Study was issued, many synagogues, federations, community centers, and other Jewish agencies, including the American Jewish Committee, have laudably redoubled their efforts to strengthen Jewish identity and appeal to ever broader segments of American Jewry.

While synagogues are sometimes accused of suffering from an "edifice complex," there is good reason for numerous synagogues, my own included, to be building these days. Existing facilities cannot accommodate all the children in the school programs, and some sanctuaries are just too small. New congregations of every denomination are sprouting up, sometimes in the most unlikely locations, bespeaking Jewish mobility. Jewish day school attendance has never been higher.

Jewish studies courses are to be found on a growing number of college campuses. Adult education courses on every aspect of Jewish life are experiencing a surge of interest.

While the Darwinian principle of the survival of the fittest applies to Jewish organizations as well, leaving some agencies in the dust, many others are thriving, as measured by membership, income, program, and reach.

Jewish political access in this country remains breathtakingly impressive, a far cry from an earlier era when American Jews could not muster sufficient clout to persuade the Roosevelt administration, in 1939, to admit 936 Jews aboard the *St. Louis* who were fleeing Nazi persecution, resulting in the ship's return to Europe with its rejected human cargo.

Discrimination against Jews in the United States is at an all-time low. True, there remain isolated pockets where Jews are unwelcome— a country club here, an executive suite there—but these are the rare exceptions, and no longer stand as barriers to Jewish professional, cultural, or social advancement.

And perhaps most importantly, Jews need not choose between their American and Jewish identities to live the American dream. In the past, many Jews believed that to achieve success and fit in they had to become "less Jewish," but that is far from the case today. There are countless examples in American politics, diplomacy, military, business, and culture of Jews who proudly affirm their Jewish identity and see it as strengthening, not weakening, their American identity.

That's the good news, and I've barely skimmed the surface. But then there's the bad news.

Demographically, we're not growing. At best, our numbers are static, but, given current trends, they're destined to decline. This is confirmed by the initial figures released from the 2002 Jewish population survey, but I confess that my primary sources are not always academic.

First, I am a regular reader of the *New York Times* Sunday Styles section on weddings. Now, I realize this isn't exactly a scientific method, but nonetheless it's a pretty revealing indicator. I knew we were headed for trouble when I saw the pièce de résistance: A Jew and a Christian being married by Jewish and Christian "interfaith ministers," who were themselves married to each other. Welcome to contemporary America and the à la carte menu of religious choices!

Second, I read obituaries. It's almost a sure bet that one or more of the deceased that the *Times* will write about on any given day is a Jew, even if religious identity is not necessarily mentioned in the article. Still, it's usually pretty obvious by a person's surname or biographical data. I look at the last paragraph of the obit, the one that mentions surviving family members—how many children, how many grandchildren, last names, places of residence, and the like. You can learn a lot about Jewish demographic trends from those few lines, and more often than not the picture isn't rosy.

Third, I just look around me. Take the world of northern Westchester County, where I live. There are welcome signs of Jewish growth and dynamism, but a closer examination reveals a decidedly mixed picture.

While there are many examples to the contrary, the number of mixed-marriage homes with barely a trace of Jewish identity is striking.

On my son Michael's high school soccer team, for instance, there were more children of mixed marriages—in these particular cases not one being raised Jewish—than there were Jews.

One extreme example of this situation is a middle-aged Jewish man with a younger Christian wife. His first wife was a Jew, and their children grew up heavily involved in both Judaism and Zionism. In his second marriage, his daughter came home from middle school one day recently and said to her mother, a friend of my wife: "Mommy, we learned about Jews today. Do we know any Jews?" To which her mother replied: "You silly goose, don't you know that your daddy is a Jew?"

But our problems don't stop there. What about endogamous Jewish marriages where there's barely a hint of Jewish content?

My children tell my wife and me about Jewish kids in school or college who come from homes where the parents just don't care, or are once-a-year Jews, or send their children to religious school only out of habit or peer pressure, while bad-mouthing the experience in front of their own children.

Is it any wonder that Jews end up all over the American religious landscape? If Jewish kids grow up in families without Jewish anchorage, pride, literacy, and joy, what will keep them loyal to their people?

Actually, Franz Kafka wrote of this phenomenon over eighty years ago in his revealing *Letter to Father* (1919):

> It was also impossible to make clear to a child who from sheer anxiety was too acutely observant that those few trivialities you performed in the name of Judaism, with an indifference corresponding to their triviality, could have any higher meaning. For you they were meaningful as small souvenirs of earlier times and that's why you wanted to impart them to me, but you could do so only by way of persuasion or threat, since they no longer had any value of their own, even for you.

In today's America, it seems, anything goes. In a very real sense, religion has become a marketplace. Some people weave in and out of religions with abandon. In fact, a few years ago, the *New York Times Sunday Magazine* devoted a cover story to real-life examples of this very phenomenon. The transmission belt that passed on religious identity from generation to generation is in acute danger, and especially for Jews who, polls repeatedly show, approach religious practice and ritual with greater skepticism than do other religious communities in the United States.

I can't even begin to count the number of times I've heard more or less the same refrains from those who have drifted away, whether from observant or secular homes or somewhere in between:

> "Hebrew school was a complete waste of time."

> "I had to sit for endless hours in synagogue for reasons that escaped me, while other kids got to sleep late, play sports, or socialize."

> "My parents didn't seem to care a whole lot about being Jewish, so why should I?"

> "I couldn't understand any of the prayers in Hebrew. The whole thing seemed so foreign."

"The rabbi wasn't a spiritual leader; he was a fund-raiser and an ego massager."

"No one ever explained to me the essence of Judaism. All I got was a bunch of stories."

"Some people around me seemed more concerned with ritual than content. It smacked of hypocrisy."

"It all seemed to be about burden and responsibility, not about happiness and fulfillment."

"I never knew if there was anything more to being Jewish than remembering the Holocaust and keeping an eye out for the anti-Semites, who for some reason wanted to kill me. Is that a sufficient guide to life?"

"All I learned about was being a good person, but Jews don't have a monopoly on ethics, so why did I need to be Jewish in order to be good?"

"I was looking for community, but instead found social hierarchy everywhere I looked in the Jewish world."

I grew up in a largely secular environment, and in my youth many of these thoughts occurred to me as well. My father couldn't tell Purim from Passover, and I couldn't wait to get my bar mitzvah behind me so that boring Hebrew school would be over and done with. But, at the same time, I always felt a visceral link to my Jewish identity and a profound connection both to the Jews who came before me and to those living around me.

And my mother, though largely unschooled in things Jewish, knew exactly who she was and where she belonged. Even without religious or scholarly grounding, in a very real sense she embodied the meaning of the legendary philosopher Martin Buber's words, written in 1923: "My soul is not by the side of my people; my people is my soul."

It wasn't until my twenties, though, that I discovered I had been cheated.

I was in Rome working with Jewish refugees from the Soviet Union. By and large, they knew even less about their Jewish heritage than I did, but at least they had a good excuse. They had emigrated from a country that had systematically denied them the chance, on penalty of imprisonment, to study about their religion and culture.

When they asked me questions about Judaism—questions that might have been bottled up inside them for years, if not decades—I was, to my embarrassment, often clueless. And they were clueless as to why I was clueless. After all, I had grown up in America, hadn't I, where opportunities to study about Jews and Judaism abounded.

I realized I was far more grounded in American and European civilization than in Jewish civilization. I was more familiar with Montesquieu than Maimonides. I could explain what kielbasa was but not Kabbalah. And, thanks to popular American culture, I probably knew more Christmas than Chanukah tunes.

I urged the Jewish organizations working with Soviet Jews in Rome and Vienna (the two European transit stops on the way to permanent resettlement) to educate these newcomers about their identity, but for one reason or another, it didn't happen. And so, by process of default, I, of all people, became a Jewish educator in my spare time. I organized programs for the refugees and eventually wrote a primer for them on being Jewish. Needless to say, to educate them I had to begin by educating myself.

And in that process of self-education, I became acutely aware of two things: First, I realized that I was the custodian, together with every other living Jew, of a magnificent heritage that covered everything from theology to philosophy, from mysticism to music, from literature to art, from language to ethnography. And second, I might have gone through life without ever stumbling on this treasure trove had I not encountered Soviet Jews.

To the extent that I can extrapolate from my own experience—and my experience, I know, was far from unique—how could it be that an otherwise highly literate group of American Jews could be so illiterate about their own Jewish identity?

To sum it up, without wishing to sound excessively banal, we've got a great "product," Jewish civilization, but we could have learned a lesson or two about promotion along the way. If religion has, as I said, become something of a marketplace, then we'd better figure out how to make certain that its inherent riches are on display for all to see and enjoy.

There are innumerable entry points to involvement in Jewish life, but they need to be better known. In fact, there are so many different opportunities that, like those twelve-page menus in some diners, surely there's something for everyone.

Jews in pursuit of a sense of community and belonging need not flock to other religions or cults. Those grappling with life's overarching questions will discover that Jews have been wrestling with the very same questions for nearly four thousand years. Those looking for ethical guideposts will find the maps. Those seeking the sense of awe that comes with the quest for the sacred need not look beyond Judaism. Those in search of spiritual fulfillment can find it in a myriad of ways.

And those Jews who desire pride of affiliation can surely find it in the extraordinary achievements of the Jewish people. Consider these sample comments from distinguished non-Jews about the Jewish role in world history:

> The Jews were the first people to break out of this cycle [i.e., the belief that the cosmos was profoundly cyclical], to find a new way of thinking and experiencing, a new way of understanding and feeling the world, so much so that it may be said with some justice that theirs is the only new idea that human beings have ever had.
> (Thomas Cahill, the author of the best-selling *The Gifts of the Jews*)

> [Moses'] life seems actually to have been the historical bridge between animistic polytheism and ethical monotheism—that is practically to say, from superstition to religion.
> (Charles Francis Potter, a Unitarian minister who wrote *The Great Religious Leaders*)

> If statistics are right, the Jews constitute but one percent of the human race. It suggests a nebulous dim puff of stardust lost in the blaze of the

Milky Way. Properly, the Jew ought hardly to be heard of, but he is heard of, has always been heard of. He is as prominent on the planet as any other people, and his commercial importance is extravagantly out of proportion to the smallness of his bulk. His contributions to the world's list of great names in literature, science, art, music, finance, medicine, and abstruse learning are also away out of proportion to the weakness of his numbers. He has made a marvelous fight in this world, in all the ages; and had it done with the hands tied behind him. He could be vain of himself, and be excused for it. The Egyptian, the Babylonian, and the Roman followed, and made a vast noise, and they are gone. Other peoples have sprung up and held their torch high for a time, but it burned out, and they sit in twilight now, or have vanished. The Jew saw them all, beat them all, and is now what he always was, exhibiting no decadence, no infirmities of age, no weakening of his parts, no slowing of his energies, no dulling of his alert and aggressive mind. All things are mortal but the Jew; all other forces pass, but he remains. What is the secret of his immortality?

(Mark Twain, writing in the September 1899 issue of *Harper's New Monthly Magazine*)

I insist that the Hebrews have done more to civilize men than any other nation.... They are the most glorious nation that ever inhabited this earth.... They have given religion to three-quarters of the globe, and have influenced the affairs of mankind more, and more happily, than any other nation, ancient or modern.

(John Adams, the nation's second president, in a letter to F.A. Van der Kemp in 1808)

One way of summing up 4,000 years of Jewish history is to ask ourselves, what would have happened to the human race if Abraham had not been a man of great sagacity; or if he had stayed in Ur and kept his higher notions to himself, and no specific Jewish people had come into being. Certainly the world without the Jews would have been a radically different place. All the great conceptual discoveries of the intellect seem obvious and inescapable once they have been revealed, but it requires a special genius to formulate them for the first time. The Jews had this gift. To them we owe the ideas of equality before the law, both divine and human; of the sanctity of life and the dignity of the human person; of the individual conscience, and so of personal redemption; of the collective conscience, and so of social responsibility; of peace as an abstract ideal, and love as the foundation of justice; and many other items which constitute the basic moral furniture of the human mind. (Paul Johnson, the distinguished historian and Christian scholar, in *A History of the Jews*)

Reading Johnson's powerful summation of the Jewish contribution to civilization, one understands why the Assembly of the Province of Pennsylvania, in 1751, turned to the Hebrew Bible, specifically the Book of Leviticus, for the inscription that was to be placed on the Liberty Bell: "Proclaim liberty throughout all the land unto all the inhabitants thereof."

Indeed, we have a great story to tell, but how do we get the word out to those who need to hear it most?

Believe me, if I had good answers, I wouldn't keep them a secret.

What is clear is that we have been endowed with the precious gift of a unique heritage and identity, one that we need to appreciate better ourselves and find ways of sharing with others. And today we have the incalculable advantage of a technological revolution that opens up all kinds of communication possibilities.

Ultimately, it requires a full-court press. Every nook and cranny of the Jewish community must examine not just what we are currently doing, but even more, what we need to do to engage as many people as possible in the Jewish experience.

At the risk of stating the obvious, there is no one address for transmitting Judaism and Jewish identity.

We cannot simply expect rabbis or teachers to do all the work for us, though much responsibility does rest on their shoulders; it must be a partnership involving, first and foremost, the family. After all, the home is where it all begins. And our children should learn to understand—by our deeds far more than by our words—that we take seriously our Jewish identity, however we may choose to practice it, and that this identity adds immeasurably to our lives, as it can to theirs.

We need to set an example for our children by conveying the message that Jewish education is a lifelong pursuit, a boon to mind and soul, that most certainly doesn't end at the age of thirteen or sixteen.

We should take advantage of Jewish experiential opportunities—camping, retreats, travel, quality time in Israel, conferences, study sessions, organizational involvement, online "virtual" communities, you name it—that give form and substance to our sense of connection.

We must make the case that to be unabashedly American and Jewish is mutually enhancing, not diminishing.

And we ought to ensure that those Jews who deliberately demean and trivialize the Jewish experience, like some authors or movie or television scriptwriters, don't have the last word. Their watered-down, caricatured, stereotyped, and, yes, occasionally self-loathing treatment of Jewish themes should not be allowed to define the American Jewish experience.

If I could wave a magic wand, there are several things I'd like to see happen, among them:

I would try to find ways to keep all children in formal Jewish education past bar and bat mitzvah, at least until the age of sixteen. Not only would that keep kids connected to Jewish education for another three years, but it would also give them a much deeper understanding of their heritage than they currently have. And a trip to Israel, whether with family or a youth group, should become an integral part of the experience of every bar and bat mitzvah child.

Moreover, American Jewry can learn from the experience of Australian Jewry—and other overseas communities—and create a network of Jewish day schools running through high school that compete with the finest secular schools at every level, including academic, athletic, and other extracurricular activities, and that appeal to the broadest possible swath of the community. While a few such schools currently exist in the U.S., many more are needed.

In the same spirit, and modeled on the visionary Birthright Israel initiative, every Jewish child in this country should have access to Jewish education, whether in day or after-school programs, without parents having to worry about the high tuition cost. Many schools, of course, offer scholarships, but much more could be done with increased communal support for those who find the costs prohibitive. The Jewish community has no higher long-term priority than education.

Further, what if those families planning to leave funds in their estates (or via other means) for their children were encouraged to designate a sum to be specifically earmarked for things Jewish? In other words, that money could only be used for Jewish activities—Jewish school tuition or camping fees, trips to Israel, donations to Jewish charitable organizations, synagogue membership fees, etc. The creation of such individual Jewish family funds would send an unmistakable message about our values and priorities.

And finally, apropos conversion and outreach, the Jewish community should make a far more concerted effort to invite people in, to make them feel welcome, and to encourage them to explore the possibilities for deepening their ties with us.

I have never understood how the Jewish community, on the one hand, can bemoan static or shrinking numbers, while, on the other hand, some Jews put up roadblocks that make it difficult, if not impossible, to pursue active participation in the life of the Jewish people.

In a post-Holocaust era, when anti-Semitism is again on the rise and Islamic radicals have declared all Jews to be fair game, should a non-Jew's willingness to identify in a meaningful way with the Jewish community be taken lightly or dismissed out of hand? Some Jews, regrettably, take just such an approach, which, in my view, is both insensitive and shortsighted in the extreme.

Extending the reach and hold of the Jewish community is a daunting task, to say the least, but eminently worthwhile and, I firmly believe, doable. In our efforts, we should always be inspired by the esteemed Jewish theologian and social justice activist Abraham Joshua Heschel, who, in 1955, encapsulated in just a few words our mission:

> To be a Jew is to affirm the world without being enslaved by it; to be a part of civilization and to go beyond it; to conquer space and to sanctify time. Judaism is the art of surpassing civilization, sanctification of time, sanctification of history.

And in the years ahead, may the good news of the Jewish community's resilience, strength, and dynamism always outweigh the bad.

Letter from an Endangered Species
January 10, 2003

Let me put my cards on the table right up front.

I consider myself a potentially endangered species. I am—gasp!—a
committed transatlanticist. Until just a short time ago that was a rather
unexceptional thing to be; most people I knew on both sides of the
Atlantic were, to varying degrees, in the same club. Now, in some
places, it could get my picture on a "Wanted" poster.

Seemingly overnight, significant swaths of European public opinion—most strikingly in Germany, but in other countries as well—
appear to have concluded that the Bush administration is hell-bent on
imposing its "imperialist" vision on the world, that the American
"infatuation" with the use of force as a solution to global challenges is
downright hazardous, and that America pays little more than lip service
to its European allies, with the possible exception of Britain, while sin-
gle-mindedly pursuing a unilateralist agenda.

According to this line of thinking—often promoted by opinion
molders, including, in the recent German elections, a few leading
politicians—America is run by a group of modern-day "cowboys,"
with precious little sophistication in the ways of the world, determined
to use their unchallenged superpower status to get their way on everything, be it Iraq, global warming, the International Criminal Court, or
genetically modified foods, and let the rest of the world be damned if
they don't like it. In response, Europe must draw appropriate conclusions and rise up essentially as a counterweight to otherwise
unchecked American global domination.

This disparaging and distrustful view extends beyond politics. A
new American Jewish Committee survey in Germany found that only
36 percent of the respondents rated America's cultural achievement as

"very substantial or substantial," while 48 percent thought it either "hardly substantial" or "insubstantial," and 16 percent had no opinion.

And a recent grisly case involving the Internet, cannibalism, and homicide in Germany produced a telling comment from the influential Munich newspaper *Suddeutsche Zeitung*, as reported in the *International Herald Tribune* (December 19): "It is all so unreal. So haunting that one thinks such a case would only happen in the movies, perhaps in America, but not in Germany...." Yes, America, of course, is capable of such bestial violence, but Germany never, we are led to believe.

Meanwhile, new generations of Europeans, increasingly fed this diet of overtly or subtly anti-American thinking, too often lose sight of the larger picture. They cannot relate easily to the backdrop of history.

That America came to Europe's rescue in two world wars of Europe's making, that America became history's most benign occupier in postwar Germany, that the U.S.-funded Marshall Plan was a key to Western Europe's astonishing reconstruction efforts, that American-led resolve and strength prevailed in the Cold War and contributed to the unification not only of Germany but of all Europe, and that America prodded a largely paralyzed Europe into decisive action against ethnic cleansing (on European soil) in the Balkans may at best have an abstract hold on younger people's thinking, but little more.

Like their American counterparts, younger Europeans are largely focused on the here and now. They may relate to American music, fashion, idiom, or, heaven forbid, fast food, but have an increasingly jaundiced view of America's larger place in global affairs.

At the same time, on too many levels, America largely ignores Europe, even as some voices emphasize the oceanic divide.

Perhaps the most talked-about recent essay on the subject was Robert Kagan's "Power and Weakness," which appeared in the June/July 2002 issue of *Policy Review*. It is a provocative piece well worth reading. Here's a brief excerpt:

> It is time to stop pretending that Europeans and Americans share a common view of the world, or even that they occupy the same world. On the

all-important question of power—the efficacy of power, the morality of power, the desirability of power—American and European perspectives are diverging. Europe is turning away from power, or to put it a little differently, it is moving beyond power into a self-contained world of laws and rules and transnational negotiation and cooperation. It is entering a post-historical paradise of peace and relative prosperity, the realization of Kant's "Perpetual Peace."

The United States, meanwhile, remains mired in history, exercising power in the anarchic Hobbesian world where international laws and rules are unreliable and where true security and the defense and promotion of a liberal order still depend on the possession and use of military might.

That is why on major strategic and international questions today, Americans are from Mars and Europeans are from Venus.

And noting the wide gap in perceptions of America between Eastern and Western Europe, columnist Charles Krauthammer suggested jokingly—I think—in the *Weekly Standard* (August 26) that had America let Western Europe fall under the sway of the Kremlin for a few decades, perhaps, like the nations of Eastern Europe today, it would be far more appreciative of America's world role.

In essence, the caricatured image of America in Europe has its counterpart here.

Europeans are seen as sanctimonious, self-adulatory, and wobbly at the knees. Rather than display a willingness to confront evil—that is, if they can even recognize it these days—they all too frequently seek to engage it through rationalization, negotiation, and, if necessary, appeasement via one Faustian bargain or another, all in the name, however it may be packaged, of realpolitik.

Look, the critics point out, at the European Union's so-called "critical dialogue" with Iran, which has been much longer on dialogue than on criticism.

Or the French flirtation with Iraq, going back to the 1970s when Jacques Chirac, as prime minister, negotiated the Osirak nuclear deal with Baghdad. Apropos, according to the *Wall Street Journal*, the last foreign country Saddam Hussein visited was France, in 1979.

Or the quiet deals several European countries, most notab
and Italy, sought to make with Palestinian terrorist groups
being targeted by them.

Or the EU's unwillingness, even post-9/11, to agree on classiᵢ
Hezbollah as a terrorist organization on the ostensible grounds that
group is also a "legitimate" political party in Lebanon, but actua. ｊ
motivated by a desire to avoid offending Syria and its satellite,
Lebanon.

Or the state visits accorded to the Syrian president in London last
month, complete with an audience with Queen Elizabeth, no less, or
previously in Paris, Madrid, and other European capitals, while Syria
illegally occupies neighboring Lebanon and cossets terrorist groups
bent on Israel's total destruction.

Or the EU's stance on Israel-related UN resolutions, almost always
opting to work out "acceptable" final language with the Arab bloc
rather than joining the United States in opposing outright those objec-
tionable texts that inevitably end up condemning Israel, regardless of
the facts on the ground.

Some Americans believe that, left to their own devices, many
Europeans would, in Winston Churchill's memorable words, be
"resolved to be irresolute" when faced with the likes of Saddam
Hussein, the mullahs of Tehran, or, for that matter, Slobodan
Milosevic. And, ironically, the Europeans can get away with it because
they know that, at the end of the day, there is an America that has both
the will and capacity to lead the fight when no other option is available.

Observing these issues being played out from both sides of the
Atlantic, I wouldn't for a moment underestimate the current chasm. It
is real, if not always as wide as it may seem at first glance. Still, we
can't ever afford to lose sight of what unites us.

Call me hopelessly irredeemably naïve, but I remain convinced that
Americans and Europeans are umbilically bound by common founda-
tional values and common existential threats, and thus, ipso facto, a
common agenda.

Those common values emanate from the very essence of our respective societies: democracy, the rule of law, and respect for the dignity of
the individual.

Even a brief glance at international socio-economic indices reveals the striking fact that the democratic nations, as a group, rank highest in personal freedoms, per capita income, life expectancy, levels of educational attainment, and overall standards of living, and lowest in infant mortality and corruption rates.

No less importantly, the democratic nations have renounced war as an instrument of resolving policy disputes among themselves.

The ties that link this precious fraternity of kindred nations must never be permitted to fray, for they represent the best—indeed, I would argue the only—hope for the ultimate realization of a peaceful and prosperous world.

And the threats are transnational.

Just as democratic nations were at risk during World War II and again during the Cold War, today those democratic nations are in the crosshairs of the radical Islamic terrorist network.

True, some European countries initially convinced themselves that this threat was about America and not them.

But as Islamic terrorist cells have been uncovered in Britain, Spain, Italy, France, Belgium, the Netherlands, Germany, and elsewhere in Europe, there is a growing realization that we are all in this together. The targets are not just specific countries, but the overarching values of freedom, secularism, religious tolerance, pluralism, women's rights, and openness that are enshrined in every democratic society.

The threat from terrorist groups and their supporters operating in just about every Western country is heightened by the prospect of increasingly available weapons of mass destruction.

Even at the risk of stating the obvious, the United States and Europe need each other, as much now as ever, in the face of this worldwide, long-term menace.

We must maintain full cooperation in the gathering and sharing of intelligence and a hundred other fields if we are to emerge on top in this daunting conflict.

We have to do a better job of coordinating policy, not only on terrorist groups, but also on those nations that help and harbor these groups. Can we afford to let such nations continue to play us off one against the other, as they so often have in the past?

And if I could be permitted to dream for just a moment, imagine our collaborating on developing alternative energy sources that would eventually wean us all off Middle East oil and gas—and, perhaps way down the road, fossil fuels in general—and do something good for Planet Earth in the process.

In the final analysis, this struggle against the radicals also entails strengthening the moderates in the Islamic world, and, here again, the United States and Europe, working together, increase the odds of success.

Put another way, we must win two epic battles, not one. We must win the war, and we must win the peace. Winning one without the other will eventually prove a Pyrrhic victory. The United States cannot go it alone on both fronts and hope to prevail. Nor can Europe.

Both of us have a profound stake in finding constructive ways to encourage the forces of democratization, civil society, and greater openness in countries that by and large have been remarkably resistant to the political and economic revolutions of recent times. Otherwise, further regression will take place, with still greater division between their world and ours, and all the attendant implications for conflict, terrorism, and the spread of fundamentalism.

Take, as an example, the case of Pakistan. Imagine for a moment the catastrophic global consequences if it descended into civil war or fell into the hands of the Islamists.

Here's a turbulent country of 150 million, twice the size of California, with 40 percent of its population under the age of fifteen. Not only does Pakistan have weapons of mass destruction, but the world was on edge recently when India and Pakistan engaged in nuclear brinkmanship.

Moreover, there are nearly one million youngsters studying full-time in Muslim religious schools, where the Koran and jihad, and not civics and biology, are the principal educational fare, and Osama bin Laden could win his share of popularity contests. What's the future for these young people, and how will their future impact on us?

The unraveling of Pakistan would hit the jackpot on the political Richter scale and send massive shock waves through its neighbors—Afghanistan, a country that has just been brought back from the edge but remains far from secure, China, India, and Iran. It would also have staggering geopolitical, strategic, and economic implications for both Europe and the United States.

Once again, therefore, we have a common agenda.

So, too, with Turkey.

Mustafa Kemal Ataturk was one of the most influential statesmen of the twentieth century. He established the modern Turkish Republic on the rubble of the collapsed Ottoman Empire, courageously separated religion from state, and recognized that the nation's future belonged squarely with Europe. Eighty years later, Turkey is closer to that goal than ever before, but the outcome is by no means certain.

Whether to admit Turkey to the European Union is a European, not an American, decision. While the United States has a profound interest in seeing this happen, it must exert its influence without overplaying its hand and infuriating the Europeans, as it managed to do last month in the run-up to the Copenhagen summit of EU leaders. Close cooperation between the United States and Europe can encourage Turkey to take the additional steps necessary to persuade Brussels that Ankara is a truly viable candidate for EU membership, and thereby outflank its European opponents.

(Valéry Giscard d'Estaing, the former French president, expressed this opposition most bluntly when, in November, he declared in the French daily *Le Monde* that Turkey "is not a European country" and inviting it into the EU would mean "the end of Europe.")

The challenges of integrating Turkey into the EU should not be minimized. At the time of accession, a decade or more from now, it would almost certainly be the single most populous—and, by far, poorest—EU member country. Further, it would extend the EU's boundaries to the turbulent Middle East. Turkey shares borders with, among others, Syria, Iran, and Iraq. And, in the process, Europe would inherit an unknown percentage of the Turkish population that is Muslim fundamentalist, adding to Europe's already considerable challenges in this regard.

Even so, the successful integration of Turkey into the European Union could create a powerful and perhaps contagious role model for other Muslim countries, beginning with those Central Asian nations in the Turkish sphere of interest, such as Azerbaijan and Uzbekistan, and extending far beyond.

The United States and Europe should have a similar interest in extending the reach of genuine democracy, especially in the Arab world, much of which is located practically at Europe's doorstep. Here, too, there's room for collaboration driven by the common overall objective of stabilizing the region and increasing prospects for peace and regional cooperation.

The United States, by dint of its size, influence, and global reach, has a great deal to offer. So does the European Union.

Let me digress for a moment. I am a long-time admirer of the European Union. The more I understand the inventive genius of Jean Monnet, the Frenchman called upon by Robert Schuman, the postwar French foreign minister, to conceptualize a structure that would prevent future wars with Germany, the more in awe I am and the more I appreciate the need for similarly bold thinking today.

(And it should be pointed out that such a structure, envisioned to fully integrate a rebuilding Germany, was a far cry from the 1944 Morgenthau Plan, named after President Franklin D. Roosevelt's secretary of the treasury, which would have converted a defeated Germany into a primarily pastoral country.)

Indeed, following Monnet's recommendations, the six-nation European Coal and Steel Community was formally established in 1952, once the member countries—Belgium, France, Italy, Luxembourg, the Netherlands, and West Germany—ratified the Treaty of Paris. Along the way, on May 9, 1950, Schuman publicly declared:

It is no longer a time for vain words, but for a bold, constructive act. France has acted, and the consequences of her action may be immense. We hope they will. She has acted essentially in the cause of peace. For peace to have a chance, there must first be a Europe. Nearly five years to the day after the unconditional surrender of Germany, France is now taking the first decisive step toward the construction of Europe and is associating Germany in this venture. It is something which must completely change things in Europe and permit other joint actions which were hitherto impossible. Out of all this will come forth Europe, a solid and united Europe. A Europe in which the standard of living will rise.

The European Union's evolution over the past fifty years has been nothing short of breathtaking.

It is a remarkable case study in the emergence of a democratic and ever more prosperous grouping based on the vision of political giants, with the core objective of preventing future wars. A European Union of fifteen nations, soon to be twenty-five, with Bulgaria and Romania poised to join a few years hence, has much to teach other regions, most notably the Arab world, about institution-building and integration.

This sounds, I realize, like the stuff of distant, perhaps impossible, dreams. Many reasons can be offered why the European experience cannot take root in the Arab world. There are, needless to say, countless political, cultural, historic, and economic differences between Europe and the Arab bloc.

Still, I refuse to abandon hope because there is no more promising alternative, certainly not over the long term, and I am unwilling to accept the proposition that the Arab people have no choice for the future but to live under corrupt, autocratic, stifling filial dynasties.

Here, too, the United States and Europe, working in concert, can help lead the way and reap the benefits of their efforts.

And while it may seem far-fetched today, it is entirely conceivable that the United States and Europe could one day be talking about Israel's entry into the European Union, and perhaps even NATO, as part of a comprehensive solution to the Arab-Israeli conflict.

In short—and I've only skimmed the surface—leaders on both sides of the Atlantic Ocean need to stress constantly our common values, common threats, and common goals.

To be sure, there are, and inevitably will always be, differences between Europe and the United States rooted in political rivalry, economic competition, divergent interests, and the like. In the larger scheme of things, however, these differences ought to be quite manageable and, in any case, must never be permitted to overshadow the commonalities.

The American Jewish Committee has long been in the business of building bridges between Europe and the United States, precisely because it understands what is at stake. At turbulent moments such as this, the work becomes only more important.

For us, it means recognizing that Europe, given its size and significance, cannot easily be ignored or dismissed even when we don't like what we see; rather, it must be engaged with skill, sophistication, and sensitivity, with ever more points of contact established.

Moreover, it means never losing sight of the larger picture of Europe and America as the likeliest of strategic allies, even when we raise tough issues with our European interlocutors, as we at AJC do regularly in Berlin, Paris, Madrid, Brussels, and other centers of power.

Among these issues currently are: (a) the slow and stumbling reaction of too many Europeans to the indisputable rise in anti-Semitism during the past two years; (b) the unacceptable moral equivalence (or worse) with which a number of European governments view the Israeli-Palestinian conflict; (c) the political expediency all too evident in molding relations with dictatorial regimes in the Arab world (and Iran); (d) the rapidly declining impact of the Shoah on European attitudes toward Israel and the Jewish people; and (e) the growing anti-Americanism that too often goes unchecked.

On a lighter but related note, I had a good laugh when I saw a cartoon in the *New Yorker* (October 28, 2002) which showed a hostess at a cocktail party introducing two men to each other. The caption read: "Francophobe, meet Francophile." In my case, though, I sometimes feel that both individuals are living within me. No European country attracts me more culturally, or exasperates me more diplomatically, than France.

At the same time, I fully understand that generalizations can be dangerous.

Not all of Europe is anti-American, anti-Israel, or anti-Semitic, far from it. Britain, Denmark, Italy, and Spain are today very close to Washington; Germany, Britain, and the Netherlands are the EU countries most sympathetic to Israel; and there are some European nations that have experienced few, if any, serious anti-Semitic incidents in recent years.

Even in France, described by *proche-orient.info* (the principal French-language source for balanced Middle East coverage) as the country that "takes the lead in the European Union's anti-Israel policies," roughly 20 percent of the parliamentarians in the National Assembly belong to the France-Israel Caucus. That may not be a sufficient critical mass to sway a nation, but it's still a rather impressive number to work with.

Moreover, though often overlooked, the situation in Central and Eastern Europe is actually quite encouraging. By and large, these countries are pro-American—Poland, Bulgaria, and Romania being three outstanding examples. They have close links with Israel, and, for a variety of reasons, have reached out to world Jewry in the past decade in a way that offers real hope for the future.

To sum it up, it would be well to revisit the eloquent words expressed by President Bush at the NATO summit in Prague six weeks ago. The American head of state said:

> The transatlantic ties of Europe and America have met every test of history, and we intend to again. U-boats could not divide us. The threats and standoffs of the Cold War did not make us weary. The commitment of my nation to Europe is found in the carefully tended graves of young Americans who died for this continent's freedom. That commitment is shown by the thousands in uniforms still serving here, from the Balkans to Bavaria, still willing to make the ultimate sacrifice for this continent's future.
>
> For a hundred years, place names of Europe have often stood for conflict and tragedy and loss. Single words evoke sad and bitter experience—Verdun, Munich, Stalingrad, Dresden, Nuremberg, and Yalta. We have no power to rewrite history. We do have the power to write a different story for our time....
>
> In Prague, young democracies will gain new security, a grand alliance will gather strength and find new purpose, and America and Europe will renew the historic friendship that still keeps the peace of the world.

These stirring words—and their policy implications—deserve a long life span, as well as permanent top-priority status, on *both* sides of the Atlantic Ocean. The question, of course, is whether they will get it.

Given the global challenges piling up one on top of another, from Iraq to North Korea, it's safe to say that we should have a pretty good idea quite soon.

Letter from France
February 5, 2003

France faces a major problem today. It's a problem without an easy or obvious solution. It's a problem that challenges the core values of French society. And it's a problem that profoundly affects French Jewry, the second largest Diaspora community in the world.

While estimates vary, there are approximately five million Muslims in France, comprising just under 10 percent of the national population. According to the French daily *Le Figaro* (October 21, 2002), half are French citizens. The vast majority come from the Maghreb—Morocco, Tunisia, and Algeria. Others hail from sub-Saharan Africa, Turkey, and the Middle East. They range from secular to fundamentalist in their religious orientation, and they represent the denominational spectrum of Islam, from Salafi to Sufi, from Shiite to Sunni, from Wahhabi to Tabligh.

It is said that in France more Muslims attend prayer services on Friday than Christians on Sunday. And it is also said that virtually all the mosques, and the imams that lead them, are funded and staffed from outside of France, principally from North Africa and the Persian Gulf.

The problem France faces is how to integrate this large community into the fabric and fiber of a nation that enshrines democratic values and secularism in the public sphere, and, since 1905, has built an impenetrable wall between religion and state. France has successfully absorbed previous waves of newcomers, including hundreds of thousands of Jews from the Maghreb, who quickly embraced the "republican" values of the country—but this time it's different.

Many Muslims resist the traditional patterns of absorption and acculturation, though there are those, notably from the Algerian region of Kabylia, who have proven the exception. And the second generation doesn't seem to have a much easier time of it than their parents; in some ways, it's even more difficult for them, though born in France. They don't fully identify with the state, but, then again, have no other state to fully identify with, either.

Often trapped in a cycle of poverty, violence, unemployment, and ghettoization, these youngsters feel alienated from French society. They are overrepresented in the prison system and underrepresented in the professional ranks. (According to a new book, *Les Territoires Perdus de la République*—"The Lost Territories of the Republic"—to which I will return in a moment, "Nearly 60 percent of the inmates in French prisons are Muslims, while the Muslim population in France probably approaches 10 percent of the total.")

This situation is by no means unique to France; Belgium, among other European countries, faces similar challenges. But France, by dint of its size and prominence, is the key country to watch. Put most starkly, will France ultimately prevail in the struggle to inculcate its prized societal values in the Muslim community, or will it fail, and, if so, with what consequences for the nation as a whole?

The 600,000 French Jews are profoundly affected by what's going on.

An ancient and proud Jewish community dating back to the first century C.E., French Jewry counts among its most distinguished members Rabbi Gershom ben Jehuda and Rabbi Solomon ben Isaac, better known as Rashi, the legendary eleventh-century scholars of Bible and Talmud. French Jews were to enjoy the fruits of emancipation in the eighteenth century, but not before experiencing mass expulsion in the fourteenth century and restrictions on their ability to return.

On the heels of the adoption of the revolutionary Declaration of the Rights of Man, full citizenship was granted to all the Jews in France in 1791. As Abram Leon Sachar wrote in *A History of the Jews*:

> At last a great European country had abolished all restrictions; the Jews had liberty, equality, and, at least in theory, fraternity. They were no

longer aliens.... The emancipated people outdid themselves in their devotion to what had at last become for them *"la patrie"* (the homeland).

History, as we know all too well, seldom follows a linear course. There were to be major calamities awaiting French Jewry, most notably the Dreyfus Affair and the Nazi occupation of France and the collaboration of the Vichy regime. But the trajectory of French Jewish history cannot be defined by these two tragic events alone.

French Jews have made extraordinary contributions to French politics, science, industry, and the arts. As but one example, how many countries in the world can claim not one, nor two, but three Jewish prime ministers—Léon Blum, Pierre Mendès-France, and René Mayer? Needless to say, this also says something important about prevailing attitudes toward Jews in French society.

Battered by the murder of more than 77,000 French Jews deported to Nazi extermination camps, primarily Auschwitz, the community made a dramatic recovery after the war, fueled by the influx in the 1950s and 1960s of North African Jews, who today constitute a clear majority of the French Jewish population. Not only did they more than double the community's size, but they also infused it with new energy, vitality, and pride, all clearly evident to this day, whether in Paris, Marseilles, Nice, Strasbourg, or Toulouse.

But now French Jews face an unprecedented challenge. In the last thirty months, with heightened tensions in the Middle East, French Jews have been the target of chilling physical and verbal violence emanating from the North African Muslim community. Literally hundreds of attacks have been documented. At first, the government was inexcusably slow to respond. The *New York Times*, in an editorial, commented that when synagogues were "defaced, sacred texts burned, individuals menaced ... the official reaction consisted of a Gallic shrug, as if to ask, What can you expect from poor Arabs when they watch brutal scenes of the Israeli-Palestinian conflict on television?"

Few suspects were arrested, even fewer prosecuted. Whether this was the result of political considerations—presidential and parliamentary elections were scheduled for the spring of 2002 and the Muslim vote was a bigger factor than the Jewish—or whether it was the fear of triggering riots in restive Muslim neighborhoods, French authorities failed to act quickly and decisively.

Instead of taking on those who would flout the law and attack Jews, the government instead took on those on the outside, mostly in Israel and the United States, who condemned the violence against Jews. "France is not an anti-Semitic country," French officials vehemently insisted, but this was never at issue in the first place. It was simply a red herring, a diversionary tactic. What was at issue was the stream of violent incidents against Jews within France, not wholesale condemnation of the country.

Regrettably, some American Jews inadvertently played into the hands of the French government by assailing France in newspaper ads and over the Internet, and calling for a travel boycott. This allowed government officials to circle the wagons and assert that their country writ large was unfairly under attack.

However well-intentioned, the boycott call was misguided. It was done without consultation with French Jewish leadership (which subsequently denounced the call, pursuing instead intensified dialogue with government officials), the Israeli government, or American Jewish organizations. With little chance of success, it would have revealed weakness, not strength. It is wiser under such circumstances to hold out the possibility of a boycott rather than to actually call for one. And a boycott could have led to retaliatory measures—not against American Jews, of course, but against Israel.

Fortunately, things have taken a turn for the better lately. Many French Jewish leaders attribute this to a toughened approach by the new government led by Prime Minister Jean-Pierre Raffarin. Much credit is given in particular to the minister of the interior, Nicolas Sarkozy, whose no-nonsense approach to law and order has proved popular. Still, French Jews aren't breathing easy yet.

At the annual dinner of CRIF, the French Jewish umbrella body, in Paris last month, Roger Cukierman, the elected president, said in a powerful speech before Prime Minister Raffarin, members of the Cabinet, parliamentary leaders, ambassadors, religious figures (among them Dalil Boubakeur, the head of the newly-established French Council of the Muslim Religion and a leading moderate), and hundreds of other guests, including an American Jewish Committee solidarity delegation:

> Last year in one breath we spoke of our fierce attachment to France and our anguish in the face of the renewed outbreak of anti-Jewish acts.
>
> Mr. Prime Minister, you heard our appeal. On July 21, 2002, at the Place of the Martyred Jews of Vel d'Hiv, you forcefully affirmed that to attack the Jewish community was to attack France and the values of the Republic. [Author's note: The Vélodrome d'Hiver was the site in Paris where, in July 1942, thousands of Jews were kept for days in inhuman conditions en route to deportation.]
>
> We thank the Minister of the Interior who, under your leadership, acted efficiently. We can confirm a decline in the number of these acts. But they have not disappeared. Far from it. What was at stake, and what is at stake, is not simply a matter of public order. What is at stake is the future of the Republic....
>
> Because we feel that we are in the front line in the defense of the Republic's values, and because we remain concerned about the risk of a resurgence of anti-Jewish acts, we have several requests:
>
> • The judicial system must punish more severely attacks that are anti-Semitic or racist in character. This looks like it will happen, given the unanimous adoption of the bill sponsored by Pierre Lellouche in the National Assembly [i.e., parliament]. We welcome this step.
> • Moreover, we believe that the penalty of three months for offenses involving the expression of racist or anti-Semitic views in France should be increased to a minimum of one year, including for offenses involving the Internet.
> • Finally, we would like to see an effort undertaken to legislate internationally against the propagation, via the Internet, of racist or anti-Semitic views.*

President Cukierman then expressed his concern about threats to secularism in French public life. He cited an important new book, *Les*

---

* This and the other translations in this letter, all from the original French, are mine.

Territoires Perdus de la République, which was published in
September 2002 and focuses on teachers' accounts of anti-Semitism,
racism, and sexism in the French school system.

This book encapsulates the Herculean problems faced by France in
trying to integrate youth of various backgrounds, especially Muslim.
Here are a few telling excerpts:

At the Lycée Bergson in Paris 19, two young girls saw the monstrous
face of anti-Semitism. In the courtyard ... they were surrounded by
some fifteen pupils who insulted them to their faces with vulgar expressions. The pupils laughed at each insult. But the humiliations weren't
only verbal. Apples and cheese were thrown in their faces. Their clothes
were dirtied. "The Jews don't wash themselves," one of the pupils commented. The torturers then pulled the girls' hair several times. They
were then ordered to get on their knees and beg forgiveness that they
were Jews. The pupils then went through their personal belongings,
without taking anything. The object of the exercise: humiliation. The
girls shivered from fear, but didn't get on their knees. They were hit.
They were warned that if they spoke about this to anyone there would
be reprisals. The ordeal lasted forty minutes.... A disciplinary committee met in May 2002. Two pupils were suspended. But one of the two
was treated more gently. She was able to go to the class where one of
the two (Jewish) girls was, and proceeded to threaten her.... The two
girls, much traumatized, changed schools.

I have taught at the elementary level in Paris for more than twenty
years and am currently in a school north of the capital. In our classrooms we have children of many backgrounds, and I have noticed that
Jewish children today are jostled and insulted because of their origin.
I've heard: "Jew dog," "Long live Bin Laden," "We're going to burn
Israel," and "Go back to your country." These comments come from the
mouths of children who are seven, eight, nine years old.

In a school in Seine-Saint-Denis something was organized that was
in large measure responsible for my desire (as a professor of history and
geography) to quit the school as quickly as possible. The town authorities, with a communist orientation, were actively looking for a school to
participate in a twinning program with Palestinian students. Our princi-

pal, himself part of the municipal council, offered our school.... He spoke of a "peace trip." I asked him if Israeli students would also participate. He said no. That's a strange way to think of education for peace, isn't it?... In February, the Palestinian delegation, with children from fourteen to sixteen, was welcomed.... During the Easter break, it was the turn of our children to go. Israel was not included in the itinerary, other than the arrival at Ben-Gurion Airport and the border crossings to reach the West Bank. The children spent ten days visiting Ramallah, Jenin, Kalkilya, and Nablus. On their return, wrapped in kaffiyehs, our students spoke more or less along the following lines: The Palestinians are poor, they have nothing. The Israelis are rich; they have everything and taunt the Palestinians....

Mr. T., a professor of history near the end of his teaching career, acknowledged with resignation and sadness that "violent criticism of Christianity and Judaism" by many pupils of Maghreb origin compelled him to touch only briefly on the curriculum on religions. When it comes to Islam, he now only speaks about it with great caution and keeping a close and uneasy eye on the reactions of the pupils.

Miss Y, a young professor of history and geography who enjoys good relations with her students, many of whom are Muslim, confided: "I believe that there is a huge problem of anti-Semitism.... I was shocked when I raised the subject of the Nazi period and the deportation. Several students ... pointed out the mistakes in my class." "But no, professor, all this is false. You repeat what's written in the history books, but you are mistaken.... We know that this was invented by the rich Jews after the war, but we've read other books that tell us the truth." "What books?" asked the professor. "People who know how to get such books because these books are forbidden by Jews who don't want them sold," a pupil replied. "But what are you saying? Give me a title." "Okay, the book of Garaudy, that's one," said the youngster. [Author's note: Roger Garaudy, a French convert to Islam, is a notorious Holocaust denier.]

Taking account of the difficulties in the French school system, Prime Minister Raffarin, in his remarks at the CRIF dinner, pointedly said:

I would like to emphasize the questions linked to teaching that you appropriately raised, President Cukierman [of CRIF]. Anti-Semitism is sometimes spread even into our classrooms. There we are experiencing the failure of integration to our republican values, which is a fundamental mission for the school. In certain educational establishments, it becomes difficult for the professors to raise the subject of the Shoah or to utter the name of Israel.... We must teach the Holocaust. The national minister of education, with absolute firmness, is mobilizing the means to assist the schools and teachers to fight against these unacceptable phenomena.

The prime minister went an important step further. Citing the campaign at the University of Paris to stop the renewal of academic cooperation between the European Union and Israel and to end exchanges with Israeli universities, he declared, to much applause, that such an initiative was "inadmissible" and that the government "has forcefully condemned it." The French government, he added, was moving in precisely the opposite direction. "We wish to develop our bilateral relations with Israel and our cooperation with foreign universities," citing as an example an agreement signed on January 14, 2003, to promote further scientific and technological cooperation with Israel.

Apropos the situation on French university campuses, an article by two leaders of the Union of French Jewish Students was published in the national daily, *Le Monde*, on January 22, 2003. Entitled "*L'Intifada des campus*," "The Intifada of the Campuses," it noted that "hatred of Jews has become a statistical fact at French universities" and that "in the name of Palestine, everything is permitted."

Two other books have recently appeared in France that are also provoking considerable discussion and much concern.

The first, entitled *Rêver la Palestine* ("Dream of Palestine"*)*, is a novel allegedly written by a teenager, Randa Ghazy, living in Milan, whose parents emigrated from Egypt. There are those who question whether Ms. Ghazy, given her youth and the fact that she never set foot in the West Bank or Gaza, actually wrote it herself, or is simply the vehicle for a clever marketing ploy.

The book appeared late last year in a French-language edition from the prestigious publishing house Flamarrion and almost immediately created a firestorm. The CRIF leadership, reacting to the book's inflammatory contents, called on the publisher to withdraw all copies. *Proche-orient.info*, a leading web site on the Middle East, commented that the book "in the guise of fiction ... is an incitement to hatred, violence, and to jihad against Israelis and Jews," citing a 1949 French law that prohibits the promotion of hate among minors. "It is a book that, given the socio-political context in France, can only encourage anti-Semitic acts."

The other book, *Mes "Frères" Assassins: Comment j'ai infiltré une cellule d'Al-Qaïda* ("My 'Brothers' the Murderers: How I infiltrated an Al-Qaeda cell"), just came out last month and has already caused a stir.

Written by Mohammed Sifaoui, a journalist, it recounts how the author ran into an old Algerian classmate in Paris, who had since become an Islamist terrorist. The classmate tried to recruit Sifaoui, and for three months the journalist pretended to go along, all the while keeping a meticulous diary and, thanks to a hidden camera, filming many of the encounters. Terrorist targets in France were discussed, including the possible assassination of two moderate Muslim leaders, Dalil Boubakeur, mentioned above, and Soheib Bencheikh, the mufti of Marseilles.

Terrorism, it should be recalled, is not new to France. In the 1990s, France was hard hit by Algerian-linked terrorism connected to the brutal civil war ravaging the North African country. More recently, German officials uncovered an Islamist cell plotting an attack on the cathedral in Strasbourg, while French authorities thwarted a plan by Muslim terrorists to blow up the Russian embassy in Paris.

In sum, France is on the front lines in dealing with the challenge of Muslim integration in Europe, trying to instill the values of democracy, secularism, separation of religion and state, respect for women, and religious tolerance in a Muslim population that, to a considerable degree, is proving resistant, while France also faces an economic and social divide that remains strikingly wide.

French Jews find themselves bearing much of the brunt of this front-line effort. Interestingly, in the 1990s it was French Jews who were among those reaching out to French Muslims and trying to find common ground in the struggle against racism and defamation.

While links with some ecumenically minded Muslims remain, French Jews have become a target for radical Muslims who rail against France, the West, Israel, or the "infidel." Vastly outnumbered, French Jews worry about the constant potential for violence. Most immediately, if there is military action against Iraq, French Jews fear repercussions in the streets of French cities. Indeed, when an American Jewish Committee delegation raised this concern with French President Jacques Chirac in a private meeting last month, he agreed that it was a distinct possibility and recognized the need for increased security and vigilance.

Recent media accounts have focused on the doubling of the immigration rate of French Jews to Israel in the past year, suggesting that these Jews, troubled by what's going on, are voting with their feet. It's true that 2,300 Jews made aliyah in 2002, and, yes, some Jews reportedly are exploring the possibility of relocating to Quebec, which is always on the lookout for French speakers, but most French Jews see France as their home and have no intention of giving up the fight.

And this is really the right note to end on. As an American Jew, I've always been inspired by the example of other Diaspora communities.

France is a perfect case in point. With a history spanning 2,000 years, today French Jewry faces daunting challenges—a large and often hostile Muslim population; a government that abstains in the vote on Libya's candidacy as chair of the UN Human Rights Commission and resists branding Hezbollah a terrorist organization; an extreme left wing that has enthusiastically embraced the Palestinian cause and challenges the legitimacy of Zionism; and an extreme right wing, with all the accoutrements of xenophobia and anti-Semitism, that flexed its muscles in the national elections last year and elbowed out the Socialists as the second top vote-getter.

Even so, the French Jewish community hasn't gone into hiding; it hasn't lowered its voice or its profile; it hasn't toned down its support for Israel; and it hasn't pushed the mute button when it comes to commenting on the outrageous behavior of the extreme left and extreme right.

To the contrary, the mobilization of French Jewry has been nothing short of remarkable. Sure, there are those who complain constantly that the leadership is insufficiently assertive and want to go to the edge. And, conversely, there are those who have never seen a petition critical of Israel they wouldn't endorse. But these groups, fortunately, are a distinct minority.

Rather than avoid France, therefore, visit and spend time with the Jewish community.

Listen to the impressive Jewish radio stations they've set up that are still a dream here in the U.S.

Go see the new feature film, *Decryptage,* that two French Jewish intellectuals have produced to defend Israel and that is now being shown in cinemas.

Attend one of the demonstrations in support of Israel or against anti-Semitism and take the pulse of the crowd.

Witness the vibrancy of organizations, synagogues, and schools.

Observe the pride of Jews, both in their identification with France and their link to the Jewish people, as they go about their daily lives.

Learn about *proche-orient.info,* the web site created by a group of top-flight mainstream journalists, who gave up their careers to bring balance to Middle East coverage that is too often skewed in favor of the Palestinians, regardless of the facts on the ground.

Watch (or, better yet, join) the steady flow of French Jewish tourists and businessmen who fill daily El Al and Air France flights to Israel, eager to deepen their links with the Jewish state at this difficult and dangerous moment in Israel's life.

Above all, let's affirm the bonds that unite us.

Letter from a Forgotten Jew
March 4, 2003

I am a forgotten Jew.

My roots are nearly 2,600 years old, my ancestors made landmark contributions to world civilization, and my presence was felt from

North Africa to the Fertile Crescent—but I barely exist today. You see, I am a Jew from the Arab world. No, that's not entirely accurate. I've fallen into a semantic trap. I predated the Arab conquest in just about every country in which I lived. When Arab invaders conquered North Africa, for example, I had already been present there for over six centuries.

Today, you cannot find a trace of me in most of this vast region.

Try seeking me out in Iraq, a nation likely to have a slew of foreign visitors very soon.

Remember the Babylonian exile from ancient Judea, following the destruction of the First Temple in 586 B.C.E.? Remember the vibrant Jewish community that emerged there and produced the Babylonian Talmud?

Do you know that in the ninth century, under Muslim rule, we Jews in Iraq were forced to wear a distinctive yellow patch on our clothing—a precursor of the infamous Nazi yellow badge—and faced other discriminatory measures? Or that in the eleventh and fourteenth centuries, we faced onerous taxes, the destruction of several synagogues, and severe repression?

And I wonder if you have ever heard of the *Farhud*, the breakdown of law and order, in Baghdad in June 1941. As an American Jewish Committee specialist, George Gruen, reported:

> In a spasm of uncontrolled violence, between 170 and 180 Jews were killed, more than 900 were wounded, and 14,500 Jews sustained material losses through the looting or destruction of their stores and homes. Although the government eventually restored order ... Jews were squeezed out of government employment, limited in schools, and subjected to imprisonment, heavy fines, or sequestration of their property on the flimsiest of charges of being connected to either or both of the two banned movements. Indeed, Communism and Zionism were frequently equated in the statutes. In Iraq the mere receipt of a letter from a Jew in Palestine [pre-1948] was sufficient to bring about arrest and loss of property.

At our peak, we were 135,000 Jews in 1948, and we were a vitally important factor in virtually every aspect of Iraqi society. To illustrate our role, here is what the *Encyclopaedia Judaica* wrote about Iraqi Jewry: "During the twentieth century, Jewish intellectuals, authors, and poets made an important contribution to the Arabic language and literature by writing books and numerous essays."

By 1950 other Iraqi Jews and I were faced with the revocation of citizenship, seizure of assets, and, most ominously, public hangings. A year earlier, Iraqi Prime Minister Nuri Sa'id had told the British ambassador in Amman of a plan to expel the entire Jewish community and place us at Jordan's doorstep. The ambassador later recounted the episode in a memoir entitled *From the Wings: Amman Memoirs, 1947-1951.*

Miraculously, in 1951 about 100,000 of us got out, thanks to the extraordinary help of Israel, but with little more than the clothes on our backs. The Israelis dubbed the rescue Operation Ezra and Nehemiah.

Those of us who stayed lived in perpetual fear—fear of violence and more public hangings, as occurred on January 27, 1969, when nine Jews were hanged in the center of Baghdad on trumped-up charges, while hundreds of thousands of Iraqis wildly cheered the executions. The rest of us got out one way or another, including friends of mine who found safety in Iran when it was ruled by the Shah.

Now there are no Jews left to speak of, nor are there any monuments, museums, or other reminders of our presence on Iraqi soil for twenty-six centuries.

Do the textbooks used in Iraqi schools today refer to our one-time presence, to our positive contribution to the evolution of Iraqi society and culture? Not a chance. Two thousand six hundred years are erased, wiped out, as if they never happened. Can you put yourself in my shoes and feel the excruciating pain of loss and invisibility?

I am a forgotten Jew.

I was first settled in what is present-day Libya by the Egyptian ruler Ptolemy Lagos (323-282 B.C.E.), according to the first-century Jewish historian Josephus. My forefathers and foremothers lived continuously on this soil for over two millennia, our numbers bolstered by Berbers who converted to Judaism, Spanish and Portuguese Jews fleeing the Inquisition, and Italian Jews crossing the Mediterranean.

I was confronted with the anti-Jewish legislation of the occupying Italian Fascists. I endured the incarceration of 2,600 fellow Jews in an

Axis-run camp in 1942. I survived the deportation of 200 fellow Jews to Italy the same year. I coped with forced labor in Libya during the war. I witnessed Muslim rioting in 1945 and 1948 that left nearly 150 Libyan Jews dead, hundreds injured, and thousands homeless.

I watched with uncertainty as Libya became an independent country in 1951. I wondered what would happen to those 6,000 of us still there, the remnant of the 39,000 Jews who had formed this once-proud community—that is, until the rioting sent people packing, many headed for the newly established State of Israel.

The good news was that there were constitutional protections for minority groups in the newly established Libyan nation. The bad news was that they were completely ignored.

Within ten years of my native country's independence, I could not vote, hold public office, serve in the army, obtain a passport, purchase new property, acquire majority ownership in any new business, or participate in the supervision of our community's affairs.

By June 1967 the die was cast. Those of us who had remained, hoping against hope that things would improve in a land to which we were deeply attached and which, at times, had been good to us, had no choice but to flee. The Six-Day War created an explosive atmosphere in the streets. Eighteen Jews were killed, and Jewish-owned homes and shops were burned to the ground.

I and 4,000 other Jews left however we could, most of us with no more than a suitcase and the equivalent of a few dollars.

I was never allowed to return. I never recovered the assets I had left behind in Libya, despite promises by the government. In effect, it was all stolen—the homes, furniture, shops, communal institutions, you name it. Still worse, I was never able to visit the grave sites of my relatives. That hurt especially deeply. In fact, I was told that, under Colonel Muammar Qaddhafi, who seized power in 1969, the Jewish cemeteries were bulldozed and the headstones used for road building.

I am a forgotten Jew.

My experience—the good and the bad—lives on in my memory, and I'll do my best to transmit it to my children and grandchildren, but how much can they absorb? How much can they identify with a culture that seems like a relic of a distant past that appears increasingly remote and intangible? True, two or three books and articles on my history have been written, but—and here I'm being generous—they are far from best-sellers.

In any case, can these books compete with the systematic attempt by Libyan leaders to expunge any trace of my presence over two millennia? Can these books compete with a world that paid virtually no attention to the end of my existence?

Take a look at the *New York Times* index for 1967, and you'll see for yourself how the newspaper of record covered the tragic demise of an ancient community. I can save you the trouble of looking—just a few paltry lines were all the story got.

I am a forgotten Jew.

I am one of hundreds of thousands of Jews who once lived in countries like Iraq and Libya. All told, we numbered close to 900,000 in 1948. Today we are fewer than 5,000, mostly concentrated in two moderate countries—Morocco and Tunisia.

We were once vibrant communities in Aden, Algeria, Egypt, Lebanon, Syria, Yemen, and other nations, with roots dating back literally 2,000 years and more. Now we are next to none.

Why does no one speak of us and our story? Why does the world relentlessly, obsessively speak of the Palestinian refugees from the 1948 and 1967 wars in the Middle East—who, not unimportantly, were displaced by wars launched by their own Arab brethren—but totally ignore the Jewish refugees from the 1948 and 1967 wars?

Why is the world left with the impression that there's only one refugee population from the Arab-Israeli conflict, or, more precisely, the Arab conflict with Israel, when, in fact, there are two refugee populations, and our numbers were somewhat larger than the Palestinians?

I've spent many sleepless nights trying to understand this injustice.

Should I blame myself?

Perhaps we Jews from Arab countries accepted our fate too passively. Perhaps we failed to seize the opportunity to tell our story. Look at the Jews of Europe. They turned to articles, books, poems, plays, paintings, and film to recount their story. They depicted the periods of joy and the periods of tragedy, and they did it in a way that captured the imagination of many non-Jews. Perhaps I was too fatalistic, too shell-shocked, too uncertain of my artistic or literary talents.

But that can't be the only reason for my unsought status as a forgotten Jew. It's not that I haven't tried to make at least some noise; I have. I've organized gatherings and petitions, arranged exhibitions, appealed to the United Nations, and met with officials from just about every Western government. But somehow it all seems to add up to less than the sum of its parts. No, that's still being too kind. The truth is, it has pretty much fallen on deaf ears.

You know that acronym—MEGO? It means "My eyes glazed over." That's the impression I often have when I've tried raising the subject of the Jews from Arab lands with diplomats, elected officials, and journalists—their eyes glaze over (TEGO).

No, I shouldn't be blaming myself, though I could always be doing more for the sake of history and justice.

There's actually a far more important explanatory factor.

We Jews from the Arab world picked up the pieces of our shattered lives after our hurried departures—in the wake of intimidation, violence, and discrimination—and moved on.

Most of us went to Israel, where we were welcomed. The years following our arrival weren't always easy—we started at the bottom and had to work our way up. We came with varying levels of education and little in the way of tangible assets. But we had something more to sustain us through the difficult process of adjustment and acculturation: our immeasurable pride as Jews, our deeply rooted faith, our cherished rabbis and customs, and our commitment to Israel's survival and well-being.

Some of us—somewhere between one-fourth and one-third of the total—chose to go elsewhere.

Jews from the French-speaking Arab countries gravitated toward France and Quebec. Jews from Libya created communities in Rome and Milan. Egyptian and Lebanese Jews were sprinkled throughout Europe and North America, and a few resettled in Brazil. Syrian Jews immigrated to the United States, especially New York, as well as to Mexico City and Panama City. And on it went.

Wherever we settled, we put our shoulder to the wheel and created new lives. We learned the local language if we didn't already know it, found jobs, sent our children to school, and, as soon as we could, built our own congregations to preserve the rites and rituals that were distinctive to our tradition.

It's unbecoming to boast, but I think we've done remarkably well wherever we've gone. I would never underestimate the difficulties or overlook those who, for reasons of age or ill health or poverty, couldn't make it, but, by and large, in a short time we have taken giant steps, whether in Israel or elsewhere.

But what has befallen the Palestinians, the other refugees of the Arab conflict with Israel? Sadly, an entirely different destiny, and therein, I suspect, lies the principal explanatory factor for the widely varying treatments of the two refugee sagas.

While we essentially disappeared from the world's radar screen overnight—if ever we were on it—as we embarked on our new lives, the Palestinians did not. To the contrary, for a whole host of reasons—partly of their own making, partly of the making of cynical Arab leaders, and partly of the making of generally well-intentioned but shortsighted third parties—the Palestinians weren't afforded the same chance to start new lives. Instead, they were manipulated and instrumentalized.

The Palestinians were placed in refugee camps and encouraged to stay there, generation after generation. They benefited from the support of the United Nations Relief and Works Agency (UNRWA), the UN body founded over half a century ago, not to resettle them, but rather to maintain them in those camps by providing a range of educational and social services.

Incidentally, the vast majority of UNRWA funds have not come from the Arab countries—many of which do not contribute a single penny—but from Western nations. In fact, the Arab nations combined donate a minuscule percent of the total annual UNRWA budget. So much for the crocodile tears of compassion and empathy that we periodically hear from the Arab world.

The UN also runs the United Nations High Commission for Refugees (UNHCR), which is responsible for the 22 or 23 million refugees in the world today who are outside the borders of their native lands and unable to return. UNHCR seeks to resettle those refugees in immigrant-receiving countries or otherwise help them adjust to new lives. Uniquely, the Palestinian refugee population is outside the orbit of UNHCR. Why?

It's obvious. Whatever the official explanation, maintaining the refugee camps provides the incubators for the ongoing war against Israel. After all, if the refugees were actually given the chance to start productive new lives, as we were, then their animus toward Israel might, heaven forbid, start to dissipate and their propensity to produce "martyrs" in terrorist operations against Israel would diminish.

I've searched high and low for another explanation that makes good sense, but I can't for the life of me find it. The sad truth is that the leaders of the Arab world never wanted to solve the Palestinian refugee problem; they preferred to nurture it, maintain it front and center, and thus keep alive their grievances against Israel for the entire world to see.

And, lo and behold, many in the world took the bait, became almost hypnotically preoccupied with the plight of the Palestinian refugees, without ever asking the hard questions, and never once thought of us—Jews from Arab lands. Out of sight, out of mind, I suppose.

Had these diplomats, politicians, journalists, and human rights activists asked the tough questions, it might have dawned on them that the Palestinian refugee problem came about because the Arab world rejected the 1947 UN Partition Plan and declared war on the fledgling State of Israel in 1948; that only Jordan, among all the Arab countries professing concern for the Palestinians, offered them citizenship and a real new start; and that the Arab countries cynically used the Palestinians when it served their purposes, but otherwise left them to fend for themselves (or worse).

Moreover, had they not abandoned critical judgment long ago, these international actors might wonder why there are still refugee camps in cities like Jenin.

The 1993 Oslo Accords provided for Israeli withdrawal from all the major cities on the West Bank and direct Palestinian rule. Astonishing, isn't it, that even under full Palestinian Authority control the refugee camps were not dismantled? Has anyone ever bothered to ask aloud why?

Another thing upsets me as well.

Sometimes I feel as if the world thinks of the Palestinian refugee problem as the only one of its kind.

Tragically, there've been hundreds of millions of refugees in history, probably more. Sooner or later, just about all of them found new homes and launched new lives. And there have been massive exchanges of populations as a result of war and territorial adjustments. Millions of people were on the move in both directions when Britain partitioned India and Pakistan in 1947, and Greece and Turkey experienced major exchanges earlier in the century.

None of this is meant to minimize the tragedy of dispossession or dislocation. I know. I've been there. Instinctively, my heart goes out to any refugee. But why are the Palestinians treated as if they were the only refugee problem worthy of boundless sympathy, and why do so many otherwise well-intentioned institutions and individuals go along with this?

And while I'm letting off steam, let me mention one other thing that troubles me.

It's when Arab spokesmen stand up and manage a straight face as they assert that there is no anti-Semitism in the Arab world. After all, they contend, Arabs are Semites, so, by definition, they cannot be anti-Semites. Give me a break. This gives new meaning to the notion of sophistry. It's well known that the term "anti-Semitism" was coined in 1879 by a German, Wilhelm Marr, no friend of the Jews, to describe a sense of hatred and hostility toward Jews and Judaism alone.

The Arab spokesmen don't stop there.

They claim that Jews were always well treated in Arab societies, pointing out that the Holocaust occurred in Christian Europe. True enough, the Holocaust did take place in Christian Europe and, equally true, there were periods of relative quiet and harmony in the Arab world, but the discussion can't end there. The absence of a Holocaust—putting aside, for a moment, the unrestrained enthusiasm with which some Arab political and religious leaders embraced Hitler and the Nazi Final Solution—does not in itself mean that Jews were always treated fairly and equally, only that the level of discrimination and persecution never reached the same heights as in wartime Europe.

And, yes, citing the experience of Jews in Andalusia under Muslim rule from the eighth to the twelfth centuries, or noting that the twelfth-century sage Maimonides settled in Egypt, is a reminder of a different—and far more promising—era. But Arab spokesmen underscore the weakness of their case by the need to go back hundreds of years to find such laudable examples of tolerance and harmony, since they don't seem able to come up with anything remotely similar in more recent times.

Finally, they assert that if Israel didn't exist, there would have been no problem with Jews in Arab lands. That's another bizarre argument. By that logic, there shouldn't be one million Arab citizens of Israel, but, of course, there are. Those Arabs who remained in Israel after 1948 were given citizenship, voting rights, religious freedom, and the opportunity to send their children to Arabic-language schools. That's pluralism and democracy at work, even if there are flaws in the system. While Israel has faced war and terrorism initiated by Arab neighbors, it never asked its own Arab populace to pay the price. By contrast, the Arab nations forced their Jewish communities to pay a very high price. I'm living proof.

I may be a forgotten Jew, but my voice will not remain silent. It cannot, for if it does, it becomes an accomplice to historical denial and revisionism.

I will speak out because my ancestors deserve no less.

I will speak out because my glorious age-old tradition warrants it.

I will speak out because I will not allow the Arab conflict with Israel to be defined unfairly through the prism of one refugee population only, the Palestinian.

I will speak out because the injustice inflicted on me must, once and for all, be acknowledged and addressed, however long that process may take.

I will speak out because what happened to me is now being done, with eerie familiarity, to another minority group in the region, the Christians, and once again I see the world averting its eyes, as if denial ever solved anything.

I will speak out because I refuse to be a forgotten Jew.

Letter from Athens
April 22, 2003

Greece, the first garden of liberty's tree.
Thomas Campbell*

It had been some time since I last saw the familiar red flag with the hammer and sickle up close. To be honest, I didn't miss it.

In 1974, I had had more than enough exposure to that flag. Teaching in the Soviet Union for several months, until my expulsion, I was treated to a daily dose of it. Watching my school—Moscow School Number 45—march in the annual parade marking the 1917 Bolshevik Revolution had immersed me in a veritable, and suffocating, sea of red. And traveling frequently to neighboring Warsaw Pact nations had only added to the experience. No surprise in any of that.

What did come as a surprise, though, in moving to Rome in 1975 to work with Soviet Jewish refugees in transit, was discovering the popularity of the Italian Communist Party and the ubiquity of that red flag with the hammer and sickle even there. Sure, Italians touted the moderation of their form of communism, in contrast, say, to the more Stalinist brand embraced by their French counterparts. But it still came as a shock to see young, well-educated Italians proclaiming their belief in anything even remotely linked to the profoundly corrupt, stifling, repressive system I had just experienced firsthand, and that Soviet Jews (and others) were fleeing in droves.

In the 1980s, the flag was still around, but its popularity was in a free fall. By the 1990s it was only to be found in a handful of places, principally China, North Korea, and Cuba.

But on that lovely Saturday only a few weeks ago, right smack in the heart of Athens, the red banners and flags with the hammer and sickle filled half of Syntagma (Constitution) Square. They were an intrinsic part of the mass demonstration organized to protest the war in Iraq. And they were in good company—the Palestinian flag was almost as popular. The signs held aloft included "Bush=Hitler,"

*Scottish poet, 1777–1844

"Bush=Sharon=Hitler," "Stop USA and British Barbarism," and "USA," with the letter S depicted either as a swastika or in the form of the Nazi SS.

> *We make war that we may live in peace.*
> Aristotle

Needless to say, there was not a single banner even remotely criticizing Saddam Hussein or his murderous regime—yet why should that come as a surprise? The organizers, purporting to defend the human rights of the Iraqi people, chose only to assail America's "imperialist" policies (and Britain's as well), while blithely ignoring nearly three decades of Iraqi-initiated war, terrorism, torture, and tyranny. But then, as the *New York Times* reported on April 7, a poll released three days earlier revealed that "94 percent of Greeks oppose the war against Iraq. Last month, another survey showed that more Greeks had a positive view of Saddam Hussein than of Mr. Bush and that a majority of those polled believed that the United States was as undemocratic as Iraq."

The strong anti-U.S. sentiment was captured by the remarks of the Greek composer, Mikis Theodorakis, quoted in the same *Times* article, who called Americans "detestable, ruthless cowards and murderers of the people of the world. From now on, I will consider as my enemy those who interact with these barbarians for whatever reason."

> *What greater crime can an orator be charged with than that his opinions and his language are not the same?*
> Demosthenes

Our American Jewish Committee delegation was in the city for meetings with Foreign Minister George Papandreou (our third meeting with him in the past seven months), the American ambassador, and the leaders of the Greek Jewish community. With our luck, the hotel housing us fronted on none other than Syntagma Square. To make matters still more interesting, our hotel was named the Grande Bretagne, a not-so-subtle reference to the other "culprit" country.

As the *New York Times* reported on April 16:

> Britain, too, has drawn Greek ire. Late last week, the organizers of an
> international book fair [in Athens] announced that they had withdrawn
> their invitation to British participants, who were supposed to be the
> guests of honor.

The night before the demonstration, the hotel management had
slipped under each door a notice urging guests not to leave or enter the
building the next day between noon and 3 P.M.

Unwilling to miss such a big event, we left the hotel at 11:30 A.M.
and waded through the assembling, and largely good-natured, crowd,
who were being treated to the blare of—you guessed it—American
rock music.

By the time we returned to the hotel at 3:30, the crowd had moved
on toward the American Embassy, leaving the façade of our hotel splat-
tered with red paint reaching up to the second floor and anti-American
graffiti scrawled on an exterior wall and the sidewalk in front of the
entrance.

It was striking to watch hotel employees on their hands and knees
trying to clean up the mess left by a crowd purported to have the
"workers of the world" at the heart of their concerns. But then, of
course, these hotel employees had committed the "sin" of working for
the "capitalist running dogs" in order to put bread on the table and,
therefore, presumably deserved their hapless fate.

As circumstances would have it, we were to meet with the American
ambassador that very afternoon in the hotel café. The meeting had
originally been set for 1 P.M., but his security detail, monitoring the
events, eventually decided on 4 P.M., by which time things were once
again deemed safe.

When the ambassador, an old friend, arrived, he told us that there
was no damage to the American embassy this time around. During the
last demonstration, forty-two windows had been broken. To our surprise, he added that the security budget for our nation's embassy in
Athens was the second highest in the world, following Beirut.

The problem, it seems, is twofold.

First, there has long been a strong current of anti-Americanism in Greece. It comes principally from the left—the hard-core elements of the ruling Pasok (Pan-Hellenic Socialist Movement) Party which, under Prime Minister Andreas Papandreou, the party's founder, took a staunchly anti-American, anti-NATO, pro-Arab, and pro-Third World (*Tritokosmikos*, or "Third Worldism") line through the 1980s; lingering resentment over America's unabashed support of the right-wing military junta, led by George Papadopoulos, that ruled Greece from 1967 to 1974; and the 5 percent to 8 percent of the population that today identifies with the communist movement, a legacy of a much stronger communist influence in years past.

It is often forgotten that the communists almost overran Greece. As Roy Jenkins writes of the years 1944-45 in his magisterial biography of Winston Churchill:

> In the run-up to the last Christmas of the war ... Churchill's preoccupation was not with the Ardennes, but with Greece. As the Germans withdrew from Greece the ELAS guerrillas made a determined attempt to take over the government of the country. [ELAS was the military wing, and EAM was the political wing, of the Greek wartime resistance. Both were under Communist control.] One of Churchill's strongest resolves was that this should not be allowed to happen. A Communist Greece, he thought, would be a disaster for the Western Allies.... This had within a few years become firmly settled American policy. The United States commitment to sustain the democratic countries of Europe against Soviet expansionism could be dated almost precisely to the proclamation of the Truman Doctrine at the end of February 1947, when America took over British commitments for the defense of Greece and Turkey.

Second, until recently Greece was known throughout intelligence circles as a weak and notoriously unreliable link in the struggle against terrorism. Only with the dramatic arrests in the last few months of members of the deadly November 17 faction, whose victims have included Americans, has this begun to change. Indeed, it was the image of Greece as soft on terrorism that almost doomed its chances to host the 2004 Summer Olympic Games.

Of course, Greek opposition to American-led military action in Iraq was far from unique in Europe. Big demonstrations were organized in virtually every major capital of the European Union member countries, Saddam Hussein's thuggish regime was a nonissue, and polls showed overwhelming percentages of the population against the war option. Still, there is something distinctive about the Greek situation.

Any excuse will serve a tyrant.
    Aesop

Americans readily—and understandably—succumb to the alluring charm of Greece, and especially its islands, as a tourist destination. Moreover, Greeks all seem to have relatives in the United States. Yet anti-Americanism runs quite deep, and it's not just from the left.

In the 1990s, the country as a whole, animated by the strong link between Greek national and religious identity, largely sided with the Serbs, fellow Orthodox, in the latest round of the Balkan wars, and thus strongly opposed U.S. support for the Bosnian Muslims and, later, the NATO bombing of Serbia.

Even so, one shouldn't exaggerate. Americans are made to feel welcome in Greece. As one Greek told us, "It's American policy, not the American people, which we object to." And, of course, Greece is a member of NATO and has a thick web of relations with the United States. Currently holding the presidency of the European Union, Athens has by all accounts handled the job, and particularly the complex transatlantic agenda, skillfully.

Costas Simitis replaced Papandreou as prime minister in 1996. The new Greek leader, though hailing from the same Pasok political party, has softened Greece's hard edge and reoriented Greek foreign policy, building smoother ties with the United States. He has been greatly assisted by the widely admired foreign minister, George Papandreou, the Amherst-educated son of Andreas Papandreou and grandson of George Papandreou, another Greek prime minister.

Greece has also come a very long way in its policy toward Israel.

In 1947, Greece voted against Resolution 181, the UN Partition Plan calling for the creation of a Jewish and an Arab state in Mandatory Palestine. In 1975, it abstained on the infamous "Zionism is racism" resolution adopted by the UN General Assembly. More shocking still, it was the last country in Western Europe to establish full ambassadorial ties with the State of Israel.

All virtue is summed up in dealing justly.
Aristotle

Though it is little remembered today, when Arafat was expelled from Lebanon in 1982, he chose to go first to Athens, asserting that the Arab nations, unlike Greece, had failed to help him. Indeed, during that decade, Papandreou reached out not only to the PLO but also embraced Libya and Syria, while giving Israel the cold shoulder. It was all part of a policy called *Anoigma*, an orientation to the Arab world, driven largely by considerations of ideology, geography, economy, and, perhaps above all, the pursuit of allies in its longstanding conflict with Turkey.

A few examples of this policy: During the 1980s, Greece became the first European Community (now the European Union) member to extend official diplomatic recognition to the PLO. In 1984, Greece signed an agreement to sell $500 million worth of Greek-manufactured weapons to Qaddhafi's Libya. And in 1986, after Britain revealed Syrian complicity in a plot to blow up an El Al airliner departing from London, Greece was the only country in the then twelve-member European Community that ignored London's call for punitive measures against Damascus.

Wrong must not win by technicalities.
Aeschylus

The American Jewish Committee first met with the Greek leader in the mid-1980s. Our primary goal was to press for closer ties between Greece and Israel. It was not our most successful diplomatic effort, though Papandreou could be rather disarming, I learned. After all, how many prime ministers of foreign lands can claim to have lived in exile in the United States for over two decades, become an American citizen, served in the U.S. Navy during World War II, and come to admire many Jews at Harvard, where he received his Ph.D. in economics, or at Berkeley, where he taught for eight years?

I particularly remember the prime minister's self-assured lecture to us, which went essentially as follows: I know Arafat. I know Assad. I know Qaddhafi. I know the Arabs, and I know the Muslims. I can tell you that Israel can trust them to make peace. Take a chance. Take my word for it. Peace is possible.

A few years later, we met with Papandreou again. It was the 1990s, the world had been turned upside down by the disintegration of the USSR and Yugoslavia, and he was back in office for a third term (1993-96) after four years in the opposition.

In the meantime, under his successor, Prime Minister Constantinos Mitsotakis of the right-of-center Nea Dimokratia (New Democratic Party), Greece had opened a new chapter in its bilateral link with Israel, strengthening ties and, in 1992, signing a bilateral cooperation agreement on culture, education, and science.

Let me add an important historical footnote before going any further.

To underscore the importance of intergroup relations, leaders of the American Jewish Committee and the Greek American community had been working collaboratively for years to usher in a new era in Greek-Israeli relations and, for that matter, in ties between Cyprus and Israel. Together we had traveled to Athens, Nicosia, and Jerusalem and met countless times with Greek and Cypriot officials, including during their visits to the United States. Enough good things cannot be said about the role played by the Greek American community, led by Andy Athens of Chicago and Andy Manatos of Washington, in encouraging the positive trend begun by Prime Minister Mitsotakis (and later followed by President Glafcos Clerides of Cyprus); the determined efforts of the late David Roth, AJC's intergroup diplomat par excellence, should certainly not be forgotten, either.

To be both a speaker of words and a doer of deeds.
Homer

In this new era, Papandreou's speech to us was rather different. It went something like this: Greece is surrounded by mortal danger from an encroaching Muslim world. Iranian mujahideen are moving into Bosnia. Albania is unraveling and hundreds of thousands of Albanians are trying to enter Greece. In Macedonia (which the Greeks call the Former Yugoslav Republic of Macedonia, or FYROM), the Albanian minority is stirring up trouble and looking to link up with their brethren in Albania and Kosovo to form a Greater Albania on Greece's northern border. Turkey, to the east, is a permanent menace to us. Who better than our Jewish friends can understand the Muslim peril we again face, having already once been occupied for centuries by Muslims? Who better than Israel can grasp the danger to our survival as a Western outpost in this turbulent region?

Papandreou's thinking had evolved to the point where, in 1994, Greece and Israel adopted a protocol for military cooperation, a quantum leap forward in the bilateral relationship. In the ensuing years, still more progress was attained in this sector. Greece came to understand the value of enhancing ties with a fellow democracy in the eastern Mediterranean. It also realized that Turkish-Israeli links were developing rapidly and, while not directed at Greece, could potentially leave Athens out in the cold. And it recognized that gestures toward Israel might be well received in Washington.

Today, according to the Greek Foreign Ministry, Israel is Greece's most important Middle East market for exports. As many as 200,000 Israelis annually visit Greece, an important source of income for a country heavily dependent on tourism. And the Greek government has noticeably toned down its anti-Israel rhetoric, while contacts between the two countries continue to increase.

The Greek media, however, is another story. It is overwhelmingly hostile to Israel and, to put it mildly, doesn't shy away from sensationalism. Ariel Sharon is never likely to get a fair hearing, and Israel is routinely portrayed as the aggressor, irrespective of the facts on the ground.

This media climate also makes it very tough for the small Greek Jewish community. Just after 9/11, for example, the American Jewish Committee received an urgent e-mail from a Jewish leader noting that the Greek media was peddling the vicious canard that the Mossad was behind the terrorist acts and that, forewarned, 4,000 Jews had stayed away from the World Trade Center on that fateful day. We were asked to provide ASAP the names of those Jews killed on 9/11 to disprove the media's claims.

The Central Board of Jewish Communities in Greece issued a report in September 2002 citing the media's irresponsibility in presenting Israel as a "Nazi country" and portraying Palestinian suicide bombers as nothing more than "persons in a state of despair."

Have I missed the mark, or like a true archer, do I strike my quarry? Or am I a prophet of lies, a babbler from door to door?
Cassandra in Aeschylus's *Agamemnon*

The report asserted that "the anti-Israeli atmosphere has led to several anti-Semitic incidents" and proceeded to describe those incidents in detail. Several press accounts, the report noted, went so far as to point a finger at the Greek Jewish community for its "apathy" in the face of "the genocide of the Palestinian people by Sharon." In effect, Greek Jews were being accused of indirect complicity in these alleged crimes.

The Jewish community's unsettling findings were buttressed by another study issued two months later by the Greek Helsinki Monitor. Entitled *Anti-Semitism in Greece, A Current Picture: 2001-2002*, the conclusions were equally disturbing:

[T]he real depth of anti-Semitism in Greek consciousness is evidenced by the ease with which it manifests itself in mainstream expression, unimpeded and seemingly unnoticed, during times of crisis. The Greek press has played a major role in this area. Since September 11, 2001, and with the increasing violence in the Middle East, the blatant anti-Semitism regularly heard on the fringe has been voiced in the print (especially) and electronic media by a spectrum of influential personalities in politics, labor, education, and culture. So widely discussed was the rumor that 4,000 Jews working in the World Trade Center were forewarned and thus escaped death, that a poll taken for state TV showed 43 percent of Greeks as believing the rumor, as opposed to 30 percent who did not.

History has amply demonstrated that if a country's leaders are silent or equivocal in the face of anti-Semitism, the message to the population is crystal clear—there are no serious consequences for expressions of anti-Semitism. Conversely, if leaders are outspoken and resolute, then it is possible, if not to eliminate anti-Semitism, at least to render it socially and politically unacceptable in mainstream society.

Unfortunately, the Greek Helsinki Monitor report offers little encouragement in this regard:

The Greek government has yet to take a strong and consistent stand against anti-Semitism. Even extreme anti-Semitic views openly expressed by Orthodox clergy members, politicians, factions, cultural icons, and journalists pass without comment. Attacks on Jewish monuments and property receive little, if any, attention in the media and faint condemnation by the political and spiritual leadership. Of course, many members of Greek society find these acts disturbing. Yet the prevailing tendency is to compare them to the larger-scale anti-Semitic violence elsewhere in Europe, and judge them to be inconsequential or at least not a serious threat.... Because anti-Semitism is a non-issue, no internal or external pressure is exerted to modify media portrayals or alter public opinion, as is the case with other forms of racism.

Against this backdrop, the Greek Jewish community is all the more remarkable for its resilience and commitment.

Numbering not more than 5,000 in a country of 10.6 million (less than 0.05 percent of the population), they are the heirs and custodians of a Jewish presence in Greece that dates back more than 2,000 years and which has played a significant role in the country's history, not to mention Jewish history. And, needless to say, the larger topic of the intersection of Greek and Jewish civilizations is a vast subject unto itself.

Where the Hebrew asked: "What must I do?" the Greek asked: "Why must I do it?" Matthew Arnold has put the differences between the two spirits in a series of famous epigrams. The uppermost idea with the Greek was to see things as they really are; the uppermost idea with the Hebrew was conduct and obedience. The Hebrew believed in the beauty of holiness, the Greek believed in the holiness of beauty.

Abram Leon Sachar, *A History of the Jews*

From Crete to Rhodes, from Corfu to Elos, from Larissa to Ioannina, from Corinth to Patras, and from Athens to Salonika—and this is only a partial list—Jews were, and in some cases still are, an essential part of the Greek landscape.

Some of these Jews are Romaniots, the original Jews on Greek soil. They are neither Ashkenazi nor Sephardi, but a direct link to the world of Hellenistic Jewry. Flavius Josephus, the renowned first-century Jewish historian and general, and Benjamin of Tudela, the celebrated twelfth-century Jewish traveler and chronicler, were among those who documented the earlier history of the Romaniots.

Other Greek Jews, in fact the vast majority, are Sephardi. They found refuge from Spain and Portugal in the Ottoman Empire, which was the occupying power in Greece during the period of the Inquisition (and until the Greek revolution in 1821). And a few Ashkenazi Jews made their way to Greece in the nineteenth century.

By the year 1537, Salonika (aka Thessaloniki) was being described as the "metropolis of Israel, city of justice, mother of Israel, like Jerusalem."

World War II brought with it the brutal Nazi occupation of Greece and the devastation of Greek Jewry, a tragedy that has received less attention than it deserves. Thousands of Greek Jews joined their compatriots in defending the homeland, but in less than two months the country fell to the invading forces. By the war's end, an estimated 65,000 Greek Jews, 85 percent of the total Jewish population, had been exterminated, principally in Auschwitz-Birkenau.

Even more Jews might have been deported and killed had it not been for the actions of the church. As Moses Constantinis, the current president of the Central Board of Jewish Communities in Greece, wrote recently in the *Forward*, "The Greek Orthodox Church in particular—and in contrast to centuries of official animosity toward the community—helped many Jews escape deportation."

Close to 45,000 of the Shoah's victims were from Salonika, leaving a once great center of Jewish life in tatters. Today only about 1,000 Jews live in this lovely city on the Aegean, seeking to preserve memory while, against all the odds, planning for the future. The community's current president is hoping to attract Argentine Jews of Greek ancestry emigrating from a country whose economy has been in a tailspin for several years.

The largest concentration of Jews is now in Athens, the nation's sprawling capital, which is in the midst of a major makeover for the 2004 Olympics, where a Jewish school, museum, synagogue, and numerous organizations all function.

The Greek Jewish community, like Jews elsewhere, is concerned with the intertwined challenges of grappling with static numbers, sustaining communal institutions, and inculcating Jewish identity in their youth.

It is also acutely aware of the external challenges—widespread lack of sympathy for Israel's situation; expressions of anti-Semitism; limited public understanding of the Shoah generally and the Greek Jewish tragedy specifically; scant political and cultural impact; and the enormous influence wielded by the Orthodox Church on the life of a country 95 percent of whose population identifies, however nominally, with the church.

To be sure, on a daily basis, life can be very good. The roots of the Jewish community—and its sense of national pride—run very deep in Greece's soil. The country as a whole has prospered in recent years thanks to its membership in the European Union. (Not so long ago its citizens emigrated in search of economic opportunity—witness the large Greek communities in places like Astoria, Queens, or Melbourne, Australia—but today Greece is experiencing immigration, principally from the Balkan countries and the Middle East.) And there is that indisputably seductive Mediterranean joie de vivre, which turns every meal, every cup of coffee, every stroll, and, of course, every vacation into something hard to beat.

> *Of all the peoples, the Greeks have best dreamed the dream of life.*
>
> Johann Goethe

When you stop to think about just what this tiny Jewish community is shouldering, it's another truly inspiring reminder of the indomitability of the Jewish spirit.

Letter from a Graduation Speaker[*]
May 1, 2003

Dear Graduates and Friends,

In preparation for this auspicious occasion, I read several commencement addresses, both those delivered at the campuses of Hebrew Union College and elsewhere.

While reading the texts couldn't give me a sense of audience reaction, I suspect among the most popular commencement addresses was the one allegedly delivered by the noted artist Salvador Dali. Let me read you the entire speech: "I will be so brief, I have already finished."

All graduation speakers should probably take their cue from him. After all, when was the last time an audience complained about a speech being too short?

Perhaps you've heard the story, presumably apocryphal, about the commencement speaker at Yale who used the four letters of the university's name as the blueprint for his speech.

For ten minutes he spoke about the "Y" as in youth, followed by fifteen minutes about the "A" as in ambition, then twenty minutes about the "L" as in loyalty to the institution, and, finally, twenty-five minutes

---

[*] This is the text of a graduation address at Hebrew Union College in New York.

about the "E" as in excellence. When he left the podium, he noticed a student who seemed particularly struck by the speech and asked what in particular had touched him. The student replied: "How lucky I am that I didn't attend the Massachusetts Institute of Technology!"

Like many given this privilege, I simply can't resist the temptation to share a few thoughts, but promise not to use the letters of Hebrew Union College-Jewish Institute of Religion as the take-off point for my remarks.

Let me first of all applaud this remarkable institution and those associated with it—administrators, faculty, trustees, supporters, and, not least, students, and, of course, their parents. And let me add a special word of admiration for your truly outstanding president, David Ellenson. For over 125 years the Hebrew Union College has made an extraordinary contribution to the life of the Jewish people worldwide.

You have impressively balanced modernity and tradition, scholarship and service, the sacred and the quotidian.

In a word, you have led by example.

While proudly committed to the Reform movement, you have opened your doors to all streams of Judaism, giving true meaning to the notion of *am echad*, one people. Just last year, I believe, Rabbi Ismar Schorsch, the chancellor of the Jewish Theological Seminary, stood here at this podium, while Rabbi Emanuel Rackman of Bar-Ilan University was given an honorary doctorate.

You have opened your doors to Christian and other religious scholars as well, underscoring the vital importance—never more so than today—of advancing interfaith dialogue and understanding. I note the fact that the Reverend Peter John Gomes of Harvard University addressed this graduation ceremony four years ago, and that my friend Father John Pawlikowski of the Chicago Theological Union was the commencement speaker at the Cincinnati graduation two years ago. And it is noteworthy that among this evening's graduates are two Christian clergy from Nigeria.

We live in a world in which the jury—that's spelled j-u-r-y, not J-e-w-r-y—is still out on the balance of forces both within and among religions and, consequently, whether religion as such will ultimately be part of the solution, i.e., as a force for harmony and peace, or, conversely, be part of the problem, i.e., as a force for division and strife. This community—your community—has long ago taken its stand, and I for one could not be more admiring.

May your example prove contagious.

And permit me to applaud you, the graduates, not only for your impressive academic achievements but, every bit as much, for taking a personal stand.

By choosing to pursue graduate studies and a career in pastoral care and counseling, education, sacred music, and, of course, the rabbinate, you say something profound about yourselves.

You say that the work of repairing this broken world is not someone else's task, it is yours.

You say that in a world where self-gratification and self-entitlement are increasingly, even obsessively, the watchwords of the day, you choose instead to focus on those in need. You stand in stark contrast to the two tycoons in the *New Yorker* cartoon sitting in luxurious armchairs, with one saying to the other: "I, too, longed to find a cause greater than myself. Fortunately, I never did."

In other words, in a world in which quality-of-*life* issues dominate, you are preoccupied with quality-of-*living* issues.

You say, in the words of Rabbi Stephen Wise, founder of the Jewish Institute of Religion, a component of this school, that life is "not a matter of extent but of content."

You say that in a world in quest of the material, you are in search of the sacred.

You say that in a world focused on the here and now, you are linked to a time line that stretches back millennia and that you are determined will stretch forward no less far.

May your example prove contagious.

As you embark on the next stage of your lives, perhaps most aptly described as "a post-tuition era," may I offer, consistent with my assigned role, a few words of reflection.

Hackneyed though it may sound, believe in yourselves and your capacity to make an imprint on the world around you, to leave the world a better, more humane place than you found it.

Today, quite naturally, you look ahead as you embark on your careers, but let me ask you for just a moment to fast-forward to the end of your careers—an unusual request on this of all days, I realize—and try to imagine the criteria you will use to assess how your professional lives were spent. In brief, did you make a difference? Were you alert both to the opportunities and, yes, dangers that emerged on your watch? How many times will you use the words "should have" in your assessment?

Let me take one decisive historical reference point as illustration.

I ask myself what the Jewish world must have looked like just after World War II ended.

Think about it.

One-third of the Jewish people had been exterminated within twelve years of the infamous prediction of American Secretary of State Cordell Hull, who said in *Time* magazine, shortly after Adolf Hitler's ascension to power in 1933, that "mistreatment of Jews in Germany may be considered virtually eliminated."

An entirely new vocabulary of genocide had been invented to implement the Nazi Final Solution—from Auschwitz to Zyklon-B.

The great centers of Jewish civilization and study from Berlin to Vilna, from Warsaw to Salonika, had been decimated.

The participants in the genocide had been many, the bystanders far more numerous still, and the blessed *Hasidei umot ha'olam*, the Righteous among the Nations, so frightfully few.

As one survivor, Dr. Hadassah Rosensaft, said:

> For the greatest part of the liberated Jews of Bergen-Belsen, there was no ecstasy, no joy at our liberation. We had lost our families, our homes. We had no place to go, nobody to hug. Nobody was waiting for us anywhere. We had been liberated from death and the fear of death, but not from the fear of life.

Palestine was largely closed to Jewish entry, as Leon Uris, whom you honor this evening, has so poignantly written in his legendary *Exodus*, a book that had a life-changing effect on so many, myself included, and that served as a catalyst for the reawakening of Jewish life in the Soviet Union. Thousands, tens of thousands, of Jews who tried to make their way to Palestine were intercepted by the British and shamefully interned on Cyprus or elswhere.

And American Jews became painfully aware of their powerlessness to influence the course of wartime events and save European Jewry, despite the indefatigable efforts of individuals like Rabbi Stephen Wise.

Can you imagine the degree of courage, fortitude, and faith required to pick up the strewn pieces of shattered lives after the war and march on?

Yet there were those who somehow found the strength, forged the vision, and navigated the turbulent waters to write a new—and promising—chapter in the Jewish saga.

There were those who never suffered from a failure of imagination, or the resolve to match. Speaking of imagination and resolve, Daniel Goldin, on whom you confer an honorary degree this evening, most certainly never lacked for either in his remarkable career at NASA.

There were those who inspired others not only by the power of their words but, more importantly still, by the example of their deeds.

There were those who believed that the Jewish mission on earth had only become more urgent—to bring God and humanity closer to one another; to remind us that we are all, each and every one of us, God's children created in the divine image; and to recall that we have been given the gift of moral choice, and that we must seek to make the right choices—to lift the falling, heal the ailing, welcome the stranger, and recognize holiness in the world around us.

There were those who resolved that the time had come for the Jewish people to become authors of history, and never again its victims.

These individuals, this determined Jewish people, succeeded brilliantly, beyond anyone's wildest dream.

Against all the odds, Israel was established and survived a crucible unlike any other nation in modern history. And not only did it survive, it flourished.

It built an army and defended itself against those who would destroy it, defying the confident predictions of many outside military experts.

A prospering state emerged, a democratic state, a growing state. Avram Burg, who is receiving an honorary doctorate this evening, symbolizes the dynamism of that state.

Distinguished universities were founded. The land was lovingly restored. And Jews the world over felt a powerful surge of pride in a nation reborn.

Israel's challenges, both internal and external, seem never-ending at times but, stepping back for a moment from the daily torrent of news, its record of achievement in state-building has been nothing short of breathtaking.

And American Jews fared remarkably well in the postwar world. They found their footing in an increasingly open and inclusive America, and raised their voices effectively on behalf of Israel, endangered Jewish communities, universal human rights, and the crying need for social justice for all Americans.

Together, in other words, leaders on both sides of the ocean moved mountains.

Can you imagine? In the 1970s—and I was a witness—many Soviet non-Jews sought to forge papers proving they were Jews, so they could attempt to leave the country and begin new lives in the West.

Just thirty years earlier, during the Nazi occupation, to be a Jew on Soviet soil meant almost certain deportation or death.

Just twenty or twenty-five years earlier, under the Stalinist regime, to be a Jew on Soviet soil could have meant arrest and imprisonment on charges of "cosmopolitanism" or other anti-Soviet activity.

Yet, by the 1970s there were those who saw in Jewish identity a ticket to life, an escape route from the pervasive suffocation of communist oppression. They saw a State of Israel committed to assisting Soviet Jews to repatriate to the historic Jewish homeland and offer them a new start. They saw the Jews of the world using whatever political leverage they could muster to part the Iron Curtain, and to let the Jews cross, if you will, from the Sea of Red to the Sky of Blue. And both Jews *and* non-Jews desperately wanted to be a part of this modern-day exodus.

And I witnessed it again in the 1980s, when some Ethiopian Muslims and Christians tried to pass themselves off as Jews to escape the grinding poverty and chronic starvation beleaguering their native land. They saw Jews being rescued and given a new lease on life, and they wanted no less.

These two examples powerfully underscore the complete transformation of the Jewish people within a span of but a few decades.

To be a Jew had become synonymous with life, with freedom and opportunity—a 180-degree turnaround.

And if that happened, it came about, again, because of the determination of those Jewish giants—some sung, others unsung—who simply refused to accept defeat for the Jewish people in the wake of the Shoah.

Now let's come back to the present.

Starting next week, next month, or perhaps next year, you will join the leadership ranks.

What awaits you?

Henceforth, you will have the chance day in and day out to touch the lives of others in meaningful ways—to awaken consciences, to stir souls, to lift spirits, to open hearts, to expand knowledge, to fortify hope, to build community, to pursue justice, and, in doing so, to mobilize those around you to stand with you.

You will have the opportunity to remind fellow Jews that, as Mordecai Kaplan said, "One cannot be a Jew without actively belonging to the Jewish people, even as one cannot be a soldier without belonging to an army."

But be warned, as if you needed such a cautionary note. You are dealing with that most inexact of sciences—human nature and human relations. Still more, you are dealing with the most infinitely complex and largely uncharted set of issues therein—faith, identity, and spirituality.

Moreover, the world in which we live is not without its complications. Just read the superb books and articles of Judy Miller, whom you honor tonight, to understand how complicated a world it really is.

And for Jews these days, that complexity is especially true. As someone once said: "Jews are just like everyone else, only more so."

We have no end of external challenges—international terrorism targeted at the West generally and at Jews in particular; Israel's age-old and unfinished pursuit of peace and security in a hazardous region where the notion of a Jewish sovereign state is still not universally accepted, much less preached from the pulpit or taught in the schools; a growing tolerance for intolerance, especially when it comes to Jews, and, as a result, a steady erosion of the postwar taboo on the expression of anti-Semitism in otherwise civilized societies; and, more broadly, a world in which too many continue to suffer from the ravages of injustice, oppression, disease, and poverty.

As if that weren't a full enough plate, our internal challenges are no less daunting.

Israel still struggles with defining the elusive nature of a Jewish democratic state; relations between Israel and American Jewry are tested by the passage of time, as well as by discontent among a sizable number of American Jews about the handling of religious issues in Israel; the ties that bind us as Jews worldwide are subject to the sometimes gale-force winds of narrow-minded, self-serving perspectives; religion in America is today a buyer's market, which provides both new possibilities but also significant hurdles in trying to make the case for Jewish distinctiveness and community; and Jewish demographic trends, to say the least, do not look particularly encouraging for our collective future.

Even so, a healthy dose of optimism is warranted.

For one thing, when in our history have we ever been without significant challenges, both external and internal? Some four thousand years have passed and, as the late Professor Simon Rawidowicz of Brandeis University famously wrote in *Israel, the Ever-Dying People*, each generation, including presumably our own, wonders whether there is Jewish life beyond our moment in time. The answer should be entirely obvious by now.

And for another, you, the graduates, are fortunate to be living in arguably the single most extraordinary period in Jewish history. Even with all the very real dangers we face, can you think of a more uplifting, more exhilarating moment to be a Jew?

To have the twin blessings of the sovereign State of Israel and the democratic societies of the West, led by the United States, as our homes is to be given a gift of an unprecedented, previously unimaginable opportunity. Use that gift wisely. Never, never take it for granted. And always bear in mind the remarkable examples of those men and women who bequeathed us that gift. May you find strength and inspiration in their exceptional lives.

I often think of Isaac Bashevis Singer's description of the Jewish people: "A people who can't sleep themselves and let nobody else sleep."

Perhaps my most fervent wish for you is to strive for the day when the Jewish people will finally get a good night's sleep. On that day, as Singer suggested, the rest of the world will also get a good night's sleep. And on that day humankind will have taken a quantum leap forward toward the prophetic vision of a world at peace, a world in harmony.

Mazal tov to you and your proud families and friends.

Letter from a Late Father's Son
June 15, 2003

Five years ago this month, my father passed away.

In his declining years he had few friends and only a tiny family, and since he was almost obsessively modest, little is known about my father outside a small circle. He deserved more. He was part of the generation that was put to the ultimate test, and he passed with flying colors. He saw nothing special in what he did, but what he did was awe-inspiring. We owe his generation more than we may ever realize.

On this anniversary, and coinciding with Father's Day, I thought it's time to put his story down on paper, however sketchily, and offer a glimpse into the complex life of a man who left no written record for posterity.

While in one sense, I realize, this is a very personal story, I believe it has broader implications for an understanding of the past and perhaps the present as well, hence my desire to share this letter beyond my immediate family.

Dad was born in Budapest in 1920. His full name was Erich Albert Loëwe.

His father, Michael, was also born in Budapest, in 1884, and died in New York in 1961. Dad's mother, Rela (neé Ettinger), was born in 1893 in what was then, under the Austro-Hungarian Empire, Lemberg, which later, under Soviet rule, became Lvov, and which today, as part of the Ukraine, is known as Lviv. Rela lived till the age of 91.

I was eleven when Mike, as we called him, died. I have warm memories of him, though there wasn't all that much interaction.

He and my grandmother lived in a modest one-bedroom apartment, with a profusion of door and window locks, on the first floor of a nondescript building on Manhattan's West Side. The neighborhood at the time was, to put it mildly, shaky, a far cry from its subsequent gentrification. Especially in the years that Rela lived there as a widow, her daily routine was largely governed by the onset of darkness. In winter, when daylight was brief, she'd make it a point to be home by dusk. She was simply too frightened to be outside after dark. I remember as a child feeling angry that my grandmother, who had endured an awful lot in her lifetime, was compelled to live such a restricted life in her waning years because of fear of crime.

Rela was a rather cold, reserved woman, especially in contrast to my mother's mother, who embodied all the grandmotherly traits of affection and generosity that I always assumed to be part of the job description. What most impressed me about Rela was her proficiency in languages. Everyone in my extended family who was older than me spoke several languages, but Rela was the champion. She spoke six that I knew of—Polish, Russian, Yiddish, German, Hungarian, and English—and probably one or two others that she never bothered to mention. Her fluency came not from demanding teachers but from the demands of life.

My father could trace his relatives on his father's side back to his grandparents, both of whom died when he was ten. On his mother's side, he could go back an additional generation. Everyone was from Lemberg. Not surprisingly, given the fate of Jews in this region, several family members, including a grandmother and an aunt, were killed in the Shoah.

At the time of my father's birth, Budapest had a large Jewish community. At the risk of gross oversimplification, there were three principal subgroups in the community—the assimilationists, the Zionists, and the traditionalists.

The assimilationists rejected traditional Judaism and the so-called "shtetl" or "ghetto" mentality, instead embracing emancipation, modernity, and universalism, whether in the form of liberalism or socialism. Indeed, Béla Kun, the Jewish-born Hungarian communist, had briefly led a government takeover in March 1919. (His inept regime, fortunately, lasted all of 133 days.)

The Zionists—and remember that the father of modern-day Zionism, Theodor Herzl, was born in Budapest—didn't believe in the possibility of assimilation. Anti-Semitism in European societies was simply too entrenched, they contended, and Jews would always be subject to the whim of the majority. Look at France. Didn't the crude anti-Semitism of the Dreyfus case, in an otherwise enlightened state where the full rights of Jews had long been enshrined under law, prove the impossibility of full Jewish acceptance? The only solution to the "Jewish problem" was the establishment of a sovereign Jewish state, ideally in the ancient Jewish homeland of Palestine.

The traditionalists, who ranged along a spectrum of Orthodoxy and included various Hasidic sects, were strong throughout this part of Europe, particularly outside such major cities as Budapest. They rejected assimilation and weren't enthusiastic about Zionism, either. By and large, they believed the creation of a Jewish state could only come about through the divine will of God, not through the political machinations of governments and individuals.

My father's family sat squarely in the assimilationist camp. He had little knowledge of Judaism and even less comfort in a synagogue. That made his decision to wear a Star of David later in life and to develop a profound emotional attachment to Israel, which he visited numerous times, all the more striking to me.

Dad's family moved to Vienna shortly after his birth and, in 1925, to Berlin, where my grandfather worked as a journalist for two local newspapers.

Berlin's Jews in the 1920s were an extraordinary presence in the city. To a large degree, they defined the cultural, medical, scientific, and commercial worlds. Jewish children like my father were expected, above all, to excel academically, to be well-mannered (i.e., seen but not heard), and to be well-versed in art, music, and literature.

Dad seemed to manage okay, in spite of having been moved around quite a bit at an early age and notwithstanding what must have been a fairly chilly, sterile home environment. He threw himself into math and science, loved to tinker with just about anything mechanical or electrical, and enjoyed skiing.

In 1933, Adolf Hitler came to power. Life as my father knew it was about to be shattered. By the time he would reemerge into a world at all resembling normalcy, he would be twelve years older, his childhood a distant memory.

His family left Germany almost immediately. They saw what was coming, in Germany at least. First, they went to Poland, and then sent my father, fourteen at the time, to Vienna to live with relatives. It would be well over a decade before this family of three would be reunited.

Anti-Semitism was a potent force in Vienna long before the Anschluss in 1938, but many Jews were nonetheless shocked by the paroxysms of hatred expressed by many Austrians after the Nazi takeover that year.

Dad recalled walking home from school shortly after the takeover. He was eighteen at the time. At the Kohlmarkt, in the center of Vienna, he was grabbed by uniformed members of the Nazi SS and SA and, together with a few other Jewish kids, ordered to get on their knees, and shine and polish the Nazis' boots. As my father later commented, "It seemed to me there were mountains of boots. I remember coming home to the Löwengasse 28 apartment of my aunt and uncle around 4 A.M., after seven or eight hours of this humiliating and backbreaking work."

My father couldn't abide the Austrians' postwar attempt to hide behind a lie. He had witnessed the throngs welcoming the Nazi takeover in 1938, and he knew that the 1943 Allied designation of Austria as the "first victim nation" of the Third Reich was utterly untrue. In the years after the war, he was struck by the contrast between Germany and Austria. While Germany, he pointed out, took full responsibility for the crimes of the Nazi era and sought to make amends, especially to the State of Israel and the Jewish people world-wide, Austria did nothing of the sort until very late in the day.

The last straw for him came just a few years before his death. He reluctantly applied to the then newly established Austrian National Fund for a one-time payment based on the suffering he had experienced. The truth is he hadn't wanted to ask for what he called "blood money." But I persuaded him that he should go ahead, arguing that it was better that he have the money than the Austrian government and, in any case, he needed it. To my dismay, though, he was turned down on a bureaucratic technicality. Once again, he pointed out to me, the Austrians had failed him.

In the final tragic irony, shortly after he passed away, I was notified by Vienna that his application had been reviewed again and approved. The money was donated in his memory to the American Jewish Committee to fund a Holocaust-related project.

While my father was coping with Nazis in Vienna, his mother, who had been living in Poland, moved east to the Soviet Union, and eventually ended up—it sounds like the stuff of fiction, I realize—as a cook in the Red Army. Her soldiers were lucky.

After the war's end, she headed for Melbourne, where two of her siblings had settled. She fell in love with Australia, proudly acquired citizenship, and came to the United States only because her husband and son, with whom she had reestablished contact after the war, insisted. Given her druthers, they would have joined her in Australia.

But she never gave up the Australian passport. Indeed, whenever she got angry with someone in the family, which was not infrequently, she would brandish that passport and threaten to return to Melbourne. It turned out to be all bluff, though.

Meanwhile, Dad's father fled west, making his way to France, England, and eventually the United States, settling first in Bethlehem, Pennsylvania, for reasons I never quite understood. He didn't stay there long, however, and managed to get a journalist's job that took him to Japan and, shortly before Pearl Harbor, China. In Shanghai, he was interned by the occupying Japanese army for "spying." Only in 1947 was he able to get back to the States, where he began working for the Hungarian-language division of Voice of America.

Back to my father. He left Austria in 1938 and moved to Paris. He enrolled in the faculty of physics and chemistry at the Sorbonne, and worked nights at an aircraft supplier.

It was in Paris that he first met his future wife, Nelly Chender. She, together with her parents and brother, had managed to leave Moscow in 1929 and resettle in France. Incidentally, by 1929 it was virtually impossible to get out of the Soviet Union. They were fortunate to have exchanged a centrally-located apartment in Moscow for four passports.

My mother wasn't quite fifteen when she first met my father. Then, she was only the kid sister; it was her older brother who befriended my father.

Dad finished his course and enlisted in the French army, or so he thought, in Sathonay, near Lyon. Through a clerical error, it seems, the French assigned him to the notorious North African-based Foreign Legion (La Légion étrangère) rather than the French army's Legion for Foreigners (La Légion pour les étrangers).

He was sent to Oran, then to Sidi Bel Abbes, both in French-ruled Algeria, where he did his gritty military service, often enduring taunts of *sale juif* ("dirty Jew") from the officers.

When France fell to the Nazi onslaught in June 1940, my father was placed in a prisoner-of-war camp in Kenadsa, in western Algeria. The prisoners were assigned to work in the coal mines.

In the camp, he met an Austrian inmate, Ollie, who was to become a lifelong friend. Ollie was the son of a Nazi general, but he himself was fiercely anti-Nazi. One day, Ollie's father, all decked out in a bemedaled uniform, showed up at the camp and offered to free his son if only he would reconsider his allegiance. Ollie told him to go to hell and went back to the barracks.

The work in the coal mines, I can only imagine, was perilous, claustrophobic, and debilitating. And being in the Sahara, with its extremes in temperature—scorching days and chilly nights—made it still worse.

Ollie told me that my father was tenacious and his spirit indomitable. Determined to return to the war against the Nazis, Dad escaped from the camp in 1943, after more than three years' incarceration. He had tried once before, but had been caught and shot in the ankle in the process.

He joined a caravan of Arab traders making their way across the desert. From his prison camp experience, he had learned some Arabic, enough to converse with them. Dressed as an Arab trader, he crossed hundreds of miles of desert on camel, and was eventually able to reach Algiers. There, after an extended period of hospitalization for treatment of the ankle wound, malnutrition, and exhaustion, he joined the British Army. Given the rank of sergeant, he supervised Algerian workers at an airport in Maison Blanche being used by Allied forces. But that wasn't the kind of military work he had in mind.

After a few months in the British Army, he was transferred to the Office of Strategic Services, the legendary American wartime espionage unit under the command of Colonel "Wild Bill" Donovan.

The story I was told is that the Americans wanted him to change his surname. It sounded too Jewish and too complicated with those two dots over the "o." They gave him someone's address book, and my father, who barely spoke a word of English, picked the name "Harris" because it looked like "Paris," the city where he had been living just prior to the war. True or not, I don't know. Dad never talked much about the war years, and when he did, it was usually nothing more than a passing remark, so that many details had to be stitched together from others. And today there's simply no one left to ask.

After participating in the invasion of Italy with the U.S. Fifth Army, he was involved in one of the war's most ferocious battles, at Monte Cassino, and then helped liberate Rome, before moving north to Livorno. Eventually, the OSS got around to training him in the craft of espionage. The OSS school in Italy fronted as a psychiatric hospital. The course was tough. Long after the war's end, my father would wake up screaming in the middle of the night, a result of having been roughly awakened during training and put through mock interrogations. And, in the same spirit, whenever we went out to eat, he would always insist on sitting with his back to the wall, another legacy of his OSS training.

In all, my father parachuted thirteen times as an OSS agent—three training jumps and ten actual jumps, the latter behind enemy lines in Austria and Yugoslavia. His assignment in the final months of the war was to help persuade the Austrians to break away from the Germans and surrender first.

After the war, the OSS helped him come to the United States. At first, he continued to work in intelligence in Washington, together with his Austrian friend Ollie, but he didn't stay long and retired with the rank of captain. He had had enough of war, both open and clandestine, and was in search of something else. He wanted to continue his scientific studies, find a job, and get married. He yearned for the security and stability that had been missing in his life over the previous twelve years.

He discovered that my mother's family had made it to New York on one of the last passenger ships crossing the Atlantic before the attack on Pearl Harbor. He located them. My mother, it turned out, was no longer just the kid sister, and they got married in 1946. Shortly thereafter, they moved to Los Angeles, and my father began working as an engineer in the MGM and Argosy film studios.

I was born in Santa Monica in 1949, but we didn't stay long. While the whole country seemed to be moving westward, my parents decided to move back to New York. Much as they liked California, they wanted to be closer to my mother's family and, in addition, to get away from what they felt was a lifestyle and mindset just too far removed from their past. New York to them was a better compromise.

My father was fascinated by every advance in technology. One of the newest frontiers at the time was television, so he gladly accepted an offer to work at CBS News, and stayed there for a decade. When CBS signed an agreement with ZDF, a German television network, in 1960, he was asked to go to Munich to help implement the agreement. He was a logical choice. He spoke fluent German and was on the cutting edge of the latest breakthroughs in video.

There was only one problem. My father hadn't set foot in Germany since 1933 and, frankly, he had no desire to return. CBS gently encouraged him to give it a shot. If he could adjust emotionally, my mother and I would follow; if not, he'd return to New York. I remember vividly the call that came a few weeks after he left for Munich. Come, he said, and we did.

Being in Germany wasn't always easy for my father or, for that matter, my mother. She had last encountered Germans in 1940, when France fell, and wasn't yearning for any new opportunities. But other than one incident in which my father confronted a group of drunken men singing Nazi-era songs, the time passed quietly and we found ourselves enjoying the city and all it had to offer. And believe me, my father may not have understood the difference between one Jewish holiday and another, but he made a point of letting neighbors and colleagues know he was a Jew. He wanted the Germans to deal with that fact. He never did it in an in-your-face kind of way; it was always a bit more subtle, but no less clear.

It was only later that I realized that my parents had taught me two very important lessons in Germany, and they did it in the best way possible—through example. Both lessons have stayed with me.

First, somehow, life goes on. Never, ever, ignore the past, but don't become its prisoner, either. There wasn't a single moment in Germany during that year when we ever forgot where we were. I was only eleven, but it quickly dawned on me. Munich, after all, was the site of Hitler's attempted putsch in 1923. It also became the quintessential symbol of British and French appeasement in 1938. It was just a few miles from Dachau. And anyone around us over the age of thirty-five, or thereabouts, could well have been involved in the Final Solution. That was at least half the population!

At the same time, I saw my parents struggling to acknowledge that the Germany of 1960-61 was different. It was a democratic country governed by the rule of law. It couldn't have been easy for them—in those years, and for very understandable reasons, few Jews were prepared to give Germany the time of day—but my father's work had brought us there and, consequently, they tried their best to be open-minded and forward-looking.

Second, be who you are. My parents were Jewish. They weren't observant or particularly knowledgeable about their religious identity, but they were proud of their heritage. They had been marked for extinction because of their identity. Their lives had been disrupted in more ways than I can count because of their identity. Yet they had absolutely no desire to deny or hide that identity, much less reinvent themselves in another guise. To affirm their Jewish identity in postwar Germany took a measure of courage. Yet perhaps they instinctively understood that the ultimate test of the new Germany—and the new

Europe generally—would be how these countries interacted with living Jews, and not only how they dealt with the memory of murdered Jews.

Our time in Germany ended on a bad note: My parents divorced. Personal differences proved irreconcilable. My mother and I returned to New York. My father stayed on in Europe, first in Switzerland, later in England for another fifteen years. He then moved with his second wife to Rochester, Minnesota, and then to northern California.

I was never to live in the same city with my father again, or even within driving distance, though we usually managed to see each other once or twice a year. To state the obvious, it wasn't ideal. There were some things I missed out on.

But with the passage of time, I've come to understand that my father was a product of a very specific time and place in world history. From an early age, he faced circumstances that were far from enviable and that couldn't help but affect the rest of his life.

At a time when many kids today are thinking about their bar or bat mitzvah, or social life, or summer camp, my father was on the run from a psychopath who wanted to wipe all the Jews off the face of the earth. When many kids today are planning for their freshman year of college, my father was forced to shine the boots of Nazi officers. When many kids today take family gatherings for granted, my father didn't see his parents from the age of fourteen to twenty-six. And when many kids today think about their post-college plans, my father was trying to figure out how to escape from a brutal prison camp in western Algeria.

So, I can't say that my father ever taught me how to drive or how to handle my first date, but, in the long run, I was exposed to something no less valuable.

I saw up close the example of a man whose courage knew no limits and who, together with like-minded men and women, saved the world from Hitler. I saw a man who never boasted about his daring exploits, but who simply did what he knew had to be done, and then, when it was over, tried as best as he could to get on with his life in a new country, a new culture, and a new language. And I saw a man who stubbornly believed that tomorrow could be better than yesterday, and who never stopped trying to make it a reality. Good lessons all.

The more time passes since my father's death, the more I miss him.

Letter from the Anti-Semitism Front
July 31, 2003

Much has been written and said—and rightly so—about changing attitudes toward Jews. There is no need to restate the case at length. Suffice it to say that an increasing number of Jews—and some non-Jews as well—have noted a growth in anti-Semitism, including new mutations of the world's oldest social pathology, and, as disturbingly, a steady decline in the antibodies that have fought it off in the postwar period.

This change appears most pronounced in Western Europe, where anti-Americanism, anti-Semitism, anti-Zionism, and anti-globalization are merging in a dangerous mix. Purveyors tend to come overwhelmingly from the precincts of the universities, the intelligentsia, the media, and the extreme left.

And, of course, the extreme right, finding new life in railing against the growing immigrant populations in Western European countries, may have put the Jews on the back burner for the moment, but the essential ingredients of racism, xenophobia, and, yes, anti-Semitism remain intact as the pillars of their ideology and pose no less a long-term threat.

The principal danger, though, emanates from within the Islamic world. Since Muslims comprise a majority in fifty-six countries and a growing minority in scores of others, in essence, this represents a global phenomenon.

It would be highly irresponsible to paint with a broad brush stroke and suggest that all Muslims are implicated, when in fact this is far from the truth. At the same time, it would be equally shortsighted to pretend that anti-Semitism is nonexistent in the Islamic world, or restricted to a tiny number of extremists, or nothing more than discontent with this or that Israeli policy. The problem is real, it is serious, and it can't be swept under the rug.

By contrast, in the United States, Jews have felt relatively secure and immune from the disturbing trends abroad, believing in the "exceptionalism" of American society. Yet a series of recent and highly publicized events on American campuses and in the lead-up to the war in Iraq has raised concerns about whether these are simply isolated and ephemeral incidents or, conversely, harbingers of more to come from a country undergoing profound sociocultural changes.

What's been less discussed, however, is what to do about all this.

Let's be realistic. Given its longevity, anti-Semitism in one form or another is likely to outlive us all. That seems like a safe, if unfortunate, bet. No Jonas Salk has yet come along with an immunization protocol to eradicate forever the anti-Semitic virus, nor is any major breakthrough likely in the foreseeable future.

Europe's sense of responsibility and guilt for acts of commission and omission during the Shoah, such as it may have been, is rapidly waning. Instead, we hear unapologetic references from various quarters to Israelis as the "new Nazis," descriptions of Jews as "manipulative," "clannish," and "excessively influential," and even paeans to terrorists and suicide bombers as "freedom fighters." Not very encouraging, is it, especially against the backdrop of a Holocaust that took place on European soil and that was preceded by centuries of mistreatment of Jews?

And not long after celebrating the milestone of an observant Jew being selected by a major political party for the second spot on its presidential ticket, American Jews have witnessed the "poet laureate" of New Jersey, who bizarrely placed blame for 9/11 on Israel, being given a standing ovation by audiences at such leading universities as Yale. Meanwhile, pro-Palestinian students are planning a national conference at Rutgers in October that calls for a Palestinian state "from the river to the sea" and glorifies homicide bombers who kill Israeli women, men, and children. And a U.S. congressman publicly called on Jews to press the Bush administration regarding Iraq, suggesting that Jews, having allegedly pushed for war, were uniquely positioned, by dint of the power ascribed to them, to stop it.

At the same time, we've learned something about how best to try to contain anti-Semitism, marginalize it, discredit it, and build a firewall around it. In other words, we've come to understand what's likely to work and, for that matter, what's not.

Given everything that's going on, this may be a good moment to review, however briefly (even if this letter is not short), various strategies. I've identified at least eight key "actors" in the fight against anti-Semitism.

First, let's get down to basics.

At the risk of stating the obvious, societies based on democracy, pluralism, and equality before the law are the best guarantors for Jews or any minority (and for the majority as well). Freedom and respect for all mean freedom and respect for everyone.

When that notion is deeply entrenched, the results can speak for themselves. Among the best examples was the Danish rescue of its Jewish population, who were targeted for deportation by the occupying Nazis exactly sixty years ago. The Jews were seen as Danes who happened to attend a different house of worship. In helping the Jews, non-Jewish Danes felt they were simply assisting fellow Danes, an entirely natural and unexceptional thing in their own minds.

Second, democratic societies are a necessary but insufficient condition for defending against anti-Semitism (or other forms of racially, religiously, or ethnically motivated hatred). Translating lofty ideals into daily realities requires many things, not least the exercise of political leadership. And this is where we meet head-on the challenge of what works and what doesn't.

Let me explain this point at some length because it is especially important. Political leaders set the tone for a country. By their words or silence, by their engagement or indifference, they are able to send messages of one kind or another to the nation as a whole.

It's hardly worth considering the role of leaders in those Muslim countries where the problem is most virulent because they've either been encouraging anti-Semitism, or else they've lacked the courage and will to tackle it. In any case, democracy, pluralism, and equality before the law are rare commodities in such places.

Still, I can't help but wonder what would happen if a prominent Arab leader like President Hosni Mubarak of Egypt woke up one morning and decided that enough is enough—anti-Semitism is not only wrong, but a stain on the Arab self-image of tolerance and moderation—and led a campaign in the Arab world against those who demonize and otherwise dehumanize Jews. The effect would be electrifying. Dream on, you probably say, and I can't argue with you, but hope does spring eternal.

In Europe, with few exceptions, leaders in recent years have fallen short when it comes to confronting anti-Semitism.

Take the case of Lech Walesa, the hero of the Solidarity movement. In 1995, as president of democratic Poland, he attended a church service in Gdansk. The priest, Rev. Henryk Jankowski, a known anti-Semite, did not disappoint. He referred to the Star of David as "associated with the symbols of the swastika as well as the hammer and sickle," and that wasn't the half of it.

What did President Walesa do in response? Did he walk out of the sermon? Did he issue a statement immediately after the service? Did he disassociate himself from Father Jankowski? None of the above. He simply chose to remain silent.

The American Jewish Committee met with President Walesa shortly after this incident took place. It was a revealing session.

We pressed the Polish leader to speak out and quickly. We argued that any further delay would only reinforce the image that Father Jankowski's venomous remarks were acceptable to Walesa and legitimate in mainstream Polish society.

He pushed back, contending that there was no point in turning a small incident into a national story.

We responded that the presence of the Polish president in the church during such a sermon made it, by definition, a national, indeed, an international, story. The onus was on Walesa to repudiate the priest's bigotry.

Our message, we feared, fell on deaf ears. We left the meeting feeling we had utterly failed in our mission.

Ten days after the sermon, though, and with pressure coming from the U.S. and Israeli governments, the president grudgingly issued a statement, but the damage had been done. A not-so-subtle message had already been sent to the people of Poland. And, in any case, there was no condemnation of the priest, only some general words about Walesa's repugnance of anti-Semitism and his appreciation of the Star of David.

Or take the case of Jacques Chirac, the French president. No one who knows him would suggest that he harbors anti-Semitic feelings. To the contrary, he has always demonstrated friendship for the French Jewish community, even if his foreign policy is heavily tilted toward the Arab world.

Yet this leader, who had the courage in 1995 to accept French responsibility for the crimes of Vichy—something none of his predecessors had done—was painfully slow to react to the wave of anti-Semitic attacks that hit France starting in the fall of 2000.

And, to be fair, since there was a government of "cohabitation" between Chirac and Lionel Jospin, the prime minister at the time and a Chirac foe, Jospin's cabinet was no quicker to respond. Yet Jospin, like Chirac, was known as a friend of the Jewish community.

Why, then, the delayed reflexes when these leaders must have understood that not only Jews were under attack, but—and this point must be emphasized again and again—the highest values of democratic France as well?

Whatever the reasons, and there is much speculation about them, the bottom line is that, inevitably, a message was sent out to the perpetrators—North African youth living in the suburbs of major French cities—that their despicable acts were not taken terribly seriously. The result: they concluded they could act with impunity.

Incidentally, in the past year since a new prime minister and cabinet have taken office, a very different—and much tougher—message has been projected, especially by the minister of the interior, responsible for law enforcement, and the minister of education. Some positive results have been achieved, even if the challenge is enormous, and the French Jewish community at least no longer feels a sense of total abandonment by the government.

Let me offer one other example, though it involves non-Jews. Nonetheless, it is instructive.

Beginning in the early 1990s, shortly after German unification, right-wing violence against foreigners erupted. The towns of Rostock, Mölln, Hoyerswerda, and Solingen became synonymous with expressions of hatred. In Solingen, for example, five women of Turkish origin were killed when skinheads torched a home. And in Rostock, not only was a shelter for foreigners, mostly Vietnamese and Romanian Gypsies, burned to the ground, but many town residents took to the streets and openly encouraged the right-wing extremists.

Chancellor Helmut Kohl, a decent man who skillfully presided over the mammoth task of German unification, underestimated the significance of these tragic events.

Rather than speak out forcefully and seek opportunities to identify with the targeted victims, he adopted a low profile, to put it charitably. When the American Jewish Committee and others urged the chancellor to be more visible, a spokesman indicated that Kohl did not engage in "condolence tourism." I wish he had.

I could offer many more examples.

It's striking how many times we've raised the issue of anti-Semitism with European leaders in the last couple of years, only to be told, in the case of a European Union commissioner, that she was "unaware of its existence," or, in the case of a foreign minister, that there was no evidence of anti-Semitism, even as a poll had just come out indicating that anti-Semitic stereotypes were a serious problem in his country. Why the blind spot? Why the denial? Again, there are several possible explanations, none of which offers any reassurance.

By way of contrast, Joschka Fischer, the German foreign minister, challenged his compatriots to confront the problem of anti-Semitism. In a newspaper article he wrote:

> Do we actually comprehend what Nazi barbarism and its genocidal anti-Semitism did to us, to Germany, its people and its culture? What Hitler and the Nazis did to Germany's Jews they did first and foremost to Germans, to Germans of the Jewish faith! Albert Einstein was as much a German as was Max Planck.... That is why the question whether German Jews feel secure in our democracy and, though even today this can only be a hope, might one day be able to feel "at home" in it again, is not a minor one, but a question par excellence about the credibility of German democracy.

More such thoughtful and courageous statements from political leaders, bolstered by appropriate actions, are precisely what's needed. In America, perhaps, we've come to expect them, as when our government publicly condemned the rash of anti-Semitic canards blaming Jews for 9/11 or, just before, boycotted the hate fest under UN auspices at Durban. But elsewhere, at least when it comes to Jews, such statements and actions have been far less frequent or forceful.

Frankly, given Europe's historical record, it should be precisely these countries—knowing as they do where the slippery slope of hatred can lead—that assume worldwide leadership in the struggle against the cancer of anti-Semitism. Wouldn't that send a powerful message about learning from the past? We've challenged many European leaders to play just such a role, but admittedly with only limited success to date.

The words of Søren Kierkegaard, the nineteenth-century Danish philosopher, ought to serve as a useful reminder: "Life must be lived forward, but can only be understood backward."

The third area for consideration is the role of law, law enforcement, and the judiciary.

This gets tricky, I realize. American and European laws on what constitutes a punishable crime in the realm of incitement can be quite different. There are varying approaches to the proper balance between protecting free speech and criminalizing the propagation of racial or religious hatred.

For instance, a number of European countries, including Austria, Belgium, France, Germany, Spain, and Switzerland, have laws that make denial of the Holocaust a criminal offense, whereas the United States does not.

As one illustration, Switzerland adopted a law in 1994 that outlaws "public denial, trivialization and disputation of genocide or other crimes against humanity," with a maximum prison sentence of three years.

Ironically, we hear persistent complaints from countries like Austria and Germany that much of their anti-Semitic material, including video games and books, originates in the United States. The problem has only grown more acute with the rapidly increasing popularity of the

Internet. We are often asked if there isn't a way around First Amendment protections to stop these unwelcome American "exports."

Meanwhile, in the United Kingdom, as we learned in a recent meeting with the parliamentary undersecretary of state:

> It is an offense to use threatening, abusive, or insulting words or behavior with intent or likelihood to stir up racial hatred against anyone on the grounds of color, race, nationality, or ethnic or national origins. Under recent anti-terrorism legislation, the maximum penalty for the offense was increased from two to seven years' imprisonment. Under the same legislation, it is also now an offense to stir up hatred against a racial group abroad, *such as Jews in Israel* [emphasis added].

The range of ways in which democratic, law-based societies seek to deal with hate speech and hate crimes could fill volumes, as would an evaluation of the impact of such efforts.

Moreover, there is an entire body of international conventions (and organizations) to consider in the struggle against anti-Semitism.

The Soviet Jewry movement relied heavily on such instruments as the Universal Declaration of Human Rights and the Helsinki Final Act to buttress the case for the rights of Jews in the USSR.

So, too, do we need to consider as tools the protections enshrined in documents like the UN Convention on the Elimination of All Forms of Discrimination and the International Covenant of Civil and Political Rights. Article 20 of the latter document, as one example, includes the following language: "Any advocacy of national, racial, or religious hatred that constitutes incitement to discrimination, hostility, or violence shall be prohibited by law."

One recent and effective use of an international organization was the two-day meeting in Vienna devoted to anti-Semitism that was convened by the Organization for Security and Cooperation in Europe. Importantly, there is agreement among the governments involved to gather again next year.

The topic of national and international law and covenants, touched on only briefly here, is unquestionably important. In the final analysis, it goes without saying, what really counts is not just the laws and mechanisms on the books, significant though they may be, but the degree of commitment to their implementation and enforcement.

Fourth, there is the media, which, as we all well know, plays an extraordinarily powerful role not only in shaping individual attitudes, but also in influencing the public policy agenda and priorities of decision-makers. As someone once suggested, "If CNN didn't report it, did it ever actually happen?"

In parts of the Muslim world, of course, the media, whether in government or private hands, or the murky space in between, is a convenient vehicle for propagating anti-Semitism. Professor Robert Wistrich, an expert on anti-Semitism and the author of a superb monograph for the American Jewish Committee entitled *Muslim Anti-Semitism: A Clear and Present Danger*, offers several examples of the media's role in peddling unadulterated anti-Semitism.

In Europe over the past three years, there have also been numerous documented instances of anti-Semitic images and stereotypes seeping into mainstream, not fringe, outlets.

Among the most disturbing developments were during the period of the Church of the Nativity standoff, when some newspapers reawakened the deicide charge—finally put to rest by the Catholic Church, in 1965, at Vatican Council II—and, more generally, the transference of Nazi images onto Israel, with the Israeli prime minister equated with the Fuehrer, the Israeli military likened to the Wehrmacht or even the SS, and the West Bank represented as an Israeli-run concentration camp.

Such depictions go well beyond any conceivable legitimate criticism of Israel to something far deeper and more pernicious, and must not be left unchallenged.

Here in the United States, while there have been some distressing images, my principal concern has more to do with belated—and insufficient—reporting on anti-Semitism in the Arab world as well as its reemergence in Europe. The media must be helped to understand the significance and newsworthiness of these issues. It's certainly not a lost cause, but it is an uphill battle.

To be sure, there have been stories here and there and the occasional column or editorial. But they have been relatively few and far between. I was especially struck by the lack of media interest in the Wistrich study, which, incidentally, makes for hair-raising reading.

Released at a press conference at the National Press Club in May 2002, it generated only a few articles, all in the Jewish or Israeli press. A Reuters reporter covered the event and filed a long story, but, we later learned, her editors apparently didn't find the topic of sufficient interest. One wonders what it would take to capture their attention on the subject. And this is not the only such example.

A study of Saudi textbooks, cosponsored by the American Jewish Committee and released in January 2003, met essentially the same fate. The major media outlets never reported on what was the first detailed report documenting the hatred and contempt of the West that Saudi children are taught from grade one. Is this not deemed relevant to a fuller understanding both of 9/11 and of the larger war on international terrorism?

Fifth, there is the role of the "values" community, including religious, ethnic, racial, and human rights leaders and their institutions.

Ideally, each of these actors should regard an assault on any one constituency, e.g., an anti-Semitic or racist incident, as an attack on all—and on the kind of world we are seeking to create—and respond forcefully. In a way, without wishing to stretch the analogy, it would be akin to a NATO member seeking support from other members under Article 5, which deems an attack on one as an attack against all.

Alas, there is no charter binding the values community, although there is an important provision in the Fundamental Agreement between the Holy See and the State of Israel, signed in December 1993, which might provide a model. Article 2 includes the following language:

> The Holy See and the State of Israel are committed to appropriate cooperation in combating all forms of anti-Semitism and all kinds of racism and of religious intolerance, and in promoting mutual understanding among nations, tolerance among communities, and respect for human life and dignity.

Virtually identical language could be used to create a charter for nongovernmental organizations committed to advancing human relations and mutual respect. What's needed, in effect, is a Coalition of Conscience in the voluntary sector.

Meanwhile, there are best-practice examples that can help guide us.

Shockingly, a cinder block was thrown through a bedroom window displaying a Chanukah menorah in Billings, Montana, ten years ago. It was the room of a five-year-old boy. Fortunately, he wasn't hurt. What followed was quite remarkable.

Led by local church leaders, the police chief, and the editor of the Billings *Gazette*, the town, previously quite apathetic, responded by placing thousands of paper menorahs in the windows of shops and homes. It was an exceptional and effective way of reacting. It said to the hate mongers: We are one community and we will not allow you to divide us.

In the same spirit, responding to the wave of arson attacks targeting African American churches in the south in the 1990s, the American Jewish Committee joined with the National Council of Churches and the National Conference of Catholic Bishops, in a display of ecumenical partnership, to raise millions of dollars to rebuild the damaged houses of worship. Moreover, AJC adopted the Gay's Hill Baptist Church in Millen, Georgia, and helped construct it from the ground up after it was completely destroyed in an act of hate.

The concept of a Coalition of Conscience also explains why the American Jewish Committee sent a delegation to a mosque in Cologne, Germany, in 1993 to attend the funerals of the five women of Turkish origin killed in their home in Solingen, and why, more recently, we chose to mobilize our resources to assist Muslim victims of Serbia's ethnic cleansing in Kosovo.

Every major religion has a variation of the golden rule. As Rabbi Abraham Joshua Heschel once remarked, "We are commanded to love our neighbor: this must mean that we can." We can, but do we?

Words are important, but timely and principled actions are what really count. And those within each faith tradition committed to the values of compassion and concern for all must lead the way.

Sixth, there is the long-term and irreplaceable role of education. As the Southern Poverty Law Center put it:

Bias is learned in childhood. By the age of three, children are aware of racial differences and may have the perception that "white" is desirable. By the age of twelve, they hold stereotypes about numerous ethnic, racial, and religious groups, according to the Leadership Conference Education Fund. Because stereotypes underlie hate, and half of all hate crimes are committed by young men under twenty, tolerance education is critical.

About 10 percent of hate crimes occur in schools and colleges, but schools can be an ideal environment to counter bias. Schools mix youths of different backgrounds, place them on equal footing and allow one-on-one interaction. Children are naturally curious about people who are different.

There are a number of tested and successful school-based programs designed to teach mutual respect. Incidentally, I'm not a big fan of using the word "tolerance" in this particular case; it strikes me as rather weak. The goal should not be simply to teach people to "tolerate" one another, but, ideally, to respect and understand one another.

That said, organizations like the Southern Poverty Law Center, Facing History, the Anti-Defamation League, and the American Jewish Committee have all developed acclaimed programs used in schools across the U.S. and, increasingly, in other countries where diversity is a factor in the population, which these days is just about everywhere. And the State of New Jersey has led the way in creating a curriculum based on the lessons of the Holocaust for all high-school students.

The challenge in the United States, given its vast size and decentralized school systems, is to reach enough schools, then to get a long-term commitment to inclusion of such programs in the curriculum. Moreover, there is a need, of course, for adequate teacher training and also for monitoring impact, both over the short term and the longer term as well.

In addition to such programs, the American Jewish Committee has developed another model for schools. Named the Catholic/Jewish Educational Enrichment Program, or C/JEEP, it links Catholic and Jewish parochial schools in several American cities. Priests and rabbis visit each other's schools to break down barriers and familiarize students with basic elements of the two faith traditions. Students who might otherwise never meet have an opportunity to come to know one another. The goal is to "demystify" and "humanize" the "other," and it works.

Again, as with the curriculum-based programs, the biggest challenge here is the sheer number of schools and the resources involved—not to mention the occasional bureaucratic hurdle—in order to reach anything approaching a critical mass of students.

(It remains to be seen what impact Mel Gibson's upcoming film, *The Passion of the Christ*, will have on Catholic attitudes toward Jews, but, given current reports, it is hardly likely to be positive.)

One more word on education. When schools in Saudi Arabia or *madrassas* in Pakistan teach contempt, distrust, or hatred of others, be they Christians, Jews, or Hindus, or, for that matter women, we face a whole other challenge.

Shining the spotlight of exposure on these school systems is vital, which is why the American Jewish Committee cosponsored the Saudi study. Sharing the information with governments that have influence in these countries is necessary. For instance, Saudi spin doctors talk of the "enduring values" between their country and the United States. Surely, then, that gives Washington some leverage in Riyadh. And from our long experience in dealing with problematic curricula and textbooks, perseverance is the key. Things seldom happen overnight.

Seventh, there is the role of the individual. In a more perfect world, the combination of family environment, education, religious upbringing, and popular culture all lead in the same direction—to molding individuals with a strong commitment to the values of mutual respect and mutual understanding, social responsibility, and moral courage.

Our world is far from perfect. We may never succeed in completely eliminating anti-Semitism or other forms of hatred. Still, we must always strive to build the kinds of societies in which the altruistic personalities of the good women and men of Denmark, or the French village of Le Chambon-sur-Lignon (described as "the safest place in [Nazi-occupied] Europe for Jews"), or the likes of an Abraham Joshua Heschel, Jan Karski, Raoul Wallenberg, Martin Luther King Jr., or Andrei Sakharov, are increasingly the norm, not the exception.

As I look around today, I see countless decent people, whether in the United States or elsewhere, who reject any form of anti-Semitism. But, frankly, there are too few prominent non-Jews of the likes of a Per Ahlmark, the former deputy prime minister of Sweden, prepared to speak out on the danger posed by contemporary anti-Semitism.

And finally, in the struggle against anti-Semitism, new or old, we must take into account the key role of the Jewish world, including the State of Israel and local, national, and international Jewish organizations.

The Jewish community looks radically different than it did, say, sixty or seventy years ago. Today, there is an Israel; then, there was not. Today, there are sophisticated, savvy, and well-connected Jewish institutions; then, Jewish institutions were much less confident and sure-footed.

Collectively, we have the capacity to track trends in anti-Semitism, exchange information on a timely basis with other interested parties, reach centers of power, build alliances within and across borders, and consider the best mix of diplomatic, political, legal, and other strategies for countering troubling developments.

We may not succeed in each and every case. But we've come a very long way thanks to a steely determination, in Israel and the Diaspora, to fight vigorously against anti-Semitism, while simultaneously helping to build a world in which anti-Semitism—and everything it stands for—is in irreversible decline.

Letter from Sasha
August 25, 2003

My name is Sasha.*

Actually, my real name is Alexander, but we Russians love diminutives. Galina becomes Galya, Konstantin turns into Kostya, and even Sasha has its own diminutive, Sashinka.

* Sasha and his family are fictitious persons. They are a composite of many Soviet Jews I have met since I first worked in the USSR as an exchange teacher in 1974 and then as a resettlement caseworker with HIAS in Rome and Vienna.

I am part of the sizable Soviet-born Jewish population in the United States. In sharing my family's story before and after arrival in this country, I'm hoping to help deepen the ties between our community and other American Jews. I don't wish to suggest that our experience is necessarily typical, but then again it may not be entirely atypical, either.

I was born in Moscow in 1966. As with many urban Soviet Jewish families of that era, I was an only child. My parents, Boris and Svetlana, were also born in Moscow—just before World War II—but were evacuated to Kazakhstan with their mothers and returned to Moscow only at the war's end. My father, a graduate of the polytechnic institute, was an engineer; my mother, a university graduate, was a high school teacher of German.

We lived in a communal apartment in a relatively nice part of Moscow. My parents and I shared a room; my mother's mother, my Babushka, slept in an alcove nearby, and another family lived in the other large bedroom. We all shared the bathroom and kitchen. It wasn't too bad, except for the occasional quarrel over who needed the bathroom more urgently or who left the dirty dishes in the sink.

I should say a word about Babushka. Her real name was Sarah. She was born in Bobruisk in 1915, two years before the Bolshevik Revolution. Bobruisk is in Byelorussia, or White Russia as some people refer to it in English. It was enough to say you were from Bobruisk and your name was Sarah for people to figure out that you were Jewish.

In many ways, Babushka was—and remains—the most special person in my life. Her husband, Abram, was killed on the battlefront in 1942, less than a year after the Nazis invaded the USSR. She never remarried. Instead, she and my mother lived together, even after my mother's marriage to my father. That was rather common. And it was also typical that she would raise me while my parents spent much of their time consumed by their jobs.

It was really from Babushka that I learned I was a Jew. It's not that my parents entirely hid it from me; it's just that they didn't talk much about it. And when they did, it almost always seemed to revolve around concerns about anti-Semitism, whether at work, in the newspapers, or on the street.

But for my grandmother, being Jewish seemed different, more expressive and substantive. For one thing, unlike my parents, she spoke Yiddish and taught me a few words. She knew the Jewish holidays and tried to explain their meaning to me. And she cooked certain mouth-watering foods whenever it was holiday time.

School, of course, loomed large in my life. I attended Special School No. 45. You had to take an exam to be admitted, and it helped if your parents knew the right people as well. The USSR had a system of special schools that focused on a particular subject, such as a foreign language, math, a science, even chess. Competition for entry was fierce, both because the level of education was high and one's chances of admission to a prestigious university or institute after graduation were substantially enhanced.

My school concentrated on English. Like other academically oriented schools in the USSR, it had ten grades. I entered first grade when I was seven, the customary age, and by second grade, I was already getting a heavy dose of English.

Pupils in the younger classes had to join the Octoberists, then the Pioneers—the very first steps on the communist ladder. (In the older grades, we were supposed to move to the third step, the Komsomol.) We wore red scarves, learned about the unparalleled achievements of the Communist Party and our country's leaders, sang patriotic songs, and were taught to believe that the capitalist world—and America in particular—was our greatest enemy. Every so often, we also heard something about the evils of Zionism and the plight of poor Arabs at the hands of bloodthirsty Israelis.

I didn't quite know what to make of this last point, as I had never in my life met Zionists and didn't have a clue as to what they looked like. But I had no reason to doubt my teachers until one day I asked my parents why the Zionists were so cruel.

I quickly realized I had stumbled onto something significant. My parents looked at each other uncomfortably before dismissing the question by telling me it wasn't worth discussing. Of course, that only made me realize it must have been well worth discussing, but they wouldn't say any more. So I went to Babushka and asked her. She began whispering to me that Zionists were Jews who wanted a state of their own and that she, my beloved grandmother, was, in fact, one of those Jews. But all this should be kept under wraps, she warned me, because it could only cause trouble for the family. It was enough to say you were a Zionist to end up in prison.

Just after I turned eleven, I began to overhear my parents talking animatedly after they thought I was asleep. This would go on night after night. I strained to listen. When I finally figured out what it was they were discussing, I couldn't believe my ears. They were going back and forth on the subject of emigration.

I could just make out snippets of what they were saying: "Did you hear that the Shapiro family has just received a *vyzov* (affidavit) from Israel, thanks to the help of a caring American Jew visiting Moscow who conveyed their request to the Israeli authorities, and want to move there?" "I learned that Kagan, the fellow I studied with at the institute, and his family left last week for Vienna and hope to join a cousin in Los Angeles." "What if we apply to leave and get turned down? How would we manage without work and money? What would happen to Sashinka at school?" "I can't take it much more. I know I deserved a promotion, but they gave the job to that nincompoop Petrov instead. We Jews just don't stand a chance here. Sashinka has no future."

Months passed. My parents never discussed anything with me, but the nightly conversations continued. The only difference was that my mother and father seemed to be in growing agreement that we should try to leave. The talk increasingly shifted to where to go, Israel or the United States.

Papa clearly wanted to resettle in Israel. He said that was the one place where Jews wouldn't have to worry about anti-Semitism and where my future was limitless. He knew there were many engineers going there, but he heard through the grapevine that the Israeli government was investing lots of money in advanced training courses, which made him optimistic he could find a job in his field. I should point out that work was extremely important to both my parents. It practically defined them.

Mama preferred immigrating to the United States. She had three main arguments. First, she was troubled by the fact that I would have to serve in the Israeli army. She had already lost her father in war; she didn't want to lose her only child too. Second, she said that since America was such a big country, it would be easier to find good jobs. And third, she was concerned about the climate. We Russians are used to the cold and snow, and Israel is practically a desert country, she would repeat over and over.

My mother prevailed.

I'll never forget the day in 1978 when my parents said they needed to talk with me. It was clear they had something serious on their minds. Babushka sat with us. Everything was said in hushed tones. They didn't want our neighbors in the communal apartment to listen in on the conversation.

This is more or less what they told me:

Sashinka, we have decided to try to leave this country and move to the United States. We want you to understand why. It wasn't an easy decision for us. This is the land of our birth. Russian is our language. We love Russian culture. Pushkin, Chekhov, Turgenev, Gogol, Tchaikovsky, and Rachmaninoff are so much a part of who we are. We love Russian nature—our walks together in the woods to pick mushrooms, our time spent near the Black Sea, the long summer nights when it barely gets dark. We have many friends here that we don't want to leave. But we can't stay any longer. We are Jews and this country has never liked Jews, neither before 1917 nor since. We can't stand the constant attacks on Israel and Zionism. We don't see any future for you here. There'll always be barriers, no matter how well you do in school. And conscription into the Soviet army, with its rampant anti-Semitism, looms ahead.

We don't know if we'll be successful in our effort to emigrate, but we must try. There's a window of opportunity. Some Jews have received visas pretty quickly; others, though, have been given a very rough time. You need to keep our plan a secret from everyone at school or else it may land you in trouble. Don't breathe a word of this to your teachers or friends. I know that's going to be tough for you, but trust us, it's the best way. And one other thing: Don't believe what they tell you in school about America, even if you have to pretend to go along. America is a great country and Jews are treated fairly. You'll be very happy there.

I quickly learned the art of living two entirely separate, if not contradictory, lives.

By day, I was an exemplary student, getting "fives" in just about every course, while being the model Pioneer.

By night, I sensed my parents' tension as they faced the difficulty of trying to obtain an affidavit from Israel, the first step in the emigration process, but running into Soviet roadblocks. Then there were a thousand other details—birth certificates, death certificates, high school and college diplomas, documents from work, police records, etc., etc., etc. It never ended, and no one in the Soviet bureaucracy had any interest in facilitating the process unless it was for a big bribe, which was beyond our means.

Franz Kafka would have had a field day describing the whole story.

Moreover, every week there were new rumors swirling around: The emigration procedure was loosening up, said one family friend who assured us he was in the know; no, said another equally confident friend, things are quickly tightening up. Officials at OVIR, the Soviet visa office, are more sympathetic to those they think are headed for Israel rather than the U.S., or is it the other way around? On and on it went. Who knew what was true and what wasn't?

It's really hard to describe our lives during this period, especially to Americans who too often take their freedom for granted.

We lived in a twilight zone. We were no longer fully part of the Soviet Union. My parents lost their jobs and had to make do with tutoring and whatever other off-the-books work they could find to earn some money. We didn't know if our exit visas would come tomorrow or ever. We were worried that our neighbors would learn our secret and clamor to have us tossed out on the street as traitors to the motherland. I was petrified that one day the Pioneers would meet and I'd be denounced as an enemy.

Even when we allowed ourselves flights of fantasy and tried to think about our new lives in the United States, we had no idea what awaited us. None of us, my Babushka included, had ever been outside the Soviet Union. Maybe, I feared, the press was right and America was a country racked with violence and injustice.

Luck was with us. In 1979, we were notified by OVIR that the four of us could leave the country on visas to Israel. As it turned out, we were part of an enormous wave that year. More than 51,000 Soviet Jews left, far more than in any previous year since emigration began as a trickle in 1968. Unfortunately, the luck didn't extend to Jewish prisoners of conscience like Natan Sharansky, languishing in the gulag, or refuseniks unable to emigrate because of alleged possession of state secrets.

That reminds me of one of the many political jokes that Jews told each other at the time, usually in the privacy of a home and with a half-empty bottle of vodka nearby:

> Rabinovich was called into the KGB and told that, as a scientist, he wouldn't be given permission to immigrate to the United States because he knew a state secret. "Are you kidding?" replied Rabinovich. "In my field, the Americans are decades ahead." "And that," said the KGB official, "is the state secret."

We were elated with our good fortune, but there wasn't much opportunity to celebrate. So many things still had to be done and there was precious little time before the visas expired. We had to arrange our plane tickets, ship whatever furniture we could to the West, sell the rest, exchange the legally enforced maximum of 90 rubles each for the $120 we would be permitted to take with us, buy a few matrushkas and other souvenirs we would try to sell in the West for extra money, say good-bye to all our friends, and pray that OVIR wouldn't have a change of heart before we left.

The big day finally came. Our friends accompanied us to Sheremetyevo Airport. All of us were crying and hugging and promising to stay in touch. We bid everyone farewell, then faced one last indignity before boarding the Aeroflot plane for Vienna.

Soviet customs officials, unlike their Western counterparts, checked travelers on the way out, not just the way in, and they reserved special treatment for departing Soviet Jews. They ripped through our luggage, microscopically examined each and every item, questioned us mercilessly, grabbed items for themselves and dared us to challenge them, and left everything in a big mess, knowing full well that we would have to rush to put things back in order and get to the gate in time for the flight.

It was toughest on Babushka. She was 64 and not in the best of health. We were her only family and she was determined to go, but you could see the strain on her face. This wasn't going to be an easy journey for her.

Not until the plane had taken off and the pilot had announced that Vienna was our next stop did we begin to breathe more normally. We had done it. We had ended one chapter in our lives and were about to start a second. For me, at the age of thirteen, this was quite an adventure.

We landed in Vienna, disembarked, and soon heard our names called. Oh, no, had the KGB followed us? When we saw the smiling face approaching us, we knew the answer. After all, KGB officials weren't exactly known for their warmth.

If I remember correctly, the man said his name was Ari and he was from the Jewish Agency for Israel. This was the first Israeli any of us had ever laid eyes on. He welcomed us to Vienna and told us there were a few other families like ours on the same flight. He asked us where we planned to resettle. My father hesitated. My mother gently poked him. That prompted Papa to say we were hoping to go to New York. Ari asked us if we had thought about making aliyah. My father explained that we had, but we decided against it and weren't open to reconsideration. Ari shook his head in disappointment.

Of the five families on our flight, two were headed for Israel and stayed with Ari; the rest of us were transferred to the care of HIAS and the American Jewish Joint Distribution Committee (JDC). We spent a few days in Vienna, which gave us our first glimpse of the West, while registering with these two Jewish organizations, answering a ton of questions, and settling into a modest hotel filled with other Soviet Jews in the same boat as we were.

I'll always remember our impressions of those days.

We were living in a dream. We kept pinching ourselves, wondering if it really was all true. Vienna was magical. The city was breathtakingly beautiful. People were polite. The stores displayed items we had never seen before. My father joked that in Russia we had money but the stores had nothing; here the stores had everything and we had no money. The supermarkets were from another planet. The Jewish organizations operated openly, not clandestinely, and they welcomed us as Jews. That was a bit confusing, as we had never before identified publicly as Jews except in trying to get out of the Soviet Union.

Speaking of the other emigrants, I'll never forget my parents' reaction. They had lived in a confined world in Moscow where all the Jews they knew were pretty much like themselves—highly educated, cultured, and secular. Now they found themselves surrounded by a profusion of diversity, and I think it was initially disorienting.

There were Bukharan Jews from Tashkent, Tat (or "Mountain") Jews from Baku, Georgian Jews from Tbilisi, and even Hasidic Jews from Uzhgorod. There were Jews from the so-called Jewish Autonomous District in Birobidzhan. There were doctors, scientists, and classical musicians, and there were truck drivers, welders, and short-order cooks. And there were even a few non-Jews, with exit visas for Israel like the rest of us, whom the Kremlin had been eager to kick out.

From Vienna, we went by train to Rome, or actually to Orte, an hour's drive north of Rome. The entire trip took about 20 hours. The security along the way was impressive. At the Sudbahnhof in Vienna, Austrian police carrying submachine guns patrolled while we boarded the railroad cars specially designated for us. Again, lots of armed guards in Italy. We were reminded that, in 1973, Palestinian terrorists had seized a train carrying Soviet Jewish refugees across Czechoslovakia en route to Vienna and demanded that Austria shut down its reception center in exchange for release of the hostages.

Buses met us in Orte and, with a police escort, took us to a *pensione* in Rome. The four of us held on to each other—and to our suitcases—for dear life, as we found ourselves in our second Western country in less than a week.

We stayed in Italy for about three months while our papers were processed for admission to the United States. After a few days in the hotel, like many of the thousands of other Soviet Jews, we moved to Ostia, the ancient port of Rome, while others found places in

Ladispoli, another seaside community. It was easy to find an apartment since it wasn't the summer high season. Actually, we shared a flat, but at least this time we got to choose our housemates.

Ah, Italy. With the stipend we received from the JDC, we were able to live modestly well, especially since prices for pasta, fruits, vegetables, and, best of all, gelato (ice cream) weren't terribly exorbitant, even if many other things were completely out of our reach. Papa tried to make a few extra lire by going on Sunday mornings to the popular Roman flea market at Porta Portese and selling some items we had brought. I felt bad for him, but he never complained. The extra money certainly came in handy.

The Italians couldn't have been nicer or more sympathetic to our situation as refugees in transit. Somehow we managed to communicate with each other, even if almost none of us spoke any Italian and few Italians understood Russian. The Italians proved patient, though, and there were some funny scenes. Did you ever notice how, when language is a barrier, people think that all they need to do is speak louder and they'll be understood? That happened a lot.

The Jewish organizations were there to assist us. Our family was assigned caseworkers by both HIAS, which took care of our migration formalities, and the JDC, which handled our living and medical needs.

We met lots of other Soviet Jewish families while in Ostia. In fact, many refugees gathered daily at the post office square, which the local Italians began calling Piazza Rossa or "Red Square" in our honor, to exchange the latest rumors about immigration and resettlement, seek information from newcomers about friends and relatives who were still in the USSR, or just shoot the breeze.

There were opportunities for me to go to school with other Soviet Jewish kids. English classes were available for my parents. Celebrations of the main Jewish holidays were organized for us. Synagogues were available for those interested.

My family and I look back on that time spent in Italy with warm feelings. We loved the country and its people, even if we couldn't quite figure out why the Italian Communist Party enjoyed such popularity. We had a much needed break from the gut-wrenching turmoil of our last year in Moscow. And we spent lots of time together.

But I noticed something that is quite normal for migrating families, but that no one had told me about at the time: I was adapting to our new circumstances far more quickly than my parents. They were emotional yo-yos. One day they were up, the next day down. They were plagued by questions: Will we adapt to the West? Can we learn to speak fluent English? Will we eventually find work in our specialties? What if we don't?

For me, on the other hand, my English from school came in handy and it didn't take long to pick up some Italian while playing soccer with local kids. My family began relying on me to get around. I kind of liked my new status.

Our American visas came through without delay. Sometimes, however, there were difficulties, we were told, especially for those who had once been members of the Soviet Communist Party or had had criminal records in the USSR.

We were informed by our HIAS caseworker that we would be resettled in New York. When Soviet Jewish families didn't have close relatives living in the U.S. whom they could join, they were sent to New York or one of dozens of other cities.

Another plane ride awaited, the longest any of us had ever been on. This time, though, there were no surly Aeroflot flight attendants, only the permanently smiling faces of the Pan Am stewardesses.

We arrived at JFK Airport and once again were met by Jewish representatives and escorted through the entry formalities. We looked around at everything with a special curiosity because this was it—our new home. Austria and Italy were transit countries for us, but America was where we would be living. There would be no turning back.

New York was different than Vienna or Rome. It didn't have the historical majesty of either city, and its size and bustle at first simply overwhelmed us. But it grew on us as we got to know it.

For one thing, we quickly came to understand how accommodating a city it was to newcomers. You didn't have to live here for three generations to make your mark. Opportunities abounded for those with the energy, drive, and vision to seize them. And for another, we were amazed by the size and confidence of the Jewish community. Jews not only lived proudly as Jews, but they also seemed entirely at home as Americans.

This, of course, was exactly the opposite of the situation in the USSR. There Jews couldn't live as Jews, yet no matter how hard many tried to assimilate—shedding every last vestige of their Jewish identity—they still were not accepted as full-blooded Soviets.

Describing our first weeks and months in New York would easily fill a book. We had no end of experiences, challenges, and mood swings. There was so much that was new and different. But slowly, ever so slowly, things began to fall into place.

We found an apartment in Rego Park, Queens, with the help of NYANA, our local resettlement agency. I went to the neighborhood public school. My studies were pretty easy for me, especially the math and science courses. Babushka found a circle of Russian- and Yiddish-speaking friends in the nearby Jewish community center and otherwise busied herself preparing us wonderful dinners of borscht, stuffed cabbage, cutlets, kasha, fruit compote, and other Russian specialties. Papa retrained as a computer programmer and subsequently landed his first job, though he quickly learned that job security in a free-wheeling capitalist society is not what it was in the centrally planned Soviet economy. Fortunately, he eventually found a stable position. And Mama announced to us that since there was no need for German teachers in New York, she was going to become a bookkeeper. Psychologically, this must have been a tough transition for her.

The years have flown by. My grandmother has slowed down, but I have no doubt that her new life in America gave her a second wind. Thanks to the miracle of satellites and cable, she's able to watch Russian-language television. With the boom in Russian Jewish life in New York, she now has her choice of two local all-Russian radio stations and a range of newspapers and magazines. And you have to see the joy on her face when she celebrates a Jewish holiday and no longer has to whisper to me—or now my children—its meaning. Her life has come full circle, she said, and it makes her feel good to know that Jewish life will continue in our family.

My parents are in their sixties and beginning to think about retirement. They have no regrets whatsoever about their momentous decision to leave Moscow twenty-five years ago.

Their English is accented, to be sure, but fluent. They've created a good life for themselves. Most of their friends here are also from the old country, but they've made a few other friends as well. Friends, you should know, are very important in our culture. We invest a lot of time in building and maintaining relationships.

My parents have traveled twice to Europe, taken a trip to Israel, which they loved and where they saw many of their old friends and colleagues, and even spent a week in Moscow last year. When they got back, their first comment was: "Moscow is a nice place to visit, but who would want to live there?"

I can't say that my parents have turned into devout Jews. The one thing communism managed to instill in them was skepticism about organized religion. Still, they have an active interest in all things Jewish—books, museums, historical sites, news. And when it comes to support for Israel, they are outspoken.

Like many Soviet Jews, they feel a strong, visceral connection to Israel and approach any peace process with deep-seated doubts about Arab intentions. They have no confidence in the word of despotic governments, be they Arab or communist.

My parents, like many other Soviet Jews here, often find themselves at odds with the majority of American Jews on key political issues. For our whole family, Ronald Reagan occupies an exalted place. He understood the true nature of communism and confronted it directly. Yet Reagan was too conservative for many of the American Jews we've met. In turn, we tend to find American Jews at times too naïve, too credulous.

As for me, I'm living proof of the American dream. I went to college, attended law school, and am now working in a good firm. I married a physician with a background similar to my own. We bought a home in Staten Island not too far from my parents' place in Queens, joined a synagogue, and send our children to Hebrew school. In just about every respect, they're typical American kids. They speak a decent Russian, though between them they always speak in English, and we're trying to give them a love of Russian culture. But that's turning out to be a steep uphill struggle. American popular culture exerts a strong pull on them.

Several times a year, we—all four generations—travel to Brighton Beach in Brooklyn, "Odessa by the Sea." We savor the sights and sounds of a bustling Russian Jewish neighborhood filled with restaurants, cafés, gourmet shops, and bookstores that continue to evoke an important part of the lives of my grandmother, my parents, and me, and perhaps will one day help explain us to my two young American-born children.

I am eternally grateful to Mama and Papa. Now that I'm a parent myself—in fact, only a year or two younger than they were when they first decided to emigrate—I can appreciate even more their courage and love. They took a leap into the unknown. They did it because they couldn't see a future for themselves, and especially for me. The step they took wasn't easy for them. Believe me when I say that. But they persevered, and I, and now my children as well, are the direct beneficiaries.

The time has come, I feel, for me to start giving back, especially to the American Jewish community and Israel. I wouldn't be where I am without them.

Through national and local organizations, American Jews—and many non-Jews as well, as I later learned to my pleasant surprise— advocated on behalf of the rights of Soviet Jewry while we were still behind the Iron Curtain. Moreover, they helped us along the way once we were able to leave. And now that I know something about the experiences of refugees from other countries who came to America, I realize all the more how fortunate we were to have such a helping hand.

Israel instilled in many of us pride and dignity, though we always had to hide it. Ask my grandmother's generation how they felt when Israel sent its first ambassador, Golda Meir, to Moscow. Ask my parents' generation how they felt when they read samizdat (i.e., secretly self-published) copies of Leon Uris's *Exodus*, translated into Russian, and came to understand the story of modern-day Israel. And ask them how they felt in 1967 when the Israeli army vanquished Soviet-equipped Arab armies in just six days.

Israel also gave us the affidavit, without which it would have been virtually impossible to emigrate from the Soviet Union in 1979. After all, officially this migration was referred to by the Kremlin, for its own domestic reasons and notwithstanding its anti-Zionist rhetoric, as repatriation of Jews to the Jewish homeland, Israel.

Organized American Jewry will find a tremendous potential resource in people like me. By now we number in the hundreds of thousands. We're roughly one-quarter of the New York Jewish population and as much as one-tenth of the total American Jewish community. We have passion, commitment, and real-life experience galore.

A number of local Federations have reached out to us, and one national Jewish organization I know of has made a special effort to integrate us into the framework of the Jewish community as full participants—the American Jewish Committee.

For the past six years, AJC has run a leadership institute specially designed for Jews from the FSU. I took the course and now feel empowered. They have a staff member focusing full-time on our community and a Russian-language web site, and they've just started regular radio commentaries on Jewish topics in Russian.

As I stop to reflect on my life, it's simply mind-boggling.

In 1979, I was still wearing the red scarf of the Pioneers. Before the year ended, I had traveled through Austria and Italy and settled in a new home in New York. Today I'm an American-educated lawyer. Were we lucky! The gates began closing shortly after we left. In the next eight years combined, fewer people left than in 1979 alone.

But then the numbers started rising rapidly. Over one million people have streamed out in the past fifteen years—most on direct flights to their countries of destination rather than through transit points, reflecting the dramatically new political climate. Some have adjusted rather quickly; others, however, have had a difficult time adapting to a new world.

The impact of this modern-day exodus, of which we were a tiny part, has been profound not only on the U.S. and American Jewry, but also on Israel, 20 percent of whose Jewish population today is from the Former Soviet Union, and on Germany, whose Jewish community is now overwhelmingly from the FSU. To a lesser degree, its impact can also be felt in Australia and Canada.

And, of course, the pièce de résistance came in 1991 when the USSR collapsed from the weight of its own tyranny, corruption, and inefficiency, to be replaced by fifteen sovereign countries and the flowering of Jewish life in just about every one of them.

On second thought, maybe we weren't such atheists after all. Perhaps someone "up there" really had heard our most fervent prayers.

Letter from a Bar Mitzvah Employee
September 17, 2003

Thirteen years ago this month, I accepted an offer to become the American Jewish Committee's executive director.

At the time, I was working in AJC's Washington office as director of government and international affairs. It was a happy period in my professional and family life. I enjoyed the front-line work and loved the city. That made the decision to uproot my family—not for the first time, I might add—all the more difficult.

Was I cut out to manage a large, complex organization? Would I have to forfeit my interest in hands-on analysis and advocacy in the new job? Could I raise money, something I hadn't previously done? And how would my family and I cope with New York, which, at the time, looked as if it was in a free fall, the butt of endless jokes in the nation's capital, especially from those who had only recently fled Gotham and insisted the city had no chance of stabilizing itself?

I wavered for some time, losing much sleep in the process, before informing Sholom Comay, AJC's president at the time, that I would take the job. And even after saying yes, I remained plagued by lingering doubts for weeks.

In hindsight, it was the best professional decision I've ever made. These past thirteen years have been the most stimulating and fulfilling of my life.

During a bar mitzvah, it is customary to express appreciation to those rabbis and teachers, family and friends, who helped make the day possible.

I couldn't even begin to list all the individuals—both lay leaders and staff colleagues—to whom I'm indebted. That would fill pages and, in the end, no doubt, I would have offended some by inadvertent acts of omission. Suffice it to say that I've collaborated with, and learned from, some rather extraordinary people during my tenure.

Instead, let me say a few things about the institution itself, beginning with the bottom line.

The longer I know the American Jewish Committee, the more in awe I am. The longer I work in Jewish communal life, the more I understand AJC's uniqueness. And the longer I live, the more I grasp how essential it is that AJC be there for the generations of Jews to come.

Some will accuse me of idealizing the organization. After all, I'm not exactly the world's most objective person on the subject. And it's true that a bar mitzvah is not normally the time to stand up and reveal everything that's wrong with life. Even so, while acknowledging that AJC is an imperfect entity with room for improvement, I can't help but sing its praises. I've been around the working world long enough to recognize something special when I see it.

I have to confess, though, that when I first began working at AJC, back in 1979, I wasn't sure I had made the right choice.

I was still rather new to the Jewish world, having spent just a few years with HIAS in their refugee operations in Rome and Vienna. That work exposed me to only one aspect of the Jewish public affairs agenda—the remarkable migration and resettlement efforts of agencies like HIAS, the American Jewish Joint Distribution Committee (JDC), the Jewish Agency for Israel, the World ORT Union, and the Federation system in the United States.

When I first encountered an AJC delegation in Vienna, I was impressed with their level of interest, even if I knew next to nothing about the organization. The Jewish organizational world beyond my narrow stratum seemed to the newly initiated like a tangled web whose component parts were difficult to separate out.

The AJC group didn't come looking for photo-ops with the refugees. Rather, they wanted to hear first-hand from the refugees about the situation in the Soviet Union and the emigration process;

from us they wanted to know what help they could provide in Washington with admissions procedures.

One result of AJC's visit to Vienna was a job offer. I did my due diligence before accepting and moving to New York. Those who knew the organizational landscape were almost unanimous in describing the agency to me as the community's "class act." But, truth be told, my first years at AJC weren't the easiest.

I went from life on the edge, dealing with the pulsating movement of Jewish refugees who were heavily dependent on our assistance, to a windowless office in a remote part of the third floor. I used to joke that when I worked in Rome and Vienna, just getting from my office to the men's room was a Herculean feat. The refugees crowded the hallways, and many had questions or requests that just couldn't, or wouldn't, wait. In AJC, by contrast, there were no such challenges in getting from here to there.

Over time, as my job assignments changed and I came to understand the larger communal lay of the land, I was increasingly able to grasp— and admire—AJC's distinctive culture. Today it provides for me a model of what a nongovernmental organization should be. Several features, in particular, stand out. In the spirit of the David Letterman Show—but without the humor, I'm afraid—let me mention my list of the top ten (in no special order).

First, like a truly great sports team, AJC seeks to attract the best professionals for every position.

Each professional is an acknowledged leader in his or her field, both within and beyond the Jewish community. There aren't many wallflowers among my staff colleagues, nor are there many yes-men—or yes-women—and thankfully so. Among other things, I should point out, this can make for exciting, even memorable, staff discussions. And it certainly guarantees good sounding boards and reality checks for all of us.

Second, AJC draws to its lay ranks accomplished and dedicated individuals who have achieved standing both in their professional and civic lives.

At a time when some major not-for-profit agencies are dominated by one leader, who by dint of wealth or prominence becomes the sun around which the organization revolves, AJC stands out for the team culture of its volunteers. To be sure, there are strong personalities among them, but they see other strong personalities in the ranks as an asset, not a liability, because together they substantially enhance the overall institution.

Third, AJC's leadership paradigm is embodied in the concept of a genuine lay-staff partnership.

Close collaboration and mutual respect are the hallmarks of that partnership, whether on the national or chapter level. Each side understands the vital—and irreplaceable—role the other plays; each makes adequate room for the other. Incidentally, when this partnership collapsed briefly in the 1980s, the agency as a whole suffered severe damage, a sobering reminder of the institutional stakes involved.

Fourth, the organization recognizes that it is grappling with some of the most difficult, complex, and intractable issues known to humankind.

In a world too often seeking a shortcut or easy answer, AJC realizes that there simply are no quick fixes, at least when it comes to attaining our goals—securing the well-being and safety of the Jewish people and universalizing democratic and pluralistic values.

Analysis, research, and deliberation are accorded a central place in the life of the agency, accompanied by the patience, perseverance, and persistence required to fashion an effective advocacy strategy. In other words, AJC's approach is to be armed with the facts and the political savoir faire to get the job done, together with the staying power for the long haul.

This approach has proven its value on many occasions in recent years. Some examples: helping prod the United Nations to admit Israel to one of the five regional blocs in New York after fifty years of exclusion; persuading the Japanese government to drop its longstanding adherence to the Arab economic boycott of Israel; and pressing a reluctant German government to extend financial assistance to thousands of Holocaust survivors in Eastern Europe.

Fifth, AJC has always put the attainment of the objective above all other considerations.

We live in a cacophonous world in which those who don't make a lot of noise and constantly call attention to themselves can easily be lost in the shuffle. But histrionics, theatrics, and decibel level are not necessarily the best yardsticks for measuring effectiveness. In fact, all that sound and fury and self-aggrandizement, while perhaps music to the media's ears, can undermine the attainment of programmatic goals.

AJC's ability time and again to suppress its ego, maintain discretion, and work behind-the-scenes on key issues affecting the Jewish people and the State of Israel—forsaking public recognition in the process— is especially noteworthy.

Whether it was the critical role AJC played in launching the National Interreligious Task Force on Soviet Jewry, or chairing the community-wide effort to raise the millions of dollars required to support Professor Deborah Lipstadt in her legal victory over Holocaust denier David Irving, or arranging meetings between Israeli statesmen and their counterparts in countries with which Israel has no diplomatic links, AJC knows how to maintain a low profile, or, if necessary, no profile, to serve a larger aim. In each of these cases, public discussion of our role at the time would have been counterproductive.

It helps explain why a retired Jewish professional who spent decades at a sister agency commented to me: "AJC did four times the work we did, yet we claimed four times the credit and got away with it only because we knew you wouldn't go public unless there was reason to."

Moreover, it means we understand the value of cooperation with other agencies. In fact, there are several Jewish organizations with which we enjoy close ties and whose work we particularly respect. Unfortunately, though, competition for turf, philanthropic dollars, and media attention occasionally leads some organizations to put their own narrow interests ahead of the community's, while deceiving themselves into believing that the two sets of interests are identical.

Sixth, AJC blends the values of Jewish ethical teachings with the ideals of American democracy and pluralism.

Not only is the agency deeply involved in seeking to advance both fronts, but it also nourishes the interconnection between the two.

To be a Jew, we believe, is to be engaged in the larger world in which we live. We are the heirs of a tradition with powerful moral injunctions:

Seek justice; relieve the oppressed, defend the orphan, plead for the widow (Isaiah 1:17).

God has told you, O mortals, what is good, and what God requires of you: only to do justice, and to love goodness, and to walk humbly with God (Micah 6:8).

What is hateful to you do not do to your neighbor. That is the entire Torah; all the rest is commentary. Go and learn it (Hillel, Talmud Shabbat 31A).

To be an American, we believe, means to stand in solidarity with fellow democracies, including Israel, to defend human rights and human dignity at home and abroad, and to build a pluralistic society based on the principles of mutual respect and compassion for the least fortunate among us.

As one of many illustrations, I'll never forget a Jewish interagency mission to Ethiopia in the 1980s. The focus was on the Jewish community on the eve of Operation Moses, the historic effort to help Ethiopian Jews realize their age-old dream of a return to Zion. But the mission also took place at a time when famine was ravaging sub-Saharan Africa and Ethiopia in particular. Millions of lives were imperiled.

AJC insisted that the mission travel both to the Jewish villages in the Gondar province and to the feeding stations and offices of international humanitarian groups working to alleviate the famine, such as Catholic Relief Service, Church World Service, and the JDC. To my dismay, there was some strong resistance to our proposal. Not only did we stand our ground, though, but when the group returned, AJC raised close to $300,000 and distributed it in equal amounts to the Catholic, Protestant, and Jewish agencies coping with the famine.

We saw no contradiction between helping fellow Jews and identifying with the suffering of fellow human beings—not then, not now.

Grandiose as it may sound, AJC truly aspires to be a model Jewish citizen and a model global citizen.

Seventh, AJC is unafraid of difference. To the contrary, it welcomes the give-and-take of debate.

By deliberately attracting to its large tent a wide array of thoughtful and caring people—with varied political, religious, professional, and social backgrounds—it practically guarantees informed, often impassioned, debate on the main issues of the day. And that's the way it should be.

Organizations of one political hue or another too often miss out on the complexity and nuance of the matters before them. Their mode of thinking and analysis tends to be heavily skewed by their ideological predispositions.

Many of the major public policy issues before us, in my view, defy simplistic precast solutions of, say, the left or right. Instead, these issues need to be examined on their own merits, critical questions must be asked, and the chips should be allowed to fall where they may—sometimes in a liberal or dovish direction, other times in a conservative or hawkish direction, and still other times in the center.

Those who try to pigeonhole AJC usually end up frustrated or just simply off the mark. They select one or two positions and then seek to extrapolate from them, only to discover later that they failed to take into account other information that might have led to a different conclusion.

Maybe in the end we're akin to the singles tennis player, whose most comfortable position is the central point of the base line, ready to move in any direction in anticipation of—or response to—a volley, but sooner or later likely to return to that central point.

Call it a spirit of independence or simply recognition that a one-size-fits-all ideological straightjacket just isn't the answer for us.

Eighth, AJC is an oasis of civility.

In a rough-and-tumble world, AJC manages its disagreements just about as well as it handles its agreements. Differences may be profound on some issues and the debate intense, but anyone who has witnessed these scenes walks away impressed by the manner in which the agency closes ranks after decisions are made. People are respectful of one another. Everyone understands going in that none of us will always get our way. Strikingly, I don't ever recall seeing tempers lost, tables pounded, or doors slammed, much less ad hominem attacks.

Ninth, AJC has an uncanny ability to peek around corners and see the future, perhaps not as clearly as any of us might wish when it comes to our investment portfolios, but certainly as it affects the societal trends with which we are most concerned.

I don't think it's by accident, either. The organization draws together insightful people who have the capacity to see the big picture and actively encourages them to think through—and plan for—not just today's challenges, but tomorrow's as well.

Whether it's Israel's quest for lasting peace, the future of Israel-Diaspora ties, the nature of American Jewish identity, the state of intergroup relations and coalition-building, the well-being of overseas Jewish communities, the use and abuse of religion, protection of human rights, or the dangers posed by the marriage of terrorism and weapons of mass destruction, AJC is constantly seeking to develop long-term, proactive strategies. In doing so, we don't pretend that we have all the answers, but history has shown that we have a pretty good record of alerting the Jewish community—and, when appropriate, the broader community—to what's coming down the pike.

And finally, AJC has never succumbed to despair.

It is a fundamentally optimistic organization that believes, consistent with our Judaic tradition, that human progress is achievable. Trust me, AJC has no illusions about the dangers that lurk, but we refuse to conclude, as a result, that hope must be thrown to the wind or that we need to retreat inside a shell. We have witnessed enough major steps forward, some the result of our own handiwork, to believe that more are within our grasp.

To sum up this agency with which I've been associated for more than two decades, it is an organization invested with anthropomorphic qualities—a mind that is sharp and quick, a heart that is filled with compassion, a spine that bespeaks moral and intellectual courage, and a soul that links us to past and future generations.

On the occasion of my thirteenth anniversary as AJC's executive director—or, as I sometimes say, chief professional worrier—I'd like to pay tribute to a remarkable institution.

The American Jewish Committee has empowered countless American Jews to have a respected and resonant voice that is heard in councils of power around the world, to have an impact on the sweep of contemporary history, and to leave the world more secure for our children than it was left for us.

Thirteen years have passed and I continue to look forward with excitement to every day in my AJC life. No two days are identical. Each one brings new opportunities. Sure, there are occasional setbacks and disappointments—is there a job without them?—but they are relatively few and far between.

In the end, I'm a very lucky person. I am blessed with not one but two precious families—the one I live with at home and the one I live with at work. That's mazel!

Now bring on the chopped liver and cha-cha. Oops, I think that puts me in the Ice Age or, should I say, the "Sculptured Ice" Age? How about the sushi and salsa?

Letter from a Diplomatic Marathoner
October 13, 2003

I've always wanted to run the New York Marathon, but the stamina just isn't there. A 10K race is about as far as I've ever been able to go, and I won't even mention my time or placement. Suffice it to say that my only goal has been to finish the race in one piece. And, believe me, that doesn't get easier with the passage of time.

The next best thing in New York is the annual Diplomatic Marathon, arguably no less taxing than the road runners' race, even if it's confined to less than a square mile on Manhattan's East Side. Actually, there's no such thing as the Diplomatic Marathon, but it's what we at the American Jewish Committee have dubbed our efforts, conducted under the auspices of our Madeline and Bruce M. Ramer Institute for Diplomatic Relations, during the two-week period each fall following the opening of the UN General Assembly. World leaders descend on New York to deliver speeches before the world body and to meet with one another.

A decade ago, following the creation of a pioneering AJC Ambassadors' Forum in Washington, which brought envoys of key countries together with Jewish audiences on a monthly basis, we decided to approach the presidents, prime ministers, and foreign ministers who flood New York in September for meetings. In the first year, we managed to schedule four meetings. Ten years later, the number has risen to over sixty-five, plus a couple we do together with other Jewish agencies.

Handling four meetings over the span of two weeks is one thing, handling sixty-five quite another. Enter the notion of a marathon. Insofar as there are ten working days in this period, it comes out to an average of more than 6.5 meetings per day. Given the fact that each meeting requires adequate preparation, that they're often back-to-back, and that getting around the East Side at this time of year can be next to impossible for security reasons, the whole process can be draining, much as it's also exhilarating.

Above all, our Diplomatic Marathon is a unique opportunity to engage world leaders on issues of immediate concern. Sure, we have ongoing diplomatic contacts year-round, as a result of travel abroad and links with ambassadors and consuls general posted in this country and at the UN, but the possibilities afforded by New York as a once-a-year world diplomatic stage are simply without equal.

Our program has grown to the point where a government official commented that, other than the Department of State, no American institution has such extensive contact with foreign leaders at this time of year as the American Jewish Committee.

What explains our formula for success? There are four basic elements.

First, the American Jewish Committee is seen as a leading representative of an influential American Jewish community. Foreign leaders believe it's important to engage the Jewish community in the world's most powerful country.

It may be because they believe that American Jews can be encouraged to use their voice and access to shape America's political attitudes toward a particular country. Perhaps they seek assistance on specific diplomatic or legislative matters. Or maybe they hope American Jews will take an economic interest, leading to expanded trade and investment. Whatever the particular reason, the thinking goes that American Jews should not be ignored. Their good will can be helpful; their ill will can be harmful to a country's interests. In other words, the bottom line is the perception of American Jewish power, personified in this case by the American Jewish Committee.

Second, the American Jewish Committee works at diplomacy twelve months a year. Thus, these meetings grow naturally out of ongoing contacts that take place in New York, Washington, other American cities where foreign diplomats are stationed, Geneva, and individual countries, as well as with Jewish communities around the world.

Indeed, for virtually every country with which we meet during the Diplomatic Marathon, there is an extensive history of previous contacts. And we don't just maintain contacts with those countries when there are particular issues, e.g., an anti-Semitic outbreak, a restitution issue, or a problematic UN vote. Rather, we stay in touch with as many countries as possible, in large part to be in a better position, with greater credibility, if a particular issue should arise.

Third, our diplomacy is two-way. Some Jewish organizations, in their approach to other countries, have adopted the attitude that the world owes the Jewish people for crimes of commission and omission during the Shoah. To the extent that this was a prevalent feeling in any country—and there weren't ever very many in this category—it's rapidly disappearing. In other words, in this day and age, Holocaust awareness does not form a foundation for long-term diplomacy. Nor does debating the history of the Arab-Israeli conflict, as if proving that right has been on Israel's side since 1948 alone will sway a country to be more sympathetic to Israel's case today. Would that it were so easy!

Diplomacy entails understanding the country with which we are engaged and assessing the way it calculates its national interests. Moreover, it means grasping how a Jewish organization can factor itself into that calculation of national interests. Much as we might wish otherwise, simply making good arguments on a given issue, or appealing to moral or ethical considerations, won't necessarily sway a foreign government. As a veteran of literally a couple of thousand diplomatic encounters over the past two decades, I can attest to this reality.

The American Jewish Committee has a proactive foreign policy that allows us to engage in two-way diplomacy. No, we don't fly F-15s, negotiate treaties, or dispense surplus grain, but we do our best to leverage the considerable strengths we bring to the table. For example, consistent with our commitment to the promotion of democratic values, humanitarian assistance, and intergroup understanding and to the protection of human rights, we have undertaken a number of important initiatives. It's worthwhile to spell out some of them, as they're a distinguishing feature of AJC.

We were the first organization of our kind to publicly support the two recent waves of NATO expansion involving a total of ten countries; to call on the Bush (41) administration to recognize the independence of Estonia, Latvia, and Lithuania; and to urge the same administration to support Ukraine's assertion of freedom from Moscow. Similarly, we successfully lobbied for an end to the application of the Jackson-Vanik Amendment to Bulgaria and Romania, and have urged similar action for Russia. And we were the first Jewish organization outside Germany to support German unification.

In the late 1980s, AJC began to devote more attention to the nations of Asia and the Pacific, and we urged Washington and Jerusalem to consider enhanced trade and strategic cooperation with the democracies of that critical region. We followed closely the independence struggle in East Timor, sending a delegate there shortly after the fighting ended and inviting East Timorese delegates to meet with the American Jewish Committee on numerous occasions. We have sought to heighten India's profile in Washington after decades of benign neglect resulting from the Cold War. We have worked closely with Turkish officials to enhance appreciation of that country's vital geopolitical role at the intersection of Europe and Asia. We have assisted Azerbaijan in its efforts to get out from under onerous U.S. trade restrictions.

We've helped Peru on trade matters. We've assisted Costa Rican political leaders to get a high-level hearing in Washington. We've taken an interest in immigration and trade issues affecting U.S.-Mexican and U.S.-Central American relations.

We were early supporters of the United Nations. Historians have credited us with a key role in the inclusion of human rights protections in the UN Charter. We were strong advocates for the Universal Declaration of Human Rights and the Genocide Convention. A former AJC president, Jacob Blaustein, originally launched the idea of a UN High Commissioner for Human Rights, which three decades later became a reality. On two separate occasions we have provided funds to assist the work of the United Nations High Commissioner for Refugees, first in the Balkans, more recently in Afghanistan.

Through the generosity of several AJC members, we have been able to undertake a number of other humanitarian initiatives. For example, we have contributed a unit for treating cancer victims in an Israeli-built hospital in Mauritania, an Arab country with full diplomatic links with Israel. We built a school in Turkey after an earthquake devastated the region, and rebuilt a school in India also hit by an earthquake. Collaborating with the German military and a German Protestant non-governmental agency, we provided medical and other relief assistance to Kosovar Muslims fleeing Serbia's policy of ethnic cleansing. And we have supported relief efforts in famine-ravaged sub-Saharan Africa, as well as in Rwanda after the 1994 genocide. Currently in South Africa, we are funding a local program to combat the impact of AIDS.

This is only a partial list, but it's meant to illustrate both the range and diversity of AJC's unrivaled initiatives in the international arena. All are entirely consistent with our core values as an agency. We would not violate those values in pursuit of short-term political gain. But, given the obvious fact that we cannot be everywhere, these initiatives are also selected with an eye toward maximizing our political objectives, which include strengthening Israel's standing in the community of nations, combating anti-Semitism, and setting an example for constructive intergroup relations.

There's still more. We are able to draw upon the stature, experience, and network of key component parts of the agency. They include the Office of Government and International Affairs, the Jacob Blaustein Institute for the Advancement of Human Rights, the Asia and Pacific Rim Institute, the Israel and Middle East Office, United Nations Watch, the Lawrence and Lee Ramer Center for German-Jewish Relations, the Harriet and Robert Heilbrunn Institute for International Interreligious Understanding, Thanks To Scandinavia, thirty-three chapter offices, the Departments of Research and Publications, the Division on Middle East and International Terrorism, our new Latino and Latin American Affairs and Russian desks, and Project Interchange, which in the past year has expanded to include seminars taking European influentials to Israel. The American Jewish Committee and two of its affiliates, it should be noted, all have UN accreditation. Further, our ten partnerships with Jewish communities around the world and extensive network of interethnic and interreligious contacts are often extremely helpful in pursuing diplomatic goals.

And not least, the participants in our diplomacy include former U.S. ambassadors and negotiators, leading experts on international organizations and human rights, veterans of our diplomatic activities who have befriended our interlocutors, and persons with business, cultural, or academic links with particular countries.

Fourth, a key to our diplomatic formula is that we're not in this for the headlines. We do this work because it's vitally important to the Jewish people worldwide. And because the stakes are so high, we don't play games, violate confidences, run to the media after an off-the-record session, or level wild accusations to embarrass others.

Our goal is to influence the thinking of governments on matters of significance, and the best way to do that is to build relationships based on trust and confidence and to appeal to their own national interests. To do that, we learn to speak truth to power, but in a way that keeps the door open and the conversation going. The key is not just to have the first meeting, but the second and third ones as well. Governments don't turn around on a dime, to say the least. I might add that we also gain much valuable information and many insights from these encounters with world leaders.

We've had our share of concrete successes. Let me mention just two.

An Israeli legal expert was just elected as vice chair of the UN's Sixth (Legal) Committee for the first time in history. This came about because Israel is now a member of one of the five regional groups (WEOG, or the West European and Others Group) that determine election to such key posts.

If Israel today is a member, it's due in no small measure to the American Jewish Committee's diplomatic efforts, over many years, to focus a spotlight on Israel's anomalous status as the only UN country not allowed membership in one of the five regional groups. When Israel was finally offered temporary membership in WEOG, Dore Gold, Israel's former ambassador to the UN, declared that "AJC changed history."

And when the fifty-five-member Organization for Security and Cooperation in Europe (OSCE) gathered in Vienna in June to spend two days assessing the state of anti-Semitism in member countries, it resulted in part from a persistent AJC campaign in Europe and the United States to garner backing for such a gathering, the first of its kind. The original concept was far from a slam dunk; many countries needed convincing that the subject of anti-Semitism warranted a separate conference. Now we are building support for a second such meeting, which we hope will take place in Berlin next year.

In the 2003 Diplomatic Marathon, once again we learned a great deal, exchanged views on key matters, measured the international temperature, and pressed certain points. It's impossible to summarize sixty-five meetings in a few paragraphs—our Office of Government and International Affairs will, as always, prepare a full report on each—but let me share with you a few of the more interesting moments.

While much discussion understandably focused on Iraq, including the possibility of a second UN Security Council resolution, there was widespread concern about Iran.

The Vienna-based International Atomic Energy Agency has imposed an October 31 deadline on Iran to provide full transparency and full disclosure of its nuclear program. Signals from Tehran are mixed as to whether the government will comply with these demands. While one Arab foreign minister with whom we met predicted that Iran would acquiesce, another confidently asserted that it would not, and foresaw a Western strike against Iran within the next three-to-four years. Interestingly, the Western leader most troubled by developments in Iran appeared to be French President Jacques Chirac. He spoke to us of his anxiety over intermediate-range missiles, with a range of 1,000 miles, displayed at a recent military parade in Tehran, and predicted that the UN Security Council would find agreement in dealing with Iran.

On Israel, it's impossible to generalize about our discussions, but one thing can be said: When it comes to bilateral relations, Israel is in pretty good shape. Indeed, some countries, including Macedonia, asked for our help in enhancing ties. But when it comes to regional or global forums, Israel hardly stands a chance.

Take countries like India, Singapore, and Turkey. The state of bilateral ties between these three countries and Israel is truly excellent. High-level contacts are frequent, trade is growing, and cooperation extends to the military and intelligence spheres. But when it comes to the UN, with few exceptions, these three countries regularly vote against Israel. All say that they seek to moderate the texts of anti-Israel resolutions, but when push comes to shove, they go along with the automatic majority because they fear a price to be paid in the world body if they vote otherwise.

In a way, the same can be said for the European Union countries. All fifteen have solid relations with Israel, especially now that Israel has returned its ambassadors to Belgium and Austria after political difficulties with each. But in the multilateral sphere, the EU, which defines itself as evenhanded, in fact leans toward the Palestinian side. At best, EU countries might abstain on an anti-Israel resolution, but seldom, if ever, will the EU join with Israel and the United States in opposing such a measure.

Most troubling for me in this round of diplomatic meetings was the infuriating lack of sympathy for Israel's extraordinary security difficulties and policy dilemmas. To be sure, some ministers evinced understanding. Noteworthy in this group were the ministers from Australia, several Pacific Island nations, and a number of Central and East European countries, including Poland, Bulgaria, and Romania.

But, by and large, we heard endless repetitions of such profoundly troubling phrases as "cycle of violence" to describe the situation on the ground. This implies a moral symmetry and an equal assignment of blame for the violence and terror. And while there isn't much love lost for Arafat, Sharon didn't fare much better.

Yet, at the same time, no one seemed to have any answers, either. There were calls for continuation of the peace process, pursuit of the Road Map, commitment to the success of the new Palestinian prime minister, and restraint by Israel, but in a way they rang hollow. The harsh reality is that, absent a Palestinian commitment to defeat the terrorism in its midst, no Israeli government, of the left or right, is likely to be in a position to move forward. And none of our diplomatic interlocutors offered any serious suggestions on how to deal with the terrorism.

One point of agreement, though, was on the irreplaceable role of the United States. It is widely recognized that Washington offers the only hope for moving the peace process forward. The EU, UN, and Russia—the other three parties in the Quartet—are simply not trusted in Jerusalem. But will the Bush administration press ahead? That was a question on the minds of many, most notably the Europeans. The fear is that, faced with a quagmire in Iraq and an increasingly tough reelection bid, the last thing in the world the Bush team now wants, rhetoric notwithstanding, is to grapple again with Arab-Israeli issues. The Road Map was launched with great fanfare. Tragically, it aborted for the very same reason that the Clinton-Barak effort had failed—Yasir Arafat sabotaged it. We are, therefore, faced with a conundrum: Peace is not possible with Arafat, yet, given his unrivaled stature among Palestinians, peace may not be possible, at least in the short term, without him.

The same reasoning that governed the administration in its first year in office, namely avoiding an issue that had consumed the Clinton team for years and ultimately failed to produce an agreement, could now return. Yet the conflict will not simply sit quietly until an administration in Washington is prepared to reengage it; it could explode at any moment, its ripple effects reaching far and wide. Thus, we saw grim faces among our European and moderate Arab interlocutors, but no well-conceived exit strategies to emerge from the current dire situation.

Another point of agreement with some of our conversation partners was the recognition that the most likely strategy to jump-start the peace process was to think big, not small, even if the chances for success are quite low. In this spirit, we offered the example of Anwar Sadat. The most transformative moment in Arab-Israeli diplomacy over the past fifty-five years was Sadat's dramatic visit to Jerusalem and his speech before the Knesset. Of course, the visit was preceded by secret diplomacy between Israel and Egypt. But once he set foot in Israel, and particularly in Israel's capital, peace became not only possible but practically inevitable; war, on the other hand, became unthinkable.

Russian Foreign Minister Igor Ivanov replied to this notion by suggesting that Saudi Crown Prince Abdullah had also tried to think big with the plan he floated. Our response was that had he taken the risk of flying to Israel and announcing it there rather than through an American journalist, he might well have had a similar impact on the Israeli people as Sadat did in 1977. Instead, his impact was minimal.

While admitting that the situation on the ground today may not be ripe for such historic gestures, we nonetheless urged leaders like EU foreign policy czar Javier Solana, Russian Foreign Minister Igor Ivanov, and Spanish Foreign Minister Ana Palacio to help plant the seeds for such a "big-vision" possibility that draws in the key Arab countries. Without them, and, of course, without the U.S., the prospects of a breakthrough are bleak.

We also consistently raised two other important issues.

The first dealt with the barrage of some twenty anti-Israel resolutions adopted by the UN General Assembly each year. Not only are these resolutions entirely one-sided, we argued, but they damage the image of the UN and undermine the search for peace. We zeroed in on three operational resolutions that fund a permanent and little-known UN structure that supports the Palestinian cause day in and day out.

This well-funded and well-staffed structure, which includes the Division on Palestinian Rights in the Office of the Under Secretary

General for Political Affairs, the Committee on the Exercise of the Inalienable Rights of the Palestinian People, and the Special Committee to Investigate Israeli Practices affecting the Human Rights of the Palestinian People and Other Arabs, is funded by member countries and is used as a battering ram against Israel.

Needless to say, there is nothing else in the UN structure that even comes close to approximating this institutionalized assault on a member state.

The truth is that many government leaders are clueless about this entire apparatus. It's too obscure. But one had to see the reaction of Australian Foreign Minister Alexander Downer when we explained the details to him. Not only was he surprised, but he immediately turned to his staff based at the UN and all but asked them why he hadn't been informed of these annual votes. He promised us he would give the matter careful consideration. Other leaders, however, were not nearly as forthcoming; sadly, they were unwilling to rock the boat.

The second issue dealt with anti-Semitism. We pressed the member countries of the Organization for Security and Cooperation in Europe to support a second conference on anti-Semitism next year, and I think we made some headway. We heard endorsements from, among others, President Chirac and Minister Palacio. We had been told that Britain objected to such a narrowly-based gathering, but Foreign Secretary Jack Straw appeared open to the idea in our meeting with him.

While there's progress to report on the second OSCE meeting, I came away from this round of diplomatic meetings once again disappointed by the general response to the upsurge in worldwide anti-Semitism. I've written on this previously (see "Letter from the Anti-Semitism Front," August 2003), but still can't quite grasp why there is such a lack of understanding. For some diplomats, the Jewish concern seems to be just another example of Jewish "overreaction," if not "hysteria." Or it simply doesn't fit with their image of Jews as powerful. Or to acknowledge anti-Semitism in their own countries is to admit to problems that they'd prefer to gloss over. Or it's an unfortunate but inevitable consequence of the Israeli-Palestinian conflict. Or to focus on anti-Semitism, in their minds, runs the risk of antagonizing the Muslim world, which they don't want to do.

The one piece of potentially good news in the discussions on anti-Semitism came in the interagency meeting with President Chirac. While painfully slow to respond to the outbreak of attacks against French Jews from October 2000 to June 2002, he told us that the French government today has a "zero-tolerance" attitude on the subject and that punishment is "swift and severe."

This year's Diplomatic Marathon is over, but the contacts continue. Next week, the Swiss foreign minister is visiting us, the following week we'll be having a meal with the Spanish foreign minister in Madrid, and then a session with the German interior minister, whose portfolio includes counterterrorism, in Berlin. And on it goes.

Unlike the New York Marathon with its precise distance, I don't know when as an agency we'll ever cross our finish line. But I do know that the collective stamina of the American Jewish Committee—our commitment to the long term and the resources we bring to bear in the effort—will ensure that there is a principled, sure-footed, and respected voice of the Jewish people in the global arena for as long as it takes.

Letter from a Town *Shrier*
November 19, 2003*

There's more bad news. This time it comes from Istanbul. Two synagogues were attacked by homicide bombers. Twenty-five people were killed, more than 300 injured.

The community, an integral part of Turkish society, had been on alert. There were warnings of possible Al-Qaeda attacks against Turkish Jews. And in 1986, a terrorist attack against an Istanbul synagogue also left twenty-two people dead. But as we now know too well, stopping homicide bombers is anything but easy.

Many governments—some with more sincerity, some with less—will condemn the bombings before moving on to deal with other issues, other demands on their time and attention. And for the media,

* I would like to acknowledge the research assistance of Adam Janvey, senior fellow at the American Jewish Committee.

it's just another bombing story in the increasingly long line of such stories stretching from Baghdad to Bali.

But what about us Jews? I'd like to think that this latest deadly attack on fellow Jews, following a string of such attacks, would have a lasting impact. For many, no doubt, it will, but for others, frankly, I'm not so sure, and this is the part that puzzles me.

George Orwell once wrote: "To see what is in front of one's nose needs a constant struggle." He might have added that for some it's easier than for others.

From my more-or-less 24/7 involvement with the American Jewish community, I'd divide us into three basic groups.

First, there are the "activist" Jews. These are the Jews who recognize what's going on around them and are engaged in the community, often in multiple ways. They care about Israel and fellow Jews around the world, and they are willing to act on their convictions.

Second, there are the "bubble" Jews. These Jews haven't left the reservation, but their level of comfort borders on outright complacency or indifference to what's going on, hence the bubble. If they follow the news, it's with a certain sense of detachment. When the going gets tough, they're incredibly hard to find.

At a prominent Westchester Reform synagogue, several lay leaders recently told the rabbi to stop talking about Israel and anti-Semitism or else they'd walk. They came to the synagogue, they said, to be uplifted, not to be confronted with depressing news.

Also, in a similar vein, I've met any number of Jews whom I refer to as "ABJs," meaning "Anyone (or anything) but Jews." These are benevolent people prepared to help almost anyone in need of assistance except fellow Jews. Laudably, they worry about AIDS victims, inner-city kids, refugees in sub-Saharan Africa, and endangered animals, and they commit time and resources to help out. But their compassion and philanthropy, for whatever reason, simply don't extend to other Jews, whether in Israel or elsewhere.

And third, there are the "apologetic" Jews. These Jews believe that our misfortunes are largely, if not entirely, of our own making. If only we'd change our behavior, everything would be just fine.

For NYU professor Tony Judt, writing in the October 23 issue of the prestigious *New York Review of Books*, that means converting "Israel from a Jewish state to a binational one."

For the financier George Soros, making a rare appearance at a Jewish event on November 5, it leads to the following proposition: "There is a resurgence of anti-Semitism in Europe. The policies of the Bush administration and the Sharon administration contribute to that…. If we change that direction, then anti-Semitism also will diminish."

According to a Jewish Telegraphic Agency report, Soros went further in an astonishing example of self-flagellation. "The billionaire financier said he, too, bears some responsibility for the new anti-Semitism, citing last month's speech by Malaysia's outgoing prime minister, Mahathir Mohammad, who said, 'Jews rule the world by proxy.'… 'As an unintended consequence of my actions,' he said, 'I also contribute to that image.'"

This letter is respectfully directed primarily to those in the second and third groups.

Let's face it. By any measure, the last three years have been pretty rough. Ever since the Palestinians rejected a landmark Israeli peace offer for a two-state solution—including the partitioning of Jerusalem—and unleashed a new wave of terror and violence, the Jewish state has been confronted with unprecedented challenges.

The normally very ordinary act of riding a city bus or sitting in a sidewalk café has overnight become a test of courage and resolve. No corner of Israel, neither inside the 1967 Green Line nor outside, is entirely safe or beyond the reach of those intent on creating havoc and mayhem. Not even the sacred space of a Passover Seder provides immunity from the murderers, any more than did the sanctity of Shabbat services in Istanbul.

The demands on Israel's military, intelligence, security, and police forces are beyond our capacity to imagine. Simply put, these forces have no margin for error. One successful infiltration overshadows dozens of foiled attempts. The infiltrators can be disguised as just about anyone—a pregnant woman, a soldier, an ultra-Orthodox Jew.

The targets could be anything—a military base, an oil storage facility, a skyscraper, or even, or perhaps especially, a simple pizzeria.

Israeli youngsters who dream of becoming NBA superstars, computer wizards, doctors, rabbis, you name it, are called on to defend their country and devote a minimum of three years of their lives if they're men, two years if they're women, while their parents live in a constant state of anxiety. The responsibility resting on the soldiers' shoulders is nothing less than the sheer existence of the state, which, fifty-five years after its establishment, remains under assault by those who continue to challenge the right of the Jewish people to self-determination in any part of the Middle East.

Is there anyone who still believes that when officials of Hamas, Islamic Jihad, or Hezbollah speak of their opposition to "occupied lands" they have in mind something other than the entire State of Israel? Can anyone confidently declare that Yasir Arafat is truly committed to a peaceful two-state solution with Israel, and not a one-state solution?

When a top adviser to Iran's supreme leader is quoted in *Agence France-Presse* as recently as November 10 declaring that "the existence of Israel is in contradiction with the national interests of Iran," and when the Vienna-based International Atomic Energy Agency reveals that Iran is much further along in its nuclear weapons program than previously believed, how difficult is it to connect the dots?

Given Israel's formidable military capacity, we sometimes forget certain basic geographic realities that are, to say the least, sobering. They're worth repeating, especially as we ponder possible political solutions. Perhaps they were best expressed by Prime Minister Menachem Begin in his first meeting with President Jimmy Carter in 1977, as retold by Yehuda Avner, who accompanied the Israeli leader to the White House:

> Referring to a three-by-five map Begin had brought with him, he ran his finger along the defunct [1967] border, and then said: "The Syrians sat on top of these mountains, Mr. President. We were at the bottom. This is the Hula Valley. It is hardly ten miles wide. They shelled our towns

and villages from the tops of those mountains, day and night." The prime minister's finger now moved southwards, to Haifa. "The armistice line is hardly twenty miles away from our major port city," he said. And then it rested on Netanya. "Our country here was reduced to a narrow waist nine miles wide.... Nine miles, Mr. President. Inconceivable! Indefensible!" The finger now hovered over Tel Aviv, and then it drummed the map: "Here live a million Jews, twelve miles from that indefensible armistice line. And here, between Haifa in the north and Ashkelon in the south lives two-thirds of our total population. And this coastal plain is so narrow that a surprise thrust by a column of tanks could cut the country in two in a matter of minutes. For whoever sits in these mountains," his fingertips tapped the tops of Judea and Samaria, "holds the jugular vein of Israel in his hands.... Gentlemen, no nation in our merciless and unforgiving neighborhood can be rendered so vulnerable and survive."

No other nation has been subjected to the same level of international scrutiny as Israel. Very few people outside the rarefied precincts of the United Nations and its specialized agencies can even begin to imagine how many resolutions are devoted to denouncing Israel, how many UN resources are allocated to maintaining a full-court press on Israel. Israel has more foreign media roaming the country per capita than any other country in the world, and they're all there to file stories. As we know too well, those stories seldom have to do with the wonders of Israeli high technology, medical research, agricultural innovations, cultural life, or social diversity.

For me, the establishment of Israel is nothing short of a miracle. The vision of Israel was made possible by the Hebrew Bible; it was made necessary by the Holocaust. We are blessed as Jews wherever we may live to witness the development of a Jewish state. That state, especially in the past three years, has faced the unrelenting trauma of homicide bombings and international vilification, as it struggles to defend itself and to find a credible Palestinian partner with whom to restart peace talks and achieve an eventual two-state solution, the only logical political outcome to the conflict.

That there are various schools of thought within and outside Israel on the best way to achieve peace with the Palestinians, I fully understand. And I fully understand, as well, that Israel is capable of making mistakes, big and small.

But I also recognize that Israel has no easy alternatives. Prime Minister Ehud Barak tried a negotiated settlement; it didn't work. Prime Minister Ariel Sharon has tried a tougher, more aggressive approach; so far it shows little sign of success, either. Are there those among us who know with certainty the precise course for Israel, a tiny sliver of a nation barely two percent the size of Egypt and one percent the size of Saudi Arabia, to pursue in its quest for a lasting peace?

I also understand that the support of the United States, and therefore of American Jewry—of us—is an irreplaceable strategic asset, pace Professor Judt, for the Jewish state's security and well-being.

We must stand strong in support of the enduring nature of the U.S.-Israel relationship. If not us, who? And if there are those among us who think that the relationship is on automatic pilot and doesn't need constant tending, they ought to think again. Our political adversaries in this country have made abundantly clear their long-term aim of driving a wedge between Jerusalem and Washington.

We need to stand together as one in expressing our revulsion against homicide bombings and our solidarity with the Israeli victims of terrorism.

We need to remind the world that no nation on earth yearns for peace more than the Jewish people. Peace is not a Madison Avenue slogan we picked up along the way for marketing purposes. Peace represents the essence of the Jewish quest throughout the 3,500 years of our existence, and peace has been at the heart of Israel's mission since its founding in 1948. Yes, different people have different approaches to the peace process, but how could it be otherwise given the tumultuous history of the past fifty-five years (and more)? And isn't the vigorous debate itself a sign of the health of Israeli democracy and Jewish pluralism?

Please come out of the bubble. All this discussion, whether regarding Israel or Turkey, is not about "them." It's about "us." Those Turkish synagogues could have been synagogues anywhere in the world.

And do yourself and all of us a favor and stop apologizing. The Jews have no less right than any other people to a state of our own; perhaps our claim, based on its longevity and source, is even stronger than most. Moreover, whatever the blemishes might be—and what country has a perfect record?—Israel's evolution as a state is worthy of our unabashed pride, even as we debate difficult issues. Also, let's never forget: Anti-Semitism is not a Jewish disease; it's a disease of the non-Jews. Do we really believe that, short of our disappearance, we can ever placate the anti-Semites? Haven't we learned this painfully obvious lesson from our history?

When a UN-sponsored conference against racism takes place in Durban, South Africa, as it did in 2001, and the most gruesome anti-Semitic and Nazi-like images and caricatures are distributed to the delegates by accredited nongovernmental organizations such as the Arab Lawyers Union, shouldn't we wake up from our stupor?

When rumors spread from Karachi to Newark that Israel—or Jews generally—are responsible for 9/11, do we dismiss the power of such rumors out of hand?

When the UN Commission on Human Rights, by a vote of forty to five, adopts a resolution implicitly endorsing terrorist acts against Israel, can we remain silent?

When Egyptian television airs a forty-one-episode series entitled *Horse without a Horseman*, which incorporates elements of the infamous czarist forgery *The Protocols of the Elders of Zion*, can we simply ignore its implications?

When an eighteen-year-old named Basu Hussain of Derby, England, is quoted in the *New York Times* as saying, "We should all get together and kill all the Jews," do we pretend to ourselves that he really doesn't mean it?

When his friend, Shaban Yasin, in the same article, adds that suicide bombing is the "wrong way" to kill the Jews, and "We should find out the best way to kill them, and do that," is this just written off as youthful fervor?

And when, in England, a young Jewish student is stabbed over twenty times while reading psalms on a public bus, an attack which

Scotland Yard labeled racist, must we not take the words of Basu Hussain and Shaban Yasin seriously?

When the imam of New York's most prominent mosque declares, shortly after 9/11, that "Muslims do not feel safe even going to the hospitals, because some Jewish doctors in one of the (New York) hospitals poisoned sick Muslim children who then died," do we fail to grasp the power of his incendiary words in the Islamic world?

And when Daniel Pearl, the *Wall Street Journal* reporter, is murdered by Islamic terrorists after being compelled to identify himself on video as a Jew, does it not send a chill down the spine of every Jew?

When European mainstream media impose Nazi images on Israel and a Portuguese Nobel Laureate likens the West Bank to Auschwitz, are we not outraged by this desecration of our history and gross distortion of a complex reality?

When an Alitalia pilot announces to the passengers of a Tel Aviv-bound flight "Welcome to Palestine," echoing an Air France pilot last June who referred to Tel Aviv's airport as "Israel-Palestine," are these nothing more than slips of the tongue?

And when a German priest named Joerg Zink appears on a popular television talk show and, referring to Palestinian suicide bombers, says that these are "courageous young folks sacrificing themselves for their cause," is it any wonder that so many Europeans naively romanticize the Palestinian cause?

When the prime minister of Malaysia opens the largest gathering of heads of state from Islamic countries in years by declaring, "The Europeans killed six million Jews out of twelve million. But today the Jews rule the world by proxy. They get others to fight and die for them," and receives a standing ovation at the end of the speech, how can we avoid the obvious conclusions?

When a volunteer application for San Francisco Women Against Rape includes a call to participate in "political education discussions" about supporting "Palestinian Liberation and taking a stance against Zionism," doesn't it hit close to home?

When a European Union survey reveals that Israel is regarded as the single greatest "threat to peace in the world" (and the United States is tied for second with Iran and North Korea), doesn't it arouse a sense of anger and injustice?

When the prominent Greek composer Mikis Theodorakis, best known for the music of *Zorba the Greek*, says that the Jews are "the root of evil," isn't he talking about all of us?

When a group of hooded men shouting "Death to Jews" attack a Jewish soccer team in suburban Paris, shouldn't it, as the *New York Times* editorialized, "prompt some profound soul-searching about whether the past has come calling"?

And when this is but one of literally hundreds of documented assaults on Jews and Jewish institutions in France, including an arson attack on a Jewish school in a northern Paris suburb on Saturday, leading as many as one-third of France's 600,000 Jews to admit in a recent survey that they are thinking about emigrating, can we afford to remain complacent?

When the president of the British Humanist Association says that "Israel as a homeland for the Jewish people was a load of crap," the French ambassador to the United Kingdom refers to Israel as that "shitty little country," and an Oxford University professor announces that "I never believed that Israel had the right to exist at all," do we simply sit still and hope it all quickly passes?

I could keep on going for pages and pages. I could cite reports of violent attacks against Jewish targets from Morocco to Tunisia and across Europe, as well as the long shadow cast by the 1992 and 1994 terror attacks in Argentina; of vitriol spewing out of the Arab media; of anti-Semitic (and anti-Christian) textbooks in Saudi schools; of thwarted terrorist attempts against Jewish targets in Germany; of Al-Qaeda threats against Jews worldwide; of calls for boycotts of Israeli products and academicians in European countries; of beefed-up security at Jewish institutions in the United States; of troubling incidents on several American and Canadian university campuses; of skewed, if not malicious, media reporting about the Middle East in many Western European media outlets; and of persistent diplomatic double standards.

My purpose, though, is not to strive for completeness. Rather, it's to try to wake up the sleeping—to puncture the bubble of complacency, denial, and detachment—and to say that we, the Jewish people, have a problem today. That problem won't go away by playing Rip Van Winkle or pretending that it's someone else's to deal with. We're all in this together, Israelis and Diaspora Jews.

I happen to believe that we'll get through this period, both because we're strong and because we have friends, chief among them the United States. We have other friends, too. Those who believe in democracy and understand that Israel is an integral part of the community of democratic nations are friends. Those who believe that democratic societies have an obligation to protect and defend the rights of all their citizens, Jews and non-Jews alike, are friends. And those who understand the dangers of the slippery slope of anti-Semitism, the world's oldest hatred, are friends.

It's also abundantly clear that a full picture of the situation should include the good news as well. This, too, would require many pages, but let me mention just a handful of examples.

The United States remains the most extraordinary setting for Diaspora Jewish well-being and success in history. Jews enjoy unprecedented freedom, opportunity, and acceptance. Today Senator Joe Lieberman can run for the Democratic Party's presidential bid without paying any price for his Orthodox religious observance. Dr. Howard Dean's wife and children are Jewish, and it's not even a topic of discussion in the elections. Both senators from Wisconsin, a state with a relatively small Jewish population, are Jewish, and no one gives it a second thought.

Australia and Canada offer models quite similar to America. In Britain, Michael Howard, a Jew, is chosen to lead the Conservative Party and his religious affiliation clearly is not an obstacle to his selection. The top echelon of the German political elite continues to stand foursquare against anti-Semitism and for close ties with Israel. Most of the Christian churches have undergone a revolution in their attitudes toward Jews, ushering in a welcome new chapter in interfaith relations. Jewish communal and religious life is burgeoning in many parts of the former Soviet empire, a far cry from the situation just fifteen years ago. And Jewish history and culture are riding a wave of popular interest from Poland to Spain.

Still, in light of the travails of the past three years, there are those who ask whether it's worth the fight. Is being Jewish sufficiently important to expose ourselves—and our children—to the very real dangers presented by those on the extreme left and on the extreme right, and especially by Islamic radicals? If even synagogues and Jewish schools are potential targets, why should we run the risk of being associated with either? If going to Israel entails possible peril, aren't we better off in Cancún or Cannes?

Such questions are serious and need thoughtful answers. Unless Jews find compelling reasons to lead a Jewish life, some will inevitably drift away, a process that could be accelerated by the current troubling atmosphere.

I've devoted a separate letter to the subject of what being Jewish means to me ("Letter from a Jewish Late Bloomer," December 3, 2002). As I wrote in that piece, I was "comfortably Jewish" growing up, but my Jewishness had little in the way of content. In fact, I didn't attend my first Shabbat dinner until I was well into my twenties. I've been playing catch-up ever since, and loving it.

Are we ready to let others deny us our identity because, for irrational reasons, they cannot abide our presence and maniacally attribute to Jews every evil known to humankind?

And there's one other thing. It may sound like hubris, but it's not. It's a simple truth. The world needs the Jewish people. Jews form an intrinsic part of the human mosaic and have for nearly four millennia. The world would be greatly impoverished in countless ways by the absence of the Jewish people.

I'll go further. A world in which there's no place for the Jews is a world without hope. It would mean, among other things, that the world had failed the ultimate challenge of overcoming past prejudice and discrimination, and couldn't find room for a people whose job description was to be "a light unto the nations" and who also took upon itself the unsought role of litmus test for a society's commitment to equality under the law for all.

Please come out of the bubble. Stop the chronic apologizing. Wake up to what's going on. We need you. We have a cherished faith and heritage that are under assault in some key quarters. We have a state, the

Jewish state, that needs our help. We dare not watch all this from the sidelines, much less avert our eyes. How will history judge us? We can draw strength from one another. Together, surely we can succeed.

If not now, when?

Letter from an Octogenarian
December 18, 2003

This year my mother, Nelly Harris, turned eighty. In the course of her life, she never spoke out publicly. She felt she didn't have the academic or professional qualifications to do so, but now she says she can no longer sit quietly. It's worth listening to her words:

My only credentials are my life experience—first as a refugee from Soviet Russia, later as a refugee from Nazi-occupied France, and, eventually, at the age of eighteen, as a new arrival to America, who went right to work and hasn't stopped.

An unknown elderly woman may not be given the time of day in our youth-oriented and celebrity-obsessed society, but I owe it to myself and my three grandchildren to at least try. My conscience demands no less.

I'm worried about the resurgence of global anti-Semitism and the ho-hum reaction it has elicited from many who should know better.

I was too young in Moscow, where I was born in 1923, to understand the gale-force winds of anti-Semitism that propelled my parents to get us out while they could in 1929 and resettle in Paris. But I recall as if it were yesterday the advent of Nazism in Germany in 1933, the introduction of the Nuremberg Laws in 1935, *Kristallnacht* in 1938, and the invasion of France in 1940.

I discovered that a seemingly quiet, comfortable, and secure life can be turned upside down almost overnight.

I learned what it is to become a refugee, to experience unbridled fear, and to be enveloped by uncertainty about tomorrow.

I saw how people I knew were prepared to abandon me the moment they realized the risk involved in being associated with a Jew.

I heard with my own ears the cries of "Death to the Jews" from Nazis and their Vichy collaborators in France.

I felt the horror of my brother's arrest by the Vichy regime and planned deportation to the death camps; he was miraculously saved, but his girlfriend was not as lucky.

I found out that my dear cousin, Mila Racine, two years older than me, had joined the *Organisation juive de combat*, the French Jewish resistance movement. She transported Jewish children to the French-Swiss border until she was arrested in October 1943 and sent to Ravensbrück. From there, she was transferred to Mauthausen and was killed five weeks before the war's end.

I experienced the world's lack of sympathy as my family rushed from one consulate to another in the south of France begging for entry visas to somewhere, anywhere, just so long as it was far away from our nightmare. Of course, had Israel existed at the time, I can only wonder how many Jews with nowhere to go might have been saved.

In the end, my parents and I were among the lucky ones. Eventually, after traveling to Spain and Portugal, we crossed the Atlantic and arrived in New York a month before Pearl Harbor. (My brother arrived separately.)

Incidentally, perhaps it is people like us—those who found refuge from political and religious persecution—who can truly savor what America stands for. The sight, through tears of happiness, of the Statue of Liberty as our ship entered New York harbor in November 1941 is something I'll never forget. I know the U.S. has its imperfections, but, believe me, it is unlike any other country in the world.

I was eighteen and went to work immediately. So did my brother. We barely spoke English, but it didn't matter. Our family needed the income, and my parents were in worse shape than my brother and me. We had no outside help, nor did we expect any. As it was, we had received the biggest gift we could have prayed for—our very lives—thanks to American visas. By comparison, the rest was a piece of cake.

In the postwar years, anti-Semitism in America existed, but it certainly wasn't life-threatening, nor was it particularly fashionable. As Jews, we encountered, at worst, small impediments in our own lives. While we heard about anti-Semitic barriers in certain elite neighborhoods, clubs, and corporate suites, that world was so far from us that it didn't really register.

The one thing I regret is that, in the 1950s and 1960s, my friends, all with backgrounds pretty similar to my own, and I were so busy trying to integrate into America that most of us didn't pay enough attention to instilling a serious Jewish identity in our children. In our immigrant milieu, our Jewish identity was pretty much taken for granted; no one really disowned it, though some played it down. In any case, it usually took a back seat to embracing an American identity.

I'm sure there are many explanations for this, not least that we had paid a high price in Europe for our Jewish identity. Moreover, I suppose we weren't all that eager to stand out as being different in our adopted country. After all, this was the time of the "melting pot" theory of America. Even so, in hindsight I realize how much we deprived our children of, though, given my son's chosen career path, maybe I'm being too hard on myself or, more probably, miracles do happen.

Now, in the waning years of my life, I smell something troubling, and it frightens me. Jews seem to be fair game. Whatever the possible reasons, they don't alter the basic bone-chilling facts. Anti-Semitism may ebb and flow, but its resilience and ferocity are astonishing. Recent events remind us that it doesn't take much of a pretext—Israel, Iraq, 9/11, currency fluctuations, Arab stagnation, Muslim resentment, you name it—for anti-Semitism to surface in one form or another.

I shouldn't be at all surprised, yet, even after eight decades, I confess I can't for the life of me understand the concept of demonizing entire groups. Of course, I've heard the explanations, but, deep down, I still don't get it. I suppose I have at least as much reason as the next person to hate, having been uprooted twice, but I find I'm not capable of doing so.

Or maybe my surprise stems from the fact that each generation clings to the belief that history moves forward, and that life will be better for our children than it was for us. And there's no question of the remarkable progress that's been achieved. The life circumstances of my son and grandchildren have been infinitely better than mine, but the story can't be allowed to end there.

The increasingly long list of attacks against Jewish and Israeli targets in the last couple of years is by now depressingly familiar, or is it?

I meet some Jews in New York who just don't seem willing, for a variety of reasons, to acknowledge the situation. Maybe either they're too self-absorbed, or they minimize the potency of anti-Semitism, or they're too convinced of their own safety, or they don't feel a visceral connection to fellow Jews around the world, or they're detached from Israel, or they principally blame Israel for the current problems, or they think that Jewish organizations are exaggerating the situation, or whatever.

While the 1930s were most assuredly another era, I saw Jews in Paris watch the events of that decade unfold and believe, until the very last minute, that somehow they were immune. Some chose not to lend credence to the eyewitness reports of Jewish refugees from Germany and Austria who streamed into France, including my future husband. Others decided that, by dint of their wealth, social standing, or connections, they were above the fray. And still others were too busy criticizing fellow Jews for bringing this on themselves.

Let me be clear. I'm not suggesting that we're witnessing a replay of the 1930s. In fact, I'm not sure it's useful to spend too much time comparing situations; they're very different. For starters, today's anti-Semitism isn't government policy in any country with a significant Jewish population—far from it. And that's not the only difference.

Nonetheless, I've learned a few things along the journey of life.

First, Jews can never afford complacency.

Second, sometimes people mean what they say. When Hitler began ranting and raving about the Jews, he wasn't taken very seriously, was he? When Islamic radicals call for the killing of Jews wherever they may live or Israel's total destruction, they shouldn't be underestimated or dismissed out of hand.

Third, things can get better. I've seen astonishing progress with my own eyes. Look, for example, at the establishment of the State of Israel, American support for Israel and the Jewish people, the Israeli peace treaties with Egypt and Jordan, the disappearance of the USSR, the onset of French-German friendship, and the Jewish success story in America. But life has also taught me that things can get worse. Our ability to imagine must go in both directions. A firm grasp of history may not be the be-all and end–all, but it does offer valuable lessons.

And fourth, freedom is a precious gift. It must be defended. Heaven forbid, we should ever take our freedom for granted.

I never thought I would live to see the day when "Death to the Jews" was again heard, as it has been in Europe, the Muslim world, and even North America, much less read the unsettling cover story in *New York* magazine (December 15) entitled "The New Face of Anti-Semitism."

I am eighty and my future is largely behind me, notwithstanding someone's foolish claim that "life begins at eighty." But my three grandchildren have their lives ahead of them. Looking around today, I can't help but worry about the kind of world that awaits them. Maybe, at the end of the day, I'm no different than every grandmother in every generation. Still, I can only hope they'll hold their heads up high as Americans and as Jews and never stop fighting for—and dreaming about—better times to come.

2. SPEECHES & TESTIMONY

The Middle East: Back to Basics
April 21, 2002

In the flood of daily news reports coming from the Middle East, too many questions about the broader nature and context of the Arab-Israeli conflict are unasked. Absent the larger picture, however, it is difficult if not impossible to understand what is really going on and how we reached this point. Here are a few of the pertinent questions:

Why did the Arab world categorically reject the UN's 1947 Partition Plan, which would have created both a Jewish and a Palestinian state in what was then British-ruled Palestine, and could have avoided over fifty years of subsequent conflict? [*]

Did those Arab countries—Egypt, Iraq, Jordan, Lebanon, and Syria—that spurned Israel's outstretched hand of peace and launched a war of destruction on the very first day of Israel's establishment believe they could do so without being held accountable for helping create a refugee problem for local Arabs? What war in history has not produced refugees either as a goal or a by-product?

Has there been any comparable situation in the world where refugees—as in this case, Palestinians—have not been resettled, but deliberately kept in camps for as long as three generations, so as to incubate hatred and garner world sympathy? Are Palestinians the world's first—or only—refugees? Why do we hear so little about the

---

[*] Palestinian spokesmen today misleadingly claim that they have ceded 78 percent of the original territory to Israel and only seek 22 percent for a Palestinian state, but they overlook one central fact. According to the Peel Commission, set up by Britain in the wake of the 1936 Arab riots against Jews in Palestine, "the field in which the Jewish National Home was to be established was understood, at the time of the [1917] Balfour Declaration, to be the whole of historic Palestine, including Transjordan [today's Jordan]." (Cited in *Myths and Facts: A Guide to the Arab-Israeli Conflict*, by Mitchell G. Bard, p. 28.)

nearly 25 million other refugees in the world today? Are they any less deserving of sympathy and support?

Why is it that none of the twenty-two Arab countries—with the single exception of Jordan—who share ethnic, religious, and linguistic ties with the Palestinians, has offered Palestinians citizenship and a new start?

Why has the world completely ignored the other refugee population created by the Arab-Israeli conflict—the 750,000 Jews from Arab countries (more or less equaling the number of Palestinian refugees at the time), many of them with roots in these countries predating by centuries the arrival of Islam, forced to leave their ancestral homes because of second-class status and pogroms? Is it because these refugees were quickly resettled in Israel rather than placed in camps and manipulated as the Palestinians were?

And why did the world conveniently overlook persistent Jordanian violations of the armistice agreement for nearly nineteen years (1949–1967), when Amman did not allow Jews any access whatsoever to Judaism's holiest site—the Western Wall—and desecrated dozens of synagogues in the Jewish Quarter of Jerusalem as well as Jewish cemeteries on the Mount of Olives?

Did Israel come into possession of the West Bank, Gaza, the Golan Heights, and eastern Jerusalem—the lands it is now accused of illegally occupying—totally out of the blue?

Is the historical record not absolutely clear that Egypt and Syria threatened Israel with annihilation in the months leading up to the 1967 Six-Day War and closed off the shipping lane to the Israeli Red Sea port of Eilat, itself an act of war under international law?

And that Israel urged Jordan, via UN intermediaries, to stay out of the unfolding conflict, which would have meant continued Jordanian control of the West Bank and eastern Jerusalem?

Speaking of these territories, if the Arab world cared so deeply about the Palestinian condition, why were absolutely no steps taken to create a Palestinian state between 1948 and 1967, when the West Bank and eastern Jerusalem were in Jordanian hands and the Gaza Strip was ruled by Egypt?

Has the world forgotten that the PLO was created in 1964, when the only "occupied" land was Israel itself, the target of the PLO's unprecedented campaign of terror that eventually spanned the globe and counted among its many victims not only Israelis but Americans, including the U.S. ambassador to the Sudan, and Europeans as well?

Are we to forget the Arab world's response to the serious Israeli peace overtures after the 1967 Six-Day War, which came most memorably in the "three noes" of the Khartoum Declaration (August 1967)—"no peace, no recognition, and no negotiation"? In the face of such a reply, is history simply supposed to stand still until one side finally gets it right?

Are we to overlook the PLO's record in Jordan, where Yasir Arafat agreed to twenty-two cease-fires with Jordan's King Hussein until he was banished from the country in 1970 after the violence of Black September resulted in the deaths of thousands?

Or subsequently in Lebanon, where the PLO created a state-within-a-state and Arafat helped launch a prolonged and bloody civil war that erupted in 1975—seven years *before* Israeli troops entered Lebanon—and during which he violated more than seventy cease-fires?

Why didn't the Palestinian leadership, if truly serious about peace, take its cue from Egypt's Anwar Sadat and Jordan's King Hussein, who concluded landmark peace agreements with Israel—involving significant territorial compromises on Israel's part—by persuading Israelis that Cairo and Amman were irrevocably committed to peace?

Even after Arafat allegedly recognized Israel in 1988, why was he always so duplicitous about his real intentions toward Israel, saying one thing in English and precisely the opposite in Arabic?

Does the world suffer from amnesia about the implications of Arafat's unbridled support for Saddam Hussein, the American-led coalition's enemy, during the 1991 Gulf War?

And for those who purport to identify with the plight of the Palestinians, where were they when Kuwait summarily expelled 300,000 Palestinians overnight, accusing them of being a fifth column for Saddam Hussein?

Once the 1993 Oslo Accords were signed between Israel and the Palestinian Authority, were we to ignore Arafat's persistent violations of just about every provision, including limitations on the size of a police force, acquisition of weapons, use of violence and terror to achieve political aims, and the teaching of incitement against Israel?

Where is the evidence that, after 1993, Arafat prepared his people for peace with Israel, based on the principle of painful but necessary compromises by both sides, rather than continued armed struggle?

Is it not true, Palestinian claims to the contrary, that the Oslo Accords made *no* reference to Israeli settlements and that the subsequent Mitchell Plan spoke of curtailing settlement activity only *after* Palestinian violence came to a halt—which, of course, has not yet happened—and a cooling-off period ensued?

Are we simply to ignore, as if it never happened, the determined efforts of President Bill Clinton and Prime Minister Ehud Barak as recently as January 2001 to achieve an historic breakthrough with Arafat, including painful compromises on such contentious issues as Jerusalem, refugees, and settlements?

Or to wonder why Arafat, rather than seize this extraordinary moment to establish the very *first* Palestinian state in history, sabotaged the talks—and thereby once again betrayed the interests of his own people—by bizarrely dismissing any Jewish historical or religious link to Jerusalem and calling for the so-called Palestinian "right of return," which would, as he knew so well, lead to the destruction of the State of Israel?

Are we to conveniently overlook the ominous implications of the *Karine-A* affair, the ship laden with fifty tons of advanced weaponry, including lethal rockets with a range of twelve miles, headed for Palestinian territory from Iran, a nation on record as denying Israel's right to exist and bent on its destruction? Or Arafat's brazen lie when he pleaded ignorance about the ship—not the first such ship, by the way—in a letter to President Bush in January?

But then hasn't a clear pattern of lies, distortions, deceptions, and exaggerations always been part of the modus operandi of Arafat and his spokesmen, too often uncritically reported by a gullible or smitten Western press?

How about the wildly exaggerated casualty figures in Lebanon in 1982 claimed by the Palestinian Red Crescent Society (chaired by

Arafat's brother), the libelous accusations about Israeli doctors inject-
ing the HIV virus in Palestinian children made by the Palestinian delegate to the UN in Geneva, the lies about Israeli use of poison gas
made by Arafat's wife, and, most recently, the effort by the Palestinian
Authority to recast a fierce armed battle in Jenin—involving
Palestinian gunmen, booby-trapped homes, and mines placed in the
midst of a civilian population—into a massacre?

Or what about the deliberate and macabre use of children—their
brainwashing and approved suicide—in the Palestinian war of terror
against Israel? Shouldn't this inhuman practice be universally condemned? Why hasn't the UN expressed itself on the matter?

Or what about the cash payments—perhaps, more accurately, incen-
tives—of $25,000 given by Saddam Hussein's Iraq to the families of
each of these so-called martyrs, actually murderers, with additional
money coming from Saudi Arabia?

Are we supposed to ignore, as if it has no relevance, the endless revelations of Arafat's direct connection to terror—the smoking-gun documents found in Ramallah, the direct links between Arafat and armed
terrorist groups under his control that have claimed responsibility for
terrorist attacks against Israeli men, women, and children, and the ties
between Arafat and Hamas, Palestinian Islamic Jihad, and Hezbollah,
all groups long committed to Israel's total destruction?

Or Arafat's refusal to arrest known Palestinian terrorists, despite
repeated pleas by the United States, or, almost as outrageous, arresting
them while the world is watching and then releasing them as soon as
he has been given credit for the arrests?

Or the use of summary justice to kill alleged collaborators, while not
a peep is heard from the international community?

Or the calculated use of homes, schools, hospitals, ambulances, and
religious sites to hide weaponry and shield gunmen, so that when
Palestinians shoot at Israelis from behind a church, say, they hope to
draw a response and then count on the Western media to report that
Israeli troops fired at Christian holy sites?

Speaking of the media, why is that no one exposes some of the dirty,
dark secrets known to many reporters covering the Palestinian-Israeli
conflict, such as the use of fear and intimidation by Palestinians, or the

fact that many of the crews for Western television are recruited from the local Palestinian population?

Did anyone notice the shockingly skimpy coverage of the media angle of the barbaric Ramallah lynching of the two Israeli soldiers in the fall of 2000? Where were the stories about the Palestinian seizure of the films of Western crews or, above all, the startling disclosure by the correspondent for RAI, Italian public television, that the film eventually smuggled out and shown worldwide was not his (it actually came from a private Italian station) because he would *never* do anything to undermine the Palestinian cause?

More recently, why were we once again subject to a virtual media blackout when thousands of Palestinians took to the streets on September 11 to celebrate America's day of agony? Why were we not told that Associated Press had footage of those celebrations but chose not to air it after threats were made on the life of its reporter on the ground?

And when, earlier this year, the media showed the world images of Israel bulldozing homes in Gaza, suggesting the ruthlessness of Israel, why did they not mention that those houses, mostly abandoned, were hiding the access points to tunnels linking Gaza and Egypt and were being used for smuggling weapons?

Moreover, isn't it long overdue for Arab spokesmen—and the world—to face head-on the steady diet of racial and religious incitement against Israel and Jews that has become a permanent feature of government-controlled media in too many countries—replete with Nazi-like images, Holocaust denial, and denigration of Judaism?

Why did it take the *New York Times*, the newspaper of record, until April 19, 2002, to write an editorial on the subject, when the problem of virulent anti-Semitism, both in the Muslim world and, as we have now seen so vividly, in Europe—has been festering for eighteen months, if not longer?

Didn't it take the same newspaper just about forty-eight hours to write an editorial condemning the alleged threats against the Brooklyn family of Adam Shapiro, the Jewish-born Palestinian activist, a story, incidentally, that died just as quickly as it surfaced?

How can a true foundation of peace ever be built if the inflammatory language of hate and calls for "holy war" fill the air in mosques and media outlets, as well as in European Union-funded schools?

Or if the Syrian president, in the presence of Pope John Paul II last spring, can reawaken the outrageous deicide charge, and then proceed merrily along his way to warm state receptions in Paris and Madrid and, a few months later, celebrate his country's election to a two-year term on the powerful UN Security Council, a body that Israel has never even been eligible to serve on since its admission to the UN in 1949?

Or if the Syrian minister of defense can proudly claim authorship of a 1983 book that accuses Jews of the infamous blood libel charge?

Or if Saudi censors can approve an article by a prominent medical professor, written on the eve of Vice President Richard Cheney's recent visit, claiming that Jews need the blood of Christians and Muslims for their Purim and Passover ritual foods?

Had today's eighteen-year-old Palestinian youths been taught peace and mutual respect since the 1993 Oslo Accords rather than hate, would they be blowing themselves up in Israeli cafés and restaurants? Or might they be enjoying the fruits of statehood, side by side with Israel, and the chance for a brighter future that they, like youngsters everywhere, so richly deserve?

Why is that we witness a vigorous and impressive debate in democratic Israel about every aspect of the conflict with the Palestinians, but there is nothing remotely comparable in Palestinian society and, what's more, few stop to note the difference, or its implications?

Why do virtually no Palestinians (or Arabs) have the courage publicly to examine their own role and responsibility for reaching this point in the conflict, and instead contentedly shift the entire blame to Israel, the United States, world Jewry, or any other convenient scapegoat—in other words, anyone other than themselves?

Where are the voices of honesty and good will to expose the unspeakably perverse historical distortions committed by Palestinians and their supporters when they obscenely choose Nazi analogies to describe Israeli leaders and their policies? Or where is the criticism of a noted Portuguese writer who outlandishly compares Ramallah to Auschwitz?

Why is it that nongovernmental groups that claim to defend democratic values and human rights are so vocal when it comes to criticizing Israel—a nation committed to those very same values—and so deafeningly silent when it comes to Israel's adversaries, none of whom make even the slightest pretense of respecting either democracy or human rights?

How much do we hear from these groups about the fact that, according to Freedom House, not one of the twenty-two Arab countries today can be labeled democratic?

Or about the tens of thousands of people killed in the Algerian civil war; the two million—yes, two million—people killed in the war against Christians and animists in Sudan; the complete denial of women's rights in Saudi Arabia, including even the right to drive a car, or the asylum granted by Saudi Arabia to one of the twentieth century's leading butchers, Idi Amin of Uganda; the total suppression of the Baha'i faith in Iran; or the unrelenting persecution of homosexuals in Egypt?

Why have we never heard a peep for twenty years from these groups about the actual perpetrator of the 1982 massacre in Sabra and Shatila—Elias Khobeika, the commander of the Phalange militia and, later, a cabinet member in the Lebanese government?

And what about the ongoing occupation of Lebanon by Syria, a country that does not even recognize Lebanon's independence and sovereignty? For those who allege concern about "occupation," why are they not heard from on this naked act of aggression?

Why is it that Israel so captures the imagination of these groups while other, truly egregious human rights situations do not?

And isn't the situation precisely the same at the United Nations, where, given the simple, unalterable fact that it's all about numbers, Israel doesn't stand a chance against a bloc of twenty-two Arab countries and a group of fifty-six countries that form the Organization of the Islamic Conference?

What are the odds on Israel receiving a fair hearing in that world body, when the deck is so overwhelmingly stacked against it? Conversely, how much attention will the UN ever pay to serious human rights abuses in the Arab world given the organization's make-up?

Are we to ignore the situation on university campuses here at home, where Jewish and pro-Israel students are increasingly harassed and intimidated if they stand up for Israel or, in the case of two students at Berkeley, physically assaulted? Or where the student leader of an Arab group at NYU that distributed a vile, anti-Semitic screed by the infamous David Duke, written shortly after September 11, was honored this month with the university's prestigious President's Service Award?

And last but by no means least, why do so many fail to understand that Israel is facing a threat to its existence and has every right and obligation to defend itself against an enemy that has no compunction about sending suicide bombers to target a Passover Seder or a bar mitzvah celebration?

That Israel, unlike any other nation on the face of this earth, has actually been fighting this war with one hand tied behind its back because of its own democratic and ethical values and because its every action is being scrutinized microscopically by the UN, Europe, the media, and human rights groups? What other country has chosen to expose its troops to far greater risks than might otherwise be the case for these reasons?

Anyone care to remember how our nation fought the war against Serbia? Wasn't it from 15,000 feet up to prevent U.S. casualties, even if some of our bombs inevitably hit civilian targets, including the Chinese Embassy?

Anyone care to remember that, during the British-Argentine war over the Falkland (or Malvinas) Islands, Whitehall deliberately kept the media far away from the war zone, yet no one questioned the British commitment to democratic values?

Isn't it painfully clear that any failure of resolve on Israel's part in the current Palestinian war of terror will only encourage its enemies to believe that the ultimate goal of Israel's destruction is within reach, and thereby diminish still further the chances for a peaceful resolution of the conflict?

And that there is a profound moral distinction, as we in the United States should especially appreciate after September 11, between those terrorist groups that destroy and those armies that seek to prevent the destruction?

Did the United States exercise restraint or rush into negotiations with Al-Qaeda and the Taliban after September 11?

Has the United States been willing to enter into face-to-face peace talks with Saddam Hussein since the 1991 Gulf War?

Has our country sat down to negotiate with Cuba's Fidel Castro, positioned just ninety miles off the coast of Florida, since he seized power over four decades ago, much less lifted the economic sanctions we imposed at the time?

Hasn't Israel time and again demonstrated its willingness to take unparalleled risks in the quest for peace, while at the very same time operating with a miniscule margin for error, since the country at its narrowest point (pre-1967) was exactly nine miles—nine miles!—wide and, given its topography and concentrated population, all the more dangerously vulnerable?

As a consequence, shouldn't those critics outside Israel—at least, those whose intentions toward Israel are honorable—show just a bit more intellectual humility about trying to second-guess Israel's life-and-death decisions?

And shouldn't they show just a bit more understanding of the extraordinary dilemmas—and dangers—Israel faces no matter which way it seeks to turn?

And shouldn't they show just a bit more recognition of the fact that Israel today does not have a credible negotiating partner in the Palestinian Authority and can't pretend that it does?

And shouldn't they show just a bit more appreciation of the fact that no people—I repeat, no people—seeks peace more than the Israelis, precisely because they've not known a single day of it since the state's founding in 1948, but that peace at any price, history has painfully taught us, is worse than no peace at all?

Muslim Anti-Semitism
National Press Club, Washington, D.C.
May 7, 2002

Out in full sight in newspaper articles, television broadcasts, and speeches of government officials is a virulent new strain of anti-Semitism that, in the words of Robert S. Wistrich, the author of the report, *Muslim Anti-Semitism: A Clear and Present Danger*, which we present to you today, "has taken root in the body politic of Islam to an unprecedented degree."

While drawing upon negative stereotypes of Jews that have roots in the Koran, and fueled by the political dynamics of the Arab-Israeli conflict, this "present tidal wave of anti-Semitism" blurs any distinctions between "Zionists" and "Jews." It is global in scope, rearing its head in literature distributed around the world and most recently at the misnamed Durban Conference Against Racism, Racial Discrimination, Xenophobia and Related Intolerance.

What is particularly spine-chilling about the new Muslim anti-Semitism is that it appropriates symbols and motifs from classic European anti-Jewish bigotry and from Nazi propaganda. Thus, in illustrations reproduced in this volume one sees images of Jews with hook noses or as devil figures, Israelis with swastikas or as drinkers of the blood of children.

Hate literature that we thought had been laid to rest, such as the notorious nineteenth-century forgery, *The Protocols of the Elders of Zion,* has been resurrected and published in numerous editions throughout the Arab world. The blood libel—the calumny that Jews require the blood of non-Jews for ritual purposes—resurfaced from the mouth of the Syrian defense minister Mustafa Tlas and most recently in an article in the mainstream Saudi newspaper *Al-Riyadh.* Arabic editions of *Mein Kampf* are selling briskly in London and in Palestinian Authority-controlled areas.

If we have learned anything from the past—both the immediate past of 9/11 and the more distant history of Nazi fascism—it is that we must not let such warning signs go unheeded, that we must not dismiss such grotesque distortions of the truth as the rantings of madmen. This publication must serve as a wake-up call to a very clear and immediate threat to Jews worldwide—and by extension, to human and Western values as well.

Sounding the alarm in the face of immediate danger to Jews anywhere has been at the core of the mission of the American Jewish Committee since its inception. This latest battle is one that we will engage fully, for it is at our doorsteps as well as half a world away in the Middle East. It will doubtless guide our agency in setting our agenda in the months and years ahead, and will hopefully be persuasive to others who have been complacent to this danger.

Let me be clear about the goals of the American Jewish Committee in this effort: to work cooperatively and in common purpose with those Muslims who seek dialogue and harmony, while standing firm and resolute against those who would seek to destroy or malign us.

We are indebted to Dr. Robert S. Wistrich, Neuberger Professor of Modern European and Jewish History at the Hebrew University, for having meticulously examined this phenomenon and having provided the documentation of its scope and virulence. His research offers abundant evidence—if any were needed—that this new wave of anti-Semitism is not merely the by-product to the Arab-Israeli conflict, as some have misleadingly suggested, but a battlefield of its own.

AJC 96th Annual Dinner
May 9, 2002

Dr. Condoleezza Rice, (Peruvian) President Alejandro Toledo, (Indonesian) President Abdurrahman Wahid, (Israeli) Minister Tzipi Livni, ladies and gentlemen:

Several years ago, I was invited to speak at an American Jewish Committee reception held at a private home in nearby Bethesda.

The guests were milling about, enjoying cocktails and hors d'oeuvres, when the hostess approached me and said: "David, shall we let the guests continue to enjoy themselves, or are you ready to begin speaking?"

So, you've been appropriately warned.

We come together tonight from all walks of life and from all the world's continents to celebrate the ninety-sixth anniversary of this extraordinary organization.

Winston Churchill once said: "The farther backward you can look, the farther forward you are likely to see."

In our case, it means looking back to 1906. From the earliest days, our founders developed a two-track approach.

Well aware of the fact that, as American Jews, they had a responsibility for the fate of less fortunate Jews around the world, they devoted themselves tirelessly to aiding their brethren in Eastern Europe who were victims of pogroms by mobilizing American and international political support.

And for the ensuing ninety-six years that sense of responsibility, kinship, and shared destiny has characterized our unstinting work in pursuit of Jewish security, equality, and well-being anywhere that Jews may live.

At the same time, our founders understood, consistent with the Jewish ethical tradition, that the ultimate guarantor of the rights of Jews was the nurturing of democratic societies that respected the rights and freedoms of all their citizens, Jews and non-Jews alike.

As the great Christian theologian Reinhold Niebuhr wrote: "Man's capacity for justice makes democracy possible, but man's inclination to injustice makes democracy necessary."

AJC's leaders put their shoulders to the wheel—or, should I say, commonweal—with uncommon gusto and determination.

This explains why, as the late Dr. Martin Luther King Jr. pointed out in his speech at the AJC annual dinner in 1965:

When few men dared to speak out, [the American Jewish Committee] launched a campaign in 1911 in New York State to end the advertisement of discrimination in public accommodations, in recreational resorts and amusement parks. This campaign resulted in the passage in 1913 of a state law which has served as a model for many other states and has thus made possible the extension of dignity for Negroes, Puerto Ricans, and other minorities.

This explains why the first major legal case that AJC entered had nothing to do directly with the rights of Jews. In 1922, the state of Oregon, influenced by the Ku Klux Klan, passed a law requiring all children to attend public schools. The real target was the Catholic parochial school system, there being no Jewish schools in the state at the time.

The American Jewish Committee filed an amicus brief in the U.S. Supreme Court in support of the Catholic schools. In 1925, the court unanimously voted to strike down the Oregon law. As a colleague has written: "This decision (known as the *Pierce* case) has been termed the Magna Carta of parochial schools."

This explains why the American Jewish Committee invested such hope in the promise of the United Nations. Indeed, as Professor James Shotwell of Columbia University wrote: "Inclusion of a human rights provision in the UN Charter was due to the brilliant leadership of the American Jewish Committee."

This explains why, again as noted by Martin Luther King, it was the American Jewish Committee that sponsored the pathbreaking research by Dr. Kenneth Clark on the damaging psychological effects of prejudice. This research became a major part of the evidence presented to the Supreme Court, that in turn led to the landmark 1954 decision known as *Brown v. Board of Education*, outlawing segregation in public schools.

This explains why, in 1980, only one person of non-Japanese ancestry was invited to a California State Legislature observance commemorating the shameful 1942 Federal order that sent 120,000 Japanese Americans to internment camps. That person was a representative of the American Jewish Committee.

As a Japanese-American leader wrote at the time: "The AJC was the first national organization to support our efforts to rectify the injustice of the World War II internment of Japanese Americans."

And this explains why the American Jewish Committee has been at the forefront of so many humanitarian efforts: assisting boat people fleeing communist tyranny in Indochina; rebuilding African American churches in the South destroyed by arson; helping feed Christian and Muslim victims of famine in sub-Saharan Africa; providing a school and medical center for an earthquake-ravaged region of Turkey; offering relief to Kosovar Muslims fleeing Milosevic's ethnic cleansing; aiding Afghan Muslim refugees; reconstructing a school in India, attended by both Hindu and Muslim children, after it was badly damaged in an earthquake; and offering help for the families of victims of the September 11 tragedy.

I could go on at length citing AJC's achievements in advancing human rights and civil rights, democracy and the rule of law, and interfaith and interethnic understanding.

Suffice it to say that we, the heirs and trustees of this organization, are suffused with the very same values and ideals as our founders.

We, like they, celebrate democracy, not tyranny; tolerance, not triumphalism; law, not whim; equality, not hierarchy; pluralism, not uniformity; debate, not dogma; humility, not hubris; and moderation, not extremism.

And wasn't it precisely these kinds of values and ideals that were targeted by those who, in the name of a twisted and demented religious faith, unleashed their venomous acts of blind hatred against this country on September 11?

Who among us will ever forget exactly where we were standing that Tuesday morning as the first plane hit the World Trade Center, or what countries the nineteen hijackers and their backers came from?

Who will ever forget the extraordinary stories of heroism and courage that we heard in the course of this tragedy?

Who will ever forget the strong and steady leadership of President George W. Bush and his administration, including notably our guest speaker this evening, Dr. Condoleezza Rice, in guiding a shaken nation through its overwhelming grief and its unflinching response?

Dr. Rice, please convey to the president our unswerving support for the global war on terrorism that he has so ably led.

Who will ever forget the laudable reaction of Congress, rising instantly above the partisan fray, to unite as one in the face of an act of war?

Who will ever forget the reassuring hand of New York's mayor, Rudy Giuliani, in lifting up a city and, in the process, inspiring a nation?

Who will ever forget the countless Americans who have put themselves in harm's way, whether abroad or here at home, to defend our nation and defeat our enemies?

Who will ever forget those nations that have stood shoulder to shoulder with us both in our agony and in our resolve?

Who will ever forget those who, openly or clandestinely, funded, encouraged, and lionized those who would destroy us?

And who will ever forget those organizations here in this country that served as apologists and fund-raisers for Islamist terror, and after September 11 scrambled to reinvent themselves as civil rights groups?

Yes, it's been quite a year for us as Americans. It's also been quite a year for us as Jews.

Dare we forget the Durban debacle, the inaptly named UN Conference Against Racism, that threatened to turn into an anti-Semitic hate fest just days before September 11?

But let us also not forget that the United States admirably chose not to attend Durban once it determined that to go would lend legitimacy to what had become an illegitimate exercise.

Dare we forget the calculated attempt to place the blame for September 11 on Jews, and the instant popularity of these malicious rumors in broad swaths of the Muslim world and even in parts of Europe?

Dare we forget the unrelenting Palestinian campaign of terror against Israel—the deliberate targeting of Israeli men, women, and children at pizzerias, discotheques, Passover Seders, bat mitzvah celebrations, and, now, billiard halls, in other words anywhere and everywhere?

Or the unprecedented effort by Prime Minister Ehud Barak and President Bill Clinton that preceded this wave of terror and that could have given the Palestinians peace, sovereignty, and development, had they only had the visionary leadership to embrace it?

Dare we forget the widespread terrorist infrastructure that has been built up on the West Bank and Gaza under the direction of the Palestinian Authority, the unforgivable manipulation of children as homicide bombers, and the financial rewards offered to the families of the bombers by Iraq and Saudi Arabia?

Dare we forget a ship called the *Karine A*, the lethal weapons it was carrying, the Iranian origin of those weapons, or the direct link between the Palestinian leadership and that ship?

Dare we forget those countries that condemn Israel for exercising its legitimate right to defend itself, accept uncritically every outrageous Palestinian claim, ignore the unmasked truths about the real nature of the Palestinian leadership, and, at the disastrous UN Commission on Human Rights session last month, affirmed the Palestinian use of terror?

Or conversely, those countries, including notably Britain, Canada, the Czech Republic, Germany, and Guatemala, among others, that resisted the herd mentality and stood up for Israel in the international community?

Dare we forget the double standard that once again prevailed in the international community, as Israel was subjected to an obsessive scrutiny accorded no other nation, even those with documented records of egregious human rights violations?

Dare we forget the revelations of what students are being taught in schools from Saudi Arabia to Pakistan about hatred and distrust of Jews, indeed of Christians as well?

Or, for that matter, what television viewers have been treated to in the Arab world—ranging from a reenactment of the infamous anti-Semitic forgery known as the *Protocols of the Elders of Zion* to the reawakening of the medieval blood libel that once caused such great Jewish suffering?

Or the kidnapping and murder of Daniel Pearl and the implications of the last words he was compelled to utter by his captors—"I am a Jew. My mother is a Jew"?

As we honor the memory of Daniel Pearl, I would like to introduce to this audience his beloved sisters—Tamara and Michelle.

Dare we forget the revival of anti-Semitism, not only at Durban and in the Islamic world, but in Europe as well?

As we meet here tonight, with leaders of European Jewish communities present, they can attest to growing concern for the security of Jews and Jewish institutions. Inexplicably, the problem is being given inadequate or only belated attention by many governments that don't seem to want to wake up to the dangerous new realities faced by Jews.

Yes, it's been a sobering year, but we remain undaunted.

We could not be more proud of the United States—this exceptional country that has stood shoulder to shoulder with Israel, a fellow democracy, through thick and thin, and which has devoted such energy to the search for a just and lasting peace for the Jewish state and for all the peoples of the region who so richly deserve a better future.

We could not be more in awe of the resolve of the Israeli people who defend their country under unimaginably difficult conditions, carry on normal lives in utterly abnormal circumstances, and continue to yearn for peace even when it may seem more elusive than ever.

We could not be more committed to strengthening the ties that bind Israel and world Jewry, all the more so when there are those who seek to break Israel's national will and cow Israel's supporters abroad. Let them know that they will not succeed—not today, not ever.

We could not be more convinced that those democratic countries facing the reality of terror, such as the United States, Israel, Spain, India, Turkey and Peru—represented here this evening by its distinguished president, Dr. Alejandro Toledo—should always recall the words of Pericles, the Athenian statesman, in his magnificent funeral oration of nearly 2,500 years ago:

> Make up your minds that happiness depends on being free, and that freedom depends on being courageous. Let there be no relaxation in the face of the perils of the war.

And we could not be more determined to strengthen mutual understanding, especially across religious lines, which makes me particularly delighted that one of the world's leading exponents of Islam, Abdurrahman Wahid of Indonesia, is here with us this evening.

Such interfaith dialogue will become only more important in the years ahead if we are to bequeath to our children a more secure and tolerant world than we found.

In closing, let me share a quick story.

When one of our sons was three and in nursery school, the teacher asked the class a question—"What do you want to be when you grow up?"

A boy answered that he wanted to be a racing car driver. A girl said she wanted to be a ballerina. Our three-year-old said that when he grew up, he wanted to be four!

In that spirit of taking one year at a time, I look forward to our celebrating the American Jewish Committee's ninety-seventh birthday with all of you next year, hopefully in a world that has moved just a bit closer to the prophetic age we so desperately seek.

A Pro-Israel Lobby[*]
Paris, France
May 30, 2002

These extraordinarily complex and challenging times require the closest possible consultation among Jewish communities and organizations, and this is one such opportunity.

I will also confess to you that I feel very close to the French Jewish community.

For one thing, both my parents lived in Paris until the war and much of my family remained in France during and after the war. As a result, I have a personal connection to this community.

For another, I have spent much time in France, meeting with the leadership of CRIF and the Consistoire, attending your demonstrations, and talking with French officials.

So thank you for the privilege of being here.

---

* This speech was delivered (in French) to an audience of 250 French Jewish leaders under the auspices of the Forum Levitique.

Ladies and gentlemen, I have been asked to talk this evening about pro-Israel lobbying in the United States. In doing so, of course, I will leave it entirely to you to determine whether anything I say has relevance for France, as I recognize the uniqueness of each society.

Let me offer ten essential elements in trying to understand the make-up of the pro-Israel lobby in the United States and its record of accomplishment.

First, the United States as a nation encourages lobbying by various interest groups. Indeed, the Constitution invites citizens to "petition the government."

Thus, the pro-Israel community is one of hundreds, in fact thousands, of interest groups organized by religion, ethnicity, values, and beliefs.

Second, in the specific sector of American foreign policy, again there is a tradition of lobbying by various groups. Foreign policy is not the sole preserve of an elite group of bureaucrats and diplomats who determine what is in the best interests of a nation. Instead, there is also a "bottom up" phenomenon, and not just a "top down" process.

Cuban Americans have been remarkably effective in shaping American policy toward Cuba for over forty years. Greek Americans take a lively interest in the American approach to the divided island of Cyprus and to the balance in American policy toward Greece and Turkey. Polish Americans were extremely active in encouraging American support for the expansion of NATO to include Poland. And African Americans are increasingly vocal on issues affecting American policy toward Africa and the Caribbean.

I could go on offering examples. Suffice it to say that the pro-Israel community is one among many such groups, and its activities are entirely consistent with recognized and accepted American political practices.

Third, the important role played by the United States Congress in the formulation and oversight of American foreign policy strengthens the hand of lobbying groups.

It is far easier for a lobbying group to reach a senator, of whom there are 100, or a congressman, of whom there are 435, than to reach the president or secretary of state.

By reaching either the well-positioned legislators or a critical mass of legislators in general, lobbying groups can exercise influence on foreign policy issues.

Members of Congress hold hearings, vote on budgetary authorization and appropriation bills such as the foreign aid bill, can defeat—though with difficulty—proposed overseas arms sales, and are in regular contact with the White House and State Department.

Fourth, in the same spirit, legislators—and, of course, the president as well—are dependent on electoral success and therefore are constantly thinking about building voting majorities. Ethnic and religious calculations do go into this thinking, whether this is always acknowledged or not.

In the case of the United States, the peculiar presidential voting system, which was on display in the year 2000, reminds us that, at the end of the day, it is the states, and not the national vote, that ultimately determine the winner and loser. Bush lost the popular vote, but won enough states to become president.

This means, as a practical matter, that certain populous states, such as New York, New Jersey, California, and Florida, are critical to any presidential candidate. Candidates will understandably pay especially close attention to the issues of interest to voters in those states.

Fifth, the complicated campaign financing laws in America mean that individuals and even groups—known as political action committees—can contribute designated amounts to political parties and individual candidates. As you know, we do not have exclusively public financing of elections. As a result, wealthy individuals and groups that join together around a common goal—for example, supporting those candidates who support Israel—can play an important role in shaping the thinking of candidates.

Sixth, Jews, though little more than two percent of the American population today, have several assets.

For one thing, on Election Day, Jews vote, whereas the rest of the American population is far more ambivalent about voting. That means that Jews comprise 3.5 percent to 4 percent of the actual voters on Election Day.

For another, Jews are very active in the Democratic Party leadership structure and increasingly active, though less so, in the Republican Party leadership structure.

Moreover, Jews contribute financially to both political parties, though especially to the Democratic Party.

And Jews are concentrated demographically in certain key states that matter on presidential election days. We all saw this in Florida in 2000, where a few thousand elderly Jews, confused by a complicated ballot, may have mistakenly voted for a right-wing xenophobe rather than Al Gore, thus giving the election to George Bush. Speaking of political power...

Seventh, from the beginning Jews legitimately sought to make the Israel issue not just a Jewish issue but an American issue. In other words, to be pro-Israel was to be pro-American, and to be pro-American was to be pro-Israel.

To a large degree, the strategy worked.

For a variety of compelling reasons, Americans embraced Israel. To begin with, Americans believe there needs to be a moral dimension to foreign policy, whether this is always the practice or not.

Americans identify with Israel's struggle to survive in a hostile environment, to build a thriving democracy, and to be a loyal American ally in the region.

Americans also identify with Israel as the source of their religious beliefs. Remember that America is one of the most profoundly religious countries in the Western world today. Religions of all kinds flourish.

Americans also came to identify with the Shoah and the recognition that the Jews deserved and needed a secure state.

All of this came about, I believe, because the pro-Israel movement from the start focused on attracting the support of labor unions, civil rights groups, Christian denominations, and other civic institutions.

Moreover, the pro-Israel movement always sought to avoid linking Israel with one or another political ideology in the United States. To be pro-Israel, in other words, was above the partisan fray.

And American Jews, increasingly comfortable and confident in American society, especially after the 1960s, did not hesitate to affirm their identification with Israel publicly. Earlier fears of accusations of dual loyalty faded away, as America recognized the emergence of multiculturalism and not divided loyalties, but multiple loyalties.

Eighth, the pro-Israel lobby in America was helped by the fact that the anti-Israel lobby was relatively weak. It was not insignificant—there have been oil companies, academics, ex-government officials, and others who have organized counter lobbies—but their success has been limited.

In addition, the Arab world and Arab culture, at least until recently, has had very little hold on the American imagination. Even if Americans had no special feelings for Israel, they usually had even less attachment to the Arab world.

This is beginning to change, as America is now home to two to three million Muslims, many, though by no means all, from the Arab world. This community, copying the Jewish community, is establishing organizations and building a lobby of its own, trying to influence politicians and shape public opinion.

To date, they have enjoyed limited success, but their influence is likely to build in the years ahead as their numbers increase and their sophistication grows.

Ironically, they are trying to use the tragic events of September 11 to their advantage. At first, they were on the defensive, but they began using the argument that America needed to build closer ties to the Arab world, understand it better, and thus defuse the anger directed at America that spawned terrorism. In some quarters, this argument has worked, but only to a degree.

Ninth, the success of the pro-Israel lobby is to a large degree due to the effective organizational structure of American Jewry. To be sure, there are lots of organizations and some overlap and competition. But, at the end of the day, the system has worked.

The principal lobby is AIPAC, which is based in Washington and is, in fact, the only American Jewish organization formally registered with the government as a lobby. Among other things, this means that contributions to it are normally not tax-deductible.

By the way, the issue of tax laws is an important factor in understanding the American scene. For instance, all donations to the

American Jewish Committee are tax-deductible, which means that every dollar contributed may, in fact, cost the donor no more sixty to seventy cents on the dollar. Needless to say, this is a huge incentive for charitable giving in American generally and, within that, benefits Jewish organizations as well.

AIPAC has a highly regarded staff of over 100, including top professionals with government, defense, and academic experience. Among their staff members, not all of whom, by the way are, Jewish, are seven full-time lobbyists whose entire focus is on the Untied States Congress.

Other staff members pay careful attention to the electoral process and ensure that candidates for office are briefed on the agenda of the pro-Israel community.

In sum, it is a highly professional operation and is consistently ranked among the top three or four most powerful lobbies in the United States.

Or take the American Jewish Committee. We have a full-time staff of 260 and an annual budget of nearly 30 million dollars, all raised through charitable donations, including from non-Jews.

A good deal of our work is devoted to strengthening support and understanding of Israel in the United States and around the world. We go about it in many ways. Let me offer just a few examples.

We have a program called Project Interchange that brings selected American influentials to Israel every month. This program has been in existence for twenty years, and in that period more than 3,000 American politicians, journalists, Christian religious leaders, university presidents, and other prominent personalities have participated.

We sponsor radio commentaries on major stations—not Jewish—in important American cities. These commentaries, many of which deal with Israel either directly or indirectly, can be heard every two weeks and are designed for a general listening public.

We do a tremendous amount of coalitional work with other ethnic, racial, and religious groups. We try to be sensitive to their needs when and where we can, and then look to them for support on issues of importance to us, including Israel, of course.

And we meet with foreign leaders on practically a daily basis, seeking to leverage our position as an influential community in a powerful country to voice our major concerns. When and where possible, we are responsive to the needs of others, as when we actively supported the entry of Poland, Hungary, and the Czech Republic into NATO.

Or another example: Roger Cukierman and the delegation that came to our Annual Dinner in Washington earlier this month heard the president of Peru say to an audience of 1,200 how much he appreciated our support on a trade matter of importance to his country. In turn, we have asked for his help on voting patterns affecting Israel at the UN.

And finally, my tenth point, a pro-Israel lobby will only succeed if it is well-funded, employs specialists in the various fields from politics to the media, and if the bulk of the Jewish community agrees on the lobby's agenda.

On this last point, if a community is hopelessly divided on issues regarding Israel, then its chances for success are greatly diminished. Or if the pro-Israel lobby is no stronger than, say, the organizations on the right and left of the Jewish political spectrum, it will only end up being one among many voices, played off against the others.

In the United States, the Jewish community has a right and a left, both quite vocal. But at the end of the day the center—those who support the democratically elected government of Israel and defer to that government on the core questions of peace and security—are by far the strongest, vastly outnumbering and out-organizing the ideologically-driven groups on the right and left.

In sum, the pro-Israel community has developed a large, multi-organizational, sophisticated, well-funded apparatus that takes advantage of a national climate conducive to lobbying and advocacy, that reaches into every corner of America, whether there are Jews or not, and that constantly emphasizes the shared values and beliefs of America and Israel.

While we can never allow either complacency or arrogance, the effort has worked remarkably well until now.

Whether it can be effectively exported will be determined by others, not me.

But what I can say is that we are all in this struggle together. Therefore, if we at the American Jewish Committee can be of help to you here in France as you discuss what more can be done on behalf of Israel in this exceptionally important country, all you have to do is ask. You will find us more than delighted to cooperate.

NATO Expansion
National Press Club, Washington, D.C.
July 30, 2002

I would like to extend a special welcome to the distinguished diplomats from Bulgaria, the Czech Republic, Estonia, Hungary, Latvia, Lithuania, Poland, Romania, Slovakia, and Slovenia who have joined us here today, as well as to Bruce Jackson, the president of the U.S. Committee on NATO, and my colleague Rabbi Andrew Baker, the director of International Jewish Affairs for the American Jewish Committee and a participant in the recent Riga Summit.

On November 5, 1997, I had the privilege, on behalf of the American Jewish Committee, to testify before the Senate Foreign Relations Committee on the first round of NATO expansion, involving the Czech Republic, Hungary, and Poland. We were the first American Jewish organization to come out publicly in favor of NATO enlargement, a fact of which I am most proud.

Moreover, I might add that, in the very same spirit and motivated by the same post-Cold War considerations, we were the first American Jewish organization to support the unification of Germany, to call for the recognition of the independence of Estonia, Latvia, and Lithuania, and to endorse the lifting of trade restrictions imposed by the Jackson-Vanik Amendment on Bulgaria and Romania.

I would like to quote from our 1997 Senate testimony on NATO enlargement:

We are convinced that opportunity is temporary, not permanent. Either it is seized or it is lost. The opportunity presented by an expanded

NATO is one that should not, must not, be lost. An expanded NATO means greater stability for Central Europe, a region that was the cockpit for the two world wars that brought such horror to the twentieth century.

Retaining the North Atlantic alliance in its Cold War configuration would have meant continuing an historic injustice—the abandonment by the democratic West of the small nations of Central Europe. Let me remind us all that it happened in 1938 at Munich and 1945 at Yalta, and the West watched from the sidelines as Soviet power squashed fledgling and promising democratic movements in Hungary in 1956, Czechoslovakia in 1968, and Poland in 1981.

An expanded NATO not only strengthens democracy in those nations embraced by the alliance at Madrid, but encourages the other countries in the region to accelerate their own democratic and economic reforms, as well as resolve long-simmering disputes. The 1994 Poland-Lithuania agreement on good neighborly relations and military cooperation and the 1996 Hungary-Romania bilateral friendship treaty are just two examples. Moreover, integration in the Western alliance offers a real safeguard for the rights of Jews and other minority communities, historically the target of national, religious, or ethnic hatreds in too many places.

It would be premature to become too specific today about the scope of a second, or a third, tranche of NATO expansion, but it is important to keep very much alive NATO's openness to further waves of expansion. To do otherwise is to dash the hopes of tens of millions of Europeans, from the Baltics to the Balkans, that their future might include membership in NATO, and to imply a recreation of European spheres of influence, a profoundly destabilizing step that could have unintended, even unforeseen, consequences.

That was 1997. At the time, we heard a number of respected voices speak out in opposition to NATO expansion.

George Kennan, the legendary architect of the U.S. postwar containment policy of the Soviet Union, said that expansion "is the beginning of a new cold war," and added that such a step "would make the Founding Fathers of this country turn over in their graves."

Tom Friedman, the *New York Times* columnist, criticized the proposed policy in a number of op-ed pieces, citing fear of the Russian reaction and worrying that enlargement would "dilute [NATO's] power every bit as much as baseball expansion diluted Major League pitching and made every ninety-pound weakling a home-run threat."

Other critics voiced concern that America could be dragged into a war not of our choosing because of Article 5, which commits all NATO countries to help defend any member that is attacked, or cited the prospect of stratospheric costs to help the three new member countries—the Czech Republic, Hungary, and Poland—modernize their forces and integrate militarily into the collective security pact.

In point of fact, the critics were wrong.

There has been no new cold war with Russia. To the contrary, we have witnessed a promising new chapter evolve in the relationship between NATO and Russia, and this development is to be heartily welcomed.

NATO strength has not been diluted by the addition of its three newest members, but rather enhanced by the laudable efforts of the Czech Republic, Hungary, and Poland to contribute to the alliance by providing additional security for the collective defense of the member nations.

Article 5 has indeed been invoked—in fact, for the first time since NATO's founding in 1949. The country that sought the decision was none other than the United States, and it happened exactly one day after this nation was attacked on September 11, 2001. In other words, America's ability to respond to the menace of international terrorism was actually helped, certainly not hindered, by an enlarged NATO.

And those who floated estimates of tens, even hundreds, of billions of dollars in costs to the U.S. taxpayer for expansion were way off. Indeed, the U.S. taxpayer has barely felt the impact.

In sum, the first round of NATO enlargement to the east has been a success. It is now time for a second round.

The American Jewish Committee urges the nineteen NATO member countries gathering in Prague on November 22 to seize the moment and extend formal invitations for full membership to Bulgaria, Estonia, Latvia, Lithuania, Romania, Slovakia, and Slovenia. Our position, needless to say, assumes that nothing will change between now and then in these countries' commitment to the core democratic values enshrined in NATO. We would also encourage NATO to make clear that, down the road and subject to performance, further enlargement is possible for other aspiring nations.

As the American Jewish Committee noted in a statement just adopted by our leadership:

> Through continued adherence to the membership action plan for new countries, these [seven] countries will demonstrate their commitment to democracy and the rule of law, peaceful conflict resolution, and the protection of human rights. Their accession to NATO membership will serve the national security interest of the United States. For these reasons, the American Jewish Committee voices its support for the continued expansion of NATO and the accession of these new member nations.
>
> The American Jewish Committee also calls on these countries to redouble their efforts in the months ahead to complete the still open process of restituting Jewish communal property and preserving Holocaust memory and its integrity. [There remains much work to be done in both respects, and any delay would only complicate matters.]

Ladies and gentlemen, this is potentially a moment of historical definition. We dare not let it pass.

The twentieth century began with territorial conflicts throughout Europe, most notably in Central and Eastern Europe. They led directly to the First World War and planted the seeds for the Second World War as well. After the massive devastation wrought by these two wars, as well as numerous regional conflicts, the second half of the century was largely defined by the Cold War and the confrontation between NATO and the Warsaw Pact, followed by the devastating events in the former Yugoslavia.

In sum, it was a brutal, bloody century, but at the end of the day the ideologies of fascism, Nazism, communism, and ethnic cleansing were vanquished and democracy, open societies, and the rule of law prevailed.

We now have the remarkable opportunity—on our watch—to extend the democratic zone of security, stability, tranquillity, and mutual assistance to embrace the seven candidate countries.

Of course, there will be significant transitional challenges in integrating the seven countries into the NATO framework. Given the scale of the project, how could it be otherwise? The fear-mongers, no doubt, will once again invoke the same issues as they did in 1997, but they will be as wrong today as they were then.

To act in Prague in November is to address the legitimate security interests of the seven candidate countries, to expand the borders of the transatlantic community at peace, to extend the reach of—and deepen the commitment to—democratic values and respect for human rights, and to strengthen America's global role, especially in the wake of September 11, as we face such transnational threats as international terrorism.

History has given us a previously unimaginable chance. The choice should be clear. The time to act is now. The beneficiary will be the collective security of the democratic family of nations.

On April 12, 1949, President Harry Truman sent the NATO Treaty to the United States Senate for approval. On that occasion, he said:

> This treaty is an expression of the desire of the people of the United States for peace and security, for the continuing opportunity to live and work in freedom.
>
> Events of this century have taught us that we cannot achieve peace independently. The world has grown too small. The oceans to our east and west no longer protect us from the reach of brutality and aggression....
>
> Together, our joint strength is of tremendous importance to the future of free men in every part of the world....
>
> We must continue to work patiently and carefully, advancing with practical, realistic steps in the light of circumstances and events as they occur, building the structure of peace soundly and solidly.

The times may have changed rather dramatically since 1949, but, strikingly, the words of President Truman are as applicable in today's world as they were then and serve to underscore the case for NATO enlargement.

We at the American Jewish Committee shall do our utmost, working with like-minded institutions, to ensure that the vision of an expanded NATO becomes a reality.

One Year Later: Remembering September 11
New York
September 11, 2002

This is a tough day for all of us.

Who among us will ever forget exactly what we were doing, where we were standing, with whom we were talking, when we first heard the news that fateful Tuesday morning?

Who among us will ever forget the sense of connection that we experienced here in this building on that day, as we were so harshly reminded both of the fragility of life and the true meaning of living?

Who among us will ever forget the welter of emotions that we experienced that day, the indelibly etched images that will forever be part of our memory bank?

Who among us will ever forget the raw display of courage of the rescue workers—the city's previously unsung heroes—who put their lives on the line, and too often gave their lives, to fulfill their sworn duty to assist others?

Or the courage of those passengers on Flight 93 who, facing certain death, prevented a still greater catastrophe?

Who will ever forget the plume of smoke, rubble, ash, and, it must be said, incinerated human remains that was visible, looking south, from our building that day?

And who will ever forget the sea of people—of all faiths, colors, backgrounds—walking as one up Third Avenue, away from the disaster zone, united by destiny and shared grief?

Who will ever forget the steady, determined response of our elected officials as they rose to the challenge of defending our nation?

Who will ever forget the blind hatred and fanaticism that drove nineteen people—and their numerous backers and supporters located in Afghanistan, Pakistan, Saudi Arabia, United Arab Emirates, Egypt, Yemen, and elsewhere in the Islamic world, in cells in Britain, Spain, Germany, Italy, Holland, and France, and in New Jersey, Florida, Minnesota, Arizona, and other states—to commit these crimes against humanity?

While there are those who would temporize, or engage in endless psychobabble, or shove books at us about the true meaning of religion, or suggest, ever so subtly, that America brought this upon itself—as some in Europe, for example, apparently believe—I beg to differ.

This was an act of war, pure and simple. It emerges from a fascist ideology that is an heir to the legacy of the totalitarian creeds of the twentieth century, and takes as its "noble" objective the obscurantist, misogynous, suffocating medieval model that was Afghanistan under Taliban rule.

If we are to study them, let it be so that we can all the better defeat them, vanquish them, and not so that we can engage in collective therapy sessions to feel each other's pain.

Shimon Peres told the AJC ten days ago that "anger is not a policy." Perhaps he's right, but it sure is a driving force in this case.

At this tender moment, let's remember September 11, 2001, yes, but let's also remember September 10, 2001, and September 12, 2001.

On September 10, we were a largely carefree and complacent country. We were an ever more self-indulgent and pampered society. We thought the blessings of geography and power could insulate us from the dangers lurking out there somewhere. As a result, we missed all the warning signs.

Never again should we allow ourselves either that excessive form of narcissism or that false sense of invulnerability as a nation.

And on September 12, at great cost to our nation, we became a more caring, more committed society. But, as a country, we suffer from a short attention span. Consequently, each of us needs to do what he or she can to extend that sense of concern and compassion for those around us, both friend and stranger.

And each of us needs to understand the importance of commitment, of determination, of resolve in this war launched against us.

Each and every day, I am thankful for the gift of this country—the world's greatest experiment in democracy, the rule of law, and pluralism. How many of us after September 11 look at the flag with a new sense of awe and respect? I know I do.

And each and every day, I am thankful for the gift of the American Jewish Committee, which has been a tenacious fighter for the values of decency, mutual understanding, and mutual respect. All of you are part of the fight. You were on September 10, you were on September 11, and you came right back on September 12, without missing a beat, and rededicated yourselves.

Through our example here as a diverse community of caring and connected people, may we reaffirm the strength of our nation, our vision, and our common humanity.

India, Israel, and the United States
National Federation of Indian American Associations
Twelfth Biennial Convention
Detroit
October 11, 2002

President [Parthasarathy] Pillai, Congressman [Joe] Knollenberg, distinguished delegates,

It is a great honor to be with you this evening at your opening dinner.

I've eagerly looked forward to this occasion, since it allows me to express to a prestigious audience, first, my admiration for India; second, my joy at the rapidly expanding bilateral ties between India and the United States and between India and Israel; and third, my desire to affirm the striking commonalties between the Indian American community and the American Jewish community that help explain our ever closer cooperation.

Representing an organization that has sought, over the years, to contribute to these very objectives by frequent trips to New Delhi, meetings here with visiting Indian officials, and contact with your member organizations, I feel a particular sense of gratification.

Yes, it took longer than we might have wished for Indo-American and Indo-Israeli relations to take off.

Indeed, it is hard to understand, even if I have heard the explanations more than once, why the world's two largest democracies—India and the United States—had such cool ties for so many years.

It was not until 1959, twelve years after India's independence, that the first American presidential visit took place, and there was a twenty-two-year gap between President Jimmy Carter's visit in 1978 and President Bill Clinton's in 2000.

And it is only in the last ten years that India and Israel have truly seized the opportunity to develop a warm and mutually beneficial relationship, but the lightning rate of this growth in ties is making up for lost time.

I want to put my cards on the table. I am a great believer in democracy.

As the legendary Jawaharlal Nehru said: "Democracy is good. I say this because other systems are worse." Indeed, democracy is the key to peaceful coexistence and mutual respect.

Again, it was Nehru who said: "The only alternative to coexistence is codestruction."

When was the last time one truly democratic nation waged war against another rather than settling their differences peacefully? But alas, in the Middle East and South Asia, democracy is a rare asset enjoyed by Israelis and Indians, but until now, too few others.

America is a great democracy. India is a great democracy. Israel is a great democracy.

May these three examples prove contagious in the world in which we live.

I am also a great believer in pluralism.

If there are better examples of diverse, pluralistic societies in the world today than India, the United States, and Israel, I would like to hear about them.

Each of these three countries has within its borders a remarkable range of linguistic, ethnic, racial, and religious groups, and all are protected, not by the arbitrary whim of individual rulers, but by the enduring power of law.

I am also a great believer in unleashing the human capacity for education, exploration, and entrepreneurship.

It is not by accident that Israel, India, and the United States are today among the most far-sighted, dynamic, and cutting-edge societies in such fields as science, engineering, technology, and medicine. After all, when creativity and discovery are encouraged, not stifled, mankind becomes the beneficiary.

And, not least, I am a great believer in the need for democratic countries to recognize the common threat to our open societies.

No three countries today better understand the nature of the global terrorist danger than the United States, India, and Israel.

And no three countries have shown more resolve, more determination to stand firm, and more willingness to take the measures necessary to prevail in this life-and-death struggle.

Ladies and gentlemen, we know—don't we?—that if terrorist bombers win anywhere, then they will feel emboldened to wage war everywhere.

We must not let them win.

And we must not succumb to the misguided thinking that would have us extend our sympathy to the grievances of those who kill innocent men, women, and children on buses and trains, and in parliaments and cafes.

And we must never forget that terrorists seldom act as individuals. They belong to groups; they are subject to indoctrination; they depend on funding; they cannot operate without training and weaponry; and they require sanctuaries.

In other words, they do not exist in a vacuum.

We cannot permit the continued coddling of those nations and groups—and we have a pretty good idea who they are, don't we?—that support this infrastructure.

We must not allow countries to have it both ways—participating in the family of civilized nations while providing vital oxygen to the terrorists.

And we must not allow our own open societies to be used by those who sanctimoniously wrap themselves in the mantle of democratic freedoms precisely to subvert those freedoms. We have seen this phenomenon right here in America and elsewhere in the democratic world.

An open society, yes. A formula for self-destruction, no.

Yet, at the same time, we cannot permit the evil deeds of some to be represented as the malevolent intentions of all.

We must never paint with too broad a brush stroke, never demonize or dehumanize an entire people or faith. That would be indefensible.

Ladies and gentlemen, if terrorism is the greatest security threat to the world today, then I daresay, without an ounce of hyperbole, that the world's fate depends to a very large degree on the successful outcome of the struggle by India, Israel, and the United States to confront and defeat that terror.

These three nations stand on the front lines. They must be strong and resolute. They merit our full—and sustained—support, for the battle will be neither quick nor easy.

Let the word go out: Political objectives will never be achieved by the deliberate targeting of innocents, regardless of whether the perpetrators think they are acting in the name of some higher calling or divine being. Murder is murder, and terrorism is, in fact, nothing more than cold-blooded murder, however it is packaged.

And if the Taliban regime in Afghanistan was the model for the terrorists' ideal of a Sharia-governed society, Lord help us all! Propped up by only three countries that formally recognized them—Pakistan, Saudi Arabia, and the United Arab Emirates—the Taliban brought nothing but misery, suffocation, and repression to those who had the misfortune to live under their rule.

I hope the world will always remember which countries are on the right side in this battle, and which are cynically trying to play all sides.

One thing is clear: The United States, India, and Israel are on the same side, and thank goodness for that.

Another word, if I may.

It is striking, isn't it, how much in common India and Israel, and, more broadly, Indians and Jews have.

We are both linked to ancient lands, proud traditions, rich civilizations, and modern countries.

We are both exceptionally tolerant people: India, where Jews have lived for centuries, is one of the very few countries in the world with no history of anti-Semitism—none. Perhaps you can teach the world a thing or two about such a remarkable record.

And, if I may say so, Jews have been leaders in the civil rights struggle for all.

As one relevant example, I am especially proud of the role played by Congressman Emanuel Celler, a New York Jew, who led the effort in 1946 to overcome discriminatory laws against Indians in the United States and provide them the chance for naturalization and citizenship.

We have both contributed disproportionately to advancing the frontiers of knowledge.

We have both created democratic, pluralistic societies that remain under threat.

And the British weren't a big help to either of us—were they?—in the period leading up to the two 1947 partition plans.

We have both known invasion, occupation, persecution, and expulsion. I vividly remember, for instance, being in the United Kingdom in 1972 when Idi Amin, now safely housed in Saudi Arabia, kicked out tens of thousands of Indians (and other Asians) from Uganda practically overnight.

We are both peoples that place the highest premium on the enduring values of education, family, and civic participation. I certainly saw this up close in my four years of graduate study at two British universities that were heavily attended by students from India and the Indian diaspora.

These values help explain your extraordinary success in this country and the imprint you have made on American society in a relatively short period of time, and I would like to believe they help explain ours as American Jews as well.

And last but by no means least, we share another thing in common. There are almost as many Indian American organizations and Jewish American organizations as there are Indians and Jews in this great land!

The American Jewish Committee has worked for nearly a century to strengthen American democracy, pluralism, and mutual understanding. We have been in the forefront of building bridges to America's diverse racial, religious, and ethnic communities. In building these bridges, we create a stronger America—and come closer, we hope, to Nehru's goal of coexistence rather than codestruction.

As we look ahead, you can count on us to be your partners in our common challenges and endeavors.

Israel at Fifty-five[*]
AJC 97th Annual Dinner
Washington, D.C.
May 6, 2003

A small town had three synagogues—Orthodox, Reform, and Conservative. All three had a serious problem with squirrels in their buildings. Each congregation, in its own fashion, had a meeting to deal with the problem.

The Orthodox decided that it was the will of God that squirrels be in the *shul* and that they would just have to live with them.

The Reform decided they should deal with the squirrels in the movement's style of Community Responsibility and Social Action. They humanely trapped them and released them in a park at the edge of town. Within three days, they were all back in the temple.

The Conservatives had several lengthy meetings, at which all members voiced opinions. They then voted the squirrels in as members. Now they see them only on Rosh Hashanah and Yom Kippur.

No matter how frequently or infrequently you are with us, it is wonderful to be together this evening and throughout the week. I am hope-

---

[*] A shortened version of this text appeared as an op-ed in the *Forward* on May 9, 2003. Also, segments of this speech were drawn from an essay of mine entitled "Israel at Fifty," which was published in 1998.

ful that, by week's end, you will feel better informed, indeed, inspired, and firmly convinced, if you weren't already, that the American Jewish Committee and you make an ideal match.

Tonight we celebrate a milestone birthday. Israel is fifty-five years old. Whatever the difficulties and challenges of the moment, and they are not inconsiderable, this is an epochal occasion for Israel and its friends to mark with unrestrained joy and pride.

It's a time to step back, if just for a moment, from the whirlwind of daily events—terror attacks against Israelis, Road Map prognostications, internal Palestinian maneuvering, Labor Party changes in Israel—and reflect on the larger picture.

Let me put my cards on the table. Just in case it was a secret to anyone in this room, I'm not dispassionate when it comes to Israel.

I believe that the establishment of the State of Israel in 1948; the fulfillment of its envisioned role as home and haven for Jews from around the world; the embrace of democracy and the rule of law, including an independent judiciary, free and fair elections, and smooth transfers of power; and the impressive scientific, cultural, and, not least, economic achievements of Israel are accomplishments beyond our wildest imagination. I am ever so grateful to witness this most extraordinary period in Jewish history and Jewish sovereignty.

And when one adds the key element, namely, that all this was accomplished not in the Middle West but in the Middle East, where Israel's neighbors were determined from the very beginning to destroy it and were prepared to use any means available to them—from full-scale wars to wars of attrition; from diplomatic isolation to attempts at international delegitimation; from primary to secondary to even tertiary economic boycotts; from terrorism to the spread of anti-Semitism, often thinly veiled as anti-Zionism—the story of Israel's first fifty-five years becomes all the more remarkable.

No other country has been subjected to such a constant challenge to its existence, to its very legitimacy, though the age-old biblical, spiritual, and physical connection between the Jewish people and the Land of Israel is quite unique in the annals of history. Indeed, it is of a totally different character from the basis on which, say, the United States,

Australia, Canada, New Zealand, or the bulk of Latin American countries were established, that is, by Europeans with no legitimate claim
to these lands decimating indigenous populations and proclaiming
authority. Or, for that matter, as Princeton University Professor
Bernard Lewis has noted, how the previously Christian lands of Syria,
Egypt, and North Africa were conquered by Arab-Islamic invaders and
totally redefined.

No other country has faced such overwhelming odds against its survival or experienced the same degree of international vilification by an
automatic majority of nations reflexively following the will of the
energy-rich and more numerous Arab states, and, in doing so, throwing truth and fairness to the wind.

Yet throughout, Israelis have never succumbed to a fortress mentality, never abandoned their deep yearning for peace or willingness to
take unprecedented risks to achieve that peace, and never flinched from
their determination to build a thriving state.

In fact, I believe this story of nation-building to be entirely without
precedent.

Here was a people brought to the brink of utter destruction by the
genocidal policies of Nazi Germany and its allies. Here was a people
shown to be entirely powerless to influence the world to stop this
unparalleled carnage. And here was a people, numbering but 600,000,
living cheek by jowl with often hostile Arabs, under unsympathetic
British occupation, on a harsh soil with no significant natural resources
in then Mandatory Palestine. That the blue-and-white flag of an independent Israel could be planted on this land, to which the Jewish people had been linked since the covenant between God and Abraham, just
three years after the Second World War's end—and with the support of
a decisive majority of UN members—is truly astounding.

To understand the essence of Israel's meaning it is enough to ask
how the history of the Jewish people might have been different had
there been a Jewish state in 1933, in 1938, even in 1941. If Israel had
controlled its borders and the right of entry instead of Britain, if Israel
had had embassies and consulates throughout Europe, how many more
Jews might have escaped and found sanctuary?

Instead, Europe's Jews had to rely on the good will of embassies and consulates of other countries and, with woefully few exceptions, they found neither the "good" nor the "will" to assist.

I have witnessed firsthand what Israeli embassies and consulates mean to Jews drawn to Israel by the pull of Zion or the push of hatred. I have stood in the courtyard of the Israeli embassy in Moscow and seen thousands of Jews seeking a quick exit from a Soviet Union that showed signs of cataclysmic change, but these Jews weren't sure if the change was in the direction of democracy or renewed chauvinism and anti-Semitism.

I have seen firsthand Israel do what no other Western country had ever done before—bring out black Africans, in this case Ethiopian Jews, not in chains for exploitation, but in dignity for freedom.

Awestruck, I have watched firsthand Israel never falter, not for a moment, in transporting Soviet Jews to the Jewish homeland, even as Scud missiles launched from Iraq traumatized the nation. It says a lot about the conditions they were leaving behind that these Jews continued to board planes for Tel Aviv while missiles were exploding in Israeli population centers. And equally, it says a lot about Israel that, amidst all the pressing security concerns, it managed without missing a beat to continue to welcome the new immigrants.

And how can I ever forget the surge of pride, Jewish pride, that completely enveloped me twenty-seven years ago on hearing the astonishing news of Israel's daring rescue of the 106 Jewish hostages held by Arab and German terrorists in Entebbe, Uganda, over 2,000 miles from Israel's border?

The unmistakable message of a Jewish state is this: Jews in danger will never again be alone and helpless.

To be sure, nation-building is an infinitely complex process. In Israel's case, that nation-building took place against a backdrop of tensions with a local Arab population that also laid claim to the very same land; as the Arab world sought to isolate, demoralize, and ultimately destroy the state; as Israel's population literally doubled in the first three years of the country's existence, putting an unimaginable strain on severely limited resources; as the nation was forced to devote a vast portion of its budget to defense expenditures; and as the country coped with forging a national identity and social consensus among a population that could not have been more geographically, linguistically, socially, and culturally heterogeneous.

Here we come to a tricky and perhaps underappreciated issue—the potential clash between the messy realities of statehood and, in this case, the ideals of a faith and a people. It is one thing to be a people living as a minority in often inhospitable majority cultures; it is quite another to exercise sovereignty as the majority population. Inevitably, there will be tension between a people's faith or ideals and the exigencies of statecraft, between our highest conceptions of human nature and the daily realities of individuals in decision-making positions wielding power and balancing a variety of competing interests.

Still, shall we raise the bar so high as to practically ensure that Israel, forced to function in the often gritty, morally ambiguous world of international relations and politics, will always fall short?

On the other hand, the notion that Israel would ever become ethically indistinguishable from any other country, reflexively seeking cover behind the convenient justification of realpolitik to explain its behavior, must be equally unacceptable.

Israelis, with only fifty-five years of statehood under their belts, are among the newer practitioners of statecraft. With all its remarkable success, look at the daunting political, social, and economic challenges within the United States fifty-five years, or even 155 years, after independence, or, for that matter, the challenges faced by our nation today. And let's not forget that the United States, unlike Israel, is a vast country blessed with abundant natural resources, oceans on two-and-a-half sides, a gentle neighbor to the north, and a weaker neighbor to the south.

Like any vibrant democracy, America is a permanent work in progress. So, too, is Israel.

Of course, the Israeli record is imperfect, but in just fifty-five years, Israel has built a thriving democracy; an economy whose per capita GNP exceeds the combined total of its four contiguous sovereign neighbors—Lebanon, Syria, Jordan, and Egypt; eight universities that contribute to advancing the world's frontiers of knowledge; a life expectancy that places it among the healthiest nations; a prolific culture utilizing an ancient language rendered contemporary; and an agricultural sector that has shown the world how to conquer an arid land.

In the final analysis, the story of Israel these past fifty-five years, above all, is the wondrous realization of a 3,500-year link between a land, a faith, a language, a people, and a vision. It is an inspiring story of tenacity and determination, of courage and renewal.

But as we all know too well, the story cannot end here. Challenges abound.

Within Israel, the major long-term challenge, I suspect, will be to ensure that the ties that bind Israelis remain far stronger than those forces threatening to pull the country apart. The most ominous of these centrifugal forces—and unquestionably the most difficult to solve—is the religious/secular divide.

Surely, the religious camp is not monolithic, nor, for that matter, is the secular camp. Still, it is fair to say that a deep rift has existed among Jews for centuries, especially since the Enlightenment, and among Israelis for the past fifty-five years, along these essential lines.

Not only has this divide not been narrowed in Israel, where regrettably, unlike in the United States, no middle ground of non-Orthodox forms of religious practice has yet taken deep root, but, in fact, the split threatens to grow ever wider. Israel increasingly encompasses two centers, or, more to the point, two worldviews, for practical purposes embodied by Jerusalem, the religious, and Tel Aviv (and Haifa), the secular.

How to manage this divide remains a daunting challenge for Israel and, I would add, the Jewish people as a whole. It is coterminous with the underlying challenge of defining the very nature of the Jewish state, still incomplete after fifty-five years. What exactly is, or ought to be, the Jewish character of the Jewish state? How Jewish ought it to be? Whose definition of Judaism should prevail? How are the very notions of religion and state to be reconciled?

Let me add a word here. I believe strongly in insuring the distinctive Jewish character of the state. At the same time, history has amply demonstrated the dangers of excessive entanglement of religion and state. Indeed, bad as such entanglement is for the state, it is still more corrosive for religion and religious leaders. Seeking God and votes at one and the same time does not a good mix make.

Moreover, to complicate matters further, Israel is a Jewish state with a non-Jewish minority numbering close to 20 percent of its citizens. Is there not a permanent tension—not easily reconciled—in embracing both its Jewish character and its non-Jewish citizens?

To underscore this problem, a recent survey among Israel's Arab citizens found that only 17 percent accepted Israel as "a Zionist, Jewish state." The results may not be entirely surprising, but surely they are sobering.

The economic divide as well cannot be ignored. A significant segment of Israel is prospering. This well-to-do crowd spends winter vacations in the Alps, is plugged into the new technologies, and is virtually indistinguishable from its counterparts in New York, London, or Tokyo. But hundreds of thousands of residents of development towns and neglected urban neighborhoods have been left behind, creating a wide income gap, not to speak of a disparity in both opportunities and services. In fact, to our collective shame, Israel is now reported to have one of the widest gaps between rich and poor of any Western industrialized nation, and the number of Israelis falling below the poverty line is growing, not shrinking.

Finally, as an American Jew, I worry about another gap or divide—that between Israel and American Jewry. In some respects, perhaps, this may be unavoidable. With the passage of time, we almost inevitably grow more distant from one another. If our grandparents were siblings, then we are now, at best, second cousins.

Here in the United States we have developed our own dynamic forms of Jewish culture, wherein Israel figures only marginally. How many Israeli authors, playwrights, poets, artists, filmmakers, philosophers or, for that matter, theologians, are even known here, much less have become integral parts of our American Jewish culture?

Whatever the gulf, though, American Jews have consistently sought to mobilize support for Israel in the United States, some adopting the secular religion of "Israelism," expressing their Jewish identity principally through political advocacy.

Inexplicably, there are some Israelis who are either dismissive or unaware of the value of this support. And, on this side of the ocean, there are American Jews, as many as 25 percent according to American Jewish Committee polls, who are totally detached from Israel.

Let's all be clear about the stakes involved. American Jewish support has been crucial in building and maintaining the U.S.-Israel relationship. Without it, and I say this from long years in these very trenches, U.S. foreign policy would far more likely resemble Europe's essentially "evenhanded" attitude toward Israel. And that is not an outcome we can afford. The American link with Israel is vital, absolutely vital, to Israel's quest for both peace and security.

While Israel, with AJC in an active supporting role, develops important links with other key countries—from Turkey to India, from Poland to China, from Germany to Singapore—the United States plays a singular role in the life of Israel. Put simply, there is no substitute. And we at the American Jewish Committee reaffirm tonight our commitment to sustaining and further enhancing that U.S.-Israel relationship.

I said at the outset that this was an occasion to look at the larger picture, as Israelis this evening mark Yom Ha'atzmaut, Independence Day. There will be other opportunities in the course of our Annual Meeting to explore the current situation in the Middle East and the prospects for the Road Map.

Let me simply say that I believe there is no nation on earth that yearns for peace more than the nation of Israel. The pursuit of peace has been central to the Jewish mission from day one, and it has been central to Israel's mission from its creation.

There are those who believe they know the best strategy for Israel to pursue in making peace. I don't count myself among them. It's not that I don't have a few ideas of my own. Believe me, I do. But I also recognize the need for a healthy dose of humility. There is a great deal of information all of us don't have, and even when we think we have it, the overlay of the Middle East makes interpretation incredibly tricky and notoriously unreliable.

And as for the self-assured ideologues, whether of the right or the left, the plain truth is that neither camp can claim complete vindication of its views—far from it. It is good to recall the words of the Chinese proverb: "Great doubts, deep wisdom. Small doubts, little wisdom." Or closer to home, as the Talmud puts it rather bluntly: "In seeking wisdom thou art wise; in imagining that thou hast attained it, thou art a fool."

Moreover, we need to bear in mind at all times what hangs in the balance—the security, indeed the very survival, of a nation precious to us beyond words. That, too, ought to humble us.

My operating philosophy here at American Jewish Committee remains as it was.

Israel is a democracy. Its citizens have abundant means to express their views. Its people yearn for peace no less than I. Its people will bear the immediate consequences of whatever decisions are made. Our role should be to help Israel achieve the time and space it needs to make the decisions that only it can make on the existential questions of war and peace, and to ensure that in the process it is not subjected to undue external pressure.

We also have another role, as friends of Israel. We share with our Israeli interlocutors in private, and as unflinchingly as we possibly can, our assessment of the potential impact of various possible Israeli actions on the key U.S.-Israel lifeline, as well as on the Israel-Diaspora relationship. At AJC we have always taken this role very seriously.

And we have a third role—not to yield to pessimism or despondency. That can be incredibly difficult at times, I realize. But Israel has shown a determination to survive and prosper that should hearten us all. Israelis have given new meaning to the will to live and taught us much about the essence of courage, resolve, and pride.

And with our own eyes we have witnessed the possibilities for progress on the ground, most notably in the peace treaties with Egypt and Jordan. Remember, Anwar Sadat had not only been anti-Israel but also pro-Nazi and anti-Semitic. Yet in 1977 he made his momentous trip to Jerusalem and the rest, as they say, is history.

I don't know how long the wait will be until Israel's birthright as a Jewish state is fully recognized and lasting peace with all its neighbors becomes a reality. Like you, I am all too well aware of the many reasons why this may not happen tomorrow or even the day after.

But we as an organization must never abandon hope. To the contrary, in everything we do, we must choose hope. And we must remind ourselves—and the world—at every opportunity that the very name chosen for the Israeli national anthem, *Hatikva*, literally means "the hope." In fact, I believe the story not only of Israel but of the Jewish people as a whole represents the best possible metaphor for the triumph of hope over despair.

I am convinced that no Jewish organization anywhere is more active regarding Israel on more diplomatic and political fronts, in more corridors of power around the world, than the American Jewish Committee. In the words of the late Abba Eban, we have stood in "vigilant brotherhood" with Israel from its very establishment. Yet proud as we are of that role, we can ill afford to rest on our laurels, for there is much work still to be done.

In sum, the agenda remains a long one, and I've only touched on elements of it. But as we consider it, how can we lose sight, even for a single moment, of the extraordinary accomplishments of these past fifty-five years?

Let me suggest that we—Israel and its friends around the world— consider the sweep of the last five-and-a-half decades. In doing so, we can more readily appreciate the light-years we have traveled since the darkness of the Shoah, and marvel at the miracle of a decimated people returning to a tiny sliver of land—the land of our ancestors, the land of Zion and Jerusalem—and successfully building a modern, vibrant, and democratic state, against all the odds, on that ancient foundation.

Am Yisrael chai!

Rally for Israel[*]
Brooklyn, New York
May 18, 2003

My dear friends,

I thank the organizers for inviting me to this wonderful event.

I thank you for being here and showing your love of Israel.

This is a critical time in history. Our voices must be heard.

Israelis need to know that we stand with them shoulder to shoulder.

Our elected officials in this great country need to hear from us often. They need to know that we care about Israel.

Let the whole world hear our voices.

We stand with Israel.

Is there another nation on earth that seeks peace more than Israel?

Is there another nation on earth that has tried harder to achieve peace than Israel?

Look at what Israel was prepared to do to make peace with Egypt and Jordan. Thankfully, there are peace treaties with those countries today, even if the peace with Egypt is colder than we might wish. Still, I'll take a cold peace over a hot war any day of the week.

With the Palestinians, what is Israel to do? It cannot make peace alone. It takes two to make peace. It needs a credible partner. Until now that credible Palestinian partner hasn't been there, has it?

Can Israel be expected to make peace with a partner who negotiates by day and plans terror attacks by night?

Can Israel be expected to make peace with a partner whose school-children are taught hatred and martyrdom?

Can Israel be expected to make peace when suicide bombers are celebrated as heroes for killing Israelis in cafés, buses, and Passover Seders?

You understand this situation far better than most other people.

You have experienced the lies, corruption, and brainwashing of a dictatorial system.

---

[*] This speech was delivered in Russian. This is a translation.

You know that words are cheap. It's actions that count. Real actions. Have we seen those actions from the Palestinians yet?

We marked Israel's fifty-fifth birthday this month.

Throughout its history, this lone democracy in the Middle East has defied all the odds. It is here to stay.

One day, God willing, peace will come. In the meantime, we Jews must stand strong. We must stand together. We must stand resolute.

Testimony on Anti-Semitism in Europe
to the U.S. Senate Committee on Foreign Relations
Subcommittee on European Affairs
Washington, D.C.
October 22, 2003

Mr. Chairman,

Permit me to express my deepest appreciation to you and to your distinguished colleagues for holding this important and timely hearing, and for affording me the opportunity of testifying before the Subcommittee on European Affairs of the Committee on Foreign Relations regarding the state of anti-Semitism in Europe.

I have the privilege of speaking on behalf of the American Jewish Committee, the oldest human relations organization in the United States. I am proud to represent over 125,000 members and supporters of the American Jewish Committee, a worldwide organization with thirty-three offices in the United States and fourteen overseas posts, including offices in Berlin, Geneva, and Warsaw, and association agreements with the European Council of Jewish Communities and with the Jewish communities in Bulgaria, the Czech Republic, Slovakia, and Spain.

Founded in 1906, our core philosophy for nearly a century has been that wherever Jews are threatened, no minority is safe. We have seen over the decades a strikingly close correlation between the level of anti-Semitism in a society and the level of general intolerance and violence against other minorities. Moreover, the treatment of Jews within a given society has become a remarkably accurate barometer of the state of democracy and pluralism in that society. In effect, though it is a role we most certainly did not seek, it can be said that by dint of our historical experience, Jews have become the proverbial miner's canary, often sensing and signaling danger before others are touched.

For nearly a century we have struggled against the scourge of anti-Semitism and its associated pathologies by seeking to advance the principles of democracy, the rule of law, and pluralism; by strengthening ties across ethnic, racial, and religious lines among people of good will; and by shining the spotlight of exposure on those who preach or practice hatred and intolerance.

Never in recent memory has that work been more important. We have witnessed in the last three years in particular a surge in anti-Semitism. Some of its manifestations are eerily familiar; others appear in new guises. But the bottom line is that Jews throughout the world, and notably in Western Europe, are experiencing a level of unease not seen in the postwar years.

I myself have been witness to the changed situation. I spent a sabbatical year in Europe in 2000–01, and continue to travel regularly to Europe, stay in close contact with European political and Jewish leaders, and follow closely the European media.

What sparked this new sense of unease? It cannot be separated from developments on the ground in the Middle East.

If I may be permitted to generalize, too many European governments, civic institutions, and media outlets rushed to condemn Israel after the promising peace talks of 2000 collapsed, despite the determined efforts of the Israeli government, with support from the United States, to reach a historic agreement with the Palestinians. Once the Palestinians returned to the calculated use of violence and terror in September 2000, for many Europeans it was as if those peace talks had never taken place. It was as if there had never been a proposal pushed relentlessly by Prime Minister Ehud Barak, with strong backing from President Bill Clinton, to achieve a two-state solution that included a partition of Jerusalem. And it was as if Chairman Yasir Arafat had not even participated in the talks, much less sabotaged them by rejecting out of hand the landmark deal offered him.

Israel was widely portrayed in Europe as an "aggressor" nation that was "trampling" on the rights of "stateless" and "oppressed" Palestinians. As Israel faced the daunting challenge of defending itself against terrorism, including suicide bombings, some in Europe went still further, seeking to deny it the right reserved to all nations to defend itself against this vicious onslaught. Such an attitude, if you will, became a new form of anti-Semitism.

I fully understand that Israel's actions, like those of any nation trying to cope with a similar threat, may engender discussion and debate or, for that matter, criticism, but what was taking place in these circles was something far more malicious. Tellingly, those engaged in portraying Israel as the "devil incarnate" for every imaginable "sin" were totally silent when it came to the use of Palestinian suicide bombers to kill innocent Israeli women, men, and children; they were even less prepared to address other compelling issues in the region surrounding Israel, such as Syria's longstanding and indefensible occupation of neighboring Lebanon, or persistent patterns of gross human rights violations in such countries as Iran, Iraq, Saudi Arabia, and Syria.

The frenzied rhetoric, especially in the media and human rights circles, kept escalating, to the point where some, including a Portuguese Nobel laureate, began recklessly using Nazi terminology to describe Israeli actions. Others, particularly at the time of the stand-off at the Church of the Nativity, reawakened the deadly deicide charge, which had been put to rest by Vatican Council II in 1965.

In highly publicized incidents, a few British intellectuals and journalists called into question Israel's very right to exist, and there were a number of attempts to impose boycotts on Israeli academicians and products. In one notorious case at Oxford University, a professor sought to deny admission to a student applicant based solely on the grounds that he had served in the Israel Defense Forces. Of course, we remember the shocking expletive used by the French ambassador to the Court of St. James regarding Israel, just as we recall that he was never punished by the French Foreign Ministry. And who can forget the travesty in Belgium as Prime Minister Ariel Sharon and a number of Israel military officials were threatened with legal action under the country's universal jurisdiction law, as were several prominent Americans, including former President George Bush, until the country's political leaders finally came to their senses and amended the law?

I could go on at length describing a highly charged atmosphere in Western Europe. Israel was accused, tried, and convicted in the court of public opinion. Furthermore, that court was encouraged, however inadvertently, by governments too quick to condemn Israel's defensive actions and by media outlets that, with a few notable exceptions, presented consistently skewed coverage, frequently blurring the line between factual reporting and editorializing. It would be enough to follow the reporting of some prominent Greek, Italian, Spanish, or even British media outlets for a few days to get a feeling for the inherently unbalanced, at times even inflammatory, coverage of the Middle East. The coverage of the Jenin episode in the spring of 2002 was particularly revealing. Israel was accused of everything from "mass murder" to "genocide," when the reality was a far cry from either, as confirmed by outside human rights experts.

Mr. Chairman, I personally witnessed a pro-Palestinian demonstration in Geneva, just opposite the United Nations headquarters, in which the chant alternated between "jihad, jihad" and *"Mort aux juifs,"* "Death to the Jews." Similar chants could be heard in the streets of France and Belgium. To the best of my knowledge, no action was taken by the authorities in any of these cases.

My children attended a Swiss international school where a sixteen-year-old Israeli girl was threatened with a knife by a group of Arab pupils. When she complained to school officials, the response was, and I quote, "This is a matter between countries. It does not involve our school." My youngest son had a more or less similar experience on the campus with, again, no action taken by the school authorities.

Is it any wonder that in such an atmosphere many Jews in the countries of Western Europe became concerned on two fronts? First, they were worried for their physical safety as they encountered a new form of anti-Semitism—the use of criticism of Israel and Israeli practices as justification for violence against Jews, who became "legitimate" targets by virtue of their real or presumed identification with Israel,

Zionism, or simply the Jewish people. This became evident in the many documented threats and attacks that took place against Jews and Jewish institutions in Europe, especially France. And second, to varying degrees, they were no longer quite as certain that they could rely on the sympathy and understanding of their governments for the physical and, yes, emotional security they needed—the certainty that the state would be there to ensure their protection.

Strikingly, those governments and institutions to a large degree professed ignorance of the problem.

For example, the American Jewish Committee met in November 2001 with the then foreign minister of France. We raised our concerns about growing threats to Jews, as well as growing tolerance for intolerance. In turn, we were treated to a revealing lecture from the minister. Initially, he denied there was any problem at all, though the facts contradicted him. Jews in France were being assaulted, synagogues were being torched, and Jewish parents were anxious about the safety of their children. Then he tried to muddy the problem by suggesting that crime had increased in France and Jews were among its many victims, but certainly not singled out. That, too, was belied by the facts, namely the specificity of the attacks against Jews and Jewish institutions. And finally, he attempted to rationalize the problem by linking it to the Middle East and inferring that, tragic though the anti-Jewish incidents were, they were an inevitable consequence of the Israeli-Palestinian conflict and would likely continue until that conflict was resolved.

Frankly, we were appalled by this response. Could it be that the foreign minister of a country which had given birth to the Declaration of the Rights of Man, and which had been the first European country to extend full protection to its Jewish community, had been unwilling or incapable of understanding and responding to what was going on in his own nation? In reality, France fell short in its responsibility to provide protection to its citizens from the fall of 2000 until the summer of 2002, a twenty-month period during which many French Jews felt abandoned and left to their own devices.

Meanwhile, French officials created a straw man—the false charge that France was being depicted as an anti-Semitic country—and went about refuting it. In reality, those concerned with developments in

France were talking about anti-Semitic acts *within* France and never sought to describe the nation as a whole as anti-Semitic, which would have been an unfair and inaccurate characterization.

While much attention has been focused on France because it is home to Europe's largest Jewish community and the greatest number of violent acts against Jews have taken place there in the past three years, the discussion by no means should be limited to France. During this period, we have also met with European Union commissioners in Brussels to discuss our concerns, but with little apparent success. Further, we have met with government leaders in other Western European countries and, with the exception of Germany, our efforts to call attention to a festering problem have fallen on largely deaf ears.

The obvious question is why there has been such a widespread failure to acknowledge and address a problem as obvious as it is real.

Could it be linked to hostility to Israel, particularly after the left-of-center Barak government gave way to the right-of-center Sharon government? Could it be an unwillingness to confront the reality that within the remarkable zone of prosperity and cooperation created by the European Union a cancer was still lurking that needed treatment? Could it be a fear of antagonizing growing Muslim populations in countries like Belgium and France, where they were rapidly becoming an electoral factor and, in some cases, were proving restive because of their difficulty in integrating? Or could it be a subliminal reaction, perhaps, to the decade of the 1990s when many countries had been compelled to look at their wartime actions in the mirror, yet resented those who held up the mirror?

Whatever the reason, it is clear that anti-Semitism still lurks in Europe, but not only in Europe, of course. Its main center of gravity today is in the Muslim world. The speech earlier this month by Malaysian Prime Minister Mahathir Mohamad at the Organization of the Islamic Conference was a prime example of the use of classical anti-Semitic themes. And not only did none of the many political leaders in attendance walk out of the hall to protest his offensive remarks, but he was greeted with a standing ovation and, subsequently, laudatory comments to the media by such leading officials as Egypt's foreign minister.

I would respectfully urge the Committee on Foreign Relations to consider a separate hearing on this pressing issue.

Mr. Chairman, European history, as we know so well, contains glorious chapters of human development and scientific breakthroughs. But it also contains too many centuries filled with an ever expanding vocabulary of anti-Semitism—from the teaching of contempt of the Jews to the Spanish and Portuguese Inquisitions; from forced conversions to forced expulsions; from restrictions on employment and education to the introduction of the ghetto; from blood libels to pogroms; and from massacres to the gas chambers at Auschwitz.

Who better than the Europeans should grasp the history of anti-Semitism? Who better than the Europeans should understand the slippery slope that can lead to demonization, dehumanization, and, ultimately, destruction of a people?

What, then, can Europe do at this moment to address the changed situation of the past three years?

First and foremost, precisely because of their history, it is the countries of Europe that could take the lead in confronting and combating the growing tide of global anti-Semitism, whatever its source, whatever its manifestation. That would be an extraordinarily positive development. And given Europe's substantial moral weight in the world today, it could have real impact.

Whether anti-Semitism comes in its old and familiar guises from the extreme right; in its various disguises from the extreme left, including the combustible mix of anti-Americanism, anti-globalization, and anti-Zionism; or from Muslim sources that peddle malicious conspiracy theories through schools, mosques, and the media to spread hatred of Jews, Europe's voice must be loud and consistent. Its actions need to match its words.

To date, experience has shown that a strong European response is far more likely when anti-Semitism emanates from the extreme right than when it comes from either the extreme left or the Islamic world. The reaction must be the same regardless of who is the purveyor.

Preserving the memory of the Holocaust is highly laudable, as many European countries have sought to do through national days of commemoration, educational initiatives, and memorials and monuments.

But demonstrating sensitivity for the legitimate fears of living Jews is no less compelling a task. Whether it is a relatively large Jewish community in France or a tiny, remnant Jewish community in Greece, the fact remains that no Jewish community comprises more than one percent of the total population of any European country, if that, and many remain deeply scarred by the lasting impact of the Holocaust on their numbers, their institutions, and, not least, their psyches.

When the Greek Jewish community awoke one morning shortly after 9/11 to read mainstream press accounts filled with wild assertions of Jewish or Israeli complicity in the plot to attack America, they understandably felt shaken and vulnerable, even if the charges were patently false. With less than five thousand Jews remaining in Greece after the devastation wrought by the Holocaust in a nation of over ten million, is it any wonder that these Jews might worry for their physical security at such a moment?

Second, political leaders need to set an example. Joschka Fischer, the foreign minister of Germany, is someone who has a grasp of the lessons of history when it comes to Europe and the Jews, and he understands Israel's current difficulties and dilemmas. He has not hesitated to speak out, to write, and to act. After all, it is political leaders who set the tone for a nation. By their actions or inactions, they send a clear and unmistakable message to their fellow citizens. When a French ambassador is not penalized for trashing Israel in obscene terms, what are the French people left to conclude? The same can be said of Lech Walesa, the former Polish president, who in 1995 remained silent in the face of a fiery anti-Semitic sermon delivered in his presence by his parish priest in Gdansk. He only reluctantly addressed the issue ten days later after pressure from several governments, including the United States.

Third, many European countries have strict laws on the books regarding anti-Semitism, racism, and Holocaust denial. In fact, to its credit, the French parliament recently toughened the nation's laws still further. These laws throughout Europe must be used. In that regard, we were pleased to hear French President Jacques Chirac, at a meeting last month in New York with American Jewish leaders, speak now of a "zero-tolerance" policy toward acts of anti-Semitism and penalties for those found guilty of such acts that would be "swift and severe." He also expressed concern about the unchecked influence of the Internet in spreading anti-Semitism and other forms of racism, and indicated a desire to explore means for restricting this influence.

No one should ever again be compelled to question the determination of European countries to investigate, prosecute, and seek maximum penalties for those involved in incitement and violence.

To cite one specific example, we are watching with particular interest what the British Home Office will do about two British Muslim youths who were quoted earlier this year in the *New York Times* (May 12, 2003) calling for the murder of Jews and whose cases were brought to the attention of the authorities.

And finally, all countries that aspire to the highest democratic values, including but not limited to European nations, must constantly remind themselves that anti-Semitism is a cancer that may begin with Jews but never ends with Jews. Anti-Semitism left unchecked metastasizes and eventually afflicts the entire democratic body.

Given the global nature of anti-Semitism, there is an opportunity for the democratic nations of the world to work cooperatively. The United States has always shown leadership in this regard. It has been an issue that unites our executive and legislative branches and our main political parties.

One venue that currently exists for such cooperation is the fifty-five-member Organization for Security and Cooperation in Europe (OSCE), which in June held its first conference devoted exclusively to the subject of anti-Semitism. This is a step forward, offering the chance to assess developments, compare experiences, and set forth short- and long-term strategies for combating anti-Semitism. This mechanism, while not in itself a panacea, should be regularized for as long as necessary, and ought to be viewed as an important vehicle for addressing the issue, but by no means the only one.

Mr. Chairman, I have deliberately omitted any reference to the nations of the Former Soviet Union because my colleague, Mark Levin of NCSJ, will address that subject in his testimony. But let me offer a positive note regarding the nations of Central Europe, ten of which have been included in the first and second rounds of NATO enlargement. I should add in this context that the American Jewish Committee was among the first nongovernmental organizations in this country to enthusiastically support both rounds of NATO enlargement.

While the history of anti-Semitism in many countries in this region runs very deep indeed, we have witnessed important progress in recent years, particularly with the collapse of communism and the ensuing preparations for membership in both NATO and the European Union. There has been a praiseworthy effort by the countries of Central Europe to reach out to Israel and the larger Jewish world, and to encourage the rebuilding of Jewish communities that suffered enormously under Nazi occupation and later under communist rule.

In other words, there is good news to report here. And one of the reasons for this good news has been the welcome recognition by post-communist leaders that their commitment to building truly open and democratic societies will be judged in part by how they deal with the range of Jewish issues resulting from the Nazi and communist eras.

Yet problems remain. In some countries, extremist voices seek votes and attempt to rehabilitate Nazi collaborators, but, fortunately, they are in the distinct minority. And some countries lag behind in bringing to closure the remaining restitution issues arising from Nazi and, later, communist seizure of property. We hope these matters will soon be addressed, with the ongoing encouragement of the United States government.

Mr. Chairman, by convening this hearing today, the United States Senate has once again underscored its vital role in defending basic human values and human rights around the world. Champions of liberty have always looked to our great country to stand tall and strong in the age-old battle against anti-Semitism.

In examining the scope of anti-Semitism today and exploring strategies for combating it, this subcommittee, under your leadership, looms large as a beacon of hope and a voice of conscience. As always, the American Jewish Committee stands ready to assist you and your distinguished colleagues in your admirable efforts.

Thank you, Mr. Chairman.

Statement to the
Senate Appropriations Committee
Subcommittee on Labor, Health and Human Services,
and Education
Hearing on "Palestinian Education—Teaching Peace or War?"*
October 30, 2003

Thank you, Chairman [Arlen] Specter, for allowing me this opportunity to submit a statement for the record.

I wish to express appreciation to the subcommittee for investigating
the current nature of the Palestinian education system so that we can
better understand how to further the process of replacing the teaching
of hatred and violence in Palestinian schools with the teaching of principles of coexistence, democracy, and mutual understanding.

The American Jewish Committee welcomes your initiative in holding a vitally important hearing on October 30 to bring to light the rampant teaching of hatred and glorification of violence in Palestinian
schools, and the concomitant incitement to violence and hate that permeates the broader Palestinian culture and is aimed in particular at
young people. We encourage the subcommittee to continue to press all
American authorities that deal with the Palestinian Authority, as you
strongly did at the hearing, to demand of the Palestinian Authority
Ministries of Education and Sport a revamping of the educational curricula that they disseminate. The basis for shared trust must begin with
clear messages from the Palestinian leadership to its children that
indeed there is a bright future for pluralism and coexistence in the
Middle East, precisely the opposite of what is being taught today. The
celebration of hate and violence that encourages children to commit
acts of terrorism, including homicide bombings, is, as Senator Hillary
Clinton noted at the hearing, a form of child abuse. The cessation of
such incitement must not await a resolution of the political issues
underlying the Israeli-Palestinian conflicts. It is a sine qua non of that
resolution.

* Richard Foltin, AJC's Legislative Director, helped draft this statement.

Of additional concern, such incitement is by no means a problem limited to the Palestinian territories, but is a malevolent trend to be found in far too many parts of the Muslim world. We are familiar with the vile anti-Semitic speech delivered by Malaysian Prime Minister Mahathir Mohamad to the Organization of the Islamic Conference last month, at which, to the everlasting shame of those attending this largest of gatherings of Muslim national leaders, his words were greeted not with condemnation, but with a standing ovation. And, as in the Palestinian Authority, one finds teaching of hatred that is directed at the young in other places as well.

This past February, the American Jewish Committee and the Center for Monitoring the Impact of Peace jointly released the most comprehensive survey ever prepared of the official Saudi worldview to which students between the ages of six and sixteen are exposed through the medium of subject textbooks. In analyzing the ninety-three school textbooks published by the Saudi Ministry of Education and in circulation between 1999 and 2002, the report reveals the widespread presence of contempt toward Western civilization and followers of other religions.

Here are the main findings from our report:

- **Islam is taught as the only true religion, and Saudi Arabia is seen as the leader of the Muslim world.** Islam is presented as the only true religion, while all other religions are presented as false. Consequently, Muslims are portrayed as superior to followers of all other religions. Islam plays the dominant role in state and society, in the judicial and educational systems, and in everyday life. Saudi Arabia assumes, in turn, a leading role in the Muslim world and sees itself as the champion of Islam.

- **Christians and Jews are denounced as infidels.** Christians and Jews are presented as enemies of Islam and of Muslims. Therefore, Muslims may not befriend them nor emulate them in any way, lest that lead to love and friendship, which is forbidden.

- **The West is a decaying society on its way to extinction, and is the source of past and present misfortunes of the Muslim world.**

Western civilization is presented as in a state of cultural and religious decline, the symptoms of which are the absence of spirituality, the practice of adultery, and the large number of suicides in Western society. The West is also blamed for desiring world domination and targeting the Muslim world by aggressively promoting Western practices, ideologies, and lifestyle habits among Muslim society. In addition, Saudi schoolchildren are taught to reject all notions of Western democracy.

- **Peace between Muslims and non-Muslims is ostensibly rejected.** Saudi Arabian schoolbooks, even grammar books, are full of phrases exalting war, jihad, and martyrdom. And though all forms of terror are rejected by the Saudi Arabian schoolbooks, it appears that such prohibitions do not apply to cases that fall in the categories of jihad and martyrdom.

- **The Jews are a wicked nation, characterized by bribery, slyness, deception, and aggressiveness.** According to the Saudi schoolbooks, the present Jewish occupation of Palestine constitutes a danger to the neighboring Muslim countries. Zionism is presented as an evil movement, based on ancient Jewish notions.

- **Israel is not recognized as a sovereign state in Saudi Arabian schoolbooks, and its name does not appear on any map.** All maps in Saudi schoolbooks bear only the name Palestine. Palestine is presented as a Muslim country occupied by foreigners who defile its Muslim holy places, especially the Al-Aqsa Mosque in Jerusalem. The occupation of Palestine is portrayed as the most crucial problem of the Arabs and the Muslims, who should all join forces for the total liberation of Palestine.

So that members of the subcommittee may familiarize themselves with our findings in greater detail, I am submitting for the record our comprehensive study, *The West, Christians, and Jews in Saudi Arabian Schoolbooks.*

The Saudi government has responded to criticism of its shameful education policies by claiming that it is working to bring about constructive reform in its curriculum and education system, but it is now high time for the Saudis to match deeds with words. As one of the strongest allies of the United States, the Saudi government needs to take a hard look at its educational system and introduce immediate reforms that remove hate and promote genuine tolerance of and respect for other faiths.

To this end, we urge that Congress move quickly to adopt a Congressional initiative spearheaded by Senators Gordon Smith (R-OR) and Charles Schumer (D-NY) in the Senate and Representatives Jim Davis (D-FL) and Doug Bereuter (R-NE) in the House. The resolution, S.Con.Res.14/H.Con.Res.242, calls on the Saudi government to "reform its education curriculum in a manner that promotes tolerance, develops civil society, and encourages functionality in the global economy."

As always, the American Jewish Committee stands with all people of good will, regardless of their race, nationality, or religion, in an effort to promote peace, democracy, and mutual understanding. My thanks go again to the subcommittee, and to its chairman, for their continued attention to these matters of utmost importance.

3. MEDIA ACTIVITY

A. RADIO COMMENTARY*

Week of January 28, 2002

When all is said and done, a lot more is said than done.

In the 1970s, we had a bitter taste of our dependence on Middle East oil. Oil-producing countries tried holding us hostage to their political aims, while sending prices sky high.

There was much talk then about cutting our oil imports. Cars and appliances became more energy efficient; conservation and alternative energy sources were being discussed.

But later complacency set in.

The drive toward higher mileage standards came to a screeching halt, gas guzzlers became popular, and our homes often resembled saunas in winter, freezers in summer.

Today, more than half our oil is from overseas, much from countries that support terrorism.

September 11 was a wake-up call. We need to press lawmakers to get serious about energy policy and reduce our nation's vulnerability. And each of us can help by saving energy starting today.

Week of February 11, 2002

There used to be a TV game show called "Name That Tune." Contestants got to hear a brief piece of music, and then had to identify the title.

---

* Beginning in September 2001, these sixty-second radio commentaries began airing on leading radio stations in major American cities, reaching millions of listeners in each cycle. Some of the commentaries were also translated into Russian and broadcast on Russian-language radio in New York.

284

This is David Harris of the American Jewish Committee asking you, in the same spirit, to Name That Country.

Here are a few hints:

It's the only democracy in the Middle East.

It's the only country in the Middle East with free and fair elections, an independent judiciary, and gender equality.

It's the only country in the Middle East with full freedom of religion and protection of holy sites for all faiths.

And, what's more, it's the leading country in the Middle East in advancing the world's frontiers of knowledge in medicine, science, agriculture, and many other fields.

Can you name the country?

It's Israel, of course, America's democratic ally and proven friend since its founding fifty-three years ago.

Week of February 25, 2002

What's that expression? Out of sight, out of mind.

Strikingly, with all the news from the Middle East, we hear almost nothing about one ongoing tragedy in the region.

Since 1975, Syria has been an occupying power in Lebanon, its multifaith Arab neighbor, yet, inexplicably, the world barely utters a word of protest.

Consider these facts:

First, Syria has never recognized Lebanon's sovereignty, instead declaring it part of so-called Greater Syria.

And second, 35,000 Syrian troops are stationed in Lebanon, where, according to our government, they're heavily involved in drug trafficking and transferring weapons to terrorist groups.

Isn't it long overdue for the world to shine the spotlight on Syria's illegal occupation of Lebanon?

Isn't it long overdue for Lebanon to regain its complete independence and freedom?

Week of March 11, 2002

When was the last time one democratic country attacked another?
Think back. It's hard to come up with an example, isn't it?

That's because democratic countries try to resolve their differences peacefully.

Look at Western Europe. Where once there were repeated wars, today there is a zone of prosperity and peace. Why? First and foremost, because all these countries enjoy the blessings of freedom.

Now look at the countries that support international terrorism—countries like Iran, Iraq, Syria, Libya, and Sudan.

There's not a single democracy among them, far from it.

Winston Churchill famously said: "Democracy is the worst form of government, except all the others that have been tried."

Our enemies hate us most for precisely those democratic values they seek to deny their own citizens.

We must never let our enemies in the war on terrorism prevail.

Week of March 25, 2002

The Yiddish word "chutzpah" means "nerve."

The classic definition of "chutzpah" is the child who kills his parents, then begs the court for mercy on the grounds he's an orphan.

Yasir Arafat has given the word new meaning.

President Bill Clinton and Prime Minister Ehud Barak offered the Palestinians a state, but Arafat said no and unleashed a wave of terror against Israel.

Then he had the "chutzpah" to claim that all he wanted was peace and that Israel was the obstacle.

Arafat miscalculated.

His plan to weaken Israel with suicide bombers won't work. Having just returned from Israel, I saw the resolve of Israelis to defend their country.

And Arafat forgot that things have changed since September 11. Terrorism is terrorism. Israel and America are fighting the same enemy.

As Jews celebrate the Passover journey from slavery to liberation, let's include a special prayer for the valiant men and women defending America and Israel.

Week of April 8, 2002

The eighteenth-century statesman Edmund Burke said: "The only thing necessary for the triumph of evil is for good men to do nothing."

The quotation came to mind as Europe has experienced a wave of anti-Semitic attacks. Synagogues, cemeteries, and school buses targeted in France, young Jews beaten up in Berlin, and synagogues burned in Belgium.

History teaches us that anti-Semitism is like a cancer. Either you catch it early, or else it metastasizes.

History also teaches us that anti-Semitism isn't just a threat to Jews; it's a danger for democracy.

It's high time for governments to deal seriously with the problem. Until recently, however, some, including the French, have downplayed it.

What can ordinary citizens do? Speak out ... and help us. For ninety-six years the American Jewish Committee has been combating anti-Semitism and other forms of bigotry, while seeking to strengthen mutual respect for all.

Week of April 21, 2002

The year was 1948. The occasion was the founding of Israel, the wondrous realization of a 3,500-year link among a land, a people, and a faith.

At the time, Israel declared: "We extend our hand to all neighboring states ... in an offer of peace."

The response? An Arab declaration of war, the first of several.

What a tragedy! Why didn't the Arab world accept Israel's offer? And why didn't the Arab world accept the UN decision for two states in the region—one Jewish, the other Palestinian?

Now fast-forward. Sixteen months ago, President Bill Clinton and Prime Minister Ehud Barak again offered the Palestinians a state. The response? The current war of terror against Israel.

As Israel marks its fifty-fourth birthday, its yearning for peace—and its resolve to defend itself against those who would destroy it—remain as strong as ever.

Happy birthday, Israel.

Week of May 5, 2002

Sometimes, as they say, it's hard to see the forest for the trees.

In the extensive daily coverage of the Middle East, three essential points are often overlooked.

First, since its founding fifty-four years ago, Israel has eagerly sought peace with its Arab neighbors.

When the leaders of Egypt and Jordan eventually stepped forward, they found a willing partner in Israel. The Palestinians and Syrians could learn from the examples of Egypt's Anwar Sadat and Jordan's King Hussein.

Second, Israel is a democracy, the only one in the region. Wouldn't it be good for everyone if Israel's democratic model became contagious in the Middle East?

And third, Israel has an obligation to defend itself against those who would destroy it. After September 11, we Americans should understand better than anyone the vast moral difference between those who promote terrorism and those who combat it.

Week of May 20, 2002

There was a cartoon in the *New Yorker* that showed a doctor and a patient in an examining room. The patient says to the doctor: "Give it to me straight, Doc. How long do I have to ignore your advice?"

In 1973, Arab oil-producing countries imposed a crippling boycott, revealing our dangerous dependence on oil from unfriendly nations.

We were shocked into action to reduce that dependence, but it wasn't long before complacency set in.

Then came September 11. Now we all know that we're importing oil from Middle East countries that fund anti-American terrorist groups and teach their children hatred of Christians and Jews.

It's long overdue to heed the doctor's advice. Let's get serious about energy policy. Let's reduce our growing dependence on oil from hostile countries. Let's make our cars and trucks more fuel efficient, let's conserve energy, and let's explore alternative energy sources.

Week of June 3, 2002

Thirty-five years ago this week, Israel fought a war for survival against Arab neighbors seeking its destruction.

It's a good moment to recall some basic facts.

Prior to the Six-Day War, the West Bank was in the hands of Jordan and Gaza was ruled by Egypt, there never having been a Palestinian state.

After the war, Israel proposed trading captured lands for peace. The Arab League rejected any talks.

Later, when partners emerged in Egypt and Jordan, Israel signed peace treaties with them.

But with the Palestinians, tragically, it's another story, as we've seen in the most recent revelations of Chairman Yasir Arafat's involvement in terrorism.

When a Palestinian leadership genuinely committed to peace emerges, it will find Israel an eager partner. Until then, Israel must defend itself against the kind of terror we Americans now understand all too well.

Week of June 17, 2002

President George Bush spoke recently about the need for democratic reform and an end to corruption in the Palestinian leadership.

Three good things can happen if the Palestinians take the president's call seriously.

First, the Palestinian people will be the beneficiaries. They deserve the prospect of a better life, but, as the president said, until now they've been poorly served by their own leadership.

Second, the chances for peace will be increased. A whole new climate will be created. Democracies settle their differences peacefully, not through suicide bombings.

And third, maybe the Palestinian model could prove contagious.

Apart from Israel, democracy in the Middle East is nonexistent. Imagine for a moment the positive impact on the region—and the world—if the democratic revolution that has swept Eastern Europe, South Africa, and large parts of Asia and Latin America spread to the Middle East.

Week of July 1, 2002

Here's a favorite story:

The legendary detective Sherlock Holmes and his aide Dr. Watson pitch a tent under the stars and go to sleep.

At midnight, Holmes wakes Watson up.

"Watson, look at the stars and tell me what you deduce."

Watson says: "I see millions of stars. There may be planets like earth out there. If so, there could also be life."

Replies Sherlock Holmes: "Watson, you fool, someone stole our tent!"

This week we celebrate our nation's birthday. It comes nearly nine months after the tragedy of September 11.

It's a good moment to reaffirm that we Americans will never stop gazing at those stars and dreaming new dreams.

And, at the very same time, we need to remain vigilant. We learned on 9/11 that there are people who will go to great lengths to destroy our democratic way of life. We must not let them succeed.

Happy Fourth of July to this wondrous and unique land.

Week of July 15, 2002

President George Bush hit the nail on the head in diagnosing the problem in the Middle East and offering a solution.

"Peace," said the president, "requires a new and different Palestinian leadership, so that a Palestinian state can be born. I call on the Palestinian people to elect new leaders, leaders not compromised by terror. I call upon them to build a practicing democracy, based on tolerance and liberty."

The question, of course, is whether the Palestinians will heed President Bush's call.

The mix of terrorism, so-called holy war, and collusion with rogue states like Iran and Iraq has achieved nothing but misery for the Palestinian people.

Conversely, the mix of democracy, nonviolence, and an unambiguous acceptance of Israel could achieve a great deal.

Let's hope this time the Palestinians will make the right choice.

Week of July 29, 2002

Here's my dream speech from Washington:

My fellow Americans,

The tragedy of 9/11 revealed three things:

First, there are those who seek our destruction. We've now taken the battle to them and victory shall be ours. May God bless those Americans serving on the front lines.

Second, our intelligence services fell short, but we're taking steps to get it right.

And third, our national independence is compromised by our energy dependence. It's time to change that, too.

We need to reduce our reliance on unfriendly oil suppliers. We can save energy by raising fuel economy standards for all vehicles. And we must step up research on alternative energy sources.

I ask everyone—from elected officials to industry leaders to private citizens—to help enact a new energy policy.

If we succeed—and we can, America will be more secure.

Week of August 12, 2002

The suicide strategy was used by terrorists against America on September 11.

It's being used by terrorists against Israel day after day—on buses, in markets, and in cafes, restaurants, and discotheques.

In both America and Israel, the terrorists, driven by blind hatred, have sought to kill as many people as possible—men, women and children of every faith and nationality.

Americans and Israelis know that if we let the suicide strategy succeed anywhere in the world, it can succeed everywhere.

The suicide strategy threatens all of us in democratic countries—all those who are hated as infidels.

Let's always remember: If we appease terrorism, we will only get more terrorism.

That's why America and Israel must prevail in the struggle against suicide bombers and terrorism. Nothing less than the future of democracy is at stake.

Week of September 10, 2002

Shalom. Peace.

The word is at the heart of the Hebrew Bible, the writings of the Jewish prophets, and prayer books in every synagogue.

And just as the quest for peace has defined the Jewish people for thousands of years, so has it defined Israel since its founding.

But peace requires partners.

When the leaders of Egypt and Jordan ended their rejection of Israel, peace treaties were signed and borders became quiet.

Sadly, with the Palestinians, it's been another story.

First offered a state by the UN in 1947, they rejected it and chose war. Again offered a state just two years ago at Camp David, they turned to terrorism instead.

Even so, the Jewish quest for peace, *shalom*, is eternal. We refuse to abandon our belief in its possibility.

As we mark the Jewish New Year, the dream of peace—for the Middle East and all humanity—is, as always, at the center of our prayers and hopes.

Week of September 23, 2002

What a difference two years make!

In 2000, the U.S. and Israel offered a peace deal the Palestinians couldn't refuse.

But Chairman Yasir Arafat did just that.

So now, instead of a Palestinian state emerging next to Israel, we witness the carnage caused by homicide bombers bent on mass murder of Israeli civilians.

But if the Palestinian aim is to break Israel's will, it's not going to happen, no more than the terrorists of 9/11 can undermine our nation's resolve.

And if the goal is to attract sympathy, again it won't work. Blowing up pizzerias, discotheques, and college buildings has only led to the world's revulsion.

The current Palestinian leadership—in power for nearly forty years—has brought its people to a dead end.

When the Palestinians finally have a leadership committed to peace, they'll find an eager partner in Israel. And all the peoples of this troubled—but ever so promising—region will be the beneficiaries.

Week of October 6, 2002

Harvard University's president recently spoke out about growing anti-Semitism.

He cited attacks on Europe's Jews in the past year.

He then warned about anti-Semitism here at home, especially on American campuses.

The Harvard president's statement was timely and laudable.

At one school, Jewish students holding a peace vigil were physically threatened by pro-Palestinian demonstrators.

At another, an Arab student leader circulated an article by David Duke, of Ku Klux Klan fame, that accused Jews of everything under the sun.

And the troubling list goes on and on.

America's colleges are usually centers of tolerance and mutual respect. When they instead breed hatred and intimidation, something's gone terribly wrong.

Such vile actions against Jews, or supporters of Israel, or any other group, have no place on American campuses, or in our country.

At moments like these, we all need to be vigilant and to speak out.

Week of October 21, 2002

Wasn't it Yogi Berra who said, "It's déjà vu all over again"?

With rogue countries developing weapons of mass destruction and terrorist groups wreaking havoc in the name of their misguided faith, we should recall a central lesson of history.

When Nazism threatened the planet, some buried their heads in the sand, while others thought that Hitler could be pacified. Thankfully, Britain and the U.S. led the free world in vanquishing an enemy bent on our total destruction.

When Communism challenged us, some chose to live in denial, while others naively underestimated its repressive nature. Again, the U.S. and Britain successfully led the free world in standing firm.

Now, faced with Iraq, Al-Qaeda, and others bent on mass murder and mayhem, fortunately, the U.S. and Britain once again fully understand the immense danger and refuse to succumb to denial or appeasement.

We must never forget that "eternal vigilance is the price of liberty."

Week of November 4, 2002

This week we marked Election Day.

We shouldn't ever take this day for granted, especially since 9/11. After all, it's our democratic values that the terrorists hate most.

Sure, there are elections everywhere—even in Saddam Hussein's Iraq. In a cliffhanger, he was just reelected by 100 percent of the voters. He's obviously got something to teach his Syrian counterpart, who managed only 97 percent in a recent presidential bid.

But real elections are another matter entirely.

We Americans should always cherish the ties that bind us to fellow democracies.

One such nation is Israel. Since its founding, Israel has been a flourishing democracy—with free and fair elections, countless political parties, and the right to vote enjoyed by all its citizens, Jews and Arabs alike.

More than anything else, it's this shared commitment to democratic values that links America and Israel, and that's cause for celebration.

Week of November 18, 2002

Remember the words of John Lennon, "All we are saying is give peace a chance"?

For fifty-four years, Israel has said to its Arab neighbors, "Give peace a chance."

With Egypt and Jordan, peace was achieved, although the airing of anti-Semitic programs on Egyptian TV this month contradicts the spirit of peace.

With the Palestinians, it's another story.

First offered a state in 1947, they refused to share the land with Israel and went to war.

From 1948 to 1967, the West Bank and Gaza were in Arab hands, but no Palestinian state emerged.

And two years ago, the Palestinians were offered a state by Israel and the U.S. Once more, they rejected it, turned to terror, and found support from Iraq and Iran.

When Palestinian leaders willing to give peace a chance emerge, they'll find a partner in Israel. Until then, Israel, like other democratic countries facing terrorism, must defend itself.

Week of December 2, 2002

Last week, in separate articles, the author Salman Rushdie and the journalist Tom Friedman called on Muslim moderates to confront those who pervert Islam through fanaticism and terror.

They cited, among other recent outrages, the horrific Bali bombing, the high death toll when Muslims rioted against Christians in Nigeria, and the rampant anti-Semitism in Egypt.

And where are our voices?

Why our silence while Iranian students courageously challenge the repressive mullahs?

Why our silence while two million Sudanese, mostly Christian and black, have been killed in a civil war?

Why our silence while women are subject to third-class treatment, unable even to drive in Saudi Arabia, and that's far from the worst of it?

It's time for people of conscience, of every religion, to speak out.

It's time to declare that no one has a monopoly on religious belief.

It's time to stand together against those who preach blind hatred and holy war.

Week of December 16, 2002

The Saudis are spending lots of petrodollars trying to improve their image here.

To help, they've even enlisted a Saudi who not only speaks fluent English but drops references to Texas football along the way. He's all over the airwaves.

Let me offer the Saudis some free advice.

To strengthen ties with America, forget the p.r. mavens and glib spokesmen. That won't do it.

What will is totally different.

Americans cherish religious freedom. There simply isn't any in Saudi Arabia.

Americans cherish loyalty. It's sometimes hard to tell if the Saudis are with us or against us in the war on terrorism.

Americans cherish women's rights. In Saudi Arabia, women's rights are a pipe dream.

And Americans cherish tolerance. Teaching hatred of non-Muslims in Saudi-funded schools around the world doesn't fuel friendships.

The bottom line to the Saudis: Forget the slick spin. It's concrete deeds that count, not well-oiled words.

Week of January 6, 2003

Two recent press headlines caught my eye.

One was "Western dependence on Mideast oil expected to grow."

The other was: "In tax twist, big vehicles get the bigger deductions."

Frankly, I don't get it.

Just when we need to reduce our dependence on Mideast oil, are we headed the other way?

And when we should be discouraging the use of gas guzzlers, are we doing the opposite?

As the new Congress begins its work, elected officials need to hear from us.

We should tell them we care about our nation's energy policy.

We should tell them that America needs higher fuel efficiency standards, better conservation, and more focus on alternative sources of energy. Today, not tomorrow.

When America puts its mind to something, it can do it. When America wanted to put a man on the moon, it did it. We need the same full-court press on energy independence.

Our future may depend on it.

Week of January 20, 2003

There's a new award-winning film worth seeing.

The Pianist is a powerful and unflinching account of the Holocaust.

It tells the true story of the survival of a Jewish pianist in Nazi-occupied Poland, against the backdrop of mass destruction and death.

The film could not be more timely.

It graphically reminds us of the potentially fatal consequences of anti-Semitism—not only for Jews, but also for society as a whole.

Let's always remember: When any group is targeted, everyone becomes vulnerable.

At a time when anti-Semitism is widespread in the Islamic world and is resurfacing in some European countries, we need to be on guard.

The Pianist helps us understand why.

Since 1906, the American Jewish Committee has been combating anti-Semitism and other forms of hatred, while building bridges among diverse racial, religious, and ethnic groups.

Week of February 17, 2003

It's said that no one is born hating.

True enough, no one is born hating.

But too many are taught to hate.

It's bad enough when the teaching comes from the home. It's even worse when a government teaches hate through its schools.

Shockingly, that's the case today in Saudi Arabia.

A comprehensive new study of Saudi textbooks reveals that anti-Western, anti-Christian, and anti-Semitic views are taught daily to millions of Saudi children.

Are some of the same books also being used in Saudi-funded schools elsewhere, including right here in the U.S.? It's worth exploring.

The textbooks cover grades one through ten and include a wide range of subjects, from literature to math. Believe it or not, these abhorrent ideas about the West, Christians, and Jews are found in all the different classes.

Saudi Arabia presents itself as a friend of America. We should tell the Saudis that real friends don't teach hatred and intolerance.

Week of March 4, 2003

Once upon a time, some thought that Israel's war with terrorism was a private war.

Now, post-9/11, we've come to see that Israel's war is linked to the wider war on terrorism that the U.S. and other democratic countries face.

The same ideology that preaches hatred of Jews preaches hatred of all so-called infidels.

The same ideology that calls for death to Israel calls for death to Western nations, and moderate Arab regimes as well.

What can we learn from Israel's struggle?

Three things.

First, there's no quick solution. It's going to take time and determination. We must face that reality.

Second, the best defense is a good offense. Preemption is the strategy of choice.

And third, the terrorists must never win the psychological battle. Our commitment to democracy, the rule of law, and pluralism only grows stronger.

Abraham Lincoln once said: "Freedom is the last, best hope of earth."

Indeed, it is.

Week of March 17, 2003

Here they go again.

In the first Gulf War, some extremist voices wove outlandish theories about the reasons for the U.S. confrontation with Saddam Hussein.

Americans rejected those theories. They understood the truth.

Now, the conspiracy peddlers are again coming out of the closet. And again these self-described patriots are resorting to wild notions about secret plots to lead our country to war. And again these bigots are dead wrong, as Secretary of State Colin Powell said last week.

Our nation is living through a tough period. 9/11 set people on edge. And the chance of war only heightens anxiety.

As Americans debate the issues, we should never forget that what unites us as a people is far greater than what divides us.

We need to be vigilant. American Muslims feel especially vulnerable to stereotyping. And American Jews have already been the targets of these conspiratorial theories.

Let's reject the hatemongers. Isn't that the true meaning of patriotism?

Week of April 7, 2003

With dramatic events unfolding to liberate Iraq, it's important to remember who America's allies are.

It's hard to say enough good things about Britain.

Australia stands out as well.

Spain has been solidly with us.

So have Denmark, Italy, Japan, Portugal, and the newer democracies, including Bulgaria, Poland, and Romania.

And it's important to mention such Middle Eastern countries as Bahrain, Israel, Kuwait, and Qatar.

As an American, I'm grateful to these and other nations for their solidarity and support.

On the other hand, I'm troubled by the behavior of some others.

France for one—though, given the history of French economic ties with Saddam Hussein, that's little surprise.

And our government has revealed that military help to Iraq is coming from Russia and Syria, while Iran, out of the limelight, has its own nuclear weapons program.

At a defining moment like this, we need to recall who are our allies—and who are not—and draw the appropriate conclusions.

Week of April 21, 2003

On April 29, we mark Holocaust Memorial Day. It's a stark reminder of the world's capacity for inhumanity.

But we also need reminders of the world's capacity for humanity. Here are three:

We know him as Mohammed. He witnessed the mistreatment of Private Jessica Lynch in Iraqi captivity and risked his life to give U.S. Marines the information required to rescue her.

On 9/11, Abe Zelmanowitz refused to abandon his disabled friend, Ed Beyea, in the World Trade Center. Both men died in the tragedy.

And a few years earlier, Christoph Meili, a Swiss bank guard, had to flee his country after he revealed that Holocaust-era bank records were going to be shredded as part of a cover-up.

These three people—a Muslim, a Jew, and a Christian—displayed extraordinary compassion for fellow human beings who happened to be of another faith.

In a world too often torn by division, such individuals serve as enduring reminders of our capacity for humanity.

Week of May 5, 2003

This week Israel celebrates its fifty-fifth birthday. It's a joyous occasion.

Against all the odds, this tiny country, no larger than New Jersey but located in a far more dangerous region, has not only survived but prospered.

It's built a vibrant democracy, advanced the frontiers of knowledge, and turned a harsh soil into a lush garden.

In fact, as Golda Meir, Israel's legendary prime minister, said, "The story of modern Israel is essentially the return to the ancestral homeland of exiles from persecution ... and fear in quest of freedom ... and peace."

Yes, Israel's birthday is another reminder of the profound link, spanning more than 3,000 years, among a land, a faith, and a people.

And for this birthday, as for the previous fifty-four, we have only one wish—that the coming year will bring Israelis the peace and security for which they've been yearning and praying from the very beginning.

Week of May 19, 2003

There are 191 countries in the UN.

There are over six billion people on earth, speaking countless languages and practicing any number of religions.

Whatever the differences might be, our common humanity is incredibly precious.

At the American Jewish Committee, we know all too well where the slippery slope of hatred, based on race, religion, or ethnicity, can lead. We've seen it happen.

That's why we extended our hand to Muslim refugees forced to flee Kosovo.

That's why, when arsonists burned down the Gay's Hill Baptist Church in Millen, Georgia, we pitched in to help rebuild it.

And that's why we're working with the Catholic Church to bring thousands of Catholic and Jewish students together in schools across the country to increase mutual understanding.

Through our actions, we help build bridges of cooperation. That's the kind of world in which we choose to live. And that's our answer to those who, blinded by ignorance or intolerance, would seek to divide us.

Week of June 16, 2003

What's the root of the Israeli-Palestinian conflict?

A recent survey, entitled the Pew Global Attitudes Project, sheds light on the answer.

The study found that 80 percent of Palestinians believe it's not possible to balance the rights and needs of the Palestinian people with Israel's existence. In other words, Israel has to go.

By contrast, more than two-thirds of Israelis believe it is possible to balance Israeli and Palestinian needs. That translates into a willingness to make compromises for the sake of peace.

The bottom line: The root of the conflict, tragically, is the same today as it's been over the past fifty-five years. A majority of Palestinians are simply not ready to accept the reality, much less the legitimacy, of Israel, whatever its final borders.

When the Palestinians finally realize they can't dislodge Israel through terror or any other means, maybe then they'll turn to the path of compromise, the path Israelis have long advocated.

Week of June 30, 2003

Amidst the fireworks and holiday fun, it's as important as ever to reflect on the larger meaning of the Fourth of July.

Freedom and democracy are priceless gifts. We owe those who've defended the cause of liberty more than we can ever express.

From the beginning, America has served as a beacon of hope for the oppressed and persecuted.

Just ask those who fled political and religious tyranny what America means to them.

And America is a permanent work in progress, always seeking to live up to its promise. This, too, reflects our nation's greatness.

We know we must always do better to achieve our founders' vision that "all men are created equal, that they are endowed by their Creator with certain inalienable rights, that among these are life, liberty, and the pursuit of happiness."

On this Fourth of July, let's recall the words from the Hebrew Bible inscribed on the Liberty Bell: "Proclaim liberty throughout all the land unto all the inhabitants thereof."

Happy Fourth of July!

Week of July 14, 2003

I'm just back from a visit to Israel.

It's a remarkable country—democratic, diverse, picturesque.

Israel's been through a lot. It's faced constant challenges to its very existence, and the threats haven't ended yet, either.

But Israel's thirst for peace remains as strong as ever. And there's a glimmer of hope today that, with American help and changes in the Palestinian leadership, progress can be achieved—*if* terrorism can be brought to an end.

And Israel's thirst for life is inspiring.

Israeli scientists are helping farmers in Africa and Asia grow crops on arid soil.

Israeli medical researchers are tackling some of the world's toughest diseases and making inroads that improve the lives of many.

And the dynamism of daily life, whether in the streets or on the beaches, needs to be seen to be believed.

In other words, Israel is a country worth getting to know. What this nation has achieved in just fifty-five years—especially given the obstacles—is simply breathtaking.

Week of August 11, 2003

Israel recently welcomed a special guest.

Christopher Reeve is the actor who played "Superman." Since 1995, he's been paralyzed from an equestrian accident. He was in Israel for a five-day visit.

He explained the trip's purpose: "Israel is an extraordinary place. I've wanted to visit for a long time…. Some of the best care for patients is happening here. Israel is among the world leaders in scientific research … and on the cutting edge in paralysis research."

Christopher Reeve visited hospitals and rehab centers. He met with patients, including an African immigrant who had been paralyzed in a Palestinian terrorist attack.

His visit, which touched the hearts of Israelis, underscored the close ties between the U.S. and Israel.

It also served as a reminder of the pathbreaking Israeli scientific and medical work that could one day help Christopher Reeve—and countless others—improve the quality of their lives.

The United States and Israel: Shared values, shared visions.

Week of August 25, 2003

In America we have no shortage of after-the-fact experts: you know, the people who appear after a major terrorist attack, for instance, and explain what went wrong.

But there are far fewer experts who foresee the dangers and try to alert the politicians and the general public.

Among the handful of experts who early on warned America about the dangers of terrorism were three courageous people, all of whom have recently written books worth reading.

The first, *Terrorist Hunter*, was written anonymously. The Iraqi-born author fears for her life. She recounts her investigation of radical groups operating, often openly, in the U.S.

The second book, by noted Middle East scholar Daniel Pipes, is entitled *Militant Islam Reaches America*. The title speaks for itself.

And the third is *Jihad in America* by award-winning investigative journalist Steven Emerson.

All three books are factual, sobering, and must-reads. They alert us to dangers here at home we simply cannot afford to ignore.

Week of September 22, 2003

The Middle East is a complicated place, to say the least.

But in the daily reporting, some essential facts are too often overlooked.

First, there's the inextricable link between the Jewish people, the land of Israel, and the city of Jerusalem. It dates back thousands of years. The Hebrew Bible tells the story; so do archaeological finds.

Second, never in history has there been a Palestinian state. But in the last three years, two separate efforts to create such a state were pursued. Tragically, both efforts were sabotaged by Yasir Arafat, as attested to by President Bill Clinton and President George Bush.

Third, Israel is a tiny country, about the size of New Jersey, and it's located in a tough neighborhood. As such, its margin for error is just about nil.

And finally, Israel's a vibrant democracy, the only one in the Middle East. It's also a reliable and tested American ally.

When you think about the Middle East, these facts are worth keeping in mind.

Week of October 20, 2003

Humanity.

It's a word that's used a lot, but can never be practiced enough.

Sixty years ago this month, the world witnessed one of the most inspiring examples ever of humanity.

After the Nazis occupied Denmark, they planned to deport the country's Jews to the death camps.

But many Danes resisted. They organized a rescue effort that brought most of the Danish Jews to safety in nearby Sweden.

It was one of the few glimmers of hope during the darkness of the Holocaust. And it remains an inspiring story of courage and compassion.

When rescuers were asked why they risked their lives to help Jews, they said they did nothing special; it was only natural. The fact that Jews worshiped in a synagogue and Christians in a church didn't matter. What counted was protecting neighbors and saving the lives of fellow human beings.

In a world that still knows too much hatred, the story of the Danish rescue serves as a powerful lesson about our capacity for humanity.

Week of November 3, 2003

Shame. That's the only word to describe it.

Outgoing Malaysian Prime Minister Mahathir Mohamad delivered a scathing anti-Semitic speech at the recent meeting of the fifty-seven-nation Organization of the Islamic Conference.

President George Bush and several other world leaders denounced his ugly comments. But the delegates assembled for the conference, to their everlasting shame, gave Mahathir a standing ovation.

Let's never forget that bigotry is bigotry, pure and simple. When an entire people or religion is assailed, all people and all religions are threatened. At such moments, voices of good will need to be heard. Surely history has taught us the danger of silence.

Please speak out.

Go to www.ajc.org to send e-mails to Malaysia's ambassador to the United States and to the Organization of the Islamic Conference. Let them know you oppose hatred and stand for a world based on mutual respect.

Week of November 17, 2003

Fifty-six years ago this month, the UN proposed an historic deal.

British-ruled Palestine would be partitioned into two countries—one for the Jews, the other for the Arabs.

The Jews agreed and Israel was created.

But the Arabs refused. Instead, they declared war on the new State of Israel. They lost.

There were other chances to establish a Palestinian state. Until 1967 the West Bank was ruled by Jordan and Gaza by Egypt. No effort, though, was made to create that state.

And as recently as three years ago, Israel, working with President Bill Clinton, proposed a far-reaching two-state solution. Tragically, the Palestinians again said no.

Peace is a strategic necessity for Israelis and Palestinians alike. But it takes two to make peace.

When a Palestinian leadership finally emerges that recognizes the need for peaceful compromise, they'll find a willing partner in Israel. And then, hopefully, swords will turn into ploughshares.

Week of December 1, 2003

There's been lots of talk lately about energy issues. Tragically, much of it misses the point.

Our country is dangerously dependent on foreign oil, a great deal of it from countries that aren't our friends.

You'd think that after 9/11 we'd finally begin to fix the problem. Think again. Nothing has been done.

Rather than raising fuel economy standards for cars and trucks, Congress has balked.

Raising those standards would mean less fuel consumption, therefore reduced oil imports.

Instead, we're at a twenty-two-year low in fuel economy standards. That makes no sense.

Energy independence strengthens national independence. Energy security strengthens national security.

We need leaders on both sides of the aisle in Washington to do what's right. Our elected officials ought to hear from us. Tell them it's high time to deal with the fuel economy issue.

It's one way of saying that we Americans, after 9/11, are all in this together and want to do our share. It's one way of making America stronger.

Week of December 15, 2003

This is a joyous holiday season.
Jews will begin celebrating Chanukah on Friday.
Next week Christians will celebrate Christmas.
It's a time for family, festivity, and fun.
It should also be a time for reflection.
Sometimes we Americans take our religious freedom for granted. We shouldn't, ever.

In too many countries, according to the State Department, religious freedom is restricted or nonexistent. Among these countries are Iran, Saudi Arabia, Sudan, and North Korea.

Mutual respect is at the heart of our nation's religious freedom. Americans are free to believe or not to believe, as we wish. But we're not free to impose our religious beliefs on others. Indeed, our religious diversity and tolerance are vital signs of our nation's enduring freedom.

And amidst all the celebrations, let's remember our brave troops overseas, in harm's way in the cause of freedom.

May this precious season usher in a more peaceful and harmonious world.

B. PRINT MEDIA

Israel's Public Relations
Move!
February 2002

In the last issue of *Move!* David Finn tackled the important and complex question of Israeli's public relations difficulties. He was right on target in diagnosing the problem, not surprising given his vast experience in the field.

I would like to add a few thoughts based on my own interaction with the media, especially over the two years that have passed since the Palestinians rebuffed the Clinton-Barak proposal for a two-state solution and triggered a new round of violence and terror.

For the pro-Israel community, there have been several challenges, among them:

First, from an Israeli perspective it can be difficult to understand the current conflict without at least some grasp of history. Yet historical explanations don't seem to resonate in a world ever more focused on the here and now.

Second, the Palestinians have quite effectively controlled both the messenger and the message. The same has not always been true for Israelis and their American supporters.

Third, Palestinian spokesmen freely use words and concepts designed to elicit immediate sympathy and which can be squeezed into the briefest of sound bites, e.g., "occupation," "humiliation," "economic strangulation," "war crimes," etc. The Israeli response to such charges, almost by definition, is reactive, and therefore less likely to have the same emotional impact. Israelis need to explain, for example, how the occupation came about in 1967, or defend their army against accusations of excessive use of force. The facts may be on Israel's side, but is anyone listening?

And fourth, media coverage of the conflict can be simplistic and lacking in context; or so scrupulously balanced as to blur moral distinctions between, say, terrorism and counterterrorism, or democracy and dictatorship; or geared toward the basic asymmetrical story line of "occupier" vs. "occupied," "soldier" vs. "civilian."

Even so, despite Israel's uphill public relations struggle, much has been done in recent months to move from defense to offense by crafting messages that are tested and work for American audiences.

For one thing, Israel is beginning to get its act together. There are now some very effective spokesmen presenting Israel's position to the media. They are articulate, credible, and quotable. Colonel Miri Eisen of the Israel Defense Forces, Ambassador Mark Sofer of the Israeli Foreign Ministry, Israeli Ambassador to the U.S. Danny Ayalon, and Ambassador Alon Pinkas, Israel's consul general in New York, are prime examples.

For another, here in the United States, with sound advice from a top-flight team of political consultants, Israel's supporters are increasingly hammering away at a limited number of themes that have been shown to work—Israel as the lone democracy in the region, Israel's fifty-four-year quest for peace, and the commonalities in the struggle against terror faced by Israel and the U.S.—and are staying on or close to the message. In this vein, the American Jewish Committee has launched an ambitious television and radio campaign in addition to an active print and web site effort. True, the poll numbers could always be better, but support for Israel in American public opinion has been consistently high.

The picture is far more problematic in Europe, where Israel has made little headway against a virtual onslaught of anti-Israel stories, editorials, images, and cartoons, and where, unlike the United States, it has all too few friends locally to call on for assistance. Speaking of public relations challenges...

Waste Not, Depend Not*
New York Times
March 3, 2002

Roaring Brook Road, normally a quiet country thoroughfare in Westchester County, becomes a frustratingly long line of cars, mini-vans and SUV's on school mornings, as hundreds of cars snake down a steep hill on their way to the local high school, which has barely 1,000 students.

The bright yellow school buses, meanwhile, arrive practically empty, carrying mostly ninth-graders. No older student would be caught dead in the "loser cruiser."

Anyone who wants to understand America's urgent energy challenge should watch this morning ritual, repeated in hundreds of suburban and rural communities across the country. With only limited public transportation, scarce sidewalks, few bike lanes, and "uncool" school buses, it's all about cars.

Of course, the problem extends far beyond high school. Parents idle their car engines while they wait for the buses carrying their grade-school children. And the traveling sports teams seldom take seriously the idea of team buses or car-pooling. Instead, players travel with their parents as far as hundreds of miles to the games, often in large family vehicles.

One concerned parent told me she approached a local school official and suggested a student-led energy conservation initiative in response to the events of September 11. The official said he wouldn't touch the idea with a ten-foot pole. Cars, clearly, are sacrosanct there.

Unfortunately, energy conservation never has been a popular subject in the United States. We all remember the ridicule President Jimmy Carter endured when he announced that he was turning down the thermostat at the White House and wearing a sweater to compensate.

But President Carter was reacting to the traumatic events of the 1970s—first, the Arab oil embargo of 1973, followed by the steep rise

---

* This op-ed piece, which appeared in the Sunday Westchester section of the *New York Times*, is based on "Letter from the Road," page 9.

in oil prices led by OPEC. He understood that America's Achilles' heel was our dependence on foreign, especially Middle East, oil, and we needed to break it.

Nearly thirty years later our vulnerability is greater than it was then. In 1973, America imported 28 percent of its crude oil. Today, the figure is 52 percent, and, according to the Department of Energy's web site, 29 percent of it comes from the Persian Gulf, principally Saudi Arabia, Kuwait, and, believe it or not, Iraq.

Americans constitute less than 5 percent of the world's population, yet one of every seven barrels of oil in the world is used on our roadways. In 1975, light trucks accounted for only 19 percent of all automotive sales. Today, that figure is 50 percent. It includes SUVs, which are subject to laxer mileage standards than cars. According to the *Toronto Star*, "The amount of extra gas they use on average in one year, compared with cars, equals the amount of energy you'd waste if you left your refrigerator door open for six years."

Meanwhile, my family's recent yearlong stay in Europe revealed some significant differences from the American appetite for energy. Cars are most assuredly an important feature of the Continental landscape, but there are at least two major distinctions.

First, Europe has invested very heavily in energy-efficient railroads, and, with few exceptions, the networks are comprehensive, efficient and fast, providing a highly competitive rival for the car.

Second, SUVs are still a relative rarity on European streets, while small cars, motorcycles, and motor scooters are more the rule. Of course, buyers are not necessarily motivated by environmental concerns. Gasoline is heavily taxed, making it two to three times as expensive as in the United States.

Europeans are also more stinting in their use of electricity. Each time I travel to Berlin, I am struck by the scant use of lighting in government offices, even those of senior officials. In Paris, apartment buildings boast wall buttons that light up darkened stairwells for barely enough time to reach the desired floor. And, I don't remember removing my sweater much during years spent studying in London.

September 11 was a wake-up call and as much of an alarm as was the 1973 oil embargo. It is imperative that we respond this time by making sure America will not be caught off guard and held hostage by unfriendly and unstable oil suppliers.

There are no simple and neat formulas for developing a national energy policy. Elected officials, foreign governments, the energy industry, car and truck manufacturers, and environmental groups have a big stake in the debate and will fight hard to defend their respective interests. But the high stakes should jolt us into national consensus.

At our suburban train station, there are now ten choice parking spots for electric cars, each fitted with a recharging unit. The wave of the future or ephemeral environmental chic? Only time will tell.

Perhaps one true test of success will be measured mornings on Roaring Brook Road and its environs. Possibly it's simply a question of spin: Now if the "loser cruiser" could be recast, say, as the "schmoozer cruiser," maybe more students would get out of their cars and back on the bus.

Questions for Arabs to Answer*
International Herald Tribune
March 22, 2002

Widespread Arab unwillingness to accept any responsibility for the evolution of the Arab-Israeli conflict, and especially for the plight of the Palestinians, is a sad reality. Instead, spokesmen cling to a narrow story line that enshrines victimology as its central motif, seeks validation from Israeli critics of Israeli policies, and ducks the tough questions. Here are a few:

Why didn't the Arab world accept the 1947 UN partition plan, which would have created both a Jewish and an Arab state and could have avoided over fifty years of conflict?

Did those Arab countries that launched a war of destruction on the day of Israel's establishment believe they could do so without being

---

* This letter is based on "The Middle East: Back to Basics" on page 222.

held accountable for helping create a refugee problem for local Arabs? What war has not produced refugees either as a goal or by-product?

Has there been another comparable situation in the world where refugees have been kept in camps for as long as three generations rather than resettled, so as to incubate hatred and garner world sympathy? Why is it that only Jordan, among the Arab countries, has offered Palestinians citizenship?

Did Israel come into possession of the West Bank, Gaza Strip, and eastern Jerusalem out of the blue? Is the record not clear that Egypt and Syria threatened Israel with extinction in the months leading up to the 1967 war? Is it not equally clear that Israel, via the United Nations, urged Jordan to stay out of the looming war, which would have meant continued Jordanian control (actually, annexation) of the West Bank and eastern Jerusalem?

Are we just to forget the Arab world's response to Israeli peace overtures after the 1967 war, which came most memorably in the three noes of the Khartoum declaration—"no peace, no recognition, and no negotiation"? Does history stand still until one side finally gets it right?

Why didn't the Palestinian leadership take its cue from Egypt and Jordan, which concluded landmark accords with Israel—involving territorial adjustments—by persuading Israelis that Cairo and Amman were irrevocably committed to peace?

Are we simply to ignore the determined effort of President Bill Clinton and Prime Minister Ehud Barak to achieve a historic breakthrough with Chairman Yasir Arafat, as if it never happened or contained no lessons?

Are we to overlook the ominous implications of the *Karine A*, the ship laden with fifty tons of advanced weaponry, including rockets, headed for Palestinian territory from Iran, or Arafat's bald-faced lie when he pleaded ignorance about the ship in a letter to George W. Bush in January?

Isn't it long overdue for Arab spokesmen to face head-on the steady diet of racial and religious incitement against Israel and Jews that has become a permanent feature of government-controlled media in too many countries, replete with Nazi-like images, Holocaust denial, and denigration of Judaism? How can a foundation of peace ever be built if the inflammatory language of hate fills the air in schools, mosques, and media outlets?

Peace is absolutely vital for both sides in a conflict that ultimately has no military solution. The suffering of all innocent people must come to an end. The region needs to harness its vast potential for development, not destruction. Encouraging at long last an honest discussion in the Arab world about past, present, and future policies regarding Israel could only help.

UN Human Rights (or Wrongs)
New York Post
March 23, 2002

Truth and fairness, especially regarding Israel, are regularly turned on their heads at the UN Commission on Human Rights by a highly selective process that is obsessively preoccupied with Israel while blatantly ignoring politically inconvenient human rights violations.

This week, the commission, absent the United States for the first time, opened its annual session in Geneva, and several Arab ambassadors, predictably, unleashed a torrent of anti-Semitism and Holocaust denigration. One asserted that "Kristallnacht is repeated daily" against the Palestinians and that "Israeli soldiers are the true disciples of Goebbels and Himmler."

Since Israel constitutes a separate agenda item, while the rest of the world comes under another heading, there are endless opportunities to attack Israel. Moreover, the makeup of the United Nations, of which the fifty-three-country commission is a mere reflection, almost inevitably ensures that there will be no criticism of Palestinians or other Arab nations.

Start with the twenty-two-member Arab League. As the ambassador of one moderate Arab country confided to me after I questioned his diatribe against Israel last March: "I had no choice. The pressure on me from other Arab countries was intense and unrelenting. Had I acted differently, there would have been negative consequences."

Nabil Ramlawi, the Palestinian permanent observer, often sets the Arab tone for the commission. At the 1997 session, he declared that Israeli doctors had deliberately infected 300 Palestinian children with HIV.

Then there's the fifty-six-member Organization of the Islamic Conference (OIC). Here, again, groupthink and identification with the Arab bloc work quite effectively.

A third and larger entity is the 113-member Nonaligned Movement (NAM). Solidarity is a powerful motivating force for many, though not all, African, Asian and Latin American nations, especially since the Arab League and OIC member nations are core constituents of NAM.

And, the pursuit of consensus within the European Union and among its thirteen associated countries permits individual European nations to duck responsibility for actions taken in the name of the group, allowing countries like France to push relentlessly for a tough European Union stance against Israel.

There's another factor. A Scandinavian diplomat, chairing a UN meeting a few years ago, blocked an Arab parliamentary move. An Arab delegation visited the diplomat with a clear message: "You will never again be elected to a post within the UN, as we control the majority; therefore your career here is as good as over."

The story was still circulating in Geneva a few years later, sobering proof of the realities that shape the way the world body works.

I brought my aunt, a native of Poland who left Europe a step ahead of the Nazis, and my wife, a refugee from the Arab world, to a commission session last year. My aunt felt physically sick after an hour of listening to vitriolic denunciations of Israel by some of the most thuggish, anti-democratic nations on earth. She couldn't sleep that night. My wife was so enraged by the self-righteous comments of the Libyan ambassador—who, incidentally, was elected a vice chairman of last year's Commission on Human Rights—that I was afraid she might be expelled from the hall.

The only difference this year is that, while the United States watches from the sidelines, Syria has replaced Libya as vice chairman.

Let France Act on Anti-Semitism
New York Times
April 7, 2002

The recent spate of anti-Semitic attacks in Europe, especially in France, is deeply worrisome. Parents are concerned about their children's safety in Jewish schools, observant Jewish men now think twice before wearing a skullcap in public, and worshipers at synagogues wonder if the next firebombing will take place with them inside.

Equally troubling has been the slow response of authorities. The American Jewish Committee has met with French officials on several occasions and with a European Union commissioner as recently as last month to discuss the anti-Semitic threats. We heard denial and rationalization.

Instead of being sensitive to the slippery slope of anti-Semitism, as Europeans above all should be, they essentially took a dismissive attitude, suggesting that the "few" anti-Semitic attacks were linked largely to the Palestinian-Israeli conflict, as if this could somehow excuse them.

It's high time for France, in particular, to get serious about the problem. Perpetrators need to be pursued, prosecuted and, if convicted, imprisoned. Public security should be upgraded at Jewish institutions. Most of all, political leaders should not wait eighteen months, during which nearly 400 anti-Semitic attacks have occurred, to wake up to the true magnitude of the threat.

Anti-Semitism Virus Strikes in France
Forward
April 12, 2002

An attempt to set fire to a Jewish school in Nice. A fire at the Jewish cemetery in Strasbourg. The burning of a synagogue in Marseilles. Shots fired at a kosher butcher shop in Toulouse. An attack on a Jewish couple in Villeurbanne, near Lyon.

These are some of the chilling attacks on Jews and Jewish institutions that have occurred in France in recent weeks. They are part of an ominous series of anti-Semitic attacks in the country since October 2000. According to a recent study, more than 400 anti-Semitic incidents have taken place during the last nineteen months.

French president Jacques Chirac has emphasized that France is not an anti-Semitic country. Unlike the periods of Dreyfus and Vichy, France today is, in fact, an open country that prides itself on its democratic traditions and values. French Jews, numbering approximately 600,000, have been among the principal beneficiaries of that openness. With the exception of the United States, perhaps no other Diaspora community has achieved such success in virtually every sector of society—politics, culture, science, economy, and academia—as French Jewry.

So, if everything's so good for the community, what's gone wrong?

One answer is that, among the four to six million Muslims, mostly from North Africa, living in France, many might be peaceful and law-abiding, but some are not.

This poses a larger challenge for French society. There are gnawingly difficult problems of social integration, unemployment, crime, and education. In fact, there are some rough districts ringing major French cities where the police are hesitant to enter.

It also poses a problem for French Jews. Many poorer and more religious Jews live in the same neighborhoods as North African Muslims. Since the Palestinian-instigated violence that broke out in September 2000, French Arab youngsters have played out their anger at home, going after Jewish targets.

Initial press reports spoke of "Muslim-Jewish tensions" in describing these incidents, but this would be akin to talking of Japanese-American tensions as an explanation for Pearl Harbor. Just as Japan attacked the American naval base in a clear act of aggression, so did Arab youth begin a wave of attacks against Jews.

French authorities responded essentially with denial, rationalization, and obfuscation. Only now, in light of the most recent events, are they finally waking up to the danger.

Over the course of many months, American Jewish Committee delegations have met with French officials several times, and we heard all three disturbing responses.

Hubert Vedrine, the French foreign minister, told us at a meeting in November that there was no problem of anti-Semitism in France. When pressed, Vedrine replied testily that he knew his country better than we. That was the denial.

Eventually, he conceded that there were a few incidents, largely because French Arab youth saw troubling television images from the Middle East, but that "when the Middle East problems are solved, the incidents will go away." That was the rationalization.

And the obfuscation has come from Interior Ministry officials who would not give us straight answers to a very simple question: How many individuals are currently in the criminal justice system because of alleged connections with the anti-Semitic attacks since the fall of 2000?

Can anything serve to justify or excuse anti-Semitic behavior, regardless of what French Arab youth believe to be happening in the Middle East, or however sympathetic they may feel France to be to the Palestinian cause?

Might it be that, rather than exercising principled leadership in the face of French Jewish anxieties, political leaders deliberately chose to "play down" these concerns—in the words of Roger Cukierman, the president of CRIF, the French Jewish umbrella organization—for domestic and external reasons? Such an attitude, however unintentionally, may have emboldened some to commit anti-Semitic attacks in the belief they could do so with impunity. Could this be a harbinger of things to come in other European countries with growing Muslim communities, such as Belgium?

France is now in the midst of a hotly contested presidential election. Has the desire for the Muslim vote deterred politicians from speaking out too strongly against anti-Semitism and its sources? Last summer, for example, several French newspapers reported on an internal Socialist Party memorandum recommending that the party take strong pro-Palestinian positions to attract more French Arab voters.

Similarly, while France maintains relatively cordial relations with Israel, though a far cry from the heyday of Franco-Israeli links until

1967, neither major French political party wants to upset ties with the twenty-two-member Arab bloc. There is simply too much at stake for the French economy, not to speak of France's enduring diplomatic ambitions.

When the French ambassador to Britain referred to Israel as "that shitty little country" at a private dinner last fall, what happened? Given the chance to retract his words, the ambassador instead only grumbled that an off-the-record conversation had been reported to the press. Meanwhile, the French government has taken no disciplinary action against the envoy. What kind of message does such an incident send within France?

Imagine that instead of Israel the ambassador had spoken of, say, Saudi Arabia. My guess is that he'd have been recalled to the Quai d'Orsay within minutes and never heard from again.

It's a tragedy that it took the latest anti-Semitic attacks in Nice, Paris, Marseilles, and Strasbourg to wake officials up to the magnitude of a nineteen-month-old threat and to get them to assign more police to protect Jewish institutions. Now we will have to wait and see if the authorities get tough with investigations and prosecutions, and abandon once and for all their tried and failed policy of denial, rationalization, and obfuscation.

Europeans, by dint of their history, should understand the dangers of the anti-Semitism virus, and France has become a modern-day laboratory.

Energy Call to Action
New York Times
June 19, 2002

Missing from David Gergen's laudable call to action for Americans after September 11 is an appeal to urgently address our country's energy challenge.

September 11 was as much of an alarm as the 1973 oil embargo. It is imperative that we respond this time by making sure that America will not be held hostage by unfriendly oil suppliers who finance terrorism and teach hatred of the West.

In 1973, America imported 28 percent of its crude oil. Today, the figure is 59 percent, and 30 percent of it comes from the Persian Gulf, principally Saudi Arabia, Kuwait, and yes, Iraq.

Increasingly popular SUVs are subject to laxer mileage standards than cars. Even for cars, fuel economy standards have not been raised since the 1980s.

There are no simple formulas for developing a national energy policy, but the high stakes should jolt us all into action.

Imposing Middle East Peace
International Herald Tribune
June 21, 2002

While urging the United States to impose a peace settlement, Hubert Vedrine (op-ed, June 18) exposes his own skewed perception of the Palestinian terror war against Israel. As the former French foreign minister should recall, Israel has been just as eager to achieve a negotiated peace with the Palestinians as it was with Egypt and Jordan, whose leaders, Anwar Sadat and King Hussein, proved to be reliable and willing partners.

Yasir Arafat is not, no matter how much Vedrine may choose to think otherwise. Arafat spurned a U.S.-backed offer made by Israel at Camp David in the summer of 2000, and again at Taba in January 2001, that would have set the stage for an independent Palestinian state on nearly all of the West Bank and Gaza with its capital in East Jerusalem. The Palestinian Authority has since encouraged escalating terrorism, a strategy initiated when Ehud Barak was still the prime minister of Israel.

Western political leaders such as Vedrine cannot want the establishment of a Palestinian state more than the current Palestinian leadership. A Palestinian state should result from direct Israeli-Palestinian negotiations, but those talks, as President George W. Bush has appropriately demanded, cannot resume until Arafat ends terrorism as a vehicle for achieving what, in the final analysis, remains disturbingly ambiguous political aims.

Anti-Semitism in Europe
Washington Post
June 24, 2002

Given the generally positive record of Germany's postwar relations with Israel, it is troubling to see anti-Semitism infecting German electoral politics. But the rise of anti-Semitism across Europe goes much farther and deeper than Jurgen Mölleman of the Free Democratic Party.

Hundreds of attacks on Jewish institutions and individuals have occurred since the Palestinians launched the Intifada in the fall of 2000. European governments are belatedly waking up to the threat. There can be no excuse, however, for the shameful delay, especially in France, where a recent report documented hundreds of anti-Semitic incidents since October 2000.

Europe should be especially sensitive to the danger posed by anti-Semitism, and should be mindful of the central lesson of the blood-soaked twentieth century: Don't ever ignore, underestimate, or rationalize hate.

Law enforcement needs clear direction from the top that the pursuit and prosecution of perpetrators of anti-Semitic attacks is a national priority. And religious leaders of all major faiths, including Islam, need to speak out much more forcefully in condemning hate-inspired violence.

The Peaceful Path to Palestinian Statehood
Asahi Shimbun (Japan)
August 4, 2002

The endgame for achieving a lasting Israeli-Palestinian peace has been clear for some time. A first-ever Palestinian state can be created alongside Israel. Most of the world, including the U.S. and Israel, is ready. The continuing obstacle, as President George Bush laudably acknowledged last month, is Yasir Arafat.

Forgotten by many is the fact that less than two years ago President Bill Clinton and Prime Minister Ehud Barak were sprinting after Chairman Arafat trying to make a historic deal. Barak was prepared at Camp David in the summer of 2000 to go further than any Israeli leader before him to achieve peace, but Arafat refused to go along. Worse, to deflect attention from Palestinian rejectionism, the Palestinian leader deliberately triggered violence against Israelis just weeks after Camp David, a fact confirmed by two of his own Cabinet ministers.

Still, in the midst of that violence Barak tried again, sweetening Israel's offer at Taba in January 2001. Arafat was offered the chance, with U.S. backing, to create a state on 97 percent of Gaza and the West Bank, captured by Israel in a war for survival in 1967, with a capital in Jerusalem. Arafat spurned that offer, too.

Foreign Minister Shimon Peres, one of the architects of the 1993 Oslo Accords, has repeatedly asked how Arafat could inexplicably turn down the chance to fulfill his own people's aspirations, much as the Palestinian leadership in 1947 rejected the UN Partition Plan. That plan would have established two states, one Jewish, one Arab, in the territory between the Jordan River and the Mediterranean Sea, then part of the British Mandate. The Arab world rejected that wholesale and then tried to eliminate the nascent State of Israel through the 1948 war.

Since its founding more than fifty-four years ago, Israel has not known a single day of peace. No people on earth yearn for peace more than the Israelis, who have too often buried their children rather than the other way around. Indeed, the concept of peace is central to the

Jewish religious and ethical tradition dating back nearly 4,000 years, just as the concept of occupation of another people is foreign to that tradition. But peace requires a partner who shares the view that the prize of peace is worth the price, and the price is painful compromise by both sides.

Peace cannot be built on shifting sands, for, ultimately, that is even more dangerous than no peace at all. Poll after poll reveals that Israelis are prepared to make far-reaching concessions for a comprehensive agreement, but only if they trust their peace partner.

They trusted Egyptian President Anwar Sadat and Jordanian King Hussein and, happily, peace became possible. They do not trust Arafat, fear that his long-range aims remain the destruction of Israel, and point to the scurrilous rhetoric coming from the mosques and media as evidence of the widespread hatred of Israel and Jews generally. That rhetoric too often trivializes the Holocaust, calls for killing Jews as the "sons of pigs and monkeys," and foresees the "liberation" of all of Palestine, from the Mediterranean to the Jordan River.

The only path to durable Arab-Israeli peace is clear—bilateral negotiations between Israel and Palestinian leaders who oppose terrorism and are committed to a durable peace. President Bush has set forth a clear path to achieve peace. Let us hope that a Palestinian leader will one day emerge who shares the president's commitment to help the Palestinian people and to offer them a path to peace and prosperity.

Israel Nearly Alone in its War for Survival
Miami Herald
September 3, 2002

What is Israel supposed to do in response to a Hamas spokesman's public reminder, just after the slaughter at Hebrew University, that the group's objective is to rid Israel of its Jewish population? He couldn't be more clear, nor could the Hamas charter. The same goes for Islamic Jihad, Hezbollah, and other terror groups.

Israel is in a war for its survival against an enemy that celebrates death, especially Jewish death.

Under then Israeli Prime Minister Ehud Barak, and with the full support of President Clinton two years ago, Israel made a breathtakingly tantalizing offer for peace and statehood on 97 percent of the disputed land to the Palestinians, only to see it turned down flat. Now the Palestinians, once again seeking to rewrite history, assert variously that the offer was never actually made in writing, or was less than meets the eye, but the people actually in the know—President Bill Clinton, Prime Minister Ehud Barak, Ambassador Dennis Ross, and Foreign Minister Shlomo Ben-Ami—all reject these contentions out of hand.

Israel has tried unilateral cease-fires, restraint in the face of severe provocation, offers to ease economic conditions, and even expressions of regret when Israeli Defense Forces mistakes occur, but that hasn't done much good.

The Palestinian leadership simply has not prepared its people for peace with Israel or even acceptance of Israel's right to exist, whatever its final boundaries. To the contrary, the years since the 1993 Oslo Accords have been devoted to the teaching of hatred and incitement, and the creation of a military and terrorist infrastructure.

After all, this is the same Palestinian leadership that introduced the world to a new era of international terrorism in the 1970s, that was expelled from Jordan, that caused a civil war in Lebanon, that has been utterly corrupt in the use of aid money, that supported Saddam Hussein in the Gulf War, and that colluded with Iran to purchase sophisticated weapons.

Since President George Bush's landmark June 24 speech, glib Palestinian spokesmen—Yasir Arafat's minions—have been appearing before Western reporters ritualistically to denounce the terror attacks against Israelis, but then never fail to add that, in the final analysis, these attacks are all Israeli Prime Minister Ariel Sharon's fault and certainly not the Palestinians'.

Palestinian leaders can look unblinkingly at the television cameras and declare that hundreds, even thousands, of Jenin residents were massacred by Israeli troops, or that Israeli doctors have injected HIV in Palestinian children, or that the Israeli army is using depleted uranium shells, or whatever other outrageous fabrication comes to mind. These spokesmen know too well that such accusations will be reported dutifully—and often uncritically—by the media that's "only doing their job." They know, too, that there are certain nations, human rights groups, and individuals who are only too ready to believe the latest charge against Israel, whatever it may be, and repeat it ad nauseam.

Meanwhile, back in Gaza or Nablus, the deaths of Israelis are cause for feverish celebration among the many Palestinians who take to the streets. Compare this to the anguished discussion within Israel when Palestinian civilians, especially children, become unintended casualties of military action to combat terror.

Israel is fighting to defend its citizens, who have been declared fair game by terrorist groups fueled by hatred and a sense that they have found the Israeli Achilles' heel through suicide bombings and remote-controlled explosions.

The United States can be counted on to quickly and unambiguously express its understanding of Israel's situation and defend Israel's right to strike back.

Europeans, by contrast, stumble all over themselves, trying, but never convincingly, to show sympathy for the Israeli victims, but unable to hide their profound antipathy for the Sharon-led government and their general dislike of military responses to what they believe to be political problems.

In fact, the European Union cannot even agree on designating Hezbollah, a group openly dedicated to Israel's destruction, as a terrorist organization. By contrast, Hezbollah, together with Hamas and Islamic Jihad, has been on the U.S. terrorism list for many years.

The media, with few exceptions, deliver the "moral equivalence," "cycle of violence," and "an eye for an eye" lines, essentially two sides in an atavistic struggle to the end, with no clear distinction between democrats and dictators. The *New York Times*, for example, is still not prepared to label Hamas—which is hell-bent on Israel's complete destruction according to its own charter—a terrorist group, instead antiseptically referring to its members as "militants."

Leaders of countries such as Egypt and Jordan, who in private express undisguised contempt for Arafat, are fearful of saying anything remotely similar in public.

The United Nations is a hostage of the numbers game, and the numbers are heavily stacked against Israel. That helps explain why the Geneva-based Commission on Human Rights, for example, was able to devote about 35 percent of its time at this year's six-week session to bashing Israel. It passed no fewer than eight anti-Israel resolutions, when no other problematic regional situation was the object of more than one resolution, if that.

Israel may not be perfect, but then neither is any other democracy. But those other nations are not faced with the same immediate threats as Israel and, therefore, the need to make tough decisions in order to defend themselves. In such situations, there are no simple or neat formulas. Yes, the United States and India, in particular, currently understand the menace of terrorism, but surely few citizens in either country ever stop to wonder whether their national existence is imperiled.

Facing the Challenge of Muslim Activism
Forward
September 6, 2002

One year ago we woke up to the stark reminder that there is such a thing in human nature as unadulterated evil. Left unchallenged, that evil can wreak unimaginable death and destruction.

The horrific events of September 11, which caught our nation totally by surprise, shattered the comforting illusion that the blessings of power and geography could somehow insulate the United States from such a daring assault. The tragedy helped many, however belatedly, connect the dots of more than twenty years of murderous terrorist attacks against American targets, at home and abroad, much of it involving Osama bin Laden and his ideological soul mates.

The tragedy has also given clarity to the reality of how the openness of American society actually allowed terrorist operatives and their supporters to establish themselves here. Wrapped in the protections of a democratic society, they pursued their war against our nation and the values of equality and openness that form the cornerstone of our way of life.

While we spoke out long before September 11—and continue to do so—against those who would paint a broad brush stroke against Islam as a religion or against all Muslims, the fact is that as Americans and as Jews we have been forced to become ever more vigilant. The events of the last year have been a shrill wake-up call both to the real physical dangers we face and, less discussed, to growing political challenges.

There has been a sharp increase in Arab and Muslim political activity in the United States. These communities know they have a steep uphill struggle. They recognize the formidable strength of the pro-Israel advocacy movement in this country, but they believe it is assailable. And they have made no secret of one of their ultimate goals—to end American support for Israel.

Indeed, in the post-September 11 environment, they believe the United States is desperately seeking to establish a broader dialogue with Islam. If Muslim organizations can persuade American opinion-molders and policymakers that they are now a force to be reckoned with in American life, the political consequences over time will be considerable.

The American Muslim population—variously claimed by Muslim spokesmen to be 6-8 million, but much closer to 2 million, as two authoritative studies revealed last fall—is variegated, but the organizations that claim to represent the community regrettably are not. Moderate groups that have sought to emerge have been kept at bay by the more extreme groups. However improbable it may seem, these extreme groups have actually been aided, if unwittingly, by the American government and media.

The Islamic Supreme Council of America is a good example. An organization that openly rejects Islamic fundamentalism and its U.S.-based apologists, the council can barely get its foot in the door inside the Beltway or have the chance to comment in the media. Just ask its leader, Sheik Muhammad Hisham Kabbani, about his attempts to deal with the State Department during the last several years. Yet such radical groups as the Council on American-Islamic Relations, American Muslim Council, and Islamic Society of North America seemingly encounter no such difficulty.

Or take the recent case of the respected director of the FBI, Robert Mueller, who astonishingly agreed to speak before the annual convention of the AMC in June, despite being presented with evidence from many sources that the group continues to be a leading advocate of Islamic extremism.

Or look at the frequency with which the media invite comment from the more extreme groups, implying that they are nothing more than the Muslim counterparts of such well-established civil-rights agencies as the NAACP and the American Jewish Committee.

Are some American institutions so fearful of being labeled anti-Muslim, or so determined to be "inclusive" at all costs, that they are prepared to ignore obvious truths about advocates for terrorism?

Predictably, any discussion of radical Islamic activity in this country is branded ad nauseam as "Islamophobia" or "McCarthyism" or a "witch-hunt" by spokesmen for such groups as CAIR and the AMC. Of course, that's nothing more than vacuous name-calling and invective designed to chill all discussion. Yet to give these spokesmen their due, this approach seems to be achieving its intended effect.

Or take the case of the shooting incident in June at the El Al ticket counter at Los Angeles International Airport, the latest in a series of Middle Eastern-related attacks against Jewish targets. Can there be any serious doubt that this was an act of terrorism, even if the FBI has inexplicably withheld its judgment?

But then again, it took the FBI seven years—and unrelenting pressure from the victim's determined mother—to reclassify as terrorism the 1994 murder of Ari Halberstam, the sixteen-year-old student killed by an Arab gunman on the Brooklyn Bridge. Until last year the crime, believe it or not, was considered an act of "road rage."

No organization has more energetically pursued Muslim-Jewish dialogue in this country over the last decade than the American Jewish Committee. But truth be told, it's been incredibly tough because finding credible dialogue partners is an ongoing challenge. Even so, we will not give up. Too much hangs in the balance.

But even as we try to go forward, we must proceed carefully, ever alert to the physical and political threats posed by the Islamic radical network to Jews and Jewish institutions in this country.

Living in denial is no longer an option for American Jewry.

One-Way Violence toward French Jews
Financial Times
January 10, 2003

To portray the violence against Jews in France as "the latest outbreak of tension between Jews and Muslims—a spill-over from the Israeli-Palestinian conflict" is dangerously to misrepresent the current situation in France ("Chirac calls for calm after rabbi stabbed," January 8). Since October 2000, French Jews have been the victims of hundreds of documented assaults by Muslims in France. Synagogues have been torched, Jewish cemeteries have been desecrated and school buses filled with Jewish children have been attacked with stones.

There can be no equivalence between the two sides in this tragic story. While French Jews have been the victims of a steady, continuous outpouring of hatred perpetrated by some Muslims, they have not responded with violence. The responsibility for the current violence falls squarely on the shoulders of those who stab a religious leader. Next time, please call a spade a spade.

What the Saudis Teach
New York Times
February 16, 2003

Discussions in the Saudi royal family about democratic reforms (front page, Feb. 9) are a potentially positive development. The values of any society are reflected in its educational system, and that would be a good place for the Saudis to begin.

Official Saudi Ministry of Education textbooks teach children intolerance and contempt for the West, Christians, and Jews. A study of the schoolbooks used through tenth grade, released this month by the American Jewish Committee and the Center for Monitoring the Impact of Peace, shows that the hatred and denigration of non-Muslims are pervasive.

Saudi Arabia represents itself as a friend of America. If so, a major overhaul of school curriculums is overdue.

Saudi Schools Keep Sowing Seeds of Hate
Forward
March 7, 2003

Meeting with leaders of the American Jewish Committee meeting in New York last September, Saudi Foreign Minister Saud al-Faisal acknowledged a problem with his country's schoolbooks and assured us that steps would be taken to rewrite them. He asserted, as he has in interviews with American media, that the problematic passages are limited to about "5 percent" of the schoolbooks.

The foreign minister grossly understated the problem. In fact, a comprehensive study of books used in Saudi schools has revealed that the Saudi government teaches children intolerance and contempt for the West, Christians, and Jews.

The study, released last month by the American Jewish Committee and the Center for Monitoring the Impact of Peace, shows that the hatred and denigration of non-Muslims is, in fact, pervasive in Saudi schoolbooks. The schoolbooks, published by the Saudi Ministry of Education, cover grades one through ten and include a wide range of subjects, from literature to math. These abhorrent ideas about the West, Christians, and Jews are found in all the different classes.

Teaching of hatred is reprehensible under any circumstances, but is especially alarming when it forms an integral part of the school curriculum in a country long viewed as a close friend of the United States and regarded as the center of the Islamic world.

Both Christianity and Judaism are denigrated in the texts we studied. Children in the eighth grade are taught, in a geography book, that "Islam replaced the former religions that preceded it," and that "a malicious Crusader-Jewish alliance is striving to eliminate Islam from all the continents."

Christians and Jews are denounced as "infidels," and are presented as enemies of Islam and of Muslims. Saudi schoolbooks implore Muslims not to befriend Christians or Jews, as in a ninth-grade jurisprudence schoolbook which states: "Emulation of the infidels leads to loving them, glorifying them and raising their status in the eyes of the Muslim, and that is forbidden."

Even grammar and math books are full of phrases exalting war, jihad, and martyrdom. Saudi youth are taught to reject all notions of Western democracy, and mutual respect between Muslims and non-Muslims is a nonstarter. Saudis are instructed that the West is a "decaying society" on its way to extinction.

Overall, Saudi Arabian schoolbooks do not comply with any of the international curriculum criteria established by UNESCO, of which Saudi Arabia is a member. The information given to students about the West, Christianity, and Judaism is totally tainted, incomplete, and biased. In fact, it's downright racist.

As long as Saudi youth are essentially brainwashed to hate others, truly amicable relations between Saudis and the West will be hard to maintain in the long term. Indeed, reading the textbooks makes it easier to understand why fifteen of the nineteen terrorists who committed the September 11 attacks were Saudi. They got an early start in seeing the world divided between Muslims and "infidels."

Moreover, Saudi schoolbooks and curricula are actively exported to other Arab and Muslim countries, where Saudi largesse funds many schools. Indeed, Muslim schools in the United States have been built and staffed with Saudi money, opening the door to the spreading of Saudi-sponsored hate on American soil. It is vital to investigate whether books published in Saudi Arabia are being used here in the United States.

It is high time for the United States, with our thick web of relations with the Saudis, to put on the table the urgent need to reform the Saudi education system, to excise the teaching of hatred from textbooks, and to monitor closely any Saudi claims of reform.

Sure, an overhaul of Saudi Arabia's education system is likely to take time before it has an impact on the current and next generations of Saudis. But to ignore the hate that is integral to Saudi education—as if through denial we could wish it away—must not be tolerated in a post-September 11 world.

Saudi Education Is in Need of Reform
Financial Times
May 20, 2003

The perceived blow to U.S.-Saudi ties in the wake of the Riyadh bombings is indeed something that should concern us ("Do not abandon Saudi Arabia," May 16). However, the sad fact is that the Saudi educational system, with its propagation of hatred toward the West, has undermined the notion of an enduring U.S.-Saudi alliance built on mutual respect. Let us not forget that the 9/11 hijackers and the Riyadh bombers were products of Saudi schools.

A recent study, cosponsored by the American Jewish Committee, of Saudi textbooks used in grades one through ten, reveals that the demonizing of Christians, Jews, and the West is pervasive.

Children in the eighth grade are taught, in a geography book, that "Islam replaced the former religions that preceded it" and that "a malicious Crusader-Jewish alliance is striving to eliminate Islam from all the continents."

Even grammar and math books are full of phrases exalting war, jihad, and martyrdom. Saudi youth are taught to reject all notions of Western democracy. Saudis are instructed that the West is a "decaying society" on its way to extinction.

What should be frightening is not just the terrorist threat but the reality, as Anthony Cordesman notes, that 53 percent of Saudis are below the age of twenty. Clearly, Saudi education reform must be an urgent priority.

Confronting Existential Questions
An Interview
Jerusalem Center for Public Affairs
August 8, 2003*

"The major external pressures of the last three years caught American Jews by surprise. They didn't expect again to have to face basic issues," says David Harris, executive director of the American Jewish Committee (AJC).

"This was even more shocking because the 1990s were such a good decade for American Jewish life. Israel appeared headed for acceptance into its region, Jews were being elected to public office in record numbers, and Jews seemed to be 'making it' in every walk of American life. Now, Israel again confronts a difficult situation—war, violence, and terror—while the issue of the right of return of the Palestinians is resurfacing. Contesting Israel's right to exist as a Jewish state is accompanied by a virulent strain of anti-Semitism, principally from the Muslim world. Their defamation activities are often denied, ignored, or minimized and rationalized by third parties, particularly the West European media, the intelligentsia, and the far left.

"Furthermore, we have felt a real sense of betrayal by many in the human rights community on issues that affect us directly, from the struggle against anti-Semitism—where there is an almost deafening silence in many circles—to the fight for Israel's right to exist. I saw this first-hand when living and working in Geneva for one year, and have written about it extensively.

"Radical Islam also represents a physical threat to Jewish institutions throughout the world—including in the United States—and thus poses immediate security questions. We now realize that American Jewry has been living in a bit of a bubble. We have come to believe so strongly in American exceptionalism—that the hatred and anti-Semitism that happen elsewhere cannot happen here—that we have allowed ourselves to be lulled into a false sense of security.

* This interview will also appear in *American Jewish Challenges: Addressing the New Century*, edited by Manfred Gerstenfeld, to be published by Rowman & Littlefield, fall 2004. Reprinted by permission of the publisher.

"It would imply dangerous self-satisfaction if I were to say American Jewry is confronting these challenges adequately. Still, we have a rather strong organizational structure, despite weaknesses such as rivalries that distract from priority issues. American Jewry is very confident about openly and publicly participating in discussions on major questions of American life. Gone is the fear of what non-Jews will think if we are 'too loud, or too visible.'"

The Lieberman Candidacy as an Indicator

"A good indicator of the community's coming-of-age is the [Joseph] Lieberman candidacy. Few people, as recently as 1998, would have predicted that within two years a Shabbat-observing Jew—whose wife's name was not Hillary or Laura but Hadassah—would be selected for what at the time seemed an anemic Democratic ticket. Yet it garnered 500,000 votes more than the other ticket in the national popular vote. This not only speaks volumes about Americans, but also seems to have caught by surprise some Jews who didn't believe the United States was ready for such a Jewish candidate.

"With Lieberman now running to become the Democratic candidate for president, a new situation emerges for American Jewry, especially because the Middle East plays a major role in international politics. Most Americans accept Lieberman's right to participate; it is not even an issue for discussion. As a by-product, Lieberman's candidacy has led some Americans to try to understand a new approach to the seven-day cycle of the week, the dietary laws, and several other Jewish traditions largely unknown to the majority of Americans.

"There is no consensus view on his candidacy among American Jews. Jews are probably more anxious about Lieberman's candidacy than non-Jews. They fear that whatever stances he may take, on the war in Iraq, for example, or energy policy, may be interpreted as the 'Jewish view.' At the same time, Jews are not lock-step voters. Unlike newer ethnic groups, they will not vote for Joe Lieberman just because 'he is one of us.' They will only gravitate to him if they accept his worldview.

"In recent years Jews have shown striking flexibility. For instance, in the 1997 New York mayoral elections, Ruth Messenger, a

Democratic Jewish woman, ran against Rudy Giuliani, a Republican Italian Catholic. Most New York Jews—though loyal Democrats—voted for Giuliani. They voted according to their ideology, not their ethnicity—an indicator of the community's healthy maturity."

Will More Jews Vote their Economic Interests?

"One wonders what this may mean for future elections. Milton Himmelfarb of the American Jewish Committee, in *Commentary,* coined the memorable phrase, 'American Jews live like Episcopalians, and vote like Puerto Ricans.'

In each election cycle there are predictions that finally Jews will catch up with the rest of America and begin voting their economic interests rather than their social consciences. In most cases, those forecasts have been proven wrong. In the 2002 elections, because of technical glitches, we unfortunately have only anecdotal information about Jewish voting patterns. One interesting case concerns Florida, where there was a considerable Jewish vote for George Bush's brother Jeb, who ran for reelection as governor.

"The real test case as to whether Jewish voting becomes more elastic will be in 2004. George Bush will run for reelection on a platform that in many respects could appeal to some American Jews. He supports the war against international terrorism, has fought the war in Iraq, and strongly identifies with the State of Israel.

"On other issues important to many Jews—such as church-state separation, abortion, and the environment—Bush's views are largely contrary to the prevailing Jewish ones. While we do not know who the Democratic candidate will be, he will probably better reflect majority Jewish domestic concerns. In the presidential elections of 2000, Bush garnered 19 percent of the Jewish vote. In 2004 he is hoping to double that figure. In a closely contested state such as Florida, that might be enough for the Republicans to win the state a bit more convincingly than in 2000."

Engaging a Younger Generation

"The younger generation of Jews is becoming more normal in a way one would not expect. Like half of all Americans, they are not voting at all. A great strength of the Jewish community—being a small minority—was that it voted. We had been taught this by our parents and grandparents because of the preciousness of this right. Younger American Jews do not reflect their parents' attitudes so much as the overall apathy or cynicism toward society. Many have not even bothered to register to vote, which is unhealthy for democracy and, of course, weakens the Jewish vote.

"A similar attitude prevails in their relationship to Jewish organizations. Many younger Jews have no strong psychological or spiritual connection to the Jewish community. The general trend in American life, affecting many groups, is to avoid encumbering memberships involving time and commitment. Robert Putnam's book *Bowling Alone* expresses this attitude. In the past, when people went bowling, they used to join leagues. Now they go with friends or alone, without adhering to formal structured groups. This is an illustration of the individualization of American life and its greatly diminished focus on the community. Of course, this may well just be a pendulum effect rather than a permanent phenomenon. Let's hope so.

"The spirit of community may reemerge, especially if there are compelling issues that manifest themselves. In the last three years, for example, the AJC has witnessed a modest influx of younger Jews. They have had various wake-up calls prompted by such issues as Daniel Pearl's murder, the mass killing of Jews at a Passover Seder in Netanya, and the threats to pro-Israel students at San Francisco State University.

"In such cases, people realize they can do very little as individuals and conclude that they have to be part of a group. They start seeking a Jewish connection. This may be with the AJC, AIPAC, or a synagogue."

Marketing Religion
"Whether we like it or not, in the past three years, negative messages about rising anti-Semitism and anti-Israelism have resurfaced and shaken people up, in some cases bringing them closer to the Jewish community. Nevertheless, we have to continue to convey to people positive messages about Judaism.

"For many, Judaism is perceived as competing in the American marketplace of religion with other 'spiritual products.' It thus has to be presented in a competitive environment to people for whom a specific religion is no longer necessarily a permanent feature of life. A paradigm figure is the musician Bob Dylan: one day a Jew, another day a Christian, yet another day, who knows what? We think we should appeal to people's need for community because those who pursue individuality discover it can be a very lonely existence. With time, a more community-oriented attitude may come back. Moreover, people will always be seeking answers to the larger questions in life. The Jewish community has to be ready to answer these questions.

"The American Jewish Committee realized this long ago. About forty years ago, AJC's Yehuda Rosenman, who worked closely with Professor Daniel Elazar, opened the first department of Jewish communal affairs. It was based on the realization that if there was not a vibrant, intellectually and emotionally connected Jewish community in America, there would eventually be no Jews left to defend. This distinguished us from the other Jewish defense agencies, whose focus was entirely external. In fact, we became a secular synagogue for some people, a place to express their Jewish commitments and to find like-minded, engaged Jews.

"As one illustration, long before the Internet existed, we created a University Without Walls, which offered Jewish adult study and literacy programs. We continue these programs today, albeit in a different form, but still in a nondenominational way. We see this not as competition to or a replacement for the synagogue. Rather, it is a way for those who approach us to explore the meaning of their Jewish connection more deeply."

Darwinian Principles in the American Jewish Landscape

"This approach is also relevant because the Darwinian principles of the survival of the fittest operate in the American Jewish institutional landscape, too. Some organizations are getting stronger in the competition for membership, financial support, young leadership talent, and media attention; others are weakening or even on life support.

"Paradoxically, one could argue that there are not enough American Jewish organizations, despite their multitude. Existing organizations appeal to only 40-50 percent of American Jews at most. Organized American Jewry must thus continuously find creative ways to reach out. New organizations will inevitably emerge that address the needs of groups that currently feel disenfranchised. One such example in recent years has been the New Israel Fund, which supports programs and groups that advance a progressive social justice agenda in Israel. It appears to be a reaction of those who, for whatever reason, feel uncomfortable with the Federation movement. Other institutions, such as Jewish cultural centers that appeal to younger tastes, are now surfacing.

"Thus the AJC, which just celebrated its ninety-seventh anniversary, can only be successful if it continues to anticipate trends and readjust itself accordingly. Flexibility is a precondition for organizational survival."

Boutique Institutions and Giving

"A recent phenomenon has emerged of Jewish charitable giving outside the existing organizational structure. Some generous philanthropists with ideas and vision have little patience for traditional bureaucracies. Instead, they create their own institutions.

"One outstanding success story is the Wexner Foundation programs: the Wexner Israel Fellowship Program, which brings Israelis to Harvard University, and the Wexner Heritage Program, which has established a two-year educational course of study for emerging American Jewish leaders. The latter aims to make the leaders feel more comfortable with Jewish learning and texts.

"Another successful program is Birthright—sponsored in part by a group of philanthropists—which brings Diaspora youngsters to Israel. Unfortunately, due to the war in Israel, fewer of them are willing to go.

"These two projects are among the most exciting initiatives to come from this community. There are many other boutique institutions around the country, which do not compete directly because they don't seek membership or funds, yet they hint at a process of decentraliza-tion. Nevertheless, even if one creates 100 such institutions—each of which does wonderful work in fields such as Jewish education, youth work, or leadership development—none is likely to replace the role of the major organizations."

New Synagogue Models

"The synagogue remains very important in American Jewish life. New models have emerged which have gained great popularity. Some have emphasized the search for spirituality. One of the greatest suc-cesses is B'nai Jeshurun on the Upper West Side in Manhattan. It has a variety of services and uses a nearby church in addition to the syna-gogue because of the overflow of attendants, many of whom are quite new to Jewish religious life. They were born Jewish but along the way became alienated.

"The Chabad (Lubavitch Hasidic) organization is enjoying some success around the world. It offers a response to the cold, detached, intellectual, or pseudo-intellectual approach of many synagogues of the last decades, where members did not feel an integral part of the ser-vice or community.

"It is difficult to determine whether, overall, the synagogue move-ment is becoming stronger. Many synagogues are in the middle of a building boom, expanding their sanctuary and classroom space and hir-ing more rabbis to accommodate a growing membership. Others are weak or even closing down because they are not attracting enough people for services.

"At the same time, one finds many people moving away from reli-gion or flirting with other religions. For example, the number of Jews among American Buddhists is strikingly large. They are drawn by a warm community and nondoctrinaire spirituality. Other spiritually-based movements have also attracted a few Jews."

Attractive Product Range, Poor Marketing

"The Jewish community must respond. Within Jewish civilization one can find mysticism, philosophy, art, music, you name it. We repre-sent an entire civilization. While we have a large 'product range,' our marketing has been weak. It is too often bound to synagogues that are perceived at times as detached, uninspiring, and remote. Conversely, those synagogues that reach out and present themselves as multi-dimensional religious, educational, and community institutions are likeliest to succeed.

"On the one hand, there is the Orthodox movement. Their approach certainly appeals to some, but not to others who may see it as too narrow or confining and out of touch with the modern world.

"On the other hand, the Reform movement has overtaken the Conservative movement and is now the largest religious denomination in American Jewry.

"For some time, the Reform movement lost the sense of boundaries or distinctiveness that defines the Jewish people. Now, Reform is swinging again toward a more traditional approach. Many congregations are reacting against the classical German 'high church' Reform movement. The balance among ritual, Jewish literacy, and social action is shifting, it seems."

Leadership: A Sociological Transformation

"This raises the question of leadership. Fifty years ago, if one were looking for Jewish leaders, one went to rabbis. A sociological transformation has occurred, as today the most visible leaders of the community are businessmen and the professionals in the big organizations.

"One cannot speak about American Jewish leaders today without mentioning Charles Bronfman, Leslie Wexner, Ronald Lauder, Michael Steinhardt, and Mortimer Zuckerman. They define the lay leadership of the community. They are very successful businessmen who have committed time and resources to the Jewish community. On the other hand, the rabbinate today largely lacks such high-profile individuals as Rabbis Joseph B. Soloveitchik, Abba Hillel Silver, and Stephen Wise, giants of the past."

Shifting Allies

"Yet another important development is the movement among our allies. To paraphrase a nineteenth-century British statesman, 'We have no eternal allies and we have no perpetual enemies. Our interests are eternal and perpetual.' The American Jewish community has realized this increasingly throughout the years. One defines one's allies according to these interests. Allies on the issue of Israel are not necessarily those on church-state separation. This shouldn't worry us. That is the way the world works.

"As American Jewish diplomats, much of our work has always been focused on trying to build relationships with other ethnic and religious groups. We do so because we believe in the importance of pluralism and intergroup harmony. And, as a minority community, we need friends to build a majority point of view in both public opinion and Congress.

"We are now facing a number of challenges. First, some of our traditional allies on key questions, such as the Middle East, have taken a leave of absence. Many ethnic or religious partners do not want to take sides in this new reality. It is a bit like the Greek and Turkish community coming to the Koreans in the United States and each asking for support on Cyprus. Koreans would probably say, 'We like both of you, but Cyprus is far from Korea, so why should we take a position? Why alienate either of you?' Thus they take a pass."

America's Changing Face
"The Jewish community confronts similar problems with the African American community. Martin Luther King Jr., Whitney Young, Bayard Rustin, and James Farmer were all very identified with the Jewish quest for sovereignty in Israel. They were among our strongest supporters in the struggle for Soviet Jewry. They are no longer alive. The support for our priority issues is still there, but it has diminished.

"The labor movement was another traditional ally of the Jewish community. Its support has decreased. Once the Jews were overrepresented in the labor movement; now we are underrepresented. A gap has grown.

"All this happens while America's face is—as the cliché says—quite literally changing. More than 50 percent of the population of California, the country's traditional pacesetter, is nonwhite. Immigration to the U.S. is principally from Asia and Latin America—populations without a historical connection to the Jewish people, or perhaps coming with preconceived prejudices. For example, many Catholics immigrating from rural Latin America have yet to adopt the changes the Catholic hierarchy made in its theology at the Second Vatican Council.

"Furthermore, they rapidly understand America's social hierarchy. Jews don't like to admit it, but we have risen close to the top and are seen as part of today's establishment. We do not belong to the Mayflower generation, but to newcomers we seem very close to it, and the result may be either envy or resentment.

"This leads to major new challenges in building intergroup coalitions, but also new opportunities. Examples are the Korean and Indian communities, with which we have much in common. It is possible to build strong relations with them, but it will take time and investment.

"Second, some of our new allies pose complications. For example, the Evangelical Christian movements have been staunch allies on Israel, but hold views on church-state and social policy issues that are anathema to many Jews."

Fighting Radical Muslim Organizations

"Third, on Israel in particular, while American public support has always been quite high, there have been important segments hostile to it—for instance, much of the foreign policy establishment and big oil. In recent years, the growing Arab and Muslim populations in the United States have been copying the Jewish communities' organizational style with the stated goal of neutralizing our influence.

"Now we are fighting so-called mirror organizations of the American Jewish Committee and AIPAC in the emerging Arab and Muslim communities. They are using the same organizational and lobbying approaches as we do.

"The $64,000 question—to which I do not pretend to know the answer—concerns the future of the Muslim community in this country. Traditionally—with the exceptions of, say, the Amish and ultra-Orthodox Jews—America's power of assimilation has been very seductive. By the second generation, American attitudes take over. The extent to which the Arab Muslim community in the U.S. will acculturate is, however, unclear."

Jews: Not Waiting on the Sidelines

"France has many more years of experience in trying to grapple with the Muslim community. While the situations are not identical, the Muslim population in Europe has largely resisted the traditional patterns of acculturation. In the U.S. the question is which will prove stronger: the traditional culture they bring to this society, or the American melting pot? The centrifugal or centripetal forces?

"The dialogue with the Muslim community may become easier once their moderates—and they do exist—organize into the equivalent of the AJC. For their own sake, I hope they will. We do not need to agree on every issue, but we need to disagree respectfully. In the meantime, we have a number of Muslim groups that have largely been hijacked by extremists, with dubious sources of funding in some cases. This is a national problem, not just a Jewish one."

The Administration's Mistakes

"On this score, the Clinton administration and the pre-9/11 Bush administration both erred, in my judgment. They were desperate to engage the growing Muslim community and could not invent new institutions for them, so they dealt with some pretty questionable groups. This approach was a mistake, which, astonishingly, in some cases still continues to this day. In their contacts with extremist groups, they inadvertently conferred legitimacy. This only made it harder for moderates to emerge.

"In confronting the Muslim community, we will not back down simply because we are out in front and exposed. Sometimes, I must admit, though, that we feel like the Greek mythological character Cassandra."

Radical Islam Has to Be Confronted

"We just copublished a book on Saudi textbooks with the Center for Monitoring the Impact of Peace. I would have been much happier had the book been published by a Catholic, Lutheran, human rights, or educational association. But they didn't do it, so we did.

"We will continue to confront and expose radical Muslims, as we believe existential questions are at stake here that go far beyond Jews.

The American Jewish community will not unilaterally withdraw itself from the public debate on central questions about America's future and the world's destiny. Let me be clear: We are not concerned about drawing too much attention to ourselves and roiling the waters—those days are over."

Arafat Never Ceded Reins of Power to Abbas
Financial Times
September 10, 2003

Contrary to the assertion in your editorial ("End of the Road Map," September 8), the primary failure of the Road Map rests with Yasir Arafat, who from day one was intent on sabotaging any chance of success by Mahmoud Abbas.

Yes, Chairman Arafat appointed Mr. Abbas as prime minister, but he never ceded the reins of power, especially in the security realm. Indeed, any possible success of Mr. Abbas in advancing the peace process would have reflected negatively on Mr. Arafat, revealing that it was Mr. Arafat all along who was unable to strike a deal with Israel.

Moreover, no Israeli government could have moved forward in the absence of determined Palestinian action against terrorist groups. Tragically but predictably, the so-called ceasefire was nothing more than an opportunity for Hamas, Islamic Jihad, and the Al-Aqsa Brigades to rearm, and the resumption of terror was only a matter of time.

When a Palestinian leadership emerges that recognizes the self-defeating nature of terrorism and pursues good-faith talks with Israel, they will no doubt find in Jerusalem a partner for the painful compromises that both sides must undertake to achieve a secure and lasting peace for Israelis and Palestinians alike.

Saudi Education Foments Hatred of the West
Boston Globe
October 14, 2003

The school year is in full swing. Across the United States children are learning civics fundamentals—democracy, pluralism, and mutual respect. These are all key values underlying our multiracial, multicultural society.

In the Kingdom of Saudi Arabia, however, children are taught contempt for anyone who is Christian or Jewish, and the West as a whole is denigrated. The daily teaching of hatred is taking place, as it has for many years, in a nation long purported to be America's closest ally in the Muslim world.

Unfortunately, amid reports about tensions in U.S.-Saudi relations, one issue largely neglected is education. That is a pity. The pervasive denigration of the West in Saudi schools is essential to grasping the root of the long dormant fissures in the U.S.-Saudi relationship, and, of course, understanding why fifteen of the nineteen terrorists on 9/11 were products of the Saudi educational system.

Saudi children are taught intolerance and contempt for the West and non-Muslims in a wide range of subjects, from literature to math. This is the central finding of a study, cosponsored by the American Jewish Committee, of Saudi Arabia Ministry of Education books used in grades one though ten.

For example, eighth graders are taught, in a geography book, that "Islam replaced the former religions that preceded it" and that "a malicious Crusader-Jewish alliance is striving to eliminate Islam from all the continents."

In a ninth-grade language exercise, Saudi youth are instructed to use the sentence, "The Jews are wickedness in its very essence," when learning the rules of the Arabic language.

Saudi schoolbooks implore Muslims not to befriend Christians or Jews. "Emulation of the infidels leads to loving them, glorifying them and raising their status in the eyes of the Muslim, and that is forbidden," states a ninth-grade jurisprudence book.

Saudi spokespeople have dismissed the indisputable fact that the demonizing of Christians, Jews, and the West is pervasive in official books used throughout the government-controlled school system.

When the American Jewish Committee raised the education issue with Saudi Foreign Minister Saud al-Faisal, he told us, as he has stated in interviews with American media, that the problematic passages are limited to about "5 percent of the schoolbooks."

Faisal and other Saudi spokespeople have grossly underestimated the problem. And, though the foreign minister and others have asserted that steps are being taken to rewrite them, there is no evidence as yet to support these claims.

Moreover, Saudi schoolbooks and curriculum are actively exported to other Arab and Muslim countries, where Saudi largesse funds many schools. Indeed, several Muslim schools in the United States have been built and staffed with Saudi money, opening the door to the spread of Saudi-sponsored hate on American soil. Probing which of the books published in Saudi Arabia might also be used here in the United States is vital.

Thus far, our government has downplayed the issue of Saudi educational reform. Members of Congress, though, are recognizing that education is at the root of the long dormant problems in the U.S.-Saudi partnership. Resolutions calling for Saudi education reform are pending in the both the House and Senate.

To continue to ignore the hate that is integral to Saudi education can no longer be tolerated, all the more so given Saudi demography. More than half of the Saudi population is under the age of twenty. What can we expect from these youngsters after years of indoctrination? The answer should be obvious.

The United States must press Saudi Arabia, which claims friendship with our country, to excise the hatred that permeates their schoolbooks. Until a new chapter, both literally and figuratively, is written in the American-Saudi relationship, truly amicable ties will be difficult to achieve.

An Anti-Semitic Speech
New York Times
October 27, 2003

Paul Krugman's October 21 column contextualized and rationalized the hateful anti-Semitic remarks of Prime Minister Mahathir Mohamad of Malaysia at the Organization of the Islamic Conference.

The unmistakable message Mr. Mahathir sent to his own citizens, as well as to Muslims worldwide, is that hatred of Jews is essential to addressing the social, economic and political challenges facing Muslims in their own countries. Mr. Mahathir has held this view for years, long before the Bush administration, seen by Mr. Krugman as contributing to the problem, came to power.

Equally disturbing was the striking absence at the meeting of dissenting voices. To the contrary, Mr. Mahathir received a standing ovation.

The Malaysian prime minister's propagation of classic anti-Semitism is crystal-clear. There should be no doubt or equivocation about the implications of his words.

4. TRANSLATIONS

Preface

As a gesture of solidarity, I began attending the annual dinner of French Jews in December 2000. Its basic format is an exchange of public speeches by the prime minister and the president of CRIF.* I was especially impressed by the latter's speech in December 2001 and translated it from the original French to allow English speakers to better understand the viewpoint and mindset of the leader of French Jewry.

Speech of Roger Cukierman, President of CRIF
Paris, December 1, 2001

Mr. Prime Minister,

Once again, you grace us with your presence at this annual meeting of the CRIF. This dialogue between the prime minister of the Republic and French Jewry permits us to air our concerns and our hopes. We are very grateful to you.

At the dawn of the third millennium, the fate of the world has been touched by a remarkable explosion of violence.

We are very anxious about the risks that weigh and will continue to weigh on the world, on France, on the Jews of France, and on Israel.

For the roots of this illness are deep and will outlive Osama bin Laden.

* * *

* CRIF is the Representative Council of Jewish Institutions of France.

Never have the promises of an era of milk and honey, of a time when the lamb will lie down with the wolf, seemed so distant.

How can one forget the nightmare of September 11, the planes striking the Twin Towers, the desperate people jumping from the buildings? At a time when we can walk on the moon, fanatics take us back to the Middle Ages.

The struggle of the American people is our struggle.

But the whole of the Muslim world must not be held responsible for these criminal acts.

In fact, as André Chouraqui said: "It is love for the Ineffable One that I discovered in each psalm of the Bible, each verse of the Gospels, each sura of the Koran—an identical song of unity and of love."

Unfortunately, the notion that Islam is a religion of love is not shared by all. How can one hope for reconciliation when the innocence of children is employed by the fanatics to foment hatred?

This enterprise of death is unfolding before our eyes throughout the entire world.

And Europe has not been spared. Must one be reminded of the terrorist attacks that struck the streets and subways of Paris or the barracks of Drakkar, Lebanon? What about the threats to the cathedral of Strasbourg?

The operations against New York and the Pentagon demonstrate the cruel efficiency of these men. The world is waking up, faced with an enemy that might have at its disposal biological, indeed nuclear, weapons.

We who live Judaism not only as a religion, but also as a moral and ethical code and a culture, cannot imagine that Islam is any different. We are sure that many responsible Muslims will finally express—in strong, audible voices—their rejection of fanaticism.

Many people have been frustrated, humiliated, persecuted, scorned—Jews among them—but no one has resorted to such barbarous acts.

The Durban Conference against Racism, which took place before these terrorist acts, escalated into a planetary concert for anti-Jewish hatred. There in Durban one heard: "One Jew, one bullet." And most virulent were those dictators who mistreat and often martyr women, children, homosexuals, political opponents, and ethnic and religious minorities—those countries where mutilation and stoning are legally sanctioned.

France, the homeland of the Rights of Man, could not sit by passively in the struggle for freedom and tolerance: Thus, the firm stance taken by the president of the Republic; thus, the actions undertaken by your government. We are proud to stand with the government of France and with the vast majority of the French people, on the side of the Americans, in the company of those who oppose the spirit of Munich.

Some suggest that America was targeted because it is arrogant and because it is too identified with Israel. They forget the sacrifice of American soldiers on French soil twice during the twentieth century. They forget the first terrorist attack against the World Trade Center in 1993, during the euphoric period of the Oslo Accords. They forget that the planning of the September terrorist attacks preceded the beginning of the intifada. The vehement search for explanations permits justification for the horrors committed. This rationalization entails a demand to stay out of the way of the conflict. In a word, it is cowardice—summed up, perhaps, by the couplet of Celine: "All this is the fault of the Jews."

We do not make a distinction between good and bad terrorism—that which can be justified and that which cannot. Terrorists are killers, regardless of their nationality. And the color of the victims' blood is the same, whether they are Americans, Israelis, or passengers on the Paris subway.

Mr. Prime Minister, you were among the first to call the terrorist movements by their real name. We hope that all those parties who at the time morally assailed you today understand their mistake.

We also hope that all the participants in the upcoming electoral campaigns will conduct themselves at the level of a debate of ideas, without lowering themselves to follow the politically expedient recommendations of the so-called experts.

We are faced with anti-Jewish hatred.

The president of the Republic, in his statement of July 16, 1995, which was both historic and essential, Mr. Alain Juppé, and you, Mr.

Prime Minister, in creating the Mattéoli and Drai Commissions, recognized the responsibility of France for the actions of Vichy. And you created the National Foundation for the Memory of the Shoah. This painful reexamination of the past was laudable.

In this land, where our blood was spilled for the homeland together with that of our fellow citizens, where many Jews have contributed to the grandeur of France in the sciences, arts, and culture, we feel threatened. Hatred of Jews has resurfaced. And for the first time in half a century, shouts of "Death to the Jews" can be heard in Paris, and some synagogues have been torched.

The extreme right is divided, but millions of French, misled, continue to subscribe to racist ideas. The climate of apprehension runs the risk of strengthening these tendencies. And theories of Holocaust denial have spread.

The democrats do not support this hatred, just as they did not understand the state visit accorded the Syrian president, author of violent anti-Jewish words.

We pay homage to the French church, which has made great strides in replacing the teaching of contempt with the teaching of respect.

Above all, we wish to avoid exacerbating the anti-Semitism of the extreme right through conflicts with the Muslim community.

We desire a trusting dialogue with the Muslims of France. We extend our hand to our Muslim fellow citizens. The majority of French Jews come from the Maghreb and are familiar with its culture. We, all of us together, have to wage a battle against the extreme right and for civic peace. We dream of uniting the "commandos" of friendship from all walks of life into a kind of pact of those who would build a more constructive future.

We are pleased to see, at the invitation of the Ministry of the Interior, the creation of an umbrella organization of Muslims of France. But if this council does not ensure a sufficient number of seats to Muslim moderates and to nonclergy, if this council does not govern itself by republican principles, the risk of a drift toward fanaticism will be very serious. We think, Mr. Prime Minister, that this risk exists.

We are experiencing verbal violence.

In 1939, French Jews, whose names were inscribed on tombstones in our cities, believed themselves protected by their presence for centuries in France, without having to trace their roots to Rashi of Troyes or to the Papal Jews in Avignon. They shared the destiny of the victims of Nazism.

We know from experience that when a Jew is threatened because he is a Jew, all Jews are in danger. And when Jews are threatened, it is liberty that is at risk. Nothing is closer to anti-Semitism than anti-Zionism.

Most certainly, every incident can be interpreted in various ways: Thus, a Palestinian terrorist, according to an international wire service, was "killed," while according to another, he was "executed," and according to a third, "assassinated." In this way a word, a single word, is sufficient to transform a news item into an op-ed piece.

Palestinian semantics have been widely used in the media. An Israeli baby, killed by a Palestinian marksman armed with a telescopic firearm, becomes a "settler baby." A newscast announces: "Two dead: a Palestinian and a female settler." As if this identification as a settler justifies the murder, as if this word does not carry a guilt-inducing connotation from our Algerian past. "The Esplanade of the Mosques" replaces the Temple Mount. "The Israelis are killed, and the Palestinians are assassinated." The term "extremist" is reserved solely for Israelis. And terrorists become "combatants," even when their targets are babies.

All this is augmented by photographs, caricatures, and the views of experts—at times, Jews—who, in this case, appear to have accounts to settle with their forefathers.

Curiously, the absence of any criticism of the Arab side becomes deafening for those with acute hearing.

Public funds, disseminated through French public institutions, support institutes, textbooks, and Palestinian television, all of which propagate hatred of Jews. This is unacceptable.

We know that journalists are driven by the need to inform, and they work conscientiously and seriously. But at times there is insufficient knowledge of the subject.

Permit me to remind them of:

- The permanent presence, since the Roman era, of Jews in Jerusalem. In 1889, there were 25,000 Jews, 7,000 Christians, and 7,000 Muslims in Jerusalem.
- The refusal of the Arabs in 1947 to accept the creation of a Palestinian state, a proposal accepted by Israel.
- The absence in the region of any democracy other than Israel.
- The creation of Israel as the result of the desire to return to Jewish roots, after centuries of persecution. This is Zionism. It precedes the Shoah. And the founders of CRIF did all they could during the Nazi occupation, to help fulfill the dream of Herzl. Of these promises, we are the heirs.
- The five million Jews of Israel, surrounded by twenty-one hostile countries and 300 million Arabs.
- The size of Israel, occupying the equivalent of three French counties, its central part the width of the distance from Vincennes to La Defense, twenty kilometers [twelve miles].

Under such circumstances, who is David and who is Goliath?

Finally, beyond the facts, some regard Israel as a colonialist and imperialist intruder. Israel has become the Jew of the nations, and if some Jews behave badly, the weight of Vichy becomes lighter.

We are sure that the journalists, media owners, and the CSA share our serious concern about the existence of a climate of extremism that takes advantage of a situation to provoke violent action.

Therefore, we fear for the security of the Jews of France.

Our community was traumatized by the attacks against our synagogues in the autumn of 2000. In the last year the situation has deteriorated further. Each day brings a further dose of insults and acts of violence. It is dangerous for a religious Jew to walk alone in certain neighborhoods. Synagogues, schools, and even a day-care center have been the targets of attacks.

We are aware of the efforts of officials to protect our schools and religious and nonreligious sites, which until now have prevented the worst from happening. But what is at stake are the fundamental freedoms of the republic.

We expect from the police and the justice system even greater efforts than in the past to pursue the culprits and to punish them. Only severe punishment can reduce the risk of violent explosion. Thus the danger of a rupture in the social tranquillity is immense. We never wanted to create our own parallel militias to defend our rights. Most of all, we don't want our youth, who are discovering this phenomenon of anti-Semitism, to become tempted to respond to the violence.

It is the responsibility of the public authorities.

In light of recent events, to support the strengthened effort of the police and judicial systems, we believe that it would be useful for governmental authorities to increase the security of schools and all meeting places, particularly through the installation of video surveillance.

You should know, Mr. Prime Minister, that security concerns touch a large part of the Jewish population, and we expect much of you in this area. To be sure, this security problem is not unique to the Jewish community; it is a societal problem.

Are we to yield to the violence, let youngsters mistreat with impunity women, the elderly, teachers, police, and judges? The violence of weapons, gestures, words, and behavior must be tamed. What is at stake is the future of French society. This must be achieved through social integration, and by an enormous effort at civic education that teaches respect for property, for individuals, and for values to which we are attached, including the national anthem and the French flag. [Note: The references are to a recent French-Algerian international soccer match in France, during which a number of French youth of Algerian origin hissed during the singing of the French national anthem and showed their disrespect for the flag.]

We are concerned not only about questions of security in France. The dangers that hang over the Middle East appear to be extremely grave.

As in 1948, Israel's legitimacy is being challenged by its neighbors. What must Israel do that its children not risk their lives?

Mr. Prime Minister, you know Israel well enough to know how much its people are concerned with peace.

In 1993, Israelis and Palestinians in Oslo said: "You and me." Since Camp David in July 2000, Arafat has responded: "You or me."

Arafat speaks with the force of a revolutionary who has never abandoned his military uniform, even when he received the Nobel Peace Prize.

Who can understand this man who said "no" to peace, against the interests of his own people? He rejected the hand that gave him all he asked for.

Israelis are not Nazis. And the butcher of Sabra and Shatila is not a Jew. He is a Christian, a Lebanese, a parliamentarian, a former minister of [Prime Minister Rafiq] Hariri: Mr. Elie Hobeika. Muslims are killed, and a Jew is accused. It's an old story.

The 600,000 Israelis of 1948 made the desert bloom; they revived a language; they built a modern economy. Their neighbors would be well served to take them as a model and not as a target.

In the sphere of foreign affairs, what does CRIF hope for from the French government?

That its Middle East policy be balanced.

Because France is generous with the Palestinians, it can pass along a message: They must accept the existence alongside themselves of their Israeli neighbors.

And this acceptance requires that Mr. Arafat stop the terrorists by arresting them. All the Arab leaders, without exception, know how to exert a strong hand, a very strong hand, with their adversaries. There will not be peace until Mr. Arafat does the same.

We are sensitive to the suffering of the Palestinian people. Fanaticism is the result of the misfortune of people and the absence of opportunities. The link between misfortune and fanaticism must be brought to an end. France should use its influence to ensure that school books, speeches, and preaching teach the Palestinian people that peace is possible, that coexistence is necessary, and that a future exists if the existence of the other is accepted.

Regarding the Israelis, what CRIF wishes is that France make some meaningful gesture, for example, by accepting the 500,000 French-speaking Israelis into the Francophone community.

The Quai d'Orsay [Foreign Ministry] is the window of France to the world. Have we seen France take sides between India and Pakistan, between Great Britain and Ireland, or between Greece and Turkey?

Those in our chancelleries who criticize violations of human rights that may have been committed by Israel would have an immense field of action if they made the effort to enlarge their field of vision.

We can understand the need for peace initiatives and France's efforts for the creation of a Palestinian state. On the other hand, could we not hope that France would become the first world power to take the initiative and formally recognize a simple fact, a reality, that Jerusalem is the capital of the State of Israel?

* * *

We are a small part of the French nation, but an active part which contributes to national harmony through mutual respect of beliefs.

Our thoughts remain faithful to our culture, our traditions, and our martyrs in a civic-minded manner that conforms with our republican traditions.

We wish security and peace for France, Israel, and the world.

We want a France strong, just, fraternal, turned decisively toward the future for all our children.

Thank you, Mr. Prime Minister, for having listened to us and, I hope, for having heard us.

Oriana Fallaci
November 26, 2002

Preface

It was a Friday in April, if I recall. I was flying from Zurich to Bologna, where I led a graduate seminar at the European center of Johns Hopkins University. As always, the airline, probably Swiss, was handing out complimentary newspapers in several languages. I picked up the two Italian papers I read regularly—*Corriere della Sera* and *La Repubblica*. Leafing through them, I found that both gave considerable attention to an essay by the noted Italian journalist Oriana Fallaci that was to appear that very day in the prominent newsweekly *Panorama*.

The essay, the papers reported, was a powerful indictment of those who ritualistically criticize Israel and side with the suicide bombers, and, needless to say, it was destined to provoke a firestorm in Italy, the target of much of Fallaci's polemic.

Arriving in Bologna, I rushed to the airport kiosk to buy *Panorama*, but no luck. The vendor told me that the magazine had sold out within minutes of its arrival. I repeated the same exercise at several news-stands in the city center, but to no avail. Finally, I found the magazine, but there was a catch. I was told that I could buy it only if I also bought a video that was being marketed by the magazine. The Italians would probably say that an American sucker is born every day, but I needed to get hold of the magazine, so I paid triple or quadruple the cover price.

I sat down in a café and began reading Fallaci's piece. It bowled me over. She's a take-no-prisoners journalist, and so she didn't mince words.

I felt it urgent that English-speaking readers have the chance to read her, so I began translating the text of what might be described as an updated version of Emile Zola's *J'accuse*. Within a few days, this translation was traveling through cyberspace. I knew that it had been widely circulated when I received my own translation from four dif-ferent people, all urging me to read it!

But Fallaci, another, briefer piece of whose I have also translated, was practically a lone voice in Europe, or so I thought.

Just prior to a recent trip to Madrid, I saw an interview, in French, with a prominent Spanish personality, Pilar Rahola. It was carried on a French web site, *proche-orient.info*, which offers insightful and bal-anced news on the Middle East—an important counterpoint to the per-vasively anti-Israel propaganda inundating France and the larger French-speaking world.

Once again, I was impressed. Here was another voice of conscience from the left who was prepared to break with the seemingly lockstep mentality of her ideological confrères. What a breath of fresh air!

Again, I sat down to translate the entire text in order to make it available to an English-speaking audience. Like the Fallaci translation, it is unofficial, but I have made every effort to be faithful both to the tone and content. It follows the two Fallaci pieces.

And I'll know if I've succeeded in my task if I receive the piece back from friends, oblivious to who the translator is, urging me to take the time to read the text!

On Anti-Semitism
by Oriana Fallaci
Panorama
Italy, April 18, 2002

I find it shameful that in Italy there was a procession of individuals who, dressed as kamikazes, uttered vile insults at Israel, held up photos of Israeli leaders on whose foreheads they had drawn a swastika, inciting the populace to hate the Jews. And in order to see the Jews again in the extermination camps, in the gas chambers, in the crematoria of Dachau, Mauthausen, Buchenwald, Bergen-Belsen, etc., they would sell their own mothers to a harem.

I find it shameful that the Catholic Church permits a bishop, moreover one housed in the Vatican, a "saintly" bishop, who, in Jerusalem was found with an arsenal of weapons and explosives hidden in special compartments of his sacred Mercedes, to participate in that procession and to place himself in front of a microphone to thank, in the name of God, the kamikazes who massacre the Jews in the pizzerias and supermarkets. He called them "martyrs who go to death as to a party."

I find it shameful that in France—the France of "Liberty, Equality and Fraternity"—synagogues are torched, Jews are terrorized, and their cemeteries profaned. I find it shameful that in Holland and Germany and Denmark youngsters show off the kaffiyeh like the vanguard of Mussolini displayed the stick and the Fascist emblem. I find it shameful that in almost every European university Palestinian students take over and nurture anti-Semitism; that in Sweden they asked that the Nobel Peace Prize given to Shimon Peres in 1994 be withdrawn, and left solely in the hands of the dove with the olive branch in his mouth—that is, Arafat. I find it shameful that the esteemed members of the (Nobel) Committee, a committee that it seems makes choices based on politics and not merit, are taking the request into consideration and thinking of fulfilling it. To hell with the Nobel Prize and hooray to those who don't receive it.

I find it shameful (we are back in Italy) that the government-controlled television stations contribute to the revival of anti-Semitism by crying over Palestinian deaths only, minimizing the importance of Israeli deaths, speaking in a brisk and dismissive tone about them. I find it shameful that in television discussions the scoundrels with the turban or kaffiyeh, who yesterday extolled the slaughter in New York and today praise the massacres in Jerusalem, Haifa, Netanya, and Tel Aviv, are received with such deference. I find it shameful that the press does the same—gets indignant because in Bethlehem Israeli tanks surround the Church of the Nativity, but doesn't get upset that in the same church 200 Palestinian terrorists (among them various leaders of Hamas and Al-Aqsa), well-armed with machine guns and explosives, are not unwelcome guests of the monks (and then accept from the tank soldiers bottles of mineral water and baskets of apples). I find it shameful that, given the number of Israeli casualties since the onset of the second intifada (412), one well-known daily felt it appropriate to emphasize in bold headlines that more Israelis die in road accidents (600 per year).

I find it shameful that *l'Oservatore Romano*, that is, the newspaper of the pope—a pope who not too long ago left a note in the Wailing Wall apologizing to the Jews—accused a people exterminated by the millions by Christians, by Europeans, of extermination. I find it shameful that the survivors of this (Jewish) people—people who still carry a number on their arm—are denied the right to react, defend themselves, avoid being exterminated again, by that same newspaper. I find it shameful that, in the name of Jesus Christ (a Jew without whom they would all be unemployed), priests from our parishes or social centers or wherever flirt with the murderers of those who in Jerusalem cannot go to eat a pizza or buy an egg without being blown up. I find it shameful that they choose the side of the very people who launched terrorism by killing us on planes, in airports, at the Olympics; and today these same people make sport of killing Western journalists—shooting them, kidnapping them, slitting their throats, beheading them. (After the publication of my piece "The Anger and the Pride," someone in Italy wanted to do the same to me. Citing Koranic verses, he exhorted his "brothers" in the name of Allah to kill me. Actually, to die with me. Since he is someone who speaks English well, I respond to him in English: "F–k you.")

I find it shameful that virtually the entire left, that left which twenty years ago permitted a trade-union procession to place a coffin (a Mafia-like warning) in front of the synagogue in Rome, has forgotten the contribution of the Jews to the anti-fascist struggle: of Carlo and Nello Rosselli, for example; of Leone Ginzburg, Umberto Terracini, Leo Valiani, Emilio Serani; of women such as my friend Anna Maria Enriques Agnoletti, shot in Florence on June 12, 1944; of 74 of the 335 victims of Fosse Ardeatine; of the infinite other deaths under torture or in combat or in front of the firing squads; the friends, the teachers of my childhood and of my early youth. I find it shameful that, in part because of the fault of the left—no, especially because of the fault of the left (think of the left that begins its congresses applauding the PLO representative in Italy, who represents here the Palestinians who seek Israel's destruction)—the Jews in Italian cities once again are frightened. And in French and Dutch and Danish and German cities, it is the same. I find it shameful that when the scoundrels dressed as kamikazes march, (Jews) shudder as they trembled in Berlin during Kristallnacht, that is, the night on which Hitler began the hunt of the Jews.

I find it shameful that, obeying the stupid, vile, dishonest, and, for them, the extremely opportunistic fashion of political correctness, the usual opportunists—no, the usual parasites—exploit the word "peace." In the name of the word "peace," now more devalued than the words "love" and "humanity," they absolve just one side of hate and bestiality. In the name of pacifism (read conformity) from the mouths of shrill voices, the same voices that earlier genuflected to Pol Pot now incite people who are confused, naïve, or intimidated. They cheat them, corrupt them, take them back half a century, that is, to the yellow star on the coat. These charlatans care as much about the Palestinians as I care about them [the charlatans], i.e., not at all.

I find it shameful that so many Italians and so many Europeans have chosen as a role model Mister—and I use the word advisedly—Arafat, this nonentity who, thanks to the money of the Saudi royal family, acts like Mussolini in perpetuity and in his megalomania believes he will go down in history as the George Washington of Palestine. This uneducated man who, when I interviewed him, could not even put together a complete sentence, an articulate thought. Therefore, to put a piece together, to write it, to publish it, is such a hard ordeal that one concludes that, compared to Arafat, even [Libyan leader Muammar] Qaddhafi becomes Leonardo da Vinci. This fake warrior who always goes around in uniform like Pinochet, who never wears civilian clothes, and yet who has never participated in a single battle. He leaves war, and has always left war, to others, in other words, to those unfortunate ones who believe in him. This pompous incompetent who, playing the role of head of state, caused the failure of the Camp David negotiations and the mediation efforts of Clinton. "No, no, I want all of Jerusalem to myself." This eternal liar who has a flash of sincerity only when (in private) he denies Israel's right to exist, and who, as I wrote in my book, lies every five seconds. He always plays a game of duplicity; he lies even if you ask him what time it is, and, therefore, you can never trust him. Never! One is systematically betrayed by him. This eternal terrorist who only knows how to be a terrorist (from a safe distance), and who in the 1970s—that is, when I interviewed him— also trained the Baader-Meinhof terrorists. And now with them, he trains (Palestinian) children who were ten years old. Poor kids. (Now they are trained to become kamikazes. One hundred baby kamikazes are ready for action: 100!) This opportunist who keeps his wife in Paris, cared for and revered as a queen, while he keeps his people in the shit. From the shit he removes them only to send them to die, to kill and to die, like the eighteen-year-old girls who, to achieve equality with men, have to fill themselves with explosives and blow themselves up together with their victims. And yet so many Italians love him—yes, just as they loved Mussolini. And so many other Europeans do as well.

I find it shameful, and I see in all of this the growth of a new fascism, of a new Nazism—a fascism, a Nazism, so much more malevolent and repulsive because it is conducted and nourished by those who hypocritically play the part of the good guys, the progressives, the communists, pacifists, Catholics and even more, the Christians, who have the gall to call those like me who shout truth at them a warmonger. I see it, yes, and therefore I will state the following: to the tragic and Shakespearean Sharon, I never gave him a break. ("I know that you came to add a scalp to your necklace," he murmured almost with sadness when I went to interview him in 1982.) With the Israelis, I've argued often and bitterly, and in the past I defended the Palestinians quite a bit, maybe more than they deserved. But I am with Israel, I am with the Jews. I am with them now, as I was with them as a young girl—in other words, from the time when I was in the trenches with them and the Anne Maries were shot to death. I defend their right to exist, to defend themselves, to avoid a second extermination. And disgusted by the anti-Semitism of many Italians, of many Europeans, I am ashamed by this shame that dishonors my country and Europe, in the best of cases, not a community of nations (e.g., Europe) but a well of Pontius Pilates. And even if all the inhabitants of this planet think differently, I will continue to think this way.

The Force of Passion (excerpt)
by Oriana Fallaci
Corriere della Sera
Italy, October 26, 2002

J'accuse. I accuse, the Westerners of having no passion. Of living without passion, of not fighting, of not defending themselves, of being collaborators because of a lack of passion.

Oh, I do have passion, you see. I am bursting with passion. But in Europe, as in America, I only see people without passion. Even the appeasers who want to send me to the stake are individuals without passion. Cold fish, larvae driven only by hatred and by envy, or by calculation or convenience, but never by passion.

And much of the guilt is yours. Because it is you who started this fashion—the fashion of rationality to an extreme, of self-control, of coldness. "Calm down, be quiet, be cool." You who were born out of passion, you who became a people thanks to the passion of your revolution.

And you don't understand what motivates your enemies, our enemies. You don't understand what it is that permits them to fight in such a global and pitiless way this war against the West. It is passion. The force of passion, my dears. It is the faith which comes from the passion. It's the hate which comes from the passion. *Allahu Akbar, Allahu Akbar, Jihad, Jihad*! They are ready to die, to blow themselves up, in order to kill us. To destroy us.

And their leaders, real leaders, [have] the same. I have known Khomeini—I spoke with him, argued with him, for more than six hours over two days. And let me tell you, he was a man of passion. What moved him was faith, passion. I never met Bin Laden. It's a pity. But I watched him closely when he appeared on television. I looked into his eyes, I listened to his voice, and I tell you that he is a man of passion. What moves him is faith, the hatred that comes from the passion.

To fight against their passion, to defend our culture—that is, our identity and our civilization—armies aren't enough. It's not tanks, atomic bombs, or fighter bombers. We need passion. The force of passion. And if you don't find within you this [passion], if we don't find it within us, I'm telling you that you will be defeated, we will be defeated. I tell you that we will go back to tents in the desert, that we will end up as wells without water.

Wake up, then! Wake up!

Judeophobia Explains the Pro-Palestinian Hysteria
of the European Left
Interview with Pilar Rahola
proche-orient.info
October 2, 2002

A Catalan from Barcelona, Pilar Rahola* is a highly colorful figure on the Spanish scene. She is known for her feminism, as well as for her frank and direct manner. A former parliamentarian, Pilar Rahola sat in the national legislature in Madrid for eight years, first as part of the Republican left, then as the founder of the Independence Party. However, she decided to leave political life just over a year ago to devote more time to her other passions. She has just published *The History of Ada*, a metaphor for abandoned children, those child-slaves or children-soldiers whom one meets all over the world, that is, when they are not transformed into human bombs.

She has also decided to step forward to denounce the flagrant imbalance in the handling of information from the Middle East. Her most recent piece, "In Favor of Israel," is to be published in a book in which fifteen Spanish intellectuals, including Jon Juaristi, president of the Cervantes Institute, and Gabriel Albiac, a well-known journalist with *El Mundo* [a Spanish daily newspaper], seek to reestablish the facts.

Marc Tobiass (of *proche-orient.info*) talks with Pilar Rahola.

Marc Tobiass: Why did you feel the need to write "In Favor of Israel," to participate in the publication of this book?

Pilar Rahola: Since the start of the second intifada, the Spanish press, on the right as well as the left, has taken a particularly aggressive approach toward Israel, an approach that leaves out the reasons for Israel's actions and tends to ignore the Israeli victims in this conflict. In this situation, a small minority of intellectuals, public personalities—sensitive to the Jewish question in general and to Israel in particular—felt deeply touched by this problem. Outraged by the return of Judeophobia in Spain, we, each in our own way, began to write some articles, to use the media to condemn this situation. And then Oracia

* Former Member of Parliament of the Spanish Republican Left

Vasquez Real, an important writer in Spain, suggested that we coordinate our activity, that we collect in one work the vision of the Middle East conflict held by fifteen well-known intellectuals.

Marc Tobiass: For whom did you write this book, and with what objective?

Pilar Rahola: Fundamentally, this book is addressed to the anti-Jewish school of thought in Spain. The goal of our book is to launch a debate about Judeophobia in Spain. We are convinced that the current view of the conflict, so Manichaean—with the good, always the Palestinians, and the evil, always the Israelis—has deep roots. It comes from an ancient anti-Jewish feeling that exists in Spain and that also explains the history of Spain. This feeling softened slightly after the Franco era [translator's note: post-1975], but today there is a virulent resurgence of this savage feeling to the point where one can find genuinely anti-Semitic expressions in the Spanish press. In essence, this is a provocative book in the face of totally pro-Arab thinking in Spain, that is completely uncritical of the mistakes of the Arab world in general and of the Palestinians in particular. We want to counter this flagrant imbalance....

Marc Tobiass: This imbalance is not specifically Spanish nor, for that matter, is the Judeophobia. You rightly recall in your piece the troubling remark of Hermann Broch [translator's note: Austrian anti-Nazi novelist, 1886-1951] denouncing the indifference of Europe as the worst of the crimes in the bloody madness of the Hitler era....

Pilar Rahola: Yes, I think that Europe was indifferent on the surface because it felt guilty within. I believe that this indifference unquestionably comes from Judeophobia. And in the ultimate paradox, the Jewish soul is part and parcel of Europe. Europe cannot be explained without its Jewish soul, but it is also explained by its hatred of the Jews. Thus, all the repeated attempts of Europe to get rid of its Jewish soul are, in fact, a kind of suicide.

After the Holocaust, after Auschwitz, that is, after the ultimate stage in the destruction of the Jewish soul—a process which lasted for centuries in Europe—Europe is shattered, many of its elements are dead, but it also has a bad conscience; it knows it is guilty. Since then, Europe has looked for and found in the Palestinian cause the expiation for its guilt. It is from this that the uncritical and Manichean attitude toward the Palestinian cause emerges—it is, primarily, the last heroic (European) adventure. Further, the more the Jews are presented as being the evil party, the bad ones, the less difficult it is to carry the responsibility and the guilt. This is a process of collective psychology. From such a perspective, there essentially is no difference between France, for example, and Spain.... It is unbelievable how Europe continues to hate its Jewish soul, even after it has expelled it!

Marc Tobiass: According to you, it is this Judeophobia that explains the "pro-Palestinian hysteria" that exists in Europe.

Pilar Rahola: I am sure of it.... There is undeniably of late a very serious effort at disinformation about everything to do with the Middle East. There is a kind of madness that excuses all the crimes, abuses, and errors of the Palestinian side, and, at the same time, there is an historical predisposition that condemns any single error of the Israeli side—and this to the point where the Palestinian victims are given maximum attention and the Israeli (victims) are ignored. It is as if the Jewish victims didn't exist, on the pretext that they were responsible for their own death!

The worst thing is that there is also a problem of terrorism in Spain, but when the crimes of ETA [translator's note: the Basque terrorist group] are mentioned, one speaks of terrorism, while when the crimes of Hamas are mentioned, one speaks of militants, activists, resistance, struggle.... When one mentions the Palestinian victims, one speaks of children, civilians, innocents, but when one mentions the Israeli victims, one speaks of people without a name, as if to suggest that they are only soldiers, members of the army. There is a distortion in the presentation of the conflict, a dangerous manipulation that feeds the hatred and the anti-Semitism.

Marc Tobiass: Your remarks add up to an indictment of the European media.

Pilar Rahola: What I want is to launch an appeal to the collective European way of thinking, and especially to the intellectuals and journalists, because, from my point of view, they are in the process of creating a collective reality that is Judeophobic. Today one must prove oneself to be on the left; it is necessary to be anti-Semitic to have credibility. Things have reached the point where, for instance, Sharon is always guilty of being guilty, while Arafat is seen as an honest figure, innocent, a tireless old resistance fighter, a heroic figure, a kind of Gandhi—in brief, a person gussied up in romantic finery, when in reality he is head of an oligarchy that has so much blood on its hands.

Israel is not (just) a country that is trying, for better or worse, to survive for fifty years, but it is reduced to one sole image: a country that occupies the territories and whose vocation is to make life miserable for the poor Palestinians. The history of the Holy Land is being reinvented. Everything takes place as if there were instructions: Never recall the faults and errors of the Palestinians, never recall their alliances with dangerous countries such as Iraq, in order to heap more shame on the United States and Israel. The profound reasons for this war are never made clear, never discussed.

Marc Tobiass: There is a comment in your text that sent shivers down my spine. You say that Judeophobia is, in the final analysis, the common denominator between Europe and the Palestinians.

Pilar Rahola: It's true that there are in Europe non-Jews who are sensitive and respect the Jewish soul, which is also part of the foundation of Europe, but they constitute a minority. The majority, the unconscious European collective, does not understand, does not absorb, nor accept, the Jewish phenomenon. And it is there that the essential meeting point between the European and the Palestinian takes place. Palestinian identity is not just a recent phenomenon, but it is, above all, built on hatred of Israel, hatred of the Jews.

If Europe can be explained by its Jewish component and by its hatred of the Jews, as if they were two sides of the same coin, Palestinian identity can essentially be explained only by its anti-Jewish component. It is for this reason that the Palestinians have such difficulty putting an end to their violence.

If the Palestinians renounced their hatred of the Jews, they would at the same time lose a significant part of their identity. To get beyond this violence, they would have to get beyond the hatred and thus change their identity. In other words, they would have to reinvent themselves. It is on the basis of this hatred that the Palestinian meets and agrees with the European. Often, this takes place with people of the left, which is a veritable calamity for people like myself, as we are of the left. We are Europeans, but we do not accept Judeophobia, just as we do not accept the anti-Zionism that justifies and nourishes the anti-Semitism of the Spanish left today.

Marc Tobiass: Isn't this legitimization of hate the true obstacle to peace?

Pilar Rahola: Without doubt. I believe that Europe is directly responsible, and not only for the conflict. In the final analysis, who, if not Europe, created the Jewish problem in the world? In a certain sense, one can even say that Europe is the actual founder of the State of Israel. Europe expelled its Jews—its Spanish Jews, its Russian Jews, its French Jews, and its German (Jews). It expelled them from its body, even though these Jews felt themselves European to the core....

Marc Tobiass: You describe yourself as being of the left and, for you, being a leftist is above all an existential position toward life, toward society. Yet, you yourself say that when this position turns into ideology, at times it becomes an excuse for channeling uncritical dogma, a simplistic Manichaeanism, indeed a racism. You, who were a parliamentarian of the left, how can you handle this contradiction?

Pilar Rahola: Those on the left in Spain have a real problem. In some respects we are the heirs of the French Revolution; we have been influenced by the great ideologues like [Jean-Paul] Sartre and [Albert] Camus, and also by May 1968. That is to say, the overall thinking of the Spanish left comes from France. Now, France is fundamentally anti-American ... from which (comes) our anti-Americanism, that at times borders on the pathological, an anti-Americanism which is also anti-Semitic. This explains why to a certain extent the Spanish left is anti-Semitic. Obviously, people like myself have great difficulty with this state of affairs.

I believe that if the left has failed as a great world ideology, it is because the left did not succeed in breaking with the worst of its dogmatic thinking. The left can be very progressive, but it can also be very dogmatic. Unfortunately, the left became infatuated with such infamous dictators as Pol Pot, Mao, and Stalin, and now it is in love with Arafat. The left should be critical, and in the first place, self-critical.

Marc Tobiass: And what is the dogma that worries you the most today?

Pilar Rahola: The most absurd thing is to watch leaders of the left today greet and celebrate Arab leaders, even when they are fundamentalists. For example, in the debates that followed the attacks of September 11, we heard an anti-American discourse here, pooh-poohing the victims, something which is in and of itself terrible! And there were those who tried to downgrade—with that tawdry third-worldism which characterizes some circles of the left—the danger embodied in individuals like Bin Laden, who is, in fact, an authentic fascist. I believe that for the moment the world remains blind to the biggest totalitarianism of the twenty-first century, which is Islamic fundamentalism. Now we must prepare ourselves seriously to face this danger: For me, this totalitarianism is without any shadow of a doubt comparable to Stalinism and Nazism, the biggest scourges of the twentieth century.

Marc Tobiass: To finish this interview, Pilar Rahola, I would like to cite a sentence from your text: You say that to be "in favor of Israel" is the most intelligent, rational, prudent, and honest way to be in favor of Palestine.

Pilar Rahola: First of all, I do not accept the use of the defense of the Palestinian cause as a pretext for a new epidemic of anti-Semitism. If Europe had had a critical discussion that did not hesitate to condemn the grave and permanent mistakes of the Palestinian side, if Europe had been more critical of the Palestinians, we would be closer to a solution today. But Arafat enjoys support and legitimacy in Europe which allows him to never miss an opportunity for missing the opportunity of peace. I believe that if Europe had been more critical toward Arafat, toward the different aspects of Palestinian violence, if Europe had been tougher in its statements, the Palestinians would have been compelled to step back from the violence and the suicide attacks.

A sense of justice calls for the establishment of a Palestinian state next to the State of Israel, but not in its place. Yet, at its core, Europe is ill at ease with the existence of Israel, and one can even say that the existence of this state provokes resentment and anger on the European left. Even if this is not acknowledged, many Europeans contend that a Palestinian state must replace the State of Israel.

But for those of us who support Israel, who are in favor of good neighborly relations—for coexistence between the State of Israel and a Palestinian state—our way of saying "yes" to a Palestinian state is also a way of saying "yes" to the existence of the State of Israel.

The Persistent Malaise of the Jews of France, by Philippe Broussard
Le Monde (Paris)
September 19, 2003

"Rupture," "shock," "fissure"—the Jews of France look for the words to express the change that has come into their lives since the start of the second intifada three years ago. This widespread unease is nourished by fear in the face of anti-Semitic violence, which calls into question for Jews their sense of belonging to the nation. It translates into a form of sectarian response, or via the temptation of exile, into aliyah to Israel ("going up" to the Hebrew state) or to North America. Their criticisms are also directed at the media, which they judge as biased in its coverage of the Middle East. Since the spring, anti-Jewish incidents have declined, but the [Jewish] organizations remain vigilant in the face of violence, which comes more often from young Muslims than from the extreme right.

Unease? Discomfort? Malaise? It's already been three years that the diagnosis of this problem stirs debate. It has been three years that the Jews of France, those 5–600,000 individuals loosely pulled together under the name "Jewish community," ask themselves about the nature of the feeling plaguing them. Depending on whether they live in Paris or the countryside, are of Ashkenazi or Sephardic origin, are exposed to anti-Semitism or not, they feel what's going on differently.

At a time when the situation in Israel is once again deteriorating, many of these Jews, including intellectuals, agree, however, that "something" has changed in their lives as Frenchmen since the beginning of the second intifada in September 2000. It's something that, at the same time, has to do with Israel and with their place in France today.

Defining this feeling isn't easy. It's fed by fear in the face of anti-Semitic violence; by anger toward the left, which is accused of passivity; by criticism of journalists who are reproached for their coverage of the Middle East; and, we shouldn't forget, by long-term questions about the future of secularism and the French Republic.

A survey conducted for the FSJU [Fonds Social Juif Unifié; translator's note: roughly equivalent to United Jewish Communities] of 1,132 heads of families underscored this phenomenon in the fall of 2002. But with the war in Iraq, the fear has gained additional ground. The schools haven't been spared, nor have the universities. Demonstrations of the extreme left turned into [forums for] anti-Zionism, that is to say, anti-Semitism. The Jewish community is worried about this, as illustrated by various meetings organized in Paris with such titles as "What future for the Jews of France?" (held in the French Senate) and "Sectarianism: Toward an Imposed Ghetto?" (held at the Espace Rachi, a Jewish forum).

Many experienced these events as a "shock," as a questioning of their belonging to the nation, from which emerges the impression of their being citizens apart, outcasts from a society that had previously engaged in important work regarding the memory of the Shoah. "There was a shock, a fissure," said David Saada, director general of the FSJU. "This didn't only touch the 30 percent of those engaged in communal life, but also—and this is new—those far from the center of activity."

The communal organizations, beginning with the Representative Council of Jewish Institutions of France (CRIF), say this using more or less carefully chosen words, but the fear this time doesn't come from the extreme right. Instead, it comes more from certain young Muslims, who are sensitive to the Palestinian cause and quick to demonstrate their "*antifeuj*" [a play on words that is meant to connote anti-Jew without saying so in so many words].

This phenomenon ... is particularly evident among Sephardic Jews, who comprise a majority of the Jewish community—70 percent—and are always ready to recall that the French Republic made them French citizens in 1870 with the Cremieux Decree [which granted Algerian Jews French citizenship]. Many of them, who live in fear of a new outbreak nearly fifty years after the decolonization of North Africa, feel deserted in favor of the Muslims. Many discussions lead to the use of numbers, along the lines of, "They, the Muslims, are six million, while we are 5–600,000." "To reason this way, one ends up with a siege mentality," says David, a Paris businessman, regretfully.

In the spring, a quick end to the Iraq conflict and the hopes for peace in the Middle East had a calming effect. In spite of a setback in the summer, the number of anti-Jewish acts declined. The lull had an impact on the political front. The president of CRIF, Roger Cukierman, often accused of populism and impolitic behavior by his adversaries, reconciled with the Socialists and the Greens, but not with the anti-globalization extreme left.

Is the crisis over? Some would like to believe so, such as the president of CRIF in the Rhone-Alps region, Alain Jakubowicz, who feels the topic is "no longer current." "The feeling of abandonment is over," insists the president of the human rights group B'nai B'rith, Edwige Elkaïm.

The representative of CRIF in Marseilles-Provence, Clément Yana, known for his commitment to dialogue, also expresses optimism. "The tendency is toward a calming of feelings," he asserts, "but we must stay vigilant in order to isolate extremists of all kinds. We need to dialogue without covering up the problems."

For many others, however, the difficulties persist, even if they are less acute than they were a few months ago. Though statistics are unavailable, everything points to the fact that the temptation to consider exile is real, whether to Israel or North America. "We haven't yet emerged from the period of malaise," suggests Saada of the FSJU.

"The Jewish community is in a post-traumatic situation. It didn't expect a return of anti-Semitism," says Patrick Klugman, former president of the Union of Jewish Students of France (UEJF, which is close to the left) and currently a member of the executive committee of CRIF. "The rupture which one could have feared hasn't taken place, but the love for the French Republic isn't as all-encompassing as it once was."

According to Klugman, known for his condemnation of both extremist Muslims and extremist Jews, the atmosphere has "strongly deteriorated" at certain universities, where "the accumulated frustrations over decades of the Maghreb [i.e., North African] community" are being given voice.

In such conditions, wouldn't Jews have a tendency to withdraw into themselves? "But it is we who are the victims of this form of sectarianism," Roger Cukierman exclaims. "We are withdrawing into ourselves as a response to being under attack. We never attacked anyone. We respect the laws of the republic, the national anthem, and the flag. You know, I was in the United States a few weeks ago. Seen from there, France is anti-Semitic; it's an absolute horror. Fortunately, that's not the case. France is not anti-Semitic."

The CRIF president continues: "Our problem is defined by some marginal elements. The vast majority of the French behave normally [toward the Jews], and we are in dialogue with responsible Muslim leaders."

The communal withdrawal is, after all, undeniable among a segment of the youth. "At Sarcelles or at Creteil, some [Jewish university students] are living in Israel in their head," asserts Klugman. In his eyes, this situation reveals the crisis that some Jews are experiencing.

"An entire segment of the [Jewish] population has broken away," he says. "This comes from the fact that the republican mold of the country, which functioned so well for 150 years, has broken. This country, which did so much for the Jews, doesn't recognize itself anymore."

Hence the affirmation of [sectarian] identity becomes more and more evident. In Marseilles, for example, Emmanuel Nidam, the local representative of the UEJF, explains: "The withdrawal is enormous. We can't deny it. Here there are clubs for the Arabs and clubs for the Jews! It's the reign of self-identity. It's difficult to get out of this logic. People have asserted their positions and are standing by them. Happily, though, there are also signs of a rapprochement. We are working tirelessly toward it."

Dissident voices, however, are having difficulty being heard. All criticism of the government of Ariel Sharon is perceived suspiciously. Any questioning of the views of CRIF is considered treason. "Write that we don't all have the same opinion," challenged Valérie, a law student in Paris. "And that's all to the good, because otherwise we'd have the triumph of sectarianism. The difficulty is to show the Jews that what's happening to them—the attacks, the violence, the hostility—is happening to everyone. In other words, this is not uniquely our problem, even if we feel it with a particular sensitivity; rather, it's a problem facing the entire republic. And barring proof to the contrary, France remains our country."

Sidebar: "A Rush to Community Schools"

From nursery school to high school, Jewish education is booming. The FSJU counts 251 educational establishments under contract with the state on French soil. For the scholastic year 2002-2003, these schools enrolled 25,884 pupils, in addition to which there were another 4,000 pupils attending schools that have no contract with the government.

According to the FSJU, the [Jewish] schools experienced a 31 percent increase in enrollment during the past ten years. Seventy-one percent of the pupils are in the Paris region. The figures for the school year starting in 2003 are not yet available, but they are expected to reveal an enrollment increase of at least 3 percent. David Saada, director general of the FSJU, has noted a "strong demand" for Jewish schools. "It is becoming difficult to find an available place in a Jewish school."

5. AJC INSTITUTIONAL

Tribute to Shula Bahat
December 8, 2003

On the occasion of Shula's twenty-fifth anniversary with the American Jewish Committee, let me take my cue from the David Letterman Show and offer my list of the Top Ten Things I Admire About Shula:

1. Shula has a big and exceptionally compassionate heart.
2. Shula has a rich and nimble mind.
3. Shula is a devoted mother to two terrific sons, a loving big sister to three wonderful siblings, and a proud aunt of a slew of accomplished nieces and nephews in Israel and South Africa.
4. Shula is a truly caring and committed friend to those she first met in Kiryat Bialik many years ago and to those she first met yesterday.
5. Shula is generous to a fault.
6. Shula is an inveterate optimist
7. Shula is indefatigable. In fact, I've never seen her yawn, regardless of the length (or content) of a meeting or the time of day. Come to think of it, I've never seen her settle back in her chair or slouch in any of the innumerable—and I mean innumerable—sessions she's attended.
8. Shula bespeaks elegance and style on every occasion.
9. Shula at any age is always open to new ideas and experiences.
10. Shula forgets jokes so quickly that, with her easy laugh, she makes a wonderful audience for the same joke over and over again.

Well, at this point it looks as if I'll need at least one more appearance on the Letterman Show because I'm only warming up. I have ten to go.

11. Shula is still capable of blushing, one of her absolutely most endearing traits.
12. Shula always finds the extra minute for everyone.
13. Shula has that unmistakable twinkle in her eye.
14. Shula is capable of charming a foreign minister one minute and willing to sew cuffs on men's pants the next—expertly, I might add—when the nearest tailor is closed for the weekend.
15. Shula's recipe for chicken soup is sans pareil. Just ask the legendary food critic, Josh Harris, our youngest son.
16. Shula has a zest for life that can be envied but rarely matched.
17. Shula has both physical and intellectual courage, a rare combination in our world.
18. Shula is totally unflappable in even the most challenging of situations. Actually, the more daunting the situation, the calmer she becomes in order to find the right solution.
19. Shula has given her soul to the American Jewish Committee 24/7 since 1978.
20. Shula has synthesized magnificently her profound love of Israel, her deep attachment to America, and her unshakable identity as a proud daughter of the Jewish people.

Happy anniversary!

Presentation to Murray Friedman, Washington, D.C.
May 7, 2002

This particular event is one that I look forward to with special enthusiasm every year. For me, it's a true family event—the family with whom I spend the bulk of my waking hours, my staff colleagues.

It allows us all the privilege to step back, if only for a few moments, from the intensity of our daily professional lives and pay recognition to one of our own.

In years past, honorees have included Gene DuBow, who was en route from his position as community services director to opening our new office in Berlin; Sam Rabinove, who was retiring after a distinguished career as AJC's legal director; and Jim Rudin, who was also leaving us after thirty-plus remarkable years as a pioneer in the field of interreligious relations.

This year's honoree will especially appreciate the fact that the award we present tonight, as always, is based solely and exclusively on merit.

It was in 1958 that Brooklyn-born Murray Friedman, then thirty-two years old, the father of two young children, a Marine Corps veteran, and a newly minted Ph.D. in American history from Georgetown, was in discussion with AJC about a vacancy in our Philadelphia office.

At that time, he had already been serving for four years, based in Richmond, as ADL's regional director for Virginia and North Carolina.

Given the era and locale, it must have been a fascinating and rather challenging assignment for the representative of an agency that was, in Murray's words, promoting human relations education and combating anti-Semitism.

Indeed, one of Murray's references, citing what he believed to be a weakness, described Murray as an "eager beaver," too engaged in the integration question, "upon which there are all shades of opinion throughout our Commonwealth, and even such understandable variances right here in Richmond." Murray's zeal, the gentleman wrote, "would be far less bothersome in the Northland, with its propensity for Civil Rights."

Prior to joining the ADL, Murray had had other interesting experiences that reflect the various sides of Murray we've come to know and admire.

The scholar in him had channeled his interests as an historian into a position in the Office of Military History, where he prepared studies on the role of the army in the Pacific theater during World War II.

The social activist in him had found expression in his work at the Washington, D.C., Housing Association, where he devoted himself to improving housing conditions in the city's impoverished neighborhoods.

The teacher in him had been a social studies instructor at a Brooklyn yeshiva.

And the writer in him had already published articles on politics and human relations in such leading magazines—friends of Murray, take note—as the *New Republic*, *Progressive*, *New Leader*, and *Commentary*. Notice something all four of these magazines had in common at the time? Right, there wasn't a conservative one among them!

To our great benefit, Murray and his family moved from Richmond to Philadelphia in 1959, though, in light of the valuable information he brought to AJC from the ADL, I can now reveal that the four of them were briefly put in AJC's witness protection program—as were Jeff Sinensky, Yehudit Barsky, and David Rosen in more recent years.

Forty-three years later, Murray Friedman holds first place for longevity among AJC's current professional staff. He could easily serve as AJC's poster boy for the physical benefits of extended employment. If you did a quick calculation a moment ago when I mentioned the year Murray joined us and his age at the time, then I think you'd agree that he wears his years extraordinarily well.

Over more than four decades, Murray has established the American Jewish Committee as a leading force in the Jewish and broader civic life of Philadelphia and beyond, and, in the process, he's become a widely admired and respected statesman of that important metropolis, one to which I feel particularly close, having lived in the City of Brotherly Love for five happy years.

His accomplishments are many—from involving the chapter centrally, as ethnic diplomats par excellence, in the fabric and fiber of the city's intergroup relations to building support for Jewish concerns overseas, especially with regard to Israel and, in an earlier period, Soviet Jewry; from building an impressive and loyal cadre of lay leaders active on both the local and national levels to creating an innovative center, in cooperation with AJC, for American Jewish history at Temple University; from producing a steady stream of well-received books and articles on history, politics, and public policy to engaging the interest of major foundations in the work of the American Jewish Committee.

Throughout his extraordinary AJC career, Murray has brought the unspent passion of a man with a mission to advance the well-being of the Jewish people; a razor-sharp mind and enviable analytical skills to explore every issue with which he has grappled; the courage to express—and defend—his convictions even when it means taking the less well-traveled road; the good sense to accept victory with humility and defeat with grace; the belief that on his watch he can make a difference in the lives of those around him; and the capacity, through his interpersonal skills, sensitivity, and good humor, to gain friends for us all.

I am proud to call Murray a friend and colleague, and absolutely delighted to present him with this year's Distinguished Professional Award. Murray will be pleased, I'm sure, to learn that this year's award comes with a lifetime membership in People for the American Way and a lifetime subscription to the *Nation*. Just kidding, of course.

Sam Rabinove: In Memoriam
New York
September 30, 2002

In 1966, a forty-three-year-old attorney for the Allstate Insurance Company decided to change jobs. He wanted to go into a field of law that would allow him to grapple with societal issues he truly cared about, affecting both this country and the Jewish community.

In supporting this idealist's application to AJC, Abe Rosenthal of the *New York Times* said he had known him since their time together at City College, where he was a "terribly bright guy." Moreover, said Rosenthal, the applicant was a "first-class man and gentleman in every way," and "highly cultured" to boot. What he couldn't comment on, though, was our applicant's legal skills since, Rosenthal noted, "I've never had occasion to find out."

Convinced that AJC had found the right person to serve as director of our Legal Division, the late John Slawson, my distinguished predecessor, wrote to Sam Rabinove on December 9, 1966, offering him a job.

Sam accepted, at a pay cut from his Allstate job, I might note, and started on January 3, 1967. And so began a remarkable thirty-year career at the AJC, a career that formally ended on June 20, 1997, when Sam retired, but which in a sense continued for another five years until Sam's death earlier this year. Not only was Sam elected to serve on AJC's National Board of Governors, but Jeff Sinensky, Richard Foltin, and others on staff continued to seek his sage counsel.

A number of years ago, in a report Sam prepared on a private visit to New Zealand and Australia, he began with a joke, quite characteristic of him. The joke went as follows: An American Jewish writer traveled to Israel for the first time, planning to do a book on his visit. Shortly after his arrival, he was interviewed by an Israeli reporter who asked him how recently he had arrived. His answer: "Yesterday." The reporter then asked him when he'd be departing. His answer: "Tomorrow." The reporter then asked him whether he still intended to write a book about Israel. His answer: "Of course! It will be entitled *Israel: Yesterday, Today and Tomorrow.*"

I'm not going to deliver either a book-length or a three-day eulogy, though the subject matter makes it tempting. After all, if anyone deserves such an encomium, it is Sam. But let me mention four attributes of Sam that particularly struck me over the many years I was privileged to call him a colleague and friend.

The first was Sam's wisdom. He wasn't just bright, as Abe Rosenthal said, and the author of countless learned articles and essays, but much more rare, he was truly wise and, as such, richly deserved the title counsel and counselor.

Second, Sam was possessed of courage—the physical courage he displayed during four years of wartime service in the U.S. Navy, and again after the onset of his debilitating stroke; and the moral courage he displayed throughout his life, the courage of an independent mind unafraid to speak out and assert his position, but always in a manner designed to bring people closer together, not farther apart.

Third, compassion. Few people I have ever met cared as much about people, especially the less fortunate, as Sam did. You know, there are those who seek to save humanity but couldn't care less about individuals. No, Sam cared every bit as much about real people as he did about the larger societal issues affecting them.

And fourth, humility. Sam was in many ways a giant among us, yet to be with him was to be with a man of quiet dignity. Joe Klein, writing in the *New Yorker* about Tony Blair, the British prime minister, said he is a man of "ostentatious humility." Sam was just the opposite, a man of authentic humility, the kind of person who drove his car every day from White Plains to North Bronx, searched for a parking spot in accordance with alternate-side-of-the-street parking rules, and hopped on the subway to come to AJC, when there were far more comfortable ways of traveling between Westchester and Manhattan. In a nutshell, that was Sam—down to earth, modest to a fault, in touch with the world around him.

He lived his life nobly, serving his country in its hour of need, always being there for his beloved wife, Anna, four children, and five grandchildren, pursuing the mandate from Deuteronomy, *Tsedek, tsedek, tirdof*, "Justice, justice, shalt thou pursue," and yes, treating his neighbor as he would himself be treated.

We live in an era dominated by the culture of complaint, the culture of celebrity, the culture of self-indulgence, and the culture of instant gratification. Sam, however, embodied the enduring—and timeless— values highlighted in Tom Brokaw's book, *The Greatest Generation*, about the Depression and wartime generation. Brokaw wrote admiringly of that generation's values of duty, responsibility, service, and family—in other words, the values that really count, the values that captured Sam's essence.

Ralph Waldo Emerson wrote: "To leave the world a bit better, whether by a healthy child, a garden patch or a redeemed social condition, to know even one life has breathed easier because you have lived. This is to have succeeded." By that standard Sam succeeded brilliantly. He redeemed countless social conditions and made so many lives breathe easier.

The American Jewish Committee owes Sam an enormous debt of gratitude that we can repay only by carrying forward the values and beliefs that motivated him and defined his illustrious career. And we shall.

Physically, Sam spent thirty years of his life in this very building. Spiritually, his presence here at 165 East 56 Street will live on forever.

Not only AJC, but the Jewish people, the American Constitution, which he cherished and protected all his adult life, and countless disadvantaged individuals of every race, religion, and creed owe this remarkable man that enormous debt of gratitude.

Sam, we miss you.

Fifth Anniversary of the AJC Berlin Office
Hotel Adlon, Berlin
March 24, 2003

I'm a former student of a country that young people will probably not remember. It was called the Soviet Union. In the Soviet Union economic policy was based on a five-year plan. For those of you with any experience with the Soviet five-year plans, you knew that each was a greater disaster than the previous one.

The American Jewish Committee ignored the Soviet experience and decided to have its own five-year plan here in Berlin, and I'm happy to say that ours was a complete success. It is that five years of American Jewish Committee presence in Berlin that you join us in celebrating tonight. In fact, we had the opening gala right here in this hall. It was a wonderful dinner. Klaus Kinkel was then the foreign minister. He spoke, as did many other dignitaries, and I could never have imagined five years ago how far the office would come.

Permit me to refer to what I said from this podium at the time. It was shortly after the establishment of the Federal Republic in 1949 that we initiated an often immensely painful and difficult conversation between Germans and Jews. With each passing year, it widened and deepened, and over time, it has allowed us at the American Jewish Committee to come to understand the evolution, indeed the revolution, in what was taking place in Germany, and to build on that in advancing relations between Germans and Jews.

Though it may be a dirty word in some quarters today, we also sought to build the transatlantic relationship. Call us antiquated if you will, but we continue to believe in that transatlantic relationship. We believed in it yesterday, we believe in it today, and we will believe in it tomorrow.

The maturing relationship between the Federal Republic of Germany and the American Jewish Committee has also allowed us to become partners in third countries. With the Bundeswehr, we have worked together to assist Muslim refugees fleeing the ethnic cleansing of Slobodan Milosevic in the Balkans. With the Friedrich-Naumann Foundation, we have worked to strengthen tolerance and pluralism in the new democracies of Eastern Europe and Central Europe. With the Adenauer and Ebert Foundations, we have worked to develop our common interests in Germany, the United States, and Israel. And, as recently as today, we held another important roundtable on U.S.-German ties with the Atlantik Brücke, a cherished partner of ours here in Germany.

Whether with religious groups, political foundations, state governments, universities, or the media, we are trying to build the human ties to thicken and broaden the relationship not only between Germans and Jews, but also between Germany and the United States and between Germany and Israel. All of this informs our anniversary celebration.

And if I may add a personal note, for me the opening of our Berlin office and this occasion have a very special meaning. Nearly seventy years ago, a thirteen-year-old boy named Erich and his parents Michael and Rela lived in Wilmersdorf, a district of this city. Erich attended the Fichte-Gymnasium. His father was the editor-in-chief of the *Lokalanzeiger*, a Berlin newspaper. Their family's world was shattered in 1933, and only after 1945 were the three reunited, each having taken a journey through hell. Erich was my father.

For me the opening of an office in Berlin and the return of my father's son to this city to plant a tree, a tree we call the American Jewish Committee, in the Mosse Palais on Leipziger Platz, speaks about the possibilities of history.

At a moment in time when we all worry about whether history can move forward, we are again reminded that indeed it can. You, our friends and partners, and we together have proven that history can go in the right direction. And were my father alive today, I believe he would be the one opening the champagne here in celebration. Yes, the world can move forward when the Bundeswehr in uniform and the American Jewish Committee go together to Macedonia to assist Muslim refugees. By doing so, we demonstrate to the people of the Balkans what human beings are capable of if only they emphasize their common humanity. And that's precisely what we're trying to do.

In closing, allow me to thank you for being here. And to express appreciation to Deidre Berger, our ambassador (without the parking privileges, though). Deidre and her staff represent us here with distinction. And I am grateful to all of you for your friendship.

Tribute to Bill Gralnick
December 3, 2003

Dear Bill:

Mazel tov on the milestone anniversary! I only wish I could be with the Chapter in person to pay tribute to your three decades of professional service to AJC and to join in the overlapping celebration of the Chapter's bar (bat?) mitzvah.

I have had the privilege of calling you a colleague for all but six of those thirty years. I don't know if it's just a function of my aging eyes, but the fact of the matter is that you look every bit as young today as when I first met you. In truth, I suspect the reason has less to do with my eyesight and more to do with your perpetual dynamism, creativity, and passion that have all been hallmarks of your remarkable AJC career.

From Atlanta to Miami to Palm Beach County, you have served as our ambassador to the Jewish and general communities. Along the way, you have made countless friends for us.

You have strengthened the fabric and fiber of America's pluralistic tapestry by being a consummate bridge builder and diplomat. You have advanced the vital link between the United States and Israel by introducing Americans of many walks of life to the wonders of modern-day and democratic Israel. You have built communities of conscience to stand up for the values of mutual understanding and mutual respect and to stand against the forces of racism and anti-Semitism. And you have been a relentless advocate in the pursuit of social justice and human dignity for all Americans.

In sum, you have made a profound difference. The American Jewish Committee has been the fortunate beneficiary of your rare talents and principles.

This is a celebration of a significant way station along a journey that is far from complete. I look forward to our continued collaboration, under the AJC banner, as we seek to advance the values of an organization that has loomed large in both our lives.

Enjoy the event in your honor. You've certainly earned it.